LUCIFER'S POWER

LUCIFER'S POWER

BELIEFS AND PRACTICES OF THE PROCESS CULT

WILLIAM SIMS BAINBRIDGE

Phenomenologist George Psathas sings, "May the Water give me Life," while sociologist of religion Rodney Stark yells, "Purify me with the Fire!"

fh

Feral House
1240 West Sims Way
Suite 124
Port Townsend, WA 98368
www.feralhouse.com
info@feralhouse.com

Design by John Hubbard | emks.fi

CONTENTS

CHAPTER 1:   Rumors of Satan   6

CHAPTER 2:   A Social Implosion   31

CHAPTER 3:   God at Xtul   66

CHAPTER 4:   In Search of the Miraculous   95

CHAPTER 5:   Paradise Misplaced   123

CHAPTER 6:   Process Society   162

CHAPTER 7:   The Gods and Their Symbols   193

CHAPTER 8:   A New Cure of Souls   219

CHAPTER 9:   The Separation   248

CHAPTER 10:   A New Beginning   274

CHAPTER 11:   The Light of Lucifer   302

ENDNOTES   330

CHAPTER 1   Rumors of Satan

IF A MAN ASKS,
"WHAT IS THE PROCESS?"
SAY TO HIM:
    It is the End,
    the Final Ending of the world of men.
    It is the agent of the End,
    the instrument of the End
    and the inexorable Power of the End.

—*If a Man Asks*, Process scripture

THIS BOOK IS PSYCHO-HISTORY of a polytheistic cult in which Satan initially triumphed by setting other gods at war, notably Jehovah against Lucifer, but eventually the wisdom of Lucifer prevailed by preserving the culture far into the following century. For the author, it was quite an adventure that required joining the Process in 1970, experiencing the Separation of the Gods when its leaders battled against each other, and then keeping in good contact for five decades. Given its English origins, the cult pronounced its name PROH-sess, and was international in its wider perspective. Journalists might want to write on this subject because they could exploit public interest in the bizarre. But why should a sociologist care? Surely Satanic cults are rare and unimportant. There is some question if any really exist at all. Yet, truth to tell, close examination of the rapid creation, evolution, and destruction of this unusually intelligent cult can offer wisdom about civilization. We must realize that *cult is culture writ small.*

Sometimes, of course, we can learn about social life by inspecting a tiny, unusual part of it. In his highly influential 1897 sociological study, *Suicide*, Émile Durkheim discovered society behind solitude, contrasting religious traditions.[1] If a real Satanic cult did exist, perhaps we could learn from its rejection of society's virtues something new about society and about virtue. The Process was only partly a Satanic cult, because it was other things as well. It began as a psychotherapy movement and evolved into a religious community. What separates psychotherapy from religion, and what happens at their common border? The Process was born among normal young adults in the English monied classes who fled London to live on a Mexican beach, then wandered the streets of Europe and America begging. How can a cohesive deviant group emerge from a diffuse network of conventional people?

The Process began with a few simple assumptions about the nature of the human personality and evolved a complex culture of Gods, symbols, rituals, songs, and social customs. What are the ways that abundant new culture can be created? The Process followed Satan but also pursued every other God and spirit that promised a unique path out of the human condition. What are the ways people seek to transcend the lives given them, and what are the results of each kind of attempt? Satan, the God beneath contempt and beyond belief, was an expression of the will to escape the inhibitions of society. In its erratic quest, the cult explored the margins of conventionality and sojourned in more than one area of deviance.

CONFLICTING REPORTS

Colorful, bizarre, even terrifying, the Process called forth interest as well as antagonism from those who encountered it in the late 1960s. The cult's striking public performance evoked a variety of metaphors from reporters. Some journalists saw only the most superficial characteristics: "They wear dark space-suits with red Satanic emblems sewn on the chests and are usually accompanied by German-Shepherd dogs." Others pretended to see far beneath the surface and called the cult "Satan worshippers" and "mind-benders." One reporter visited the cult and was surprised to discover that Processeans were not really fiends from Hell: "What I found was no secret cult of drug-taking Devil worshippers, but one of the most curious, and curiously attractive, of all the unorthodox religions in America." Another reporter was impressed by the mysterious ambiguity surrounding the Process: "They have been charged with devil worship, rumored to perform ritual murder, accused of drinking dog's blood. While their church services and hierarchy would make a pope proud, their symbols and secrets are a gossip's playground."

The Process came to national attention in 1970 and 1971, when journalists publicly charged that it was ultimately responsible for the infamous Tate-LaBianca murders committed by Charles Manson and his followers. Without any good evidence, they wrote that Manson had been a member of the Process and indoctrinated in Satanism by it. The prosecutor in the Manson case said a direct connection with the Process could not be proved, but he felt the ideologies and structures of the Manson Family and the Process were so similar that some connection was quite likely. One journalist reported that the Process was extremely deviant sexually. He explained its success with converts as the natural result of this deviance:

> The Process, as did Manson, employs sexual excesses as a means by which to shake loose any influence society may still hold over the initiates. Both groups practice communal living and indiscriminate sexual relations among members.... Savage and indiscriminate sex is forced on the entrants into the cult not as a means of religious communion but as a means of purging the initiates of any residue of Grey Forces [conventionality] that might be latent in them. Sex is a means of cutting members off from the outside and subjecting them to the will of the group, or the wills of the group leaders.

When I first published a more limited book in 1978, with the title *Satan's Power*, Robert de Grimston was still trying to revive it in its original form, so I avoided giving his actual name and renamed the Process "the Power." That required me to avoid citing some of my information sources, because they would have revealed identities I had some duty to protect. That is no longer the case, not the least because a Wikipedia contributor posted an article about the Process in 2001, citing my book as the primary source. I did not save the reference for the paragraph quoted above, and just now had an interesting experience googling some of its text and finding that websites claiming to have the paragraph were rated suspicious by a security software system: "This webpage is a known malicious webpage. It is highly recommended that you do NOT visit this page."

My years studying the Process convinced me that the specific claims of wickedness made by some outsiders were false, but that a quasi-sociological hypothesis hidden behind these stories was correct. I found no actual connection between Manson's murders and the Process. "Savage and indiscriminate sex" was not forced on new recruits. The Process was, however, a closed social universe created and maintained by intensive emotional interaction between participants. In this it resembled the Manson Family or any other small sect or deviant subculture embodied in a specific social group. Processeans often spoke of "sexual energy" as the glue that held them together, referring not to orgiastic group experiences but simply to intense bonds of positive feeling that tied members together in a strong, closed social network.

Processeans enjoyed projecting a wild image. Their black uniforms and red emblems excited cult members as much as they worried the general public. In its own imagination the Process was a Satanic cult. "Black is the color of the Bottomless Void to which the human race is doomed by its insistence upon a GODless compromise of living death. So Black we shall wear in mourning for the doom mankind has brought upon itself." Announcing themselves with such lurid rhetoric, the Beings of the Process stalked Europe and America in the late 1960s and early 1970s, dressed in sinister black uniforms with flowing cloaks, accompanied by huge Alsatian hounds and plagued by the vilest rumors, bearing on their chests the sign of the Devil, the red Mendes Goat badge. "And upon the Black we shall wear Red for the blood that man has shed amongst his fellow men. We shall wear Red for the blood of CHRIST that man has shed and still sheds to his own damnation. And we shall wear Red for the rivers of blood that shall be shed in the Latter 10 Days, for man has taken blood and blood shall he give in recompense. And we shall wear Red for the Fires of Hell where the Lord SATAN shall execute the Final Judgement of the world."

An outsider observing a Sabbath Assembly would have had few doubts that this was a real Satanic cult. Through the haze of heavy incense he would have seen swastika-like symbols carved in a wooden altar. The amber light of flickering candle flames was lost in the black uniforms of cult members but infused faces with the appearance of harsh strength. The outsider would have heard alien chants and terrifying proclamations. He might have been intimidated by the haughty tone of the officiating priests.

Yet anyone who visited the local chapter of the Process more than a few times would have acquired a very different and probably positive perspective. The Sabbath Assembly was a beautiful grand opera, and the performers were great actors. The music was very well composed, while the garments and symbols were extremely artistic. The Process seemed ready to abandon the existing world, but it was honestly preparing to create a better one. Figure 1 shows a Sacrifist and Evangelist from the Process's Sabbath Assembly, dressed in their sacerdotal robes, standing in front of the painted face of Satan that dominated the Alpha ritual room.

In this book, the historically correct "sacred names" will be given only for leaders who served as Fathers or Mothers, given that they were public figures, even sometimes having their words and pictures in the many magazines published by the Process. For those who were still alive when this book was published, privacy is protected by the fact that their sacred names were temporary, identifying them only when they were serving essentially as priests of the cult. Yes, I know many of their secular names, what Processeans called "grey names," but will not reveal them here. For members who did not play the roles of public figure and priest during my research, I will use pseudonyms invented for this book.

FIGURE 1. **Two Process priests presiding over the Sabbath Assembly.**

Dominic is Sacrifist and Christian is Evangelist.

To preserve their privacy during the time the cult was still active, this drawing from the 1978 edition of this book was based on a photograph I had taken of two public leaders who posed for it, Father Christian on the left and Father Dominic on the right. Both are still alive in 2024 but completing their admirable lives under different names. They wore different tabards, cloth vestments that hung down over their chests and backs. Christian was playing the ritual role of Sacrifist and wore a light purple tabard over his black gown, while Dominic was playing the Evangelist role with a bright red tabard. They carried red and black books of secret scriptures in their left hands and wore silver rings available only to priests of Master rank on their right hands. Those rings and the Sacrifist icon on Christian's tabard displayed a mysterious symbol of a narrowed Greek letter alpha inside an open omega, representing God as the sexual copulation of a male Lucifer with a female Jehovah. Dominic's tabard, and the silver prophet's rings on their left hands displayed a swastika-like symbol representing the wider contest between the four warring gods, adding Christ and Satan. Did they really worship the ultimate Evil?

Indeed, first impressions are often wrong. The Process was easy to misunderstand because it was complex and richly metaphoric. Founded by young adults of the English middle class, it drew on occult and countercultural traditions to create a vivid lifestyle reminiscent of a theatrical performance or a particularly innovative primitive tribe. Processeans wore many colorful uniforms and emblems, enacted dramatic rituals, composed touching songs and chants, conducted intense public demonstrations, traveled over a range of seven thousand miles, and planted communes in several cities. Organized as a hierarchical secret society, the Process put neophytes through a series of occult therapeutic exercises called Telepathy Developing Circles, Progresses, Sessions, Processcenes, Mediumistics, and Enactments. Through scriptures and seminars it instructed them in a large corpus of doctrine.

The Process was a Satanic cult, but Satan had a very special meaning for Processeans that no outsider could easily grasp. The complicated Process theology identified four Gods: Lucifer, Jehovah, Christ, and Satan. Lucifer, God of the air, represents sensuousness, liberality, and intellect. Jehovah, God of the earth, represents austerity, authoritarianism, and emotion. The cult believed that cosmic forces were working for the Union as if in marriage of Lucifer and Jehovah, even using that symbol suggesting radically that Jehovah was female, but never openly stating so. Christ, male God of the waters, gave himself in love for the unification of all beings and the resolution of conflict. Satan, perhaps female God of fire, reserved herself in hatred to achieve the separation of all beings and the propagation of conflict. The cult claimed that it was the terrestrial manifestation of the coming Unity of Christ and Satan, a force moving to achieve the end of the world in service of Satanic destruction so that a Christian Golden Age might dawn.

RESEARCH METHODOLOGY

The evidence on which this book rests was collected intermittently in two main phases: (1) over a period of nearly six years through a variety of participant observation and ethnographic methods, and (2) for another forty-eight years initially through close personal ties to a few members, then more extensively online. I first encountered Processeans in Boston near the end of 1970, when I was just completing six months' study of Scientology. At first I planned to investigate the Process only briefly, along with other groups, and develop a comprehensive theory of culture-creation through comparative analysis. Consequently, I began my research following the classical anthropological approach exemplified by Bronislaw Malinowski's work.[2] Although I allowed myself to be initiated into the cult, I did not become a core participant but developed the status of friendly associate, an unobtrusive observer of Process rituals and interviewer of native informants. Although I felt my main task was documentation of the official culture of the group, I kept a detailed diary of field observations that included many reports of member interactions, problematic disruptions, and other revealing incidents. I observed the Boston chapter of the Process consistently throughout 1971, then switched to relatively infrequent contact for the next three years.

A leading Harvard professor, Seymour Martin Lipset, was sufficiently impressed by a term paper I wrote about the spaceflight social movement for his seminar about intellectuals that he convinced me to make that the topic of my doctoral dissertation, published as my first book, *The Spaceflight Revolution*, in 1976.[3] That monopolized my time, so I could not continue constant field research on the Process while I was locked in Harvard's libraries. This limitation turned out to be a blessing in disguise. Because I was unable to devote my full time to research on the cult, my observations were stretched out over a long span of time, and I was able to witness many changes in group society and culture. Over this period of less intense contact, I documented changes in the rituals and shifts in cult policy and also was able to increase my collection of documents and descriptions of relatively rare events such as weddings, but my contacts became quite rare.

A page from my field notes documents that on Monday, August 19, 1974, about six in the evening, I was walking home past the Cumberland Farms store on Huron Avenue in Cambridge, Massachusetts, when I saw a young man walking toward me wearing a large red and silver Process cross. I said, "As it is …" He replied, "So be it." We stopped to talk and I asked what has been going on. He began to tell me, and after a few moments I invited him to my apartment to chat. He gave me his name, but here I will apply a pseudonym, as I will do for all other members other than very public leaders, so let us say he was Bob Stone.

He said there had been a split in the Process in May. The "hierarchy" had rejected the public leader of the Process, Robert de Grimston, and his teachings, and set up the Foundation Church of the Millennium. His "Oracle" in creating the Process, Mary Ann MacLean, had remained, perhaps to lead the Foundation. De Grimston had gone to New Orleans, where the Process had been rather well established, but was at the moment visiting New York. A leader from the Boston chapter I had known quite well had taken a new sacred name in the Foundation, given that all high-level members other than Robert and Mary Ann took new identities, and was wearing a white robe indicating high status. Bob Stone said the Foundation had taken on some Jewish customs, for example saying "Shalom" rather than "As it is …" The schism between Process and Foundation had been announced in a nation-wide radio talk by one of the leaders I knew best, who said that the old ways of the Process had proven not to work. Bob did not agree with that and had become the treasurer of a new Boston area chapter of the Process, taking the middle-status role of Brother.

I reestablished contact with the two main fragments of the broken Process at the end of 1974, with help from George Oberhofer, a Harvard freshman who did his own study for two term papers. We closely observed the Boston Processeans join in setting up their chapter in nearby Waltham, Massachusetts. Many of the Processeans I had come to know well in 1971 were then transforming the existing cult headquarters in New York City, so I began visiting them as well. In 1975, I made excursions to see the groups in Chicago and Toronto. Robert de Grimston, original founder and charismatic figure of the Process, had come to Boston late in 1974, a victim of the great schism, and over a period of six months I came to know him quite well.

The ethnographer Rosalie Wax commented that of all the factors that contribute to good field research, "no technique or talent is quite so valuable as luck."[4] My own experience supports her observation. I was extremely fortunate throughout my Process research. Threatened disasters never materialized; several times, as Robert himself commented, I happened on the scene just as something revealing was happening. The schism that tore the cult in 1974 was a great advantage for my research, although a sad misfortune for members. The breakup not only produced much interesting material in itself, but also made possible many rich interviews and the collection of hundreds of pages of previously secret documents.

The Process was a closed secret society that kept members in the dark until years after they joined, so without the schism it would have been far too expensive of my time and spirit to penetrate to the heart of the cult. Of course, it is common for groups like the Process to suffer fragmentation, and they occasionally expel their charismatic leaders, so my luck consisted merely in being at the right place at the right time. In 1975, researching the Boston dissidents, I had to take a much more participatory role than before. I helped the group beg for food, did many errands with my car, and lived part-time in the chapter house, sleeping on the floor or a couch. Conscious of the necessity of preserving my intellectual independence, I nonetheless felt it was justified to perform whatever tasks were given me. Therefore, I participated in the rituals, playing the role of priest in the Sabbaths, Telepathy Developing Circles, Meditations, and even three Baptisms. After being asked to do so, I also conducted doctrinal seminars for the cult; it was not necessary that I believe the doctrine, but rather that I understand it and be able to communicate it. Robert de Grimston included me in a committee working to develop a formal correspondence course based on his Teachings.

These tasks gave me the opportunity to test my understanding of Process culture in the most direct way, by demonstrating cultic competence. The most important tool of data collection was of course my lengthy field diary. In the early months of my research I was a detached observer, forced to write my observations down a few hours after the fact, and therefore forced to memorize the rituals, chants, and interactions as best I could. It was actually rather easy to document the cult's official practices this way, because each ritual or therapy exercise would be repeated many times, permitting me to refine my descriptions until they were just right. By the end of my research I also had the benefit of the cult's own training and possessed copies of all the "ritual formats," documents written for Process priests delineating each step in each ritual. As time went on, there came to be more and more occasions when it was appropriate for me to take notes while actually in the field. Although my status with the group was ambiguous in the beginning, after the first year or so members were quite content to see me as both a sociologist and a friend. At the end, Processeans saw me as the historian of their cult.

Photography proved to be a very useful tool. The Process was extremely visual, quite literally a colorful cult. I began in 1971 by taking pictures of Processeans on the streets, then gave copies of color prints to some of the cult members in them. The results convinced the leaders of the Boston chapter to employ me to do photography work on a regular basis. The Process used my pictures in television appearances, in its magazines, on photo-identification cards for inner members, and for a variety of private purposes. Throughout the last half of 1971, I was able to document not only the clothing, physical setting, and work activities of the cult but also some rituals and informal behavior. The photography allowed me to develop a relationship of happy reciprocity with the group, giving it useful services in return for sociological data. Tape recordings proved invaluable. I made tapes of about two dozen rituals, including several Sabbaths, a Telepathy Developing Circle, an Evening Assembly, a Processcene, midnight meetings, and even a marriage ceremony. The cult was happy to sell me recordings of about thirty of its radio programs to add to the half dozen I had taped off the air.

In 1974 and 1975, my able research assistant George Oberhofer conducted recorded interviews with most members of the dissident Boston group. Subsequently, from March 1975 through September 1976, I used a tape recorder in interviewing cult members in Boston, New York, and Chicago. Many of the direct quotations in this book were taken from transcripts of these recordings. Field research in the Process gave me many opportunities to collect cult artifacts. In this respect my project followed anthropological rather than sociological traditions. My collection included many badges and other physical symbols of Process membership and rank: rings, crosses, other jewelry, Satanic emblems, priests' badges, and even a cultic belt buckle. I also obtained a hooded cloak and a priest's ritual tabard that were made by Processeans, two paintings of the Lord Satan, and a complete set of ritual furniture, including two carved priests' chairs and a circular altar with fire and water stands. Over the years I was able to amass a large collection of Process literature, comprising every magazine and book that was publicly available, and also all the doctrinal scripture available to most inner members and many of the cult's administrative documents. My priest's Missal counted as both artifact and literature because it has an elegant black binding imprinted in red with the Process symbol.

Although I constantly refer to cult scripture, administrative documents, and some correspondence in this book, I have not peppered my pages with footnotes, although of course I often name scriptures. One reason is that the publications have not been preserved in public libraries, and the Process always distributed the publications themselves rather than selling in stores. In recent years, online Process groups have made electronic copies available, and the concluding chapter of this book will survey that remarkable cultural phenomenon. But exactly which website will survive for the reader to visit is uncertain. As of July 15, 2024, a copy of *The Gods and Their People* by Robert de Grimston can be purchased online from eBay for $1,359.99 (or best offer), but that may be of value only for a collector, because Google finds more than one scanned copy online for free.

The social forces and structural principles I observed in this tiny, deviant cult are quite common in society and are found in settings and institutions of many kinds. My original research aim, to discover ways that novel culture is socially generated, is partly achieved in this book. Here I do show the basic processes by which Process culture was derived from Scientology and from the experiences of core Processeans and describe the cultural transformations effected by the Foundation when it sought to break with the old Process. After my first contacts with the Process, I developed a second theoretical interest. The Process appeared to be the only modern polytheistic group available for me to study. The gods Lucifer, Jehovah, Christ, and Satan represented alternate moral systems, competing models of the ideal person, and even different intellectual conceptions of the world. Perhaps the really radical cult, that arose from various Dark Ages, was Monotheism, and it is time for humanity to return to the inherently diverse Polytheism that may be more natural for us.

How could a social group maintain mundane authority in the face of celestial conflict? To what extent did the Process theology actually support multiple social and phenomenological realities? More generally, what happens when radically different ideologies attempt to co-exist within the same organization? The Process looked like a combination of medieval authoritarian and modern liberal values, and I wondered whether such a hybrid could possibly be viable. These two theoretical interests immediately point to the body of theory that was most important for my project: the indigenous theory of the Process itself. Of course I was interested in the group's beliefs as an ethnographer. But beyond that, the ideology of the Process is a collection of alternate social theories. By and large, the occult is more of a deviant social science than it is a deviant description of the physical universe. The Process drew its inspiration not only from pseudo-social sciences like Scientology but also from standard sources.

The cult's Teacher, Robert de Grimston, was influenced by classical Psychoanalysis, for example, although it must be admitted he never studied the subject in a formal way. He accepted Sigmund Freud's idea of the unconscious, Arthur Adler's goal theory, and Carl Jung's notion of the collective unconscious but acknowledged, "I've read hardly anything of these things. It's just what I pick up, what I hear people talk about, or what occasionally I see in some book that I happen to pick up in a bookshop and flip through." So the ideologies of cults may in part be loose extensions of standard social-scientific thinking as well as deviant alternatives to it. Sometimes a cult may independently invent a system of thought that is accepted within some branch of social science.

As we will see, the Process developed a structuralist analytic perspective very similar to that of the anthropologist Claude Lévi-Strauss; Processeans used this perspective not only to create their own ideology but also to interpret the mythological systems of other groups.[5] Beyond their similarities with and connections to standard social science, the beliefs of the Process provide a valuable source of theory because they were developed through the living experience of the members. Just as I do not accept all the theories of my sociological colleagues, I am not a believer in the Process's ideological system. But it was an important source of theories and hypotheses. My approach to sociological theory is thoroughly eclectic, with its main emphasis on the social-psychological level.

A CONCEPTUAL BASIS

At one point in my early research on the Boston chapter of the Process, actually located in Cambridge, Massachusetts, within walking distance of Harvard Square, a tiny magical accident contributed greatly. Visiting a bookstore near the Square, I noticed the corner of a book sticking out from under a bookcase and picked it up to restore it to the shelf above. It was *Doomsday Cult* by John Lofland, with which I was not familiar, so instead I bought and read it avidly.[6] It mysteriously described a radical cult without revealing its identity, which I later learned was the first branch to reach America of the Korean messiah Sun Myung Moon's Unification Church. A single middle-aged woman had been sent over to launch the church in the States, and a small group of converts had clustered around her. Today the church is quite successful, but its growth was probably the result of a second importation attempt. Consequently, while its theoretical model is intended to apply to a wide range of phenomena, it was developed using data from a group that may not be entirely typical. Although the Process may not be typical of religious communities either, it is sufficiently different from the Unification Church to provide a valuable comparison.

Published in 1966, *Doomsday Cult* connected to a journal article titled "Becoming a World-Saver," which Lofland wrote in partnership with Rodney Stark, when they were graduate students at the University of California, Berkeley. When I completed my doctorate at Harvard and interviewed for an assistant professor job at the University of Washington in the spring of 1975, my familiarity with this work encouraged Stark, a tenured professor there, to advocate my hiring. After *Satan's Power* was published in 1978, Stark and I began work on development of a general theory of religion, emphasizing innovation, in part based on our experiences studying these two doomsday cults. Lofland and Stark theorized that for conversion to a radical cult, it is necessary that a person:[7]

1. Experience enduring, acutely felt tensions
2. Within a religious problem-solving perspective,
3. Which leads him to define himself as a religious seeker;
4. Encountering the group at a turning point in his life
5. Wherein an affective bond is formed (or pre-exists) with one or more converts;

6. Where extra-cult attachments are absent or neutralized;
7. And where, if he is to become a deployable agent,
   he is exposed to intensive interaction.

This model is very much like a synthesis of the three competing theories in *Causes of Delinquency* by their colleague, the criminologist Travis Hirschi: strain theory, control theory, and subcultural deviance theory.[8] *Strain theory* is fundamental in *Theory of Collective Behavior* by the Harvard-trained Berkeley professor Neil Smelser, often attributed to the Harvard-trained Robert K. Merton, and may be described as the motivation felt by an individual who cannot succeed in achieving goals set by the wider culture through following its behavioral norms.[9] Thus strain is related to Durkheim's concept of *anomie*, lack of effective norms to guide behavior, while control theory connects to his concept of *egoism*, namely the weakness of social bonds that may not be sufficient to control the individual's behavior.[10] Steps 5, 6, and 7 of the Lofland-Stark model clearly draw upon *differential association theory*, proposed by Edwin Sutherland, who had been trained in the first influential American sociology department, at the University of Chicago, which continued to compete with Harvard and Berkeley.[11] So at that point in the history of sociology, creative and adventurous researchers were able to combine elements of several well-developed social theories to explain the complexity of deviant behavior.

What I added when I began collaborating with Stark was a combination of two very different cognitive theories, the Behaviorism of B. F. Skinner and his friend Goerge Homans, which I studied while serving as teaching assistant for Homans, and the Phenomenology and Ethnomethodology I had studied at Boston University with George Psathas, who advised my senior honors thesis based on my months of field research in Scientology.[12] At the same time I was first engaged in ethnography of the Process, I was unintentionally studying an equally unusual but more respected psychotherapeutic parareligion that was led by Paul A. Walters, who half a century ago was the director of mental health services at Harvard University.[13] He had a private psychiatric practice as well and taught an undergraduate class each spring, in which I was twice one of his graduate teaching assistants. Also, he chaired my pre-dissertation graduate oral examination on Sociology of Mental Disorder, in which he awarded me honors for summarizing well the twenty-five books and 100 articles I had selected to study.

Summarizing his subculture is difficult, but it is an example of how a professional in the areas covered by this chapter could do parareligious innovation without many of the people around him fully realizing. When I was Walters' teaching assistant, the main textbook was *Playing and Reality* by Donald Woods Winnicott, which offers a Psychoanalytic theory that infants live in a world of illusions and can achieve disillusionment through *transitional objects*.[14] Children can discover their own existence as independent entities by playing with toys, but they begin life believing they are still parts of their mothers.

A cultic task for the teaching assistants was leading many student discussions of three books by Carlos Castaneda that Walters assigned his class to read: *The Teachings of Don Juan: A Yaqui Way of Knowledge*, *A Separate Reality: Further Conversations with Don Juan,* and *Journey to Ixtlan: The Lessons of Don Juan*.[15] Castaneda claimed these were parts of an anthropological study in which he primarily became the student of a Yaqui sorcerer he called Don Juan. A news article that suggested this study of a cult had itself become a cult summarized the books: "Under don Juan's tutelage, Castaneda took peyote, talked to coyotes, turned into a crow, and learned how to fly. All this took place in what don Juan called 'a separate reality.'" "The godfather of the New Age led a secretive group of devoted followers in the last decade of his life. His closest 'witches' remain missing, and former insiders, offering new details, believe the women took their own lives."[16] The reader will see hints of another Harvard cult in this description of Walters' course from the university's 1972 catalog:

> SOCIAL SCIENCES 130. Drug Use and Adolescent Development. Uses a controversial form of adolescent behavior, drug use, as a vehicle towards understanding some aspects of adolescent development. Emphasis is on intra-psychic variables such as types of object relationship, maturation of mental processes, and concepts of defense and adaptation, and their possible relationship to types of drugs used by individuals and groups.[17]

Controversial indeed, because the course was an offshoot of a prominent cult of the previous decade, the International Federation for Internal Freedom (IFIF), founded by the Harvard psychologist Timothy Leary, that promoted transcendental experiences from LSD and other psychedelic drugs: "Turn on, tune in, drop out!" As the online encyclopedia of new religious movements, World Religions and Spirituality Project, reports, the name and face of his organization changed after his departure from Harvard: "Leary sought to create his own religion as a means of protection against law enforcement and as an attempt to fully portray psychedelic use as a truly religious experience. In September, 1966, Leary announced to the media the creation of the League for Spiritual Discovery and shortly thereafter he published the pamphlet 'Start Your Own Religion,' which acted as 'how-to' guide for creating one's own psychedelic church."[18] I never directly studied the various meanings of LSD, but at 10:30 on Sunday morning, April 24, 1983, I attended the reunion of Timothy Leary with his most prominent disciple, Richard Alpert, who in 1967 had converted to Hinduism and become Baba Ram Dass. Held at Harvard's Sanders Theater in Memorial Hall, it celebrated the twentieth anniversary of their firing from the university's psychology department.

Given that Rodney Stark had already published extensively in the sociology of religion, the new theoretical aspects of our joint work tended to begin with the different set of ideas I delivered from Harvard, including the relevance of psychiatry. In 1979 we published a journal article about three compatible models of cult formation. (1) The *Psychopathology Model* describes cult innovation as the result of individual mental illness that finds successful social expression, often when the founder can convince more normal people that a psychotic episode he experienced was actually supernatural. For example, I had interviewed Love Israel, founder of a cult called the Love Family, who honestly reported that his religious vision was triggered by hallucinogenic drugs but considered the drugs to be magical. (2) The *Entrepreneur Model* notes that cult founders often may consciously develop new rituals and beliefs in order to exchange them for great rewards. If social circumstances provide opportunities for profit in the field of cults, then many perfectly normal individuals will be attracted to the challenge of achieving financial success in that business. (3) The *Subculture-Evolution Model* emphasizes group interaction processes. It suggests that cults can emerge without authoritative leaders, and it points out that even radical cultural developments can be achieved through many small steps. The example we gave for the third model was indeed the Process, which was unusual for having been created by a couple, rather than an individual, and for constantly creating new culture as it faced difficulties achieving the collective goals of the members.[19]

The general Stark-Bainbridge theory of religion began with seven simple Behaviorist axioms, including these two: "Humans seek what they perceive to be rewards and avoid what they perceive to be costs." "Human action is directed by a complex but finite information-processing system that functions to identify problems and attempt solutions to them."[20] Framed by formal definitions of 104 terms, the theory derived 344 *propositions*, which were not fully proven, but offered as hypotheses that might guide empirical research or could eventually be derived as theorems using more complete logical deductions. Here is a key sample:

PROPOSITION 6: In pursuit of desired rewards, humans will exchange rewards with other humans.

PROPOSITION 14: In the absence of a desired reward, explanations often will be accepted which posit attainment of the reward in the distant future or in some other nonverifiable context.

DEFINITION 18: *Compensators* are postulations of reward according to explanations that are not readily susceptible to unambiguous evaluation.

DEFINITION 19: Compensators which substitute for single, specific rewards are called *specific compensators*.

DEFINITION 20: Compensators that substitute for a cluster of many rewards and for rewards of great scope are called *general compensators*.

PROPOSITION 22: The most general compensators can be supported only by supernatural explanations.

DEFINITION 22: *Religion* refers to systems of general compensators based on supernatural assumptions.

These ideas connect back to the Lofland and Stark concept of *problem-solving perspective*. In their article they focused on religious problem-solving, but mention two alternatives, psychiatric and political. Thus, my research on both Scientology and the Process connected creatively, because both had aspects of both religious and psychiatric problem-solving, even shifting the balance between the two perspectives over the years, especially as psychotherapy separated culturally from medicinal psychiatry and became more like a collection of new religious cults. The *general compensators* Stark and I placed at the center of our definition of *religion* provided hope for solution of a major problem that actually lacked one, such as faith in a supernatural afterlife, while more specific compensators might stimulate some reliance upon *magic*. Thus, from moment to moment, or year to year, a cult and its members might migrate back and forth between religion and magic, depending upon their current emotional needs.

My interviews with early converts to the Process indicated that the *religious seekership* emphasized by Lofland and Stark was unimportant for this middle-class cult. Few of the original Processeans said anything that indicated they were actively seeking a specifically religious solution to life problems at the time they converted. The *turning point* item is a bit ambiguous. Although some Processeans said they were at loose ends, others did not. Many seemed to join during very early adulthood, when they had completed their educations and a transition was experienced by most members of their generation. Looking backward, they saw their conversion as constituting a turning point, so perhaps this item is tautological or poorly articulated. In itself, the idea may not explain anything not already explained by other elements in the Lofland-Stark model. It can be interpreted either as a subjective feeling held by a person that some life decision is necessary, or as an objective description of a time when a person's social relations and institutional commitments are temporarily quite weak and he is open to new involvements.

My observations suggest that a cult can arise without the necessity of either strain or cultural deviance. Therefore a theory of cults need not be a theory of deviance, and at some future time hundreds of them may be respected as normal religions. But, although times and standards are changing, cults were very deviant from the standpoints of most people when the Process was born. Until they are so numerous as to define acceptable variance, if not conventionality itself, cults will be implicated in many kinds of social deviance in ways that conventional churches may not be. And, in a sense, my definition of a cult suggests a quality of deviance: in that a cult is *innovative*, it is deviant with respect to the past; in that it is *cohesive*, it is deviant with respect to outsiders; and in that it is *oriented to the supernatural*, it is deviant with respect to everyday concerns. The complex interplay between deviance and conventionality in the formation and persistence of a cult is a major theme of this book. The Process was deviant, but it cannot be understood merely through theories of deviance nor from a narrow social-problems perspective. In analyzing the formation of cults we have to bring to bear everything we know about cultural and social differentiation. To understand the life and customs of a cult we must use all the intellectual tools of social science developed for understanding human society. We must indeed realize that *cult is culture writ small*.

AN OUTLINE

The structure of this book is dictated by my historical, ethnographic, and theoretical purposes. Following this introduction, chapters 2 through 5 recount the history of the Process from its birth in 1963 to its height just before the schism of 1974. The historical survey first describes the emergence of the cult as a deviant subculture born from conventional middle-class English society through the mechanism of a pseudo-psychotherapy group. Next, it follows the Processeans to a wild beach on the Yucatan peninsula and shows the steps through which the group came to be a church. Then, the story follows the erratic wanderings of Satan's Horde all over Europe and North America on their quest for a door out of this world and examines the paradoxical period in which they reversed course and tried to gain acceptance in the world as an established and progressively more conventional church.

The next three chapters describe the Process at its height, when six branches of the church were founded in North America, the culture was most perfectly developed, and the unusual lifestyle blossomed. These chapters describe Process life, the procedure of joining and the communal existence of members, the Gods, symbols, and chief rituals, and the variety of deviant psychotherapy practices followed by the cult. The historical narrative resumes in chapter 9 with the Great Separation, the schism in which the nominal leader of the cult was expelled and Processean culture disappeared in the formation of the Foundation Church of the Millennium. There follows the rocky tale of the second Process created by the exiled charismatic leader and a band of dissidents who clustered around him. The concluding chapter describes the survival and diversification of Process culture, in such social media as rock music and the World Wide Web. Its conceptual basis is the suggestion that Rumors of Satan evolved into Revivals of Lucifer, leading to this moment in time when each individual person can decide which forms of magic to inherit from the Process for whatever our future faith will be. We begin our memorialization with a vignette taken from my own experience.

A SABBATH IN THE WOODS

We had to get out of the city. The sun was setting, and it was nearly time for our Sabbath Assembly, the most sacred hour of a Processean's week. Providence, Rhode Island, was not in fact a place of providence, and gave us no freedom to shout the praises of Jehovah, Lucifer, Christ, and Satan. We drove north along the river in our Champion camper, seven of us searching for a secluded place. We had just come from the Rubicon, a second-floor, scruffy, antidrug youth hangout, where we had flashed our capes and spoken of the Unity of Christ and Satan. An Italian guy in a checked shirt had liked the idea of Satan and made us explain why we wore not only silver crosses but also red and black badges showing the head of the Prince of Darkness, half goat and half man.

"I think it's wild," he said, "because I agree with the whole idea. I'm not so sure I feel it's necessary to have symbols, but I do agree with the concept, very much so. I recognize that there's a lot of crap in me. A lot of bullshit. I'm fucked up in a lot of ways. All my life, eighteen and a half years, I spent pushing that down, saying. 'If I think about these things, and I feel these things, they make me unique.' You know what I'm saying? Or maybe the way I treated my mother. Of my parents, the little screw-up things I did against them. All these things, I kind of stuffed them down." He had gone on at length about the intensity with which he used to despise himself. Even now, the Christ and Satan within him were not entirely reconciled: "I mean, I'm screwy. I'm crazy. I'm a little perverted."

Then we realized he was not really responding to us, to the message of the Process, but was giving a testimonial for the Rubicon, explaining how much comfort and release he had been given. These were among the products the Process was selling, but without the deviant religious packaging of our polytheistic cult. He continued his spiel: "I sat down with a guy and I was talking with him about some of these things, and he said, 'Yeah. I feel the same way.' I says, 'Oh, shit! Wait a minute,' I says, 'what are you talking about?' And he got into it, and he explained how everyone feels these things at some times and acts this way and that way. And at first I said maybe it's just him and me. I got into it, and holy shit! It was like three hundred pounds of cement off my back!" We nodded and told him the Process had also lifted many burdens. We were glad his were lighter through the realization that everyone is dominated by the Power of Satan at one time or another. "With Satan there is no right or wrong, no success or failure. There is simply what is. Satan demands nothing." We took our leave from the Rubicon and from this poor guy who was not ready to join with us. "As it is . . . " we gave the Process's passwords, " . . . so be it."

We definitely had to get out of the city. After seven o'clock, Saturday, October 23, 1971, we were driving north out of Providence, hurrying to find a setting for a makeshift Alpha. Then, on the left, there were trees at the other side of a meadow. It was some kind of park. We suddenly realized we didn't have a single candle! Sister Eve and Sister Roxana ran down the road to a line of houses, ringing doorbells looking for someone willing to donate a half dozen candles for "a religious ceremony." Sister Hagar turned the pages of our Sabbath Assembly Book, choosing hymns and pointing them out to Brother Thomas, who would be Music Officer. We needed a bowl of water, to symbolize the life-giving power of Christ, and a bowl of fire, to symbolize the purifying power of Satan.

Christ's water was easy enough—a plastic cereal bowl filled from the camper's sink. Satan's fire was a problem. Brother Matthew struggled to make an oil lamp out of a shoe polish can. Brother Eros looked on with his always vaguely interested, always vaguely friendly expression and agreed that the shoe polish can had promise. Sister Hagar was convinced it would never work. Eve and Roxana climbed back into our van. They had candles! Wonderfully red Satanic candles. Matthew punched a hole in the top of the can and inserted a torn bit of shoe polishing cloth for a wick. He poured vegetable oil into the can and struck a match to give Satan's fire a trial run. It burned perfectly, a steady, bright flame.

The sky was dark now. We crossed the field and went into the woods a short distance along a narrow path. There was a little clearing ahead, just large enough for us to form a tight circle. We arranged everything where it belonged and sat on the dry leaves. Brother Matthew placed himself at one end of the circle, and Sister Hagar sat opposite him. They were both of Prophet rank, senior to the rest of us, and would soon become leaders named Father Matthew and Mother Hagar. He would be the Sacrifist in the ceremony, she the Evangelist. The other four Processeans in this ritual were dedicated members who used sacred names, but they were not public figures, so they have been given pseudonyms: Thomas, Eros, Eve and Roxana.

We lit the shoe polish lamp and opened our Assembly books. Eros lit candles and gave them to us to hold or stick into the soft earth. The wind threatened to blow out the flames, so we sat close together and spread our capes on each other's shoulders. We began the first chant, a proper chant to sing outdoors at night beneath the Heavens:

> Contact reaching to the stars
> Through the Spirit of the Christ;
> Knowledge of the Universe,
> He is the way to life.

Brother Matthew began the Declaration. "The Final Reckoning."

Sister Hagar responded. "An End and a New Beginning."

Matthew continued. "And for this purpose Christ and Satan joined."

Hagar answered him. "The Lamb and the Goat."

"Pure Love, descended from the pinnacle of Heaven, united with pure Hatred raised from the depths of Hell."

"Repayment of the debt."

"Fulfillment of the promise."

"All conflicts are resolved."

"An End and a New Beginning."

"The End of Hell and the Beginning of Heaven."

"The End of Darkness and the Beginning of Light."

"The End of War and the Beginning of Peace."

"The End of Hatred and the Beginning of Love."

"The End is now. The New Beginning is to come."

Brother Thomas announced the first hymn, "And the Clarion Calls." We sang joyously of the joining of the Gods and the birth of new life. "Beauty and power in the light of the sun, now that the Gods are One. We have the gift of love through the Gods. And the battle is won!"

Eros turned the pages of one of our magazines and read by the glow of a dancing candle flame. "Brethren, the Relevance is taken from The Process on Death." It was a passage about Lucifer, the quiet God of sensuous love, opponent in the Conflict of the Mind to the harsh, aggressive Jehovah. "Lucifer is the God of Rebirth and Immortality; have faith—in yourself, in your undying spirit, in your future, most of all in your immortality. This is what matters: that in the end, you are infinite; in God you are infinite. For you, there is no death without rebirth. Death is the gate to life. And no man passes through the gate, but he reaches the other side. Before death is birth, and after death is rebirth. In your death you will be reborn." While Eros read, Thomas played a quiet melody on his guitar. "As it is ... ," Eros concluded.

We responded, " ... so be it." Thomas plucked a strong, harmonious chord on his instrument to simulate a stroke on the big brass gong we used back at the Boston chapter house.

Matthew, Eve, and Thomas recited the Convocation of the Gods, explaining who the Gods were and how they were coming together, playing their roles in the End. We sang the hymn "Rise Up, Rise Up," then meditated for a while "on the purpose of our lives in service to Christ and the Gods." Matthew read the Prophecy of the End, describing in horrendous language the coming apocalypse. After each terrifying phrase we chanted, "And we shall conquer fear with love!" There was more recitation, then we sang again:

> Cleanse us in the Water of Life,
> Purify our Souls in Your Fire,
> Holy Father, Holy Mother,
> Christ and Satan, Unity and Love,
> God and Goddess, Salvation to our God.

Sister Hagar rose to her feet to begin the evangelical Revelation. "Brethren!" She looked down at each of us, an expression of pride and comradeship on her face. "There aren't many religious groups, or any kind of group really, that would consider this a religious ceremony, or be able to sit out in the woods with a can of shoe wax as a fire and scrappy pieces of paper as religious articles. But we are. And the reason we are is because we don't need the materialistic things to bring the presence of the Gods and the Beings to us. While we were invoking the Gods, a leaf fell down right in the middle of us, which was in a way a message of them telling us, 'We're here.'"

An expedition from Providence to Heaven.

She had seen how often we looked around us in the dark, expecting to be disturbed, chased by police or interrupted by strangers. She assured us, "There are no physical beings here, but there are thousands and thousands of Beings and Superbeings which are gathered here right now. Because they can feel our presence. They can feel our worship."

Hagar spoke of the great purpose each of us has, however much it may be hidden beneath the triviality of each mundane day. "We each have a particular relationship to one another in terms of the Hierarchy, and in terms of the Game." The Sabbath was one way of validating the Gods and reasserting our sense of purpose. "We're given energy and spurts of energy at particular times during the day to fulfill particular kinds of functions. Ten minutes ago we were all exhausted. And now we're all out here completely filled with energy, because there's a service that we have to give to the Gods. And They're all here."

"This is a very special trip," she told us. "It's the first one of its kind. We're making history." It was the first evangelical tour of southern New England in the camper which was just brought up from the New Orleans chapter. I was the first person of lowly Initiate rank to go on a Boston Process expedition. It was to be the most documented trip, because I took photographs for the Love issue of our magazine, and Roxana took notes for an article to go around them. But for the seven participants, two Prophets, one IP Messenger, three OP Messengers, and one Initiate, it was an historical trip because it placed their lives within a meaningful historical context, within the Latter Days leading to the Final Judgement. We make History by our every act. "Without The Process, we wouldn't be able to do this. We'd be nothing. And with The Process we're able to know that we belong and that we have a purpose in life."

Hagar turned toward me. "And now, all those Initiates who would like to rededicate their lives in service of Christ and the Three Great Gods of the Universe, come forward now and kneel before me."

I knelt and bowed my head, gripped by emotion and by paradox. In my own mind I rededicated myself to the research project which has produced this book. Ironically, I now feel that in a sense that was the same as dedicating myself to the Process and to the Great Gods. All six of the others, Matthew, Hagar, Eve, Thomas, Eros, and Roxana, remained together for a while in a Church, but the Church is no longer itself. Matthew and Hagar became respected leaders of the church, which evolved in a series of amazing steps into a non-religious non-profit organization serving humane goals. Half a century after the Sabbath Assembly in the woods, a few of us are Facebook friends.

Two and a half years after our Sabbath, the organization expelled its charismatic leader, Robert de Grimston, expelled the Gods Lucifer, Christ, and Satan, leaving only rigid, narrow old Jehovah. It rejected the living essence of the cult by discarding the dynamic name Process for the static name the Foundation. In 1975, after that gray revolution, Hagar would use her "telepathic powers" in a Psychic Workshop to discover that my chief secret virtue was "Loyalty." In our increasingly chaotic culture, it is hard to define the word "loyalty," yet I imagine if we discussed it today, each would agree the other had been loyal to the Process over many decades. In the woods, in 1971, she stood over me and said, "In the Name of the Lord Christ, and in the Name of the Lord Satan, I accept you as Initiate of the Process–Church of the Final Judgement. As it is."

I replied, "So be it."

We sang two more hymns, ending with the phrase, "The evils of the world of men are perishing, Satan's Hordes consume them. Out of the ashes of the old shall arise the beginnings of a New Age." "Brethren," said Roxana, "the Assembly is now ended. As it is … " We responded together, "So be it." We rose and walked along the forest path. Process means change. That Sabbath in the woods captured the living Process as it was at that instant. It was never the same.

We had to return to the Rubicon to hold a Midnight Meditation for the troubled teenagers there. We were about to drive off when we saw a young man and young woman walking hand-in-hand beside the road. They stopped near the place we had held our Assembly, and knelt, facing the spot, with bowed heads. Had they seen our service? Had they sensed the magic we had drawn to earth? They meditated for a moment, then went on their way.

CHAPTER 2   A Social Implosion

> But when all is brought together, when space and time no longer channel all existence into a chaos of tiny pieces divorced by the dimensions from each other, but instead feed back the splinters, concentrate them outside the separating limits of dimensional existence, so that all may become one, having one nature, one substance, one being, one orientation, one power, one truth, one knowledge, one awarenes ... then we can say ... "god is."
>
> — *God Is*, Process scripture

THE PROCESS IS NOT A THING but a force, an unfolding, a mode of evolution. One of the sisters told me, "It's been said the only thing that's absolutely definite about us is change." This chapter will continue to mention the real sacred names of leaders who were public figures, such as Father Aaron, but will be cautious about naming rank-and-file members, so her pseudonym will be Sister Samantha. Looking back on the changes over a dozen years of his membership in the cult, Father Aaron said, "The whole evolution was a continuous revelation experience." Not only was it different at different times, but each Processean experienced his own Process. To Robert de Grimston, the cult's Teacher, The Process was the projection of his own mind's subconscious processes, linked magically to the cosmic processes of universal history. To other Processeans, it was the collective adventure they shared in their quest for an unnamable goal. In the beginning, it was the personal, private relationship between Robert de Grimson and Mary Ann MacLean. For a dozen years they worked as partners in love and partners in building a movement. They shared high intelligence and an interest in uncovering the secret nature and hidden powers of the mind. In every other way they were exact opposites. They discovered Gods in each other and invented a world in their imagination.

ROBERT AND MARY ANN

Robert de Grimston Moor was born in Shanghai, China, October 8, 1935, the son of an engineer and the grandson of a barrister and of a vicar. Before he was a year old, Robert's mother returned with him to England. He says, "My upbringing was fairly conventional middle-class English, reasonably happy and uneventful." After the Second World War, his father became managing director of a time recorder company, "built the company up from virtually nothing when he took it over … to a thriving enterprise when he sold out a few years before his retirement." Robert's family was large and extended. In addition to an older sister and two younger brothers, he enjoyed the proximity of many relatives, a number of them fairly well connected. One great-uncle was an earl. Another served in Parliament for a decade at the turn of the century. One was an unsuccessful inventor, devising a horse race game, a tennis ball practice set, and an air raid turret shelter, among other things that did not sell. Uncle Prim, who was wounded at the capture of Delville Wood in 1916, was a haughty and proper gentleman. The family seems thoroughly respectable, hovering just at the bottom of the English upper class. This impression is given not only by Robert himself but by the reports of those who knew his parents and in the pages of a family genealogy printed by a grandfather. Robert's sister married and settled in Canada to run a riding academy. All three of the brothers wound up professional members of cults. The youngest joined Robert in the Process and became Father Phineas.

Robert received a strict Christian training at an exclusive private school. He was offered a slot at a leading university to study toward an engineering degree, but, unsure in motivation, he decided to satisfy his military obligation before continuing his schooling. In 1954, he began training for the elite Life Guards display cavalry unit but then transferred to the more active 15th-19th King's Royal Hussars. For six months he was stationed with the Hussars in Malaya, where the British were successfully fighting Communist insurgents. He says the Hussars, like the Life Guards, were too "twee," that is, too affected. A transfer brought him back to England and lodged him first in a unit made up of men who shared the single characteristic of being misfits. He ended his service in 1958 as transport officer in a unit stationed in Wareham, Dorset.

Robert reckons that his time in the cavalry was excellent training and experience. There he developed aristocratic poise and a dignified bearing, great assets for the charismatic leader of a cult. At discharge from the military he was entitled to only a single month of educational benefits, which he invested in an art course. He then spent three years studying at an architectural institute. He completed the training necessary for his Intermediate Certificate but did not go the full five years to get an architectural license. Robert learned basic principles of design, useful not only for designing cult symbols, but also transferable in a more abstract way to the designing of doctrinal structures.

Robert vividly described his struggle with sexual inhibitions given him by his prudish Anglican training. He says it wrongly convinced him that religion and sex were incompatible. His first marriage, bland and uninspiring, did not last, and he says very little about it. I am told he fathered two children, but I know nothing about them. In 1962 he was ready for a change.

I never met Mary Ann MacLean, because my extensive interactions with Robert began only after their separation, and she died in 2005, so I cannot interview her. A modern source of information is an essay by Christian Giudice which implies I was quite ignorant of her significance, claiming incorrectly that I did not begin my study of the Process until after the Separation in 1974, rather than the correct year of 1970. Giudice states: "It is my firm conviction that, far from being the uncontested leader of The Process, Robert de Grimston was but the mouthpiece of Mary Ann, the (not-so) charismatic facade, behind whom the real leader of The Process could act, detached and isolated from the majority of members: Mary Ann de Grimston."[21] I had been quite aware that the Process was created by the partnership of Mary Ann with Robert and viewed their Separation as a split between the organization (Mary Ann) and the culture (Robert). True, Robert had not himself created all the hymns and rituals, but he was primarily responsible for writing the scriptures, and he kept the name "Process" for his sect, while hers was renamed the Foundation and rapidly erased first the theology, then more gradually the rituals. Giudice offered little information about Mary Ann's background beyond the fact she "had grown up in a very poor area of Glasgow and had learned to fend for herself since a very early age, her father abandoning the household soon after her birth, while her mother repeatedly entrusted her to the care of relatives." That sentence paraphrases what I had already published.

Perhaps I should say she was not raised by anyone but simply grew up on her own. She was poorly treated as a child and learned quickly how to take care of herself. Mary Ann boasted that she came from the wretched Gorbals section of Glasgow, and claimed she never had a single day of formal education. The only person who ever gave her love in those years was an older man who died of exposure sleeping off a drunk behind a warehouse. He had vainly wrapped himself in newspapers against the cold. At least that was a tale she told.

Mary Ann apparently learned well the skill of giving men what they wanted at her price and rose to become the favored companion of prominent Londoners. She was a keen observer of other persons' feelings and used her insight to control them for both her protection and her gain. A famous actor and a world-renowned comedian were among her series of male friends, and rumors claimed at one time she was going to marry a famous prizefighter. She was maintained well by her London friends, kept in furs and comfort by their generosity.

Mary Ann's lifestyle was not, however, one of great security. She had many friends and admirers, but there was only one certainty ahead—as she aged, her successes would be gained with greater and greater difficulty. There was no obvious resting point. She had no conventional career and had experienced a long series of temporary intimate relationships. If she were to find security while still maintaining the excitement to which she was accustomed, she would have to strike out in a new direction. She was a demanding and emotionally volatile person. Relatively indifferent to the sufferings of humans in war, she became furious at any mistreatment of animals. It is said she once smashed a television set because it was showing pictures of a bullfight. Perhaps she identified with the powerless, abused creature fighting gallantly in a hopeless struggle. In 1962, she also was ready for a change.

Two kinds of personal characteristics of Robert and Mary Ann deserve analysis, two areas of personal qualities that guided them in the creation of the Process and made success possible: *skills* and *needs*.

First, they possessed skills and native abilities that when combined made them an extremely effective team. Both had high native intelligence. Their minds had been educated in opposite and complementary directions. Robert had learned to write elegantly in school, to project an aristocratic bearing in the military, and to design logical structures in his architectural studies. Mary Ann had learned the effective manipulation of other persons' emotional needs, based on deep understanding of each individual; her power was sufficient to make some individuals thoroughly dependent on her. Robert was trained in those skills necessary to make him the doctrinal Teacher of the cult and its charismatic leader, while Mary Ann could provide the personal analysis and intense emotional commitment required to bind and control the first ranks of members.

Second, they were driven by intense, complementary needs that guided their actions and resulted in a highly creative synthesis. Robert had been unsure of himself and of his future for a long time, suffering acutely in a struggle to cast off the inhibition that had dominated his upbringing. Mary Ann's life had always been chaotic and devoid of stable focus. Because the kinds of tension they experienced were nearly opposite, the solutions they sought were in opposite directions. Robert, depressed and dependent, wanted someone to intervene in his life to repair it. He wanted to explore his own feelings, escape from his inhibition, and receive Love. Mary Ann, anxious and aggressive, wanted absolute control over other people so they would serve her, yet never betray her. She wanted to develop her already strong personality, bend people perfectly to her will, and achieve Power. Having experienced repression, Robert sought liberation. Having experienced disorganization, Mary Ann sought control.

In Lofland's terminology, Robert and Mary Ann had opposite problem-solving perspectives. One might construct many typologies of these perspectives. Lofland suggested that our society primarily offers members a choice of three "alternate perspectives, or rhetorics, that specify the nature and sources of problems and offer some program for their resolution," the psychiatric, the political, and the religious.[22] These three types are only distinct, I believe, because each is connected to a different standard societal institution. The Process was created apart from any other church, political party, or medical institution. It was both religious and psychotherapeutic. If we define *problem-solving perspective* broadly as constituting any cluster of major assumptions about how human problems can be solved, rather than identifying it with one or another standard societal institution, then the orientations of Robert and Mary Ann are opposite but complementary perspectives. His was a *liberation perspective*; hers was a *control perspective*. The two could fit together in the same way that a masochist and a sadist can achieve a complementary relationship; to some extent each provided what the other wanted.

These opposing tendencies equally guided the Process in its development, at times conflicting, at times cooperating. When the theology was in its most developed state, Mary Ann's control orientation was expressed in the personality of the aggressive, God Jehovah; Robert's liberation orientation was expressed in the personality of the passive, God Lucifer. We will discuss the Great

Gods of the Universe later, but it is important to realize from the start that the beliefs of the Process were projections of the personalities of its founders.

Their needs and their perspectives on how to satisfy them derived from their individual life experiences. But these experiences in turn derived from their social origins. Robert came from the respectable, repressed middle class. Mary Ann came from the despised, chaotic underclass that lurks beneath the stable working class. Using language slightly different from mine to describe the strata of society, John Howard has written on the Hippie movement of the 1960s, a type of deviant people who tended to find the Process attractive. Howard thought he saw consistent differences between the classes in their attitudes toward drugs and therapy groups. He said there is a "common middle-class belief in the need to 'break out'" of a confining culture. "The socialization experience of middle-class children probably gives them the sense of a 'divided self,' the sense that there is an inner self which is more joyous, more buoyant, freer, and more innocent than the controlled, proper, achieving outer self."[23] This desire to break out, to liberate the inner self in all its narcissistic glory, was important for most early members of the Process, but not Mary Ann. Howard believed that other social classes typically have other needs:

> It is not clear that lower-class people feel this bifurcation, this schizoid burden. Indeed, middle- and lower-class people appear to have opposite problems. Whereas middle-class people exert themselves to facilitate impulse expression, lower-class people strive for impulse control. Whereas the middle class strives to be less "proper," lower-class people strive for propriety. Encounter groups encouraged people to touch each other; group members were encouraged to get outside themselves, experience others in sensate ways which violate middle-class conceptions of personal boundaries. It is not clear that lower-class people feel constrained in the same way.... Whereas middle-class people want to break out of lives experienced as too confining, lower-class people seek to forget lives experienced as too harsh and painful.[24]

The anthropologist Anthony F. C. Wallace framed a similar general hypothesis about which kinds of therapy will be emphasized in cultures experiencing different social conditions:

In a highly organized sociocultural system, the psychotherapeutic needs of individuals will tend to center in catharsis (the expression of suppressed or repressed wishes in a socially nondisturbing ritual situation); and ... in a relatively poorly organized system, the psychotherapeutic needs will tend to center in control (the development of a coherent image of self-and-world and the repression of incongruent motives and beliefs).[25]

Many sociological studies of psychiatric health care delivery done immediately before the birth of the Process supported the idea that the higher social classes seek, if not liberation, at least warm, personal expression in therapy, while the lower classes seek means to establish quick and firm control over their lives.[26] It is possible that this class difference is not a necessary one, the result of either accidental historical circumstances or the imposition of an unjust system by the dominant classes. In any case, Howard's and Wallace's observations apply well to the people who created the Process, and to those who came later to become members. The issue of liberation-versus-control was one of the most powerful forces in the history of the cult and is a major theme of this book.

ALFRED ADLER

Both Robert and Mary Ann independently became interested in the work of the psychoanalyst Alfred Adler, most particularly in his extremely simple theory of human goals. Robert described it as a theory of *compulsive goals*, saying Adler assumed each person "was in pursuit of something, and he wasn't speaking of the conscious aims and ambitions that we all have, but the unconscious driving forces that really motivate our actions. This both Mary Ann and I were in agreement with. And we also agreed with Adler that bringing these unconscious goals to consciousness could relieve the tensions, the pressures, the conflicts, the problems, and the sense of failure to which every human being is subject."

Adler said many things; Robert and Mary Ann adopted some of his ideas and rejected others, apparently according to the emotional response each idea elicited from them. They liked the theory that each individual lives according to a specific set of principles that can be identified, agreeing with Adler that "the psychic mechanism pursues a definite aim according to a definite interpretation of the world, and along the lines of an ideal behavior pattern."[27] Robert's goal was unconditional love and nurturance; Mary Ann's was unlimited power and security. In the theory, each person had a hierarchy of goals built on top of the basic one because of failure to satisfy the basic goal. For example, we might conjecture that Mary Ann's basic goal was security, and, because she assumed that people could not be trusted, she believed security could only be achieved through power. So power became her manifest goal, serving the deeper goal of security.

Adler says that each individual builds a world-view, or cosmic picture, to match his primary goal. It could be described in Lofland's terms as a problem-solving perspective, but, Adler feels, it is really broader than this, coloring all the person's perceptions:

> The ever-present goal which determines all our activity influences also the choice, intensity, and activity of those particular psychic faculties which serve to give shape and meaning to the cosmic picture. This explains the fact that each of us experiences a very specific segment of life, or of a particular event, or indeed, of the entire world in which we live. Each of us values only that which is appropriate to his goal. A real understanding of the behavior of any human being is impossible without a clear comprehension of the secret goal which he is pursuing; nor can we evaluate every aspect of his behavior until we know that his whole activity has been influenced by this goal.[28]

Adler had been the first of Freud's major disciples to break away from the master psychoanalyst, and Philip Rieff, an admirer of Freud, has complained that Adler oversimplified, looking for quick solutions and abandoning scientific analysis for magical commitment: "Adler's passion for finding what he called a 'guiding line,' a master doctrine, was the precise opposite of what Freud had trained himself to achieve: to tolerate uncertainty and always entertain multiple analytic perspectives until, in the cruel competition of ideas, some few survived."[29] For Reiff, Freud's critical, stoical approach was the most noble. He condemned schismatics like Adler for pressing "commitment therapies" on their clients:

> Both Adler and Jung sought in psychoanalysis a total theory, to which a patient could commit himself wholly. But all such therapies of commitment belong to the religious category of cure: that of souls.

More modestly, Freud sought to give men that power of insight which would increase their power to choose; but, he had no intention of telling them what to choose.... Adler and Jung sought, each in his own way, a cure, while Freud, knowing there was no cure, in the classical sense of a generalizable conversion experience, sought an increase in human power without reference to any of the established ideals.[30]

Reiff was a passionate supporter of Freud and may have exaggerated Freud's virtues while correctly distinguishing the two ideal types of therapy. The direction he says Freud took may lead to Science. The direction Adler took certainly leads to Religion. Several social scientists suggested, however, that psychotherapeutic cure is indistinguishable from religious cure.[31] Both may be vain hopes that often encourage unrealistic expectations. J. A. C. Brown has written that there were several reasons why Adler's brand of Psychoanalysis might appeal to people, including the optimistic impression he conveyed that "treatment was a relatively simple matter which could be conducted on the basis of friendly chats with one's analyst who would point out the style of life with its fictive goals and give some practical advice for a more sensible future strategy."[32]

Although inspired by Adler's writing, Robert and Mary Ann did not become patients of an Adlerian analyst. Certainly, few people have social connections to such a professional; there were not many in the world. But there was another barrier. One of the great costs of participating in Psychoanalysis, aside from the monetary expense, has been the expense to self-esteem. One must accept the role of *patient*, admit that one suffers from *neurosis*, and bear the stigma of *mental illness*. In recent years, several therapies have appeared that do not demand this sacrifice of honor. Scientology is one.

SCIENTOLOGY

Quite independently, Robert and Mary Ann discovered the innovative alternative to Psychoanalysis, Scientology (originally Dianetics). Invented by L. Ron Hubbard, an American science fiction writer, and announced to the world in a 1950 science fiction magazine, Scientology had grown into a thriving "technological religion" with world headquarters in England by the early 1960s.[33] Robert told me how he made contact:

I first heard about Scientology from a young man who came to stay in my father's house for a while in 1960—or thereabouts. My brother was in a very rough state at the time. My parents were worried about him, were willing to try anything, and packed him off to Scientology, where he got back on his feet and found a purpose in life, especially by meeting Mary Ann.

My own interest was aroused by the fact that here seemed to be a way of helping people to get out of a state of intense confusion and dissatisfaction. A workable form of therapy, no less. My first wife was in such a state, and I'd not been able to get her out of it. (Her state was nowhere near as bad as my brother's.) So I went there to find out what it was all about.

I took a course (I can't remember how much it cost), and became a therapist within fourteen weeks. I didn't pay very much attention to the theory. Most of it was science fiction. But I liked the practical applications, the stress on communication, between people and on helping people to discover their inner blocks and motivations in a systematic way.

Mary Ann was already on the therapist's course part-time when I joined it. We had little contact to begin with, but later discovered that our interests coincided at many points and so did our assessment of Scientology.

They were most impressed by the simple, easily learned techniques that seemed effective in uncovering the unconscious goals postulated by Adler's theory. The basic purpose of Scientology therapy does not assume the client is neurotic; instead, he could be entirely normal, because its goal is a mental condition far above normal, called *Clear*. In the early 1960s, this was an ideal condition devoutly to be desired but that had not yet been fully achieved. Not only would a Clear suffer from no psychosis, neurosis, compulsions, repressions, or psychosomatic ills, but in principle he would also enjoy being highly intelligent, vigorous, and satisfied. Scientology offered two basic routes toward Clear. In the more passive, a person becomes simply a client, submitting to the therapy as he might in Psychoanalysis. In the more active, he enrolls in a series of courses to become a Scientology practitioner, receiving therapy from fellow students while learning how to give it. Both Mary Ann and Robert chose the latter route. Thus they completely avoided being put in the low status of neurotic psychiatric patient but were elevated quickly to the apparent status of mental health professional.

In the most basic practice therapy sessions, they would sit on opposite sides of a small square table with a little electrical device called an E-Meter (electrometer) between them. Robert would hold two electrodes connected by wires to the E-Meter. Some machines had fancy, chrome-plated, cylindrical electrodes, but most that I had seen used emptied tomato juice cans. A tiny electrical current is passed through the body of the client, and the meter measures changes in his electrical resistance. Mary Ann would ask Robert questions, and he would respond. As his emotional state varied, so would the sweatiness of his palms, and thus also the electrical resistance measured by the E-Meter and indicated by a moving needle. Mary Ann would pay close attention to the reactions, writing down responses and asking new questions to follow up on the most interesting ones. All the time she would turn various knobs on the E-Meter, adjusting the sensitivity and returning the needle to its center position. It seemed to help Mary Ann uncover Robert's subconscious feelings, memories, and assumptions, disclosing his thoughts and feelings to her. The history of the E-meter is complex, but one of the methodologies explored by Carl Jung's branch of Psychoanalysis was the use of an electronic device to measure the emotional reactions of a client during analysis.[34]

For Robert there were at least two major consequences of the fourteen-week course. First, he found such mental excavations extremely interesting and his work with clients and other students abundantly rewarding. Second, his many hours in practice with Mary Ann as his therapist bound him to her in a most powerful fashion. Looking back, he analyzed it in Freudian terms, commenting that a *transference* had taken place, making her the center of his life for the next decade. He also described it in more popular language. In their sessions together, Robert fell deeply in love with Mary Ann.

They worked for the London Scientology organization as Certified Therapists for six weeks after graduating from the course. Mary Ann and Robert chafed at the rigid system of therapy demanded by their superiors. One of Hubbard's favorite slogans, simultaneously a boast and a demand, is "100% Standard Tech!" This means Scientology's spiritual technology is to be followed exactly, without the slightest variation. Mary Ann was especially anxious to experiment in the sessions she ran, changing the questions slightly or departing from the established order of procedures. Robert says he was less inventive than she at first, but both of them wanted the freedom to try out their own ideas. So they left Scientology and soon established their own therapy business.

The doubt and constraint they felt in Scientology became focused when Mary Ann came to believe that the session rooms were bugged. She accused her superiors of listening in on her sessions through hidden microphones. If they were in fact doing this, it was to make sure she and other therapists performed correctly and gave their clients 100% Standard Tech. There had been no complaints about her or Robert. Both of them were considered excellent therapists. They felt the bugging was an invasion of their privacy which neither of them could accept. They left Scientology, according to Robert parting amicably with the Scientology organization.

Founders of a new cult often served an apprenticeship in an earlier cult, and one consequence is that cults are historically connected in the equivalent of a social network. I explored those facts in a book chapter titled "Cultural Genetics" that used the example of Scientology and the Process to illustrate how concepts from biological genetics might be used to understand better how new religions are born.[35] It was already clear among scholars of sects and cults that many of them cluster in family lineages, as illustrated by the 1978 *Encyclopedia of American Religions* by J. Gordon Melton, which for example reports that L. Ron Hubbard had been active during 1945 in the Ordo Templi Orientis, prior to founding his Dianetics therapy, then Scientology religion.[36] Rather magically, the book that included my "Cultural Genetics" chapter was published by the Unification Church which Lofland and Stark had studied, was edited by Rodney Stark, and derived from a rather unusual conference also funded by that new Korean religion. In his introduction, Stark suggests what an adventure it was:

> Essays included here were originally prepared for an international conference held in May 1982 on Orcas Island, Washington, located in Puget Sound. There, more than a dozen scholars from the United States, Canada, Australia, England, and Northern Ireland spent three days sharing their most recent work. We arrived on the island after a five-hour cruise from Seattle aboard the "Viking Star," a chartered yacht. We returned in a squadron of single-engine float planes that picked us up on the beach and then landed on Lake Union in downtown Seattle.[37]

"Cultural Genetics" gave some emphasis to the Process but also mentioned several other groups that other authors had labelled "cults" and had suggested had been at least partially derived from Scientology. The earliest example was the flying saucer cult studied ethnographically by Festinger, Riecken, and Schachter in their 1956 book *When Prophecy Fails*, the founder of which had deeply studied within the Dianetics phase of Hubbard's movement.[38] The authors gave the pseudonym "Marian Keech" to the founder, setting the privacy standard I followed in my earliest publications about the Process, but today we know her real name was Dorothy Martin and she died in 1992.[39]

In order to consider how cults could be combined with other components of modern culture in developing cultural genetics, I also gave examples from classical music, using a fairly simple categorization system to classify these four composers: Johann Sebastian Bach, Richard Wagner, Arnold Schoenberg, and Carl Orff. Yes, Bach was Christian, even naming his composer son Johann Christian Bach. There is room to debate whether Wagner's glorious quartet of grand operas, *Der Ring des Nibelungen*, was really intended to revive Norse Pagan religion, but that was certainly one of its consequences. In the case of Schoenberg, I pointed out how he had created an essentially pseudoscientific cult within twentieth-century classical music by abandoning Wagner's romantic tradition to compose "12-tone" music following mathematical rules. Some day I must do a study of Orff's glorious attempt to revive European Paganism in his trilogy of cultic cantatas: *Carmina Burana, Catulli Carmina,* and *Trionfo di Afrodite* (*The Triumph of Aphrodite*).

COMPULSIONS ANALYSIS

Founders of new cults learn many practical skills during their apprenticeships as lieutenants to the leaders of other cults, before going into business for themselves. The word "business" is the right one. It is appropriate to view the founding of a new cult as an entrepreneurial act, on the same order as the founding of any new small business. If the cult succeeds, its founders will become rich in both material wealth and honor. For those in the cult business, there is nothing crazy about founding one.

Mary Ann and Robert did a little more exploring before setting up the Process. For a short while they exchanged ideas with a group of four amateur psychological experimenters bankrolled by a lawyer who hoped the "Fearsome

Foursome" would achieve a spiritual breakthrough that he could share. They, too, were using E-Meters and hunting for subconscious goals. Robert said this "friend of Mary Ann's was helping them to set up their own consulting business as therapists, and the precise structure of the original Process therapy was his idea."

Soon, Mary Ann and Robert established themselves under the name Compulsions Analysis and began looking for clients. They found that their talents combined were much more effective than they would have been separated. "Mary Ann was the real drive in the situation," Robert says; "I was the intellect. She had the certainty; I had the answers. She had the eye for an opening; I had the means to navigate it. She knew the move to make; I knew how to make it. Without her, I'd have been too uncertain to plunge ahead; without me she'd have been too ill-equipped to plunge ahead. But between us we had the essential elements, and in no time at all we were in business."

Like Scientology, Compulsions Analysis did not present itself primarily as a paramedical means for transforming disabled mentally ill patients into functioning members of society. Robert explained its orientation to a reporter in late 1965: "Our aim is to make people become aware of themselves, and so more responsible to themselves and to other people. We are not so concerned with healing the mentally sick as are the more orthodox psychoanalysts. We want to help people fulfill themselves." Unlike Scientology, however, Compulsions Analysis did not promise infinite benefits. Once Robert and I discussed mystical groups that try to reach beyond this life into an occult realm on the other side of existence. He said, "We are not offering super-powers but a means that people can live on this side more effectively." It is important to realize, however, that Compulsions Analysis and the Process never set any limit to what might be achieved. Psychiatry sets normal functioning as its limit as well as its goal. For Mary Ann and Robert's movement, the sky was the limit.

Their first client was an old boyfriend of Mary Ann's whose real purpose was to get back into her favor. When he saw that he had no chance with her, he dropped out. The next two clients were good friends of Robert's and later were named Father Joel and Father Micah. Compulsions Analysis recruited clients through Robert's friendship network. Mary Ann's lively but jaded and chaotic network did not contribute. Joel and Micah knew each other, but Robert feels he was closer to them than they were to each other. They were very different men with different styles and different friends of their own. Robert said, "They were my friends. And somewhere they knew I had the answers. And after them came their friends. A whole group of them, male and female, eager to discover what they had discovered."

Like Robert, Joel and Micah were students of architecture, so it was not surprising that they quickly brought in two other architects, later named Mother Greer and Father Raphael. The five were already somewhat close together and were quick to mobilize their energies as a group. Micah recalled, "Robert and I were very close for some time. Joel and I were very close. Raphael and I went to India together, and Morocco, so we were very close." They had already conspired on one rather rebellious project. The architectural school they attended put out a magazine, *Polygon*. Micah said, "We decided to take it over. Two days away from publishing, we took it over and rewrote it. We worked solidly for about fifty-two hours." They were not even members of the *Polygon* staff. "We just took it over." The issue they produced "really represented for the first time a psycho-humanist approach to architecture, as opposed to a design-aesthetic approach."

The rebellious future Processeans wanted their architectural profession to grow in new directions. Micah delighted in designing buildings that could not be seen, mirror buildings. Like many energetic young people, they did not want to submerge their creativity in the drab monotony of the commonplace. If there were a practical way of achieving a superhuman style of life and work, they would seize it. If we were offered such an opportunity at the right points in our lives, perhaps all of us would. Compulsions Analysis seemed like their best chance.

Robert and Mary Ann were the only trained therapists, so there was a limit on the number of people that could be gathered in by Compulsions Analysis. Some of their analytic hours were wasted on people just passing through—people who did not like the therapy or did not like the therapists. They began training their associates and over the period of about a year developed a large clientele of people involved to various degrees. They charged clients three guineas per fifty-five-minute session. Often the sessions were sold in blocks of six. There was no limit to the number a person might receive. One disgruntled woman reported getting three hundred sessions before she quit, while the angry father of two satisfied customers gave up after sixty. The early sessions were E-Meter therapy interactions, but, once a handful of clients had assembled, Compulsions Analysis organized group meetings at which several exercises adapted from similar Scientology meetings were practiced. They offered a Communications Course patterned on the one given at Scientology centers.

Whatever good the therapy sessions may have been as personal exploration, they functioned to give people an opportunity in which they might develop powerful bonds with Robert and Mary Ann, bonds like the transference relationship between them. The participants in the Communications Course practiced psychological exercises with each other, like the ones I will describe in chapter 8. Thus, clients could build intense personal relationships with each other. Some knew each other already, while others were strangers. They were already members of the same extended social network, and as their interactions continued the network became more highly interconnected and evolved into a group.

All the people who later formed the core of the Process community entered therapy in the two and a half years from the middle of 1963 to the beginning of 1966. It is impossible at this late date to determine what personal characteristics might have distinguished those who joined from those who did not. Most were effective middle-class young adults. Some were experiencing greater tension in their lives than others. I doubt that any were mentally ill. Perhaps only one or two exhibited the "enduring, acutely felt tensions" predicted by Lofland and Stark. Based on interviews I had with them, I will describe how seven came to join: Hathor, Rhea, Malachi, Dominic, Aaron, John, and Joshua. The original version of this book gave each a pseudonym, because the Process and the Foundation were both still active, so the groups as well as the leaders were temporarily anonymized. Here it is historically appropriate to use their actual sacred names, which functioned as pseudonyms they had been given by the Process for use in their public activities, which included many statements they published in the cult's magazines. Half a century later for this revised edition when all had long abandoned those names, we shall restore them, given that they served as public figures of Mother and Father rank when playing these sacred roles.

EARLY RECRUITS

Hathor

Mother Hathor was a student at an English art college where she met a young man who had been studying to be a concert pianist, whose later sacred name was Father Christian. His older brother was Raphael, a close friend of Micah, who was an intimate friend of Robert. Hathor was drawn into Compulsions Analysis through this long chain of strong social ties. Robert brought in Micah, who brought in Raphael, who brought in Christian, who brought in Hathor.

She had no particularly intense life problems. "Nothing dramatic was happening at that point in my life. I wasn't going through a vast trauma, or anything like that. I was at a crossroads, really, in terms of a career. Would I do teaching? Which I didn't really look forward to with a great deal of pleasure, 'cause . . . with the qualifications I had it would have meant teaching art in grade school. It really didn't excite me terribly. Or should I go on and do further training in order to qualify for a different kind of teaching position? Or should I take up painting? It was a period of indecision. But nothing deep or wrenching."

When she came into contact with the group, it was indeed "a kind of psychotherapy"; perhaps one might call it an "encounter group." For Hathor "it was quite a profound experience of self-discovery." She had no contact with other groups or techniques where she could feel emotions as profoundly within a symbolic context that seemed to describe vividly her thoughts and desires. "I had no contact, or very little, with any kind of psychotherapy. I mean, I don't think I would have known at that point what a psychoanalyst was. It just wasn't in my background. My background was the arts. I had read a bit, as a child. I'd been an avid reader in the public library, and I had got out books on weird things like metaphysics and Freud and Bertrand Russell and Jung, and couldn't make head nor tail of it." She used to read with a dictionary, trying to make sense of the unfamiliar words, attracted by something but not yet gripped. When she encountered Compulsions Analysis, she was amazed "that such a thing existed."

Her first few sessions had a tremendous impact. She saw herself and her emotions in an entirely new light. "The big thing was knowing that there was an unconscious mind." The therapy "answered so many of the almost unasked questions that I had. And that was how it was. It was quite: Good Heavens! It was really almost like a revelation to me, and opened up for me a whole area of exploration and discovery. And I decided, after contact with the group for a short time . . . not to pursue a teaching career in art but to study there, with that group, and become a part of it, become a worker. At that stage we weren't a community. I simply wanted to do that kind of work, which was helping people to uncover what was going on deep down inside that was maybe causing problems." The aspect of Compulsions Analysis that Hathor said was most important was the intensity of social interaction: "It wasn't something I was used to at all and could use quite a lot of." She said that few people in England at that time were involved in such experiences of self-discovery and sharing such intense, intimate feelings. For Hathor and the others, Compulsions Analysis "was quite radical and new."

Rhea

Mother Rhea met the group in the early days after she had already begun a career as an actress. "I had done a lot of repertory." English repertory theater is a bit like summer stock in America, except that it goes on all the time. "At that time I was doing radio, the BBC. I subsequently then did a play in the West End and television and this sort of thing." Rhea denied she had any problems in her work. "I was having a successful career … was becoming better known. So far as that was concerned it was very good. But I wasn't totally satisfied. I was very happy to entertain a lot of people at one go. I was not particularly happy with the way I related on a personal level. The idea of a conventional marriage to a doctor, or lawyer, a psychiatrist, a whatever, which is what my background would have supposed would happen. Something like that and the raising of a family in a conventional setting absolutely—for some reason, I don't know why—just appalled me! I could not imagine that kind of existence as being too fulfilling."

Rhea knew Greer, one of the original group, and John, who came in a little later. Although she had no prior interest in developing her inner self, she went along to a meeting to see what was going on. "The thing that struck me was the degree of intensity at which the work was being done. The kind of questions the people were asking, and not only asking themselves but asking one another. The degree of intense personalizing that went on, which I was unaccustomed to. One didn't ask those kinds of questions!" Rhea laughed when she recalled how unconventional the intimacy and openness were. "The absolute commitment to truth about self, and ownership of the answers. Like owning, 'I feel this. I do X,' or whatever. Discovering that people didn't fall apart. I didn't fall apart. In fact, it made me feel a lot stronger, and it made other people feel stronger too. I thought that it would end up with people not being able to speak to one another at all. In fact, it had the opposite effect." Rhea laughed again to remember how "fascinating"—indeed, "more than fascinating"—the experience of sharing such psychological intimacy had been.

There were group sessions as well as the individual therapy sessions with Robert and Mary Ann. Which did she feel were most striking or most successful? "I thought, to begin with, that it was the individual ones, because I like attention. I felt I was getting a lot of attention. But, in fact, more happened in the group situations than happened in the one-to-one situations."

She came to a decision point. Should she give up her acting career and throw body and soul into Compulsions Analysis? The safe thing would be to stick to her career and keep the therapy for a hobby. "As my friends kept telling me, 'Things are really opening up for you. Why do you want to give up a career which is now beginning to completely open up for you and give you promises of films?' I said, 'Because I know what it's going to be like from here on in. Even though I don't know the exact jobs, I know where it's going to go.' I had a whole vision of what my life would be like if I followed that career, and I suddenly felt there was no challenge. I thought, Oh, I see. And from that point I lost interest [in acting] and became much more interested and fascinated" by Compulsions Analysis. It was "like I was interested in knowing the answer to questions, and I didn't even really know the questions. But I knew that it was more challenging than what I had been doing previously. There was a certain amount of fear in that decision, but that was part of the challenge."

Malachi

Father Malachi joined the group in January 1966. He had known some people who were already members for a number of years. He knew Joel well and had shared an apartment with Micah for an extended period. Malachi had many friends outside Compulsions Analysis and was successful in his work. He was a management consultant, had already worked eight years for the same company, and "was considered one of the bright young people who would go far." There was nothing pathological about his life, and yet he was not entirely happy. Perhaps, if we were honest with ourselves, we would have to admit we are all somewhat dissatisfied with our lives, but for most of us there never comes a moment when we see a glimpse of something better, a way out of a gray life into a vivid existence full of excitement and triumph. Malachi was an effective, normal member of the middle class. He could be attracted away from his conventional lifestyle only by the convincing promise of a route to supernormal existence.

Malachi said, however, there were two factors that disposed him to join the group. First, he had found adulthood disappointing and disillusioning. In childhood he had hoped for a great and exciting life, but when he grew up he "found a fantastic discrepancy between what I expected of life and what actually transpired. I think one has to be dedicated to keeping a degree of excitement and interest and stimulation and constant development." But in his conventional career, as in most, that excitement was lacking. His contacts with Compulsions Analysis suggested that a splendid life could be enjoyed within it. "I remember very specifically my first reactions in going to my first meeting of all the people, which was one of an absolute whirlwind of energy, stimulation, intensity! Dynamic! All of the things you'd wish. Extraordinarily intense! It happened purely on the basis of the intense involvement of people, which was something that was completely new and nice."

Second, Malachi said, "I'd always had the feeling that I was a special person who was intended to do special things in their life and to rise beyond what I would call a normal life." It bothered him that he was caught in an ordinary life. "Obviously I equate normality with something less than exciting." At first he participated in the therapy exercises in the hope that they would give him greater effectiveness in his job and his outside personal life. But he began to feel that his unique personal identity flourished when he was within the group. "I don't think I ever said to myself, 'Oh, here is a situation where I can be special.' But it felt like I was employing some talents that I had" in a special way. Over the years, Malachi's involvement in the group permitted him to feel special, both in the intensely personal social life of the group and in flamboyant public presentations.

Malachi described his decision to join the group and abandon his earlier lifestyle in terms of investment, risk, and return on investment. "The idea of moving into a community was not something I did very easily. I had my own place and my own situation, friends, job. That was one of the investments." The group put no pressure on him to join. "When I was having problems whether I was going to be coming into the community or not, I was told, 'Well, whatever you want to do. You make up your own mind.' Nobody was making any attempt to get me involved." But he became totally involved. His hours inside the group were more gratifying than his hours outside it. Compulsions Analysis offered the possibility of greater gain but at greater risk. In the end, he left his job and moved in to live with other future Processeans. The people where he worked thought he was "quite insane to leave," but then they had not experimented with Compulsions Analysis and found it exhilarating.

Dominic

Father Dominic is a man of charm and ability who left science for the cult not because of failure but because the cult gave much greater personal and social gratification than laboratory research work. His actual conversion involved some temporary strain and a tortured personal reevaluation but was highly situational rather than the result of any longstanding problems. Like Malachi, Dominic came to feel that conventional life alternatives, however good, were inferior to the unconventional alternative, Compulsions Analysis.

Dominic grew up in Australia and did well in college. He earned a B.A. in Chemical Engineering from one university and a master's degree in Chemical Engineering Science from another. In 1965, he and his master's thesis advisor submitted two technical articles for publication, based on Dominic's research. Both were published in scientific journals. Like most successful student theses, the project was neither radical nor particularly creative but a solid example of careful journeyman science. Dominic's work did not give evidence yet of scientific genius, but a successful scientific career was definitely open to him.

Rather than complete his Ph.D. in Melbourne, a very practical course because he could do it in a short time, Dominic decided to accept a studentship at London University. He said he did this "mainly because I wanted to see Europe." He had no friends in London and did not quickly make friends at the university. In Australia he had been surrounded by people close to him, but now he was isolated from social support. His previous academic work had been closely supervised, not only in the technical sense that the details of his work were closely monitored, but also in the social sense that his attitudes were supported by those of others.

Dominic had looked forward with such anticipation to London University that it was a bitter discovery to find that he "didn't like it at all when I got there . . . found the work extremely tedious and completely lost concentration on it there." Scientifically, he should have found the work very rewarding. "I did Biochemistry in the same department with people who had made real breakthroughs in Biochemistry. And I was very excited about genetics research at that time. They were first discovering the DNA molecule, and the RNA was very recent and I was drawn towards that area. But I couldn't take the Biochemistry at all! The tedium of Biochemical Engineering sterilization procedures and all that sort of thing drove me crazy. My mind was working much faster, but my concentration span was shorter by that time."

Despite the gloom spreading from the tedium of his work, there were bright points because "I got off to Europe and the British Isles as much as possible." He filled his senses with exciting but unconnected impressions of the world outside the Laboratory. "I found most things quite unsatisfying at that time." He had "a number of hobbies" but lacked the vital feeling that his life had a stable core.

The friends Dominic made in London were not scientists but architects. One had some contacts with Compulsions Analysis. He told Dominic about the group and suggested he attend one of the public meetings. On impulse one evening, Dominic dropped in: "It was just like walking into an alternate universe! It seemed to be so lively, so interesting, and so challenging. And people's faces were so alive! The questions that were being asked and the answers that were being given were so much on what I really wanted."

One night, several meetings later, Dominic was riding home on his motor scooter with his friend who asked, "Are you thinking of joining?" Dominic liked the occasional meetings, but was he ready to commit himself further? Dominic replied, "Oh, I can't. I'm doing a Ph.D. at London University." Then his friend asked, "Would it matter to you if you didn't get your Ph.D.?" Dominic remembers "it was just an incredibly placed question in that moment of time. It was a very odd thing. Nobody had ever asked me a question like that before." He realized that his degree did matter to him, but he was not sure how or why. His course seemed compulsively aimed at the degree, rather than being the result of free, conscious choice. "I was on a compulsive pattern where I didn't even stop to think. It was a fantastically freeing question." As he thought it over more, he realized that in a very real way his spirit had died: "My life was a closed cycle. I was going to get a Ph.D. in Chemical Engineering, therefore I would become a Chemical Engineer, and therefore I would join an industry, and therefore I would get married, and therefore and therefore to the grave. Which was a totally compulsive path! That [realization] opened up the possibilities infinitely, you know? Because if it didn't matter to me, I could do any number of things. And I determined that very night to resign, to resign my Ph.D."

The immediate consequences were emotional and social: "I felt so incredible, like I'd never felt for years. Chills up and down my spine. I felt completely euphoric. I couldn't sleep. I was so excited about not getting a Ph.D., I felt more alive than I'd felt in years. And the next morning I went in and resigned, and the euphoria lasted for months. I never looked back, and I never once wished I got a Ph.D." His fellow graduate students were not happy with Dominic's decision: "They all thought I was crazy. They'd all gotten used to the rather dead, academic student that I was. That was the only recourse for them, really, to assume that I was crazy. That way they could rationalize it and still accommodate their own work. Because If I'd truly had a revelation, and in fact the best course for me would have been not to get a Ph.D., that would have involved them having to review what they were into."

The cultural relativity of norms for the expression of joy is shown in a study by Myron Sandifer and others in which British and American psychiatrists were shown sound films of mental patients and asked to list their symptoms.⁴⁰ The British were much more likely than the Americans to list symptoms "that overshot the mark," symptoms of too much activity, too much elation, according to English standards. The American doctors were more likely to see depression in the same patients. The national standards for the expression of joy were quite different. Dominic's joyful excitement may have been entirely healthy, yet it violated the standards of those around him. So when Dominic began exhibiting euphoria to his fellow students, they took it as a clear symptom of serious mental derangement.

For example, there was the famous cartwheels incident. This was a story of happiness that so violated the standard norms that it became a legend among outsiders who knew about the cult. "I remember that we used to go out to lunch at the cafeteria, any number of the research students, a fairly routine deal. But this time I was feeling particularly good, and did a series of cartwheels down Galloway Street. They really couldn't accommodate this!" The other students continued walking soberly to lunch, but the acrobatics "must have really shocked them, because some months—even years—later I was selling Process magazines somewhere in central London and somebody looked at the magazine and said, 'Oh, yes, I know about this organization. A friend of mine knew someone who joined it, and he used to do cartwheels down Galloway Street!'"

In a series of capricious moves, Dominic rearranged his personal life, living for a short time in an apartment with Micah and Malachi, then following these two men when they joined a larger group of Robert's clients. "One of my big problems in life before was making decisions, I always found it hard to make decisions, and I'd drive myself crazy trying to think of what I should do. But I lost that problem as soon as I joined up with the group. I felt the last decision I made was to join, and I've never really had a problem with decision-making since then." What did the initial impulse to visit Compulsions Analysis for the first time feel like? It was a "total experience where I felt that in a sense the decision was made for me, that it wasn't actually a decision I made. It was like something was taking control of me. Anyway, I was propelled through the street and went to that meeting. I got dressed very quickly and ran through the streets of London to get to the meeting on time. Hop in the elevator, out of the door, open a door, and there they all were." Was Dominic driven by a powerful subconscious desire, or by the will of God? Processeans say they are the same thing.

Aaron and John

Two of the earliest recruits, Father Aaron and Father John, were consciously dissatisfied with the course of their lives, investigated Compulsions Analysis as a possible solution, and grew quickly to become leading figures in the cult. Neither had close ties with the original members.

Aaron was a student at Oxford University, concentrating in Politics, Philosophy, and Economics. He found little joy in his studies or in the turmoil of student life: "I couldn't relate to what everybody was getting terribly worked up about. I could see the time at Oxford was leading nowhere, leading just into more education." Somebody he met at Oxford had a friend who was attending meetings at Compulsions Analysis. "It was a very tenuous connection" but enough to give him the idea of attending a meeting himself. His first visit was striking, but, despite his articulateness, he found it hard to describe: "There wasn't anything about it itself so much as the people. Walking into the room. Joel was there. Raphael was there. Mother Hathor. Maybe one or two others." There was an "inexplicable sense that we belonged together working towards whatever." Aaron believed each person there had a special feeling: "There is somewhere I have to go. There is something I have to do." Something extraordinary, something not possible in the context of the lives they had been leading.

John was the most disturbed of the first permanent recruits. Robert said John was depressed to the point of suicide. By his talents, John was a superior man, but he was also an unhappy one: "For about as long as I can remember, I've had the feeling of watching, looking, wanting something, occasionally touching something, usually losing it." He experienced this longing "often quite acutely, usually with a sense of despair, because I felt I couldn't touch or hold or reach, and I felt very unworthy." He was employed as an accountant, successful but unhappy in his work. Dissatisfied with his own life, he contemplated the courses of his friends' lives and found them dreary: "I could see that in my terms they were dying." They were "marrying and settling down and being very good citizens," but the life was draining out of them: "I could see compromise and defeat, or defeat in the form of compromise, entering into their lives. And that they were ceasing to aspire in terms that were meaningful to me. I wasn't particularly interested in becoming director of a company or top of the civil service. It didn't hold my attention, that kind of thing." The firm of accountants for which John worked offered him a partnership and a big boost in salary. Instead of accepting, he resigned from the company and began to look in new directions. He was accepted at Harvard Business School, where he thought he might improve his prospects from good to excellent, but he never went. An old friend put him in touch with Compulsions Analysis and its "interesting bunch of people." It was just the prospect he was looking for.

Joshua

Father Joshua was the only original Processean recruit from a working-class background. He grew up in Paisley, a textile town near Glasgow, Scotland. His mother worked in a thread mill and was able to invest in seven years of piano lessons for Joshua when he was a boy. At fourteen he flunked his abstract music theory exam for the third time, and the piano lessons stopped. His next interest was soccer. He hoped to become a professional player. A little later he also became interested in rock bands and other kinds of popular music. At the end of his teens he saw that his soccer was coming to nothing. Some of his friends began to make money at it, but no soccer scout ever recruited Joshua to a professional team. That left performing popular music as the only apparent chance to escape the drudgery of factory work. "I worked in a factory for four years," he recalls with little pleasure. "Rubber. Making vacuum brake pipes on a train. It was only a way of making money. The faster you did it the more money you made."

At the age of twenty he joined a semi-professional band. After playing together for a while around Glasgow, the group of five men decided to quit their regular jobs and try their luck in the big city, London. They called themselves the Pinnacle but in London took a new name, the Silhouette. They hung on in London for nearly a year, playing wherever they could get a gig, and cutting a few single records. They clung to their hopes. A new record was scheduled to come out at the beginning of 1966, so when Joshua went home to Scotland for the Christmas holidays he was dejected but not yet desperate. "And who should walk into my house in Scotland but Robert de Grimston. He was a friend of a friend of mine. I was given a card for The Process, 14 Wigmore Street, London. Put it in my pocket."

Joshua had no interest at all in deep questions about the human psyche and had drifted away from the Catholic religious training of his childhood. When his band's failure became more acute and hope ran out, he had no thought of seeking any kind of "therapy" to improve his condition. He needed a job. "This was a very rough time for me." A painful time. He did not want to return to the rubber hose factory. But what else could he do? "I remember walking around, thinking, Well, where to next! Needing help, needing support

... money." Money was the main thing. He remembered the card in his wallet that Robert had given him. Robert had seemed prosperous, and what little he had heard about his group suggested there was money to be found there. "It was mainly money and a little curiosity" that brought him to visit the group on one of its open evenings.

He found "lots of nice people" and a "very nice atmosphere. Father Joel, I remember, answered the door, and he was very charming. There was an air of success, and a good feeling." Robert invited Joshua to return the next day and bring the entire band with him. On his second visit, Joshua saw a good chance he could make some money off the group. "The band that I was playing with was invited to join and write music for the Process. We were offered to be put on a wage, fifteen pounds a week, which was very nice for us." It was more than they had been earning. On that basis Joshua joined. He discovered other reasons for staying and was, as it happened, the only member of his band to continue with the cult until it disintegrated. That left him free to develop a successful, independent life that combined musical performance with conventional Christianity.

THE PROCESS EMERGES

Compulsions Analysis evolved from a therapy service into a social group. Robert and Mary Ann settled into their roles as cult leaders. There came a time when participants realized they were a group, something above and beyond the original therapy. They began inventing new words, new symbols to express the emerging reality. Although Mary Ann has often been described as the strongest personality in the group, she did not become its charismatic figure. Rather, she gave that role to Robert and withdrew from public sight to exert her influence through more hidden means. Mary Ann felt Robert's name was not grand enough. He should change it. Robert Moor was the name of an ordinary person. His middle name, de Grimston, had more class. It pointed to a glorious ancestral past. Legend has it that Sylvester de Grimston came to England with William the Conqueror in the grand year of 1066. Knightly forebears included Sir Roger de Grymeston (1273-1343), his son Sir William, and Sir Gerard de Grymeston (1318-1396). A Marmaduke Grimston was knighted in 1603. Robert received this heritage through his paternal grandmother. At Mary Ann's insistence, Robert dropped the plebeian name Moor and became Robert de Grimston. Among cult members he was often called *the Teacher*. Mary Ann, now Mrs. de Grimston, was called *the Oracle*.

Compulsions Analysis needed a new name, too. Various alternatives were suggested, but no one idea received enough support to get adopted. Eventually, the group merely capitalized a common word they had been using to describe their therapy, and this became the evocative name of the cult. Members of the Process were Processeans. A couple of years later, the group began staging theatrical presentations called Processcenes. The uniforms worn in later years were called PGear (Process Gear). Automobiles and campers were P-Cars. Soon after Compulsions Analysis became the Process, the E-Meter used in the sessions was renamed the P-Scope.

In 1965, or possibly even earlier, Robert began writing Process literature of two kinds. He composed many bulletins giving instructions for performing the different therapy exercises. Eventually there were hundreds of different bulletins, some written by Joel or John, giving authoritative instructions for carrying out each ritual, each activity, and each aspect of church work. Robert also began composing the first pieces of semi-religious scripture, *The Logics*. These are short dissertations on the human personality that provided theoretical background for the actual therapy procedures. No other member of the group could write scripture the way Robert could.

The group also needed a symbol. One day several of them were sitting around a table, sketching various symbols and looking for one that was eye-catching and expressed something about the Process. Cassandra invented the winner: four thick lines that came together something like a Nazi swastika. They outlined the letter P for Process, seen from four different directions. This was very symbolic, since the Process was a coming together of contrasting people from different directions for a common purpose. The symbol is shown in Fig. 9a on page 211.

Finally, the Process needed a headquarters, something better than the Wigmore Street apartment they had been using, a place large enough for public activities. They took a lease on a large stone house at 2 Balfour Place, in London's fashionable Mayfair district. They put a big version of the new symbol on the door and began moving in around the beginning of 1966. At first, Malachi said, "We didn't conceive of people moving into it and it becoming a community. It was just that various people would live there, and that would be the center of operations. But that began to change in character very rapidly. January, February, March. We began to feel that what we should do is live as a community, create a community, because there already was one in terms of our interests. We were all interested in the same things, so we would all live together."

ANALYSIS

Many factors made the Process what it was, but two related sociological phenomena explain its origin and the recruitment of new members. First, people who participated in Compulsions Analysis saw it as a rational and initially low-risk step that might lead to increased personal effectiveness and satisfaction. Second, the structure of social relations was transformed because of the new standard of intimacy set by the therapy procedure itself. An originally extended social network collapsed into a closed, cohesive group. We can call the first phenomenon *optimization*, the second, *implosion*.

Optimization

Lofland and Stark told us, "For conversion it is necessary that a person . . . experience enduring, acutely felt tensions."[41] They needed a concept about the motivation of people who found and join strange cults. The early California converts to the Unification Church they studied were unsuccessful people suffering various chronic life problems. They were so incompetent in presenting their own doctrines that Lofland had to rewrite their literature for them, and Stark was pressed into service as the voice of the cult in tape-recorded lectures. The life stories of these folk, published by Lofland and Stark, depict them as chronically miserable, maladjusted, untalented people. Clearly they did suffer "enduring, acutely felt tensions." They could not be more different from Processeans, most of whom were quite able and seemed reasonably successful in their careers.

How did Lofland define his tension? "This tension is best characterized as a felt discrepancy between some imaginary, ideal state of affairs and the circumstances in which they actually saw themselves."[42] If we look back at the life stories of founding Processeans I have just told, we do see evidence of tension, so defined. At least when people decided to give up their old lives in favor of the Process, it seems they had become dissatisfied with their ordinary careers and reached for a more ideal state. In a 1976 doctrinal lecture, Father John, who had been the most intensely disturbed of the original group, pointed to a felt discrepancy such as that predicted by Lofland. But John said all people feel it, not just a few pathological types. "The only lack is the lack of Love. If there was lots of Love, I think problems wouldn't exist. I'm saying that from the point of view of assuming that everybody feels there are problems, there are difficulties. There is a gap between what we want to be and what we actually are. There is a gap between the reality as it is right now and the ideal out there in the future as we would like it to be." John said we all want to receive more love and give more love than is possible in conventional society. The Process was a grand attempt to approach the ideal life which would be drenched with love.

Lofland's definition of tension does not really describe the pathological tension his converts suffered, but the normal tension required to motivate any organism. It explains little about cults per se that it does not explain about everything. Social psychological literature is rich with theories and studies indicating that people (and animals) tend to act so as to maximize their rewards. The first of George Homans' famous Five Propositions states: "For all actions taken by persons, the more often a particular action of a person is rewarded, the more likely the person is to perform that action."[43] The related Third Proposition makes a similar point: "The more valuable to a person is the result of his action, the more likely he is to perform the action."[44] These axioms concern normal action, not pathological behavior.

Joining a deviant cult may often be perfectly reasonable behavior. If the Processeans had left their ordinary, successful lives to become movie stars or U.S. Senators, we would hardly feel their behavior demanded an explanation. It would be obvious to us that they had improved their situations, and we would not immediately assume that the lives they left had to be unattractive. We might all want to be movie stars or senators. Therefore we are quick to agree that a fairly happy person might leave a cozy and familiar occupation for the advancement such splendid careers would offer. But when a person leaves a conventional life to join a crazy cult, we tend to feel that a special explanation is required.

Why are we so foolish? I can think of two reasons. First, we judge the Processeans' actions from our own position, hindered by our own prejudices and lacking the evidence they had in deciding the Process was a positive alternative. Second, the Process developed its own norms and values, a counterculture we do not share. When the Processeans grew close together, they pulled away from us to form their own society, thereby opening a gulf of mutual deviance between their group and ours. The first point is a statement about *optimization*, the second about *implosion*.

We have to remember that people choose alternatives according to their own momentary estimations of the payoffs, not according to what the real payoffs are going to be or according to the views of outsiders not caught up in the situation. People will do what they think is best for them, not what we might imagine they ought to do. My interviews with founders of the Process suggest that seven factors made future Processeans more likely than other people to place their bets on the side of the cult.

1. The ideologies of the artistic training many members had received were congruent with that of the Process. There were five architects, a couple of musicians, an artist, a research scientist, and an actress in the original group. In these fields creativity is said to be a prime value. Unfortunately, the actual opportunities for creativity are strictly limited. Architects and industrial engineers may believe they are creative artists, but most of them are simple workers employed to do completely mundane jobs. Technological gurus like Victor Papanek and Buckminster Fuller urged designers to fulfill a revolutionary, Utopian role in society.[45] In the Process, people were able to realize these goals and values better than in their original occupations, even though the socialization to the role of creator had taken place in the conventional institutions. Micah told me the work he and the others performed building the Process was a natural extension of their architectural training: "It's a very architectural thing, building up a [group like the Process]. I call it religious engineering."

2. The founders of the cult were isolated from social control, from social forces that would have inhibited their cult involvements. All had left the homes of their parents. Some had recently lost social ties with outsiders, Dominic by leaving Australia, Aaron by leaving college, John by leaving his job. The others counted many fellow Processeans among their friends. None was deeply involved in a conventional religious organization. Apparently, none was involved in any conventional psychiatric treatment. None had been trained in academic psychology, which might have inhibited participation. Resistance from friends and co-workers only came when people were already deeply involved in the cult, because initial experiences with it in no way interfered with the maintenance of conventional jobs or friendships. In short, the future Processeans were all free to experiment with the cult.

3. Compulsions Analysis offered something new, an alternative that was plausible because it had not ever been discredited. In the history of therapy and self-improvement techniques, we see many examples of new ideas that gain tremendous support for a while, then are rejected just as vigorously when their limitations become manifest.[46] This phenomenon encourages the emergence of fashion cycles. The newest idea has the least evidence against it, so at first it triumphs over the tired ideas of the past that have already been found wanting. People who commit their lives to a new fad, perhaps by becoming

professionals in it may promote it until the ends of their lives. Today, many well-educated middle-class people encounter a pseudo-therapy cult and exclaim, "Oh, not another one of those! I've seen so many others, and they're all bunk!" Future Processeans could not react this way. Pseudo-therapies were so new in their social circles that they had not yet been discredited.

4. The founders of the Process were all young adults, at that time in life when adventure and risk are most normal, when idealism and hope can be high, and when a person's talent and energy can make it most possible to act decisively.[47] The 1960s were the decade of youth, in which radical students, young rock stars, and colorful hippies amplified the usual vitality and adventuresome character of young people.

5. Several, but by no means all, of the future Processeans joined at a period in their lives when some kind of decision was necessary anyway. Lofland and Stark would say they were at turning points. John was consciously searching for a radical change. Hathor had to decide whether to take a job or continue with her schooling. Aaron didn't know what he wanted to do. The Process was not the only game in town, but it looked like a good bet to these three partly because they were ready to bet on something new, rather than hang on where they were. The others also needed to be convinced that betting was in order.

6. People were able to sample Compulsions Analysis and the Process at little risk before committing themselves. They could try it out, decide whether they liked the therapy, and develop friendships in the group. Much of the literature on religious conversion emphasizes the striking, sudden, emotional transformation of people who join almost instantaneously.[48] This cult allowed newcomers to take their time. At each step in a ladder of increasing commitment, the risk and immediate cost were low.

7. The people who did join report they found the experience extremely satisfying. They saw direct evidence that the claims of the cult were substantiated. Dominic, for example, saw his compulsions just as Compulsions Analysis said he might. To the extent that people did find participation rewarding, they could anticipate that continued and even greater participation would be still more satisfying. While the therapy claimed objective benefits of personal improvement, I think the real rewards were social. But these social rewards looked like the improved personal effectiveness that was promised.

The most important returns from high-status conventional occupations are social in nature. Conventional status symbols happen, not surprisingly, to be expensive and rather remote from direct social interaction. Costly houses and exalted titles convey symbolic status but are often difficult to transform into the direct respect and appreciation given by close friends. Who has the greater feeling of personal power, the bureaucrat who shuffles thousands of lives with his administrative papers, or the cult leader who has intimate influence over a dozen individuals? In the Process, members could experience immediate social benefits—*immediate* not only in the sense of *instantaneous* but also in the sense of *direct*, that is, *not mediated* by any complex chain of cultural symbols or social institutions. Sociation is the stuff of society. We want the constant, warm attention of other human beings. In "alienated" complex societies we must take much of our social gratification second-hand, displacing or sublimating our needs for love and stimulation onto abstract social constructions. In sharing intensive, positive social interactions of a kind unusual in English society at the time, Processeans could achieve their desired social gratification without the necessity of laboring toward distant, indirect satisfactions in conventional institutions. Therefore, the experience of participating in the Process could convince them, at least over the short run, that the cult was in fact a better alternative than the conventional ones open to them.

Those who had remained with the cult from the beginning right up until the time I interviewed them told me they did in fact maximize their satisfactions by betting on the Process. The cult shifted course many times, sometimes in radical ways, in continual optimization of its perceived chances of reward.

Social Implosion

The Process emerged from Compulsions Analysis, a pseudo-therapy. In chapter 8 we will examine the specific therapy exercises used by the Process and see that all functioned to build unusually intense, intimate bonds between participants. We have already seen that Robert used the technical language of Psychoanalysis to say that his therapy sessions with Mary Ann caused him to develop a *transference relationship* with her that lasted a dozen years. In pure psychoanalytic theory, this would mean that Robert had displaced powerful feelings onto Mary Ann that had their origins in his childhood relationships with his parents. Psychoanalysis may be mistaken. But it is certain that for him, and for other participants in Compulsions Analysis for whom the therapy was effective, an overwhelming involvement developed with the therapist, a relationship of such intense dependency that it overpowered other relationships in the person's life. Because every therapist in Scientology and Compulsions Analysis was also a patient to some other therapist, the sessions created intense, interlocking bonds of transference and countertransference. The basic therapy interaction forces the disclosure of the patient's inner feelings and builds a powerful if asymmetrical intimacy between the two participants. The tie between them can become the dominant social reality for the patient, and the therapist develops a number of rather strong ties to his several clients.

John Lofland, Mark Granovetter, and many other sociologists stress the importance of a "pre-existing friendship net" in the growth of a brand-new cult or other kind of movement.[49] Essentially all of the early recruits were members of Robert's own friendship network or contacted Robert through a chain of social relationships. As Raphael said, "It was all friends of friends." Compulsions Analysis recruited outward through this network until Robert and Mary Ann had as many clients as they could handle.

As soon as there were many clients, this fragment of a network began to develop into a cohesive group. Clients began interacting more frequently with each other. Group therapy sessions were set up in which they shared intimate feelings. Compulsions Analysis provided participants a supremely rewarding, exciting, vivid social life. It established a new norm for the quality of social interaction. Consequently, social ties between members strengthened markedly, while the network was becoming more thoroughly interconnected. The rudiments of a group culture evolved. Several of the members I interviewed spoke of coming to feel that only other participants understood them completely and said it grew more and more difficult to communicate with friends who were not participants. At the same time that ties were strengthening with other participants, ties with nonparticipants weakened. What I call a *social implosion* took place.

In a *social implosion*, part of an extended social network collapses as social ties within it strengthen and, reciprocally, those to persons outside it weaken. It is a step-by-step process. I suppose that social implosions may be set off by more than one kind of circumstance. In this case, the introduction of a new element of culture, a "therapy" technique that increased the intimacy of relations around a point in the network, triggered the implosion.

The key factor was the sessions with Mary Ann and Robert. They did not quickly train other therapists from among the recruits; had they done so, this new culture might have spread widely in English society rather than producing an implosion. Although we are not in a position to quantify the parameters of the social situation, the implosion required that the growth of intimacy among participants proceed in some measure more rapidly than the growth of the group through recruitment.

Mary Ann and Robert did train a couple of their closest lieutenants to do some of the therapy routines. But at the same time, new routines were being constantly invented, and participants' schedules increased to take advantage of the new processes. Thus the invention of new techniques counteracted the tendency of training to aid diffusion. Raphael, for example, "worked in the morning as an architect, and in the afternoon as a therapist. In the evening we would have courses in communication, sensitivity development." The density of social relations increased faster near the center of the network than the wave front of participation could expand.

For a certain distance out along the ties of Robert's network, Compulsions Analysis was strengthening ties in the direction of Robert and Mary Ann. This distance was a function of the amount of time its therapists could give divided by the amount of time required each week by a deeply involved client. Beyond that distance, ties began to weaken. The social fabric tore along the periphery at this social distance. People quit their jobs and let friendships lapse with people further out along the network. They moved in together, all living as one small society at Balfour Place. They developed a consciousness of creating and joining a group. They invented a name and a symbol for it.

The phenomenon of social implosion may be very common, and many examples have undoubtedly been reported in the sociological literature, though not analyzed in exactly the same way. E.L. Quarantelli and Dennis Wenger reported on a Ouija board cult that apparently experienced a short-term social implosion. This is another example of an implosion that followed the introduction of a social mechanism that increased the intensity of social relations among participants, in this case the use of a Ouija board supposedly to communicate with spirits but actually to share powerful emotional experiences and intimate communication. The cult developed among eight female students at a large university after a particularly intense Ouija board session. Afterwards they met regularly at midnight to work the board:

> The more the cult members participated in using the Ouija board,
> the more they were seen and saw themselves and their behavior as
> different. Negative reactions expressed by outsiders intensified this
> process. Cult members became increasingly secretive so as to protect
> their activities and themselves from "nonbelievers." This had the
> dual effect of increasing the separation between participants and
> nonparticipants and of bringing the participants even closer togeth-
> er in sharing something exclusive.[50]

This social implosion was only temporary; it did not produce a permanent group that could successfully maintain its integrity for a long period. Members' participation in the Ouija board cult rested upon their attendance at the university. The cult dissolved when two members left the university, another left the dormitory they had been residents in, and the informal leader lost interest.

A social implosion can be reversed at any point if relationships within the group lose their special quality or members begin having especially rewarding contacts with outsiders. An implosion is most likely to become permanent if the initial phase of actual implosion is immediately followed by a period marked by an absence of involvements with attractive outsiders or enticing career alternatives. The social implosion that created the Process became permanent after the entire cult packed up, abandoned London, and went to live on an isolated Mexican beach.

At a place called Xtul on the Yucatan Peninsula, geographically separated from the society in which it had emerged, the Process took its social implosion to the logically extreme conclusion: the generation of a thorough-going alternate society which described itself in religious terms. In this chapter we have seen how the Process came into being as a deviant psychotherapy group. In the next we will see how it evolved into a religious cult.

CHAPTER 3

God at Xtul

We traveled on into Mexico
And on through Yucatan
And in a ruin on the Maya coast
We found our promised land.
Xtul, you simplify our lives
Xtul, you clarify our love for our GOD.

— A Process Song

The Process became an "Army of God upon earth," a deviant religious group following the four Great Gods of the Universe, over a period of two years, from late 1965 through late 1967. Originally a therapy cult, it evolved into a religious sect and finally became legally incorporated as a church. Six factors combined to produce this social and conceptual shift. First, although many of the Processeans considered themselves agnostic, all had received some religious training, so religious concepts and language were available to them and they were able to use the general religious culture of England as an interpretive structure through which to understand themselves and their experiences. Second, the Adlerian analysis of personal goals was open-ended in design, encouraging participants to discover magical desires within their psyches, wishes that could not be accommodated inside conventional, mundane reality. Third, the effect of the social implosion was to incorporate the individual people in a social personality, perceiving the presence of a group mind that they felt existed quite apart from their own personalities, and which they identified as God. Fourth, the events and emotions of those years seemed to confirm their religious assumptions and provide ever deeper glimpses of divine intervention in their lives. Fifth, the claim that God provided guidance and made demands was a kind of excuse made by members, and especially by the leaders, for acting impulsively, for avoiding responsibility to any human law or to the welfare of followers. Sixth, the religious label was used strategically, to control the response of the general public. These six factors operated in various combinations at different times. At the end of the chapter we will suggest what their unifying principle might be.

BEFORE DEPARTURE

Some Processeans say their group became religious before it visited Mexico, while others say the change happened in a ruined plantation on the Yucatan coast. The date each assigns to this transformation depends, I think, on when each individual's consciousness changed. The term *religious* refers not to a well-marked objective reality, but to a particular consciousness, to a particular interpretation of social reality. Malachi had a religious orientation almost from the beginning. For Rhea, the word "religion had so many negative connotations" that "presentation of ourselves as a religious group was not readily acceptable" until her feelings changed "simply as the reality of God became much more of a personal experience."

By late 1965, many Processeans had recognized that their concerns went beyond the strictly psychological to include religious feelings and desires. Robert explained to a newspaper reporter how this had happened: "The Process started off purely as psychotherapy. But the more we worked with our clients, the more we realized we were closer to a religious approach. Nearly everyone kept coming up with their religious goals—with their own concept of God."

As another reporter noted about the same time, the Process was becoming "increasingly religious and introverted." This is a good observation, because the early development of religiosity in the Process came from two parallel changes going on that could each be described as introversion: (1) as Robert said, individuals were discovering and admitting their secret magical desires in the therapy sessions; and (2) the group was becoming intensely cohesive and all-encompassing. The first was individual introspection, the second, social implosion. Raphael's view agrees with mine. He noted that the Process began as a group of normal people who encouraged each other to aspire to the supernormal and as a result became a religious cult:

> The initial stage was more psychotherapeutic than it was religious. But we were not people with problems. We were normal people ourselves, and so were our friends. We had good jobs. We had reasonable situations. I was an architect. I had also written a number of stories, a couple of which had been published, and I'd been commissioned to do a mural. So I wasn't a failure in worldly terms. We weren't struggling, or in the hands of psychiatrists. We were essentially looking for something more than society was apparently capable of delivering. We were looking for greater fulfillment than we could see stretching ahead of us in the careers society provided.... We essentially researched both using ourselves and the people who came to us for help, and reached, about the middle of 1965, a recognition that underneath everything (in every person who we helped or in our own research on ourselves) we came to what we would call a basic religious reality . . . a sense of religious purpose, or a sense of purpose in life.

Raphael had been raised Catholic but was agnostic at that time. His religious background made it possible for him to define the end result of his own therapy as a religious consciousness. But his experiences in therapy really were supernatural, if by "supernatural" we mean phenomena beyond the normal ability to understand and describe. "We recognized that essentially we were talking about religion in the broadest sense, so in our public presentation we began to become more religious and talk about God and religion more than we had up to that point."

Mother Hathor believed the emergence of the Process's community facilitated the development of a religious conception. When people were still living apart, "we had very private things, private realities, private thoughts." Once they were sharing many intimate hours together, private thoughts and feelings "started coming out. And we all found that there was a thread in common, and that was that somewhere deep inside there was a very strong belief in God. It quite amazed me as much as the preliminary discovery of the unconscious mind." Her comment is apt. The religious discovery was both an *extension* and a *reversal* of the discovery of the subconscious. As an expression of personal desires that had been repressed by society's disdain for them and were now liberated by the developing subculture's tolerance, religiousness was a product of the subconscious. But the new religion was also the product of a superconscious mind, the cognitive and emotional currents that began to flow in the group, around and beyond the individuals that constituted it.

The intimacy produced by the implosion stimulated mystical feelings. Individuals lost a sense of independence. Decisions were often made subliminally in group meditation sessions. Individuals contributed fragments of feelings and ideas to the social decision-making process, and no one could readily distinguish his own feelings and ideas from those of the others. Ideas, feelings, and decisions were therefore perceived as coming out of the blue from an obscure, uncanny, occult source. The appearance of occult and pseudo-telepathic subjective events in Psychoanalysis has been documented,[51] and similar phenomena are common in Scientology. People who know each other extremely well respond to the nuances in each other's behavior, coming to know things that have not been said and predicting behavior without conscious analysis. I do not happen to believe that real telepathy or clairvoyance take place. But people do communicate without knowing how they do it and do anticipate each other's behavior without the slightest conscious idea what information they used. However much the outsider might disbelieve, for the participant these experiences can be very convincing evidence of the supernatural.

And the same therapy that produced these uncanny phenomena also stimulated a will to believe. In psychoanalytic language, one might say that patients in any intensive analytic therapy *regress*. Whether or not we want to conceptualize this as a return to the habits of childhood or merely a transformation that resembles such a return does not matter. The patients lose some of the veneer of maturity and begin admitting their autarchic, magical, infantile desires. As they mutually liberated themselves from any external control over the expression of fantasies, Processeans came to express completely unlimited desires, oceanic feelings, longings for absolute power and absolute dependence. These wishes could not be accommodated within ordinary reality. They are the kind of thing banished from polite society, even though all people might feel them. I believe we will see why this is true when we examine the later history of the cult.

If my analysis is correct, then it ought to be very easy for psychotherapy groups to become quasi-religious cults. Why doesn't this happen often? Why don't Psychoanalysis and its more recent descendants follow the same pattern? First of all, the fact is they often do, perhaps when therapists forsake Freud's skeptical *analytic* approach and adopt commitment therapies.[52] Second, the medical metaphor used by psychiatrists and others trained thoroughly in university settings both defines the goals of therapy narrowly and identifies the patient's mystical sensations as symptomatic of his neurosis. Third, after his didactic analysis, the therapist is not commonly expected to receive intensive therapy himself and will, therefore, remain relatively unmoved by patients' religious urges. From a different perspective, we can say that the tendency of a psychotherapy to evolve into a full-blown religious cult is inhibited if the therapist keeps himself aloof from the intense experience of his patients and is stimulated if the therapist enters completely into the experience himself, accepting alongside the patient the role of suppliant and permitting his own consciousness to be transformed by intense social intercourse. A therapy is most likely to remain pedestrian if its administration is securely locked into a standard medical institution and is most likely to become a cult if it is practiced independently of any restraining institution of conventional society.

THE DEPARTURE

Almost as soon as the Processeans had moved into Balfour Place, they were talking about leaving London altogether. Relations between members and their old outsider friends were now rather painful. Malachi, Dominic, and Rhea were serious when they said their friends thought they were crazy to give up normal lives for membership in a deviant cult. They made several attempts to tell London how wonderful the Process was. Malachi recalled they often gave public presentations: "One of my first evenings out was to go with a group of people speaking up at Oxford. And we went there and created quite a stir. I didn't feel it was fantastically effective! We were talking too much above people's heads, or too wide of where they were at. A lot of what we were doing was shaping our own identity, and you only get that from being different to somebody else, so already there was a strong situation to have a conflict. Maybe one makes a few converts, but basically what you're doing is creating an argument and a conflict." I am not aware of a single convert made at those public presentations. Apparently the Processeans would harangue their audiences mercilessly.

Rhea believed this breakdown in communication was at the heart of the decision to leave London: "My own recollection was the feeling of not being understood. It was a feeling of having found something very important and discovering that there was no understanding from other people. We couldn't communicate it basically. It was non-communicable at that point.... Certainly in terms of my friends, there was non-understanding on both sides. I couldn't explain what I was doing... what made me want to do it... And they couldn't understand, because I couldn't explain it . . . It was like having a germ of a feeling, a sense of something which was definitely not being confirmed in that environment. It was at odds with, and therefore non-communicable." The social reality of the Process was at odds with the social reality of London, so the perceptions and values conflicted as well. Robert de Grimston told me the group left London because the city was "a miasma." Miasma means a noxious influence or atmosphere. Contact with outsiders had become unpleasant. By 1965, the first aggressive newspaper reporters had begun invading the cult, writing extremely unfriendly stories expressing scorn and disapproval.

Malachi said, "I wasn't surprised when we began talking about moving away from London. The concept of creating our own community, a self-supporting community, where we were away from the distractions and the effort of convincing somebody" was very attractive. "So the idea of moving away from London everybody thought was a great idea."

Hathor said the decision to leave London was a step forward in the attempt to become a cohesive group: "We still weren't much of a community. We'd just started living that kind of a lifestyle, i.e., a lot of people in one very large building. We didn't have much contact with each other. Everybody had their own room; maybe two people were in a room, I don't even think we had meals together at that point. We may have just started. It was still very isolated.

And so we didn't have the same kind of group feeling that we've since developed—on decisions, and knowing exactly what things were going on—that kind of feeling. I remember for myself the decision to go to Nassau, and then later to go to Xtul, was based on a feeling of 'It would be nice to create something a bit more cohesive.' Because there was a lot of isolation at that point. And there didn't seem to be anything within that situation that we could work with, living in the middle of London." Raphael said the only clear feeling was "to get away from civilization and to see what we really wanted to do. We weren't really sure. We didn't know whether we were packing our bags for good, maybe never coming back to civilization as we knew it, or whether we were going away for a period of time." Where would they go? The Process rejected the all-too-modest standards of conventional life and reached out for the ideal. Robert said they decided to search for "a tropical island paradise." Malachi put it this way: "We thought, 'We'll get an island. We'll get some land. We'll get an island, and we'll become self-sufficient and self-supporting.'"

In May 1966, Raphael was sent out to look for a suitable tropical island. He went to Nassau in the Bahamas and began shopping around "for an island where we could set up a self-contained community." The Processeans pooled their resources, contributing everything they had to a central fund. According to one report, Raphael himself contributed more than £10,000 from his inheritance. After a few weeks, he found some property that looked suitable, a small, uninhabited island in the Bahamas that was for sale.

On June 23, 1966, the core group of Processeans, numbering about thirty, left London by ship bound for Nassau. With them went six German shepherd dogs. In mid-July, a reporter for a London newspaper interviewed Raphael, who admitted, "Our plans are fluid." The Process rented a large colonial house for everyone to live in. Group therapy sessions continued, and many participants had the conscious desire to grow closer to each other. The house was so big, however, that individuals retained some privacy. Compared to later years, Hathor said, "It was a time when we didn't have a lot of contact," and "We still were strangers to each other in many ways."

Nassau was not a megalopolis like London, but it was a city, and the house was right in the middle of it. Most Processeans took jobs, wandering off in different directions during the day, leaving the house almost empty. There were many distractions, Hathor said: "We still had a lot of attention outwards, in a sense, because we were working. People were going out in the morning, working in an office, then coming back at night. So we were very much connected to *the world* and the ways of the world." Raphael, for example, worked in his old profession of architecture. He took a job with the city and helped to design a police station.

They stayed in Nassau for about three months. They never bought the island. Nassau had been intended merely as a way station, and it was time to move on. Raphael recalled the next decision vividly: "One night we sat down in the garden of the house, by the swimming pool, and we had a Meditation. This was something we'd developed over the years, the idea of meditation. We hadn't started out with that, but by going into a gradually more religious lifestyle, obviously meditation was a part of it that had grown up. We meditated on where we should go next from the Bahamas, what the next move was. And it came down to either we would go to Mexico City, or we would go to Caracas. Both of them were about equidistant, as I remember, from Nassau. And we decided on Mexico City. It seemed to have the more positive projections. And so, quite shortly after that we ended our jobs, we ended our lease on the building, and we took off with our savings for Mexico City." They stayed there for only a few days before wandering on. "And again, very much following signs and portents given to us in meditation, we traveled south in a rather rickety old bus that eventually took us up to Sisal, which was a little coastal village where they used to make hemp until nylon came in."

XTUL

Near Merida, the largest town in the state of Yucatan, lies the little fishing village of Sisal. The group of about thirty Processeans arrived there in early September 1966. Micah found a fishing cottage they could rent. There were coconuts hanging from the trees, and the Mayan Indian villagers let some members come along on their daily fishing expeditions into the Gulf, so there was enough to eat. About a week after they arrived in Sisal, they held another Meditation. Process meditations are not like Transcendental Meditation or any similar brands. There is no mantra or other standard stimulus upon which the meditator fixes his attention. Rather, the Meditation leader suggests a fresh topic each time. The participants close their eyes and let images and feelings about the concept drift through their minds. After a little while, the Meditation is over, and they describe what they saw, sharing their sensations with each other. Thus, Process meditation is *directed group fantasy*, free association to a common stimulus, an exploration of the collective subconscious of participants. This time, as always, they sat on the ground in a circle, joined hands, and closed their eyes. "What should we do? Where should we go?"

Images came. The Meditation ended. They opened their eyes and described what they had seen. Raphael said, "It was like putting a jigsaw puzzle together. Everybody had a bit of a vision, and also indications of what we would see along the way" to our destination. "I saw some ruins ... a long wall, very white ... " "Near the sea, but you can't see the sea." "Very green, like an oasis." "Lots of little lights in the sky." Rhea predicted an explicit sign: "We'll see the man with the stick and the dog." "How do we get there?" they asked themselves. "Start walking in the morning." "What direction?" Since the coast ran east and west, the choice was narrowed to these two directions. The nearly unanimous response was "East." Only one member, the daughter of a world-famous scholar and architect, said "West."

They did not sleep that night. About eight o'clock the next morning they began walking east, singing enthusiastically. After a couple of hours, their spirits sagged. They trudged along, searching in vain for the realization of their fantasies. It was terribly hot. Endless walking. Late in the afternoon they turned a corner and saw, to their happy amazement, exactly the sign Rhea had predicted—a man with a stick and a dog! The thirty ran madly past him. Here was their destination! Here indeed was a cluster of half-ruined buildings surrounded by coconut palms, a place they could stay, a place the real Process could come into existence.

It was called Xtul (pronounced sh-tool), a Mayan word they thought mean *terminus*, marking the end of a journey. From Xtul onward, a couple of special Process words would always be spelled with "X" to indicate an initial "sh" sound. Both of the words appear to derive originally from Yiddish or German slang, but to be in use in London circles and merely adapted for Processean use. One is *Xpiel* (spiel), meaning the flow of words from a therapist or patient in one of the group's sessions. The other is *Xtumm* (stumm). This is an important concept, defined in the notes to a series of essays Robert wrote at Xtul, the *Xtul Dialogues*:

> To xtumm (pronounced "Shtoom"; oo as in "good") is to "kill," either
> physically, spiritually, or mentally, depending on the context. The
> extent of the "death" can vary. For example: to xtumm someone
> could mean simply to silence him, to knock him senseless, or to
> destroy him completely. Also atmospheres can be xtummed, conver-
> sations can be xtummed, contact between people can be xtummed,
> etc. In the present context, a "xtummer" refers to one who kills

contacts and atmospheres on a spiritual level, with heavy deadening projections and attitudes.

Xtul was the opposite of xtumm. Xtul, the endpoint of the spiritual voyage of the last three years, was a turning point in the history of the Process. They came to Xtul a group of thirty individuals tied together by their involvement in a deviant psychotherapy process. They left Xtul slightly reduced in numbers but members of a cohesive community and founders of the Process Church. Physically Xtul was an abandoned coconut plantation, but in the mythology of the Process it was the Land of Oz, a magical place worthy of legend and song. Years later, many Processeans who joined after Xtul would still think of it as their magical beginning.

Come to Xtul, cries the voice of angels in the wind.
Come to Xtul, where the wonders of this world begin.
For you the glory of Xtul!
For you the glory of Xtul!

The Xtul mythology was very poetic. Was Xtul really an exact substantiation of the meditation image? Was a man with a stick and a dog a true sign or a coincidence? And the magic name? A year later, when Sister Rebekah joined the Process, she told Father Malachi she doubted that *Xtul* meant *terminus*. Rebekah had a master's degree in Anthropology and had spent a year in Mexico studying Mayan linguistics. She thought *Xtul* was one word in a phrase the Indians used to name the plantation, the entire name meaning "Place of the little she-rabbit." Malachi agreed the Indians used a whole phrase, with Xtul just a part, but wanted to stick with the official definition even after Rebekah's professor from the University of Chicago supported her theory.

In a Process magazine five years later, Malachi stressed the magical-poetic feeling of Xtul: "We had found Xtul by taking a jump of faith. We had found Xtul by a miracle. And the place was miraculous: we knew that we had been guided to it. Some of the Mayan Indians at the nearby village, Chuburna Puerto, told us they had been waiting for us." The Processeans took possession of Xtul by the simple act of living in it. There were three principal buildings. Nearest the sea was a large wooden house with a tile roof, relatively intact. Inland from it was the biggest building, a roofless and overgrown stone structure that came to be known as "the Monastery." A smaller stone building in similar condition was a short distance to the east.

At the village, about a mile's walk down a dusty road, they met a fellow named Balthazar who was supposed to look after the ruined plantation for the owner who lived in faraway Mexico City. With some trepidation, the Processeans wrote a letter to the owner, explaining how they had found Xtul and offering to pay a small rent for the right to stay there. The owner agreed in a letter which commented, "Thank you for your distinguished letter. I understand completely that you were led to my property by 'voices.' There is, however, one thing that slightly worries me. What if the voices tell you not to pay the rent?"

They slept on straw mats and in hammocks. Hathor recalled, "The weather was so fine that many of us chose to sleep outdoors. I did myself." Only on the rare nights when it rained did everyone cram together in the imperfect shelter of the old house. There was no running water, of course, and the water in the well was saline. No problem! They had a bona fide hydraulic engineer, Dominic, expert in fluid dynamics. He rigged up a system of bamboo pipes. Expeditions went out daily to get good drinking water and other necessities from the village.

There were coconuts to eat, but as Hathor told me, "Coconuts get awfully boring after a while, Bill, I can assure you." Greer started a vegetable garden. The fishing was good. And then there were the prickly pears, many of them, growing wild. They are not pears, exactly, but an edible cactus, with hair-like little spines. Hathor explained, "Unless you clean off the fruit very well, you'll get them stuck in your tongue. . . . I got quite scared of them after a while. I wouldn't touch them, because I hated this feeling [of getting the prickers in my tongue]. It was awful." Everyone warned everyone else to be careful and be sure to cut away all the spines before eating. But again and again, some poor fool would impulsively bite into one that still had a few prickles. It was almost impossible to remove the spines from one's own tongue. Somebody else had to do the job. Often, a little group of victims would gather, sticking out their tongues piteously. One of the women would operate on them with a pair of eyebrow tweezers. There was one solution to the prickly pear problem that both produced safe food and allowed Processeans to exact vengeance on the nasty fruit: they squashed the cactus into prickly pear jam.

Most members of the group did "an enormous amount of physical work," Hathor said, "building, repair work, because the place wasn't in good condition when we took it." They spent a lot of time clearing out the Monastery and made such useful items as a log table and sleeping mats woven of palm fronds. One fellow succeeded in making a functional musical instrument out of a gourd and accompanied Brother Joshua, who began composing songs. Few of the members were used to hard physical labor. It was a good body-building experience. Individual P-Scope sessions and even the group therapy sessions had temporarily given way to much more fluid, more religious activities: Meditations, Vigils, prayer, fasting, much discussing and dreaming. As an anonymous Processean wrote later in one of the cult's magazines, "Without really realizing it, we were developing our own civilization in Xtul. Much of the theology, religious observance, and day-to-day community ethos and life-style came through intense discussing and enactment. And through simply observing what worked—and what didn't."

Hathor spoke for the entire group when she recalled the two most important lessons she learned at Xtul. First, she discovered that many of the modern conveniences she had taken for granted in London were not really necessary for a comfortable life. Electricity, flush toilets, and supermarkets are not in fact vital necessities. This insight, learned on a deep emotional level through living at Xtul, is parallel to one of the major doctrines of the Process: our lives are distorted, impoverished, imprisoned by "human agreements." These are assumptions, like Dominic's compulsion to become a chemical engineer, false beliefs that some specific thing, goal, or behavior is absolutely necessary for our survival. In the original therapy sessions, Processeans hunted for these human agreements in order to uproot them—and liberate themselves. At Xtul, the same process occurred through day-to-day life in this new environment. In later years, the Process chanted this discovery that turning away from the compulsions of the mind toward a magical destiny, abandoning civilization for something transcendental, was the best course:

> Freedom from the human game,
> Freedom from the mind;
> In service of the Purpose
> Lies freedom for the soul.

Hathor's second lesson is the mirror image of the first, the discovery of the bountiful miracle that is Nature: "I can remember having strong feelings about sleeping on the beach at night, looking up at the sky … feelings of space and dimension and size and scope and wonderment—something I really hadn't been into before. And just feeling and acknowledging the Higher Presence, really." She describes her experience of Nature as intensely *spiritual*, the rapturous psychological opposite of that human miasma that was London.

On his weekly radio show, six years later, Father Dominic expressed his wonderful feelings about the animals that shared the ruined plantation with them: there were "iguanas, like prehistoric monsters in miniature. They would lie in the sun all day. And then when our dogs got near them, they would look around, and with their legs out sideways they would run off as fast as they could and get up a tree before the dogs could get to them. . . . We had wild horses as well, gray and white and black and tan, grazing, nomadic, and free. And pelicans would fly overhead in formation, going who knows where on some migration. We also had snakes, some big ones something like a boa. We had vipers in the water and coral snakes, pink and writhing in the grass. Scorpions—very scary—but nobody ever got hurt, fortunately. Jumping spiders as well, and fish, lots of fish. They used to jump around while we swam in the waters of the Gulf... beautiful place! One day I remember the birds danced outside the window while we watched them. It was a real magic. A place called Xtul in Mexico."

On another broadcast, he said, "When we lived in Mexico, way back at the early days of the church, we lived very close to the earth. And we had a rule of only using local materials when we were doing things, building things. And we made our roofs out of thatch, walls out of rocks and limestone. We ate corn and beans like the Mayans around us. And somehow the countryside and the colors seemed much more vivid. And we were much more conscious of animals and plants and birds and insects than we are in the cities."

This romanticizing of Nature included the local Mayans. In later magazine articles about Xtul, Malachi reported a number of occult speculations about the superiority of Mayan civilization as though they were authenticated facts. The Mayans were said to be descendants of the Chaldeans who brought the pyramid with them when they migrated across the Atlantic. Their great wisdom is demonstrated by their invention of the zero and the related concept of illusion or nothingness called *maya*. Of course, *maya* is actually a Hindu concept and only sounds related to the Mayans. From this jumble of pseudo-historical free association, Processeans concluded that "the Mayas had developed a super-religious civilization and a super-detached concept of reality."

Along with a new consciousness of the world came new personal identities. Several members of the group assumed bold new names during their sojourn at Xtul. Joshua, one of them, explained how the names were chosen. It just kind of happened. We drew them out of a hat!" He laughs. "It felt right at the time. We were very much into an Old Testament, Biblical time." The earliest names all came from the Old Testament. "We were thinking about who" in the Bible each of us resembled, and only half-seriously decided, "He looks like a Malachi, he looks like an Aaron, and he looks like a Joshua." Some members did not take new names until several months later. For example, Hathor adopted this ancient Egyptian name a whole year later. This practice of adopting a Sacred Name later became a standard step in becoming a member of the cult.

Father Dominic told a reporter years later that he had gotten "completely absorbed" in the identity of St. Stephen. The events at Xtul, both psychological and physical, convinced him he was being swept away by powers much greater than his own will. "I thought of all the ways I could escape my fate. But I could see the time when I was meant to die." Dominic told me he experienced many visions—auditory hallucinations—in which voices predicted everything that was going to happen to him. At Xtul, the reporter said, Dominic "felt worthless. He felt that he had nothing to contribute to the group." Dominic may indeed have felt somewhat cut off from the group, coming from a scientific rather than an artistic background. Robert de Grimston once exclaimed to me that he never understood what Dominic had in common with the others. At Xtul, feeling worthless and identifying himself with St. Stephen, Dominic felt he should duplicate his saint's martyrdom by stoning. "I went through how it would feel. I could see stones hitting my body, I felt the dizziness, felt the stones hit my head." He proclaimed to the group, "I'm completely unworthy, but I can give my life." The others were quite surprised to discover how isolated Dominic felt and quickly assured him there was no need to die.

HURRICANE!

A week before the end of September, Mr. Macmillan, the British Consul stationed in Merida, paid a surprise visit to Xtul. He drove over to warn the Processeans that Inez, a great hurricane, was headed directly toward Yucatan. "You must move away," he said. "Come and stay with me in Merida. The hurricane will sweep you away. There will be 200 mph winds. A great wall of sea will come in and sweep you to kingdom come." The group gathered and discussed their situation for a few minutes. Their resolve was clear. They thanked Macmillan for his concern but said they had decided to stay. Consul Macmillan abandoned the Processeans to their fate.

They immediately started getting ready for Inez. For safety's sake they removed the tiles from the roof of the wooden house. Swept off by the hurricane winds, they could be as dangerous as cannonballs. They decided to build a shelter inside the roofless Monastery, taking advantage of its eighteen-inch-thick masonry walls. The five architects held a technical conference. They agreed that the best site would be on the inside face of the thick north wall, on the sea end of the building but best shielded against waves. Quickly they constructed a large lean-to using old doors, stone blocks, beams, and pieces of burlap and canvas to plug gaps against the expected wind and rain.

The sky turned dark and the wind rose. Palm trees bent and the air filled with blown missiles, coconuts, and branches. The sea chewed away at the shore, in some places eating as much as thirty yards of land. An entire section of the wooden house was crushed, and its pieces scattered. Weeks later, the official count of people killed by Inez reached 293 and could easily have included all the members of the Process. Looking out from the fragile shelter of their lean-to, they saw the solid walls of the Monastery sway, then lurch "like so much plastic foam." Their strongest protection became their greatest danger. The heavy south wall collapsed inward! Had they built their shelter there, many would have been crushed. They ran terrified out into the storm.

They huddled under blankets, drenched by the rain and chilled by the wind. Flying branches lashed them. They sang songs to boost their miserable spirits. Hurricane Inez ravaged Xtul for two whole days. It was a time of agony but also of a fascinating psychedelic consciousness. The air was so dark it was often impossible to know if it was day or night. The interplay of internal psychological turmoil and external meteorological chaos made it seem they were in the grip of transcendent, cosmic forces. The wrath of God! Daemonic powers, black magic. A falling limb almost crushed one of the men. He could not believe his escape was a meaningless, chance event. It was a meaningful moment, in which he was the center of a cosmic struggle.

Inez passed, and the weather began to clear. Everyone was safe. The beach was littered with junk, some of it interesting fare for beachcombing. A fishing boat from the nearby town of Vera Cruz had washed ashore. The Processeans helped the fishermen secure it and shared some of the catch. Three Processeans walked to Chuburna Puerto for food. After their return, most of the group went to the village to offer help in repairing the damaged houses. They divided into four or five groups and energetically set to work, earning the gratitude of the villagers, who rewarded them with thanks and food. Nobody in the village had been seriously injured, so, despite the devastation, rebuilding was a time of joy and festivity. Joshua sang some of the first Process songs he had composed. Dominic danced with the mayor's daughter.

Several joined in a rousing song popularized by the Beatles. The Processeans remember Xtul in poetic terms. One began chopping up a fallen coconut tree, when "the axe-head cut into a hive of tiny black stingless Mexican bees. Most of them had deserted the nest. With a little finger I tasted the honey on the blade of the axe. It was sweet, so fresh and with a wonderful subtle flavor of coconut."

The cult shared in the disaster relief sent by the Red Cross and the U.S. and Mexican governments. They were given tortilla mix and black beans and some building supplies. The villagers gave them roast ducks in thanks for their help. They began putting Xtul back together. The hurricane and its aftermath heightened the social processes and spiritual development that were in progress. They had experienced both sides of the God of Nature: His benevolence and His wrath. Later they explained, "Xtul was the place where we met God face to face. It was the experience that led to the establishment of the Church. In terms of commitment, it was the point of no return where each one of us, plucked by fate out of a workaday world, found that we had a God-vocation."

A few members lost commitment, while the majority gained. Both were given religious interpretations. One week, Dominic said, two or three people "were deciding the pressure at Xtul was too much for them, and they were leaving." When each person actually left, a large limb fell from one of the trees. "We would sit around under the tree, talking. And there was appearing some stress. People decided they would like to leave, and a branch fell on each occasion. That's rather dramatic! The sort of thing a passerby would not notice or would attribute to coincidence. But when you were actually involved on the scene, it was a very poignant moment."

Robert began writing the *Xtul Dialogues*, writings that only real insiders would be allowed to read in later years, composed in the form of eight conversations between a student and his teacher. Robert *wrote* his teachings, yet he said he merely *channeled* them. He stored up ideas, impressions, phrases, perhaps taken from the conversation and experiences of the entire core group of the Process. Then, in long, intense bouts of lightning writing, he spilled doctrine out onto the page. I had photocopies of many pages of his handwritten first drafts in my collection, as well as the final typed draft, and it is clear he did a significant amount of editing and some rewriting, but the basic draft was produced very rapidly. Robert wrote several short pieces while living with me in 1975, so I am familiar with his work habits. He was aware that he composed the literature but still spoke of it as *recorded* or *channeled* from some Higher Source. In theory he was only the medium through which it expressed itself.

Robert has not clarified whether this Higher Source was God, in the traditional sense of the word, or the collective mind of the Process, or his own personality. Processeans dispute the degree to which Robert, their Teacher, composed the writings on his own or as the mouthpiece for the entire group.

One of the most striking features of the mature Process theology was the doctrine of the Great Gods of the Universe: Jehovah, Lucifer, Satan, and Christ. The only God specifically identified by name at Xtul was Jehovah, God of strength, wrath, and Nature. The second *Xtul Dialogue* discusses the connection between the psychological level of perception and the higher consciousness a man can have of God. It begins with a question:

> Is there more than one universe?
>> Yes. On various levels there are many universes, but they are all only part of the One True Universe, which exists on all levels. That is to say, there are many Gods, but only One True God who embodies all of them.
> Is each God, then, a universe?
>> Or an aspect of a universe. Jehovah, for example, is the Knowledge of the Physical Universe.

As we will explain in a later chapter, the Gods were projections of different human personality types, discovered among the original Processeans. This passage written at Xtul is the first scriptural hint of their emergence, and the theory of the Gods did not reach a developed form until two years later.

Official church stories of Xtul do not mention the last disaster that struck, a calamity made by men, not gods. Sir John Verney, father of Sabrina Verney, a nineteen-year-old girl in the cult, conspired with two other parents whose Processean children were just twenty. They sent a solicitor from London to Xtul to drag the three youngsters home. Under the law, they were still minors, subject to parental control. The solicitor arrived at Xtul accompanied by an official of the British Embassy and an immigration official of the Mexican government. The three were told they would be deported unless they went along with the solicitor willingly. In the third week of November, they arrived in London.

The solicitor told London newspaper reporters he had found twenty-two Processeans at Xtul, fifteen men and seven women. All were wearing casual and tattered clothing except Mary Ann, who "was wearing a bikini and silver-painted fingernails. She seemed to be treated like a kind of high priestess by the others. They acted like her slaves." His impression of their lifestyle was unfavorable: "They were living like hermits, dressed in rags and many without shoes. The men wore beards and the girls were working like peasants, growing, or trying to grow, vegetables to eat." Xtul offended his strict sense of propriety. The three officials carted away the three young Processeans.

The remaining Xtul group sat right down, discussed the crisis, and held a Meditation. They decided quickly that most of them should return to London for a while, both to rescue the three that had been taken and to prevent the abduction of the two remaining under-age members. Christian, Raphael's brother, one of the captives, was indeed ultimately rescued and grew to be one of the leading figures in the cult. About eight Processeans stayed behind to hold the fort. The cult still intended to make Xtul its long-term headquarters. One member humorously told a reporter, "We have nothing to hide, and we all plan to return to Mexico. We just decided, suddenly, to come home for Christmas." Three of the eight remaining at Xtul left a bit later, and the last five did not vacate the plantation until a year after they arrived. Hathor recalled the last months with special joy. She gave birth to her first child, a son, in Mexico and talked about returning someday to visit that "very special place," Xtul.

BACK TO CIVILIZATION

Despite the troubles with the authorities, the return to London was triumphant. The Processeans had gained a feeling of immense strength at Xtul, Rhea said: "I remember coming back to England with a sense of invulnerability and power that, so help me, I never had experienced in my life." Where did the feeling originate? What was it like? "I was convinced that it came from God. It was a bit like feeling like Superwoman!" She laughed. "Which was a very nice feeling . . . invulnerable . . . . The idea of not having ready food, the idea of having your house burnt down, the idea of not having anything on the physical level was no longer a threat." At Xtul, "God" had provided. "This was a fantastic strength. I no longer needed to put my faith in the insurance companies. I was very happy to sell my life insurance without a single qualm, which I did."

Xtul had the same effect on Raphael: "When I went back to London three months later, I really realized at that point how invulnerable I had personally become to the pressures and problems that in normal life one is totally vulnerable to. In so many ways those didn't matter anymore." Xtul gave not only a sense of security but also a special pride, a sense of self-worth. "What came out of that was a recognition, to put it in religious terminology, that God had a mission for us in the world. That we weren't meant to be an isolated community for the rest of our days. That our experiences in Xtul and the time leading up to Xtul we were in fact meant to take out to the world. We were meant to relay those experiences, particularly since all of us had a real feeling of close contact with God … that God does care, that God does love us."

Back in London, Raphael said, "We started off with quite a bang! We started off by opening a coffeehouse" in the old Balfour Place headquarters, which was still on lease to them. They were active "running courses, having lectures and services. We also started publishing a magazine." The first issue was titled *The Common Market* and criticized Britain's projected entry into the European Economic Community. "There is a prophecy in the Book of Revelation that calls about the Ten-Headed Beast, and many interpreters of prophecy do relate this to the EEC. One of these ten heads is England, and it's not a very nice prophecy!" They interviewed a few members of the House of Commons for this inaugural issue, then gave copies to every member of Commons. The topic of the issue was an entirely perverse choice for the cult, newly returned from Paradise, but this irrationality set the pattern for many future Process public relations.

A great deal of work was invested in the invention of many aspects of the "church." Rituals were invented step by step. The therapy exercises were expanded and further codified. Processeans began wearing black uniforms and constructed unusual church decorations for Balfour Place. A church rhetoric developed.

It seemed natural to express the communal experience of the group in religious terms. Mother Rebekah said that, so far as she was concerned, the Process was really "a community" but called itself a church because that was the nearest thing that outsiders could understand. Malachi looked at it the other way around: "The thing about a community is that there has to be commitment and involvement. It's a way of living." But it is a special way of living that seeks a high quality of life for all members, therefore demanding a high level of performance from them. "And so, you see, that automatically puts you into a religious, spiritual sort of space, because there's nothing else which is going to produce that kind of commitment. It's impossible [without a religious orientation]. We live in very unspiritual days, and I think you see the result in people. They're unhappy because they don't have that core or that perspective on what they're doing." So the religious conception of the Process was a way both of calling forth from each member the greatest possible commitment and of giving him or her the most powerful hope.

This new religion elevated Robert to the status of prophet. Despite his passive temperament, Robert de Grimston was the man for this important job. His physical presence and manners radiated dignity. A slim man, over six feet tall, his leonine features and sandy mane projected strength. His regal bearing was the outcome of his elite cavalry training, and his intelligence was refined in his private school education. Robert once told me he had briefly belonged to Mensa, the social club for underemployed intelligence, and had scored 163 on the I.Q. entrance test. More a philosophical than a benevolent man, he was happier composing doctrine than sharing the problems of his followers. He said it was Mary Ann's idea that he withdraw from public encounters and play the role of charismatic leader from a distance. But this haughty, imperial detachment suited Robert. His dramatic photograph and thundering scriptures became key elements in the Process presentation, while Robert the man withdrew from sight into private mystery.

Yet Mary Ann retained great power at the center of the cult, concealed from the general public. Two witnesses at Xtul long afterwards wrote books that indicated Mary Ann was the real leader, suggesting Robert was merely an image. In 2011, Sabrina Verney published *Xtul: An Experience of The Process*, saying Mary Ann was "the undisputed leader of the group."[53] Yet Verney was only briefly involved, and Robert's key role in producing most of the sacred scriptures had begun just as Verney was leaving the group.

Far more central to both the group and the culture was Timothy Wyllie, who later became Father Micah, with major responsibilities for producing the publications of the Process, before experiencing his own separation from Mary Ann. In the 2009 book, *Love Sex Fear Death: The Inside Story of The Process Church of the Final Judgment*, Wyllie put great emphasis on his own emotional relationship with Mary Ann, rather than on connections with the other central members who helped create the culture through interaction with each other.[54] Clearly, the social implosion that essentially ended with Xtul had begun with the central couple and produced a group, and together they created a culture. Externally, Robert represented the culture, while Mary Ann was central to the internal family, each playing a different important role in the supernatural drama.

CHURCH STATUS

In April 1967, Robert, Mary Ann, John, and Mary Ann's mother left London on a grand tour. From this time on, the pair of top leaders would usually be separated from the rank and file. Calling themselves the Omega, Robert and Mary Ann would travel independently, live outside the church chapters, and rule from afar. The Omega went first to Greece, Robert recalls: "We arrived in Athens the day before the military took over." That means they landed in Greece April 20, 1967, the day before George Papadopoulos and a clique of military officers seized power. "There were tanks in the streets and all kinds of things" that the Omega found exciting and impressive. They stayed for several days in Piraeus, the ancient port of Athens.

"Then we went to Israel," Robert says, "and that must have been in May, because we left Israel the day the war broke out." Israel triumphed in the famous Six Day War, June 5 through June 10, 1967. This must have pleased Mary Ann a great deal because she was an admirer of Israel and of both the ancient and modern Jews, although not Jewish herself. As their boat pulled away from the Israeli shore, they heard booming noises that sounded like gunfire but did not know a war was on until a few hours later.

When Robert recounted his trips to Greece and Israel, he hinted that perhaps it was not chance that they arrived in Greece just as a coup began and left Israel at the start of a war. Those conflicts seemed to have a connection with the Process. They were signs that the cult was at the center of History, headed in the right direction. They were signs that repressive "civilization" was crashing down to make room for something new.

They sailed to Turkey, where they stayed as tourists near Izmir. Here Robert began to write the first sections of a work called *The Tide of the End*, an apocalyptic condemnation of the world, an analysis of the human condition, and a prophecy of the coming Millennium. It is the most emotional and poetic of his writings, yet also contains many of the most important intellectual concepts of Process doctrine. It continues on a higher literary and philosophical plane the basic ideas of Compulsions Analysis but adds the social and religious experience of the early Process. It continues the search for ways of overcoming ordinary human limitations and, as a natural extension of this, expresses the social gulf and antagonism that had developed around the Process as a result of the social implosion. The first phrase of the first book of *The Tide of the End* proclaims: "Humanity is doomed!"

Written from October 1967 to May 1971, *The Tide of the End* is a collection of thirteen short books in seven "phases." One of the books, *Christ Came*, may have been written by Mary Ann. It is the shortest, only a single page long, and not very intelligently written. John and Aaron also wrote books of the type collected in *The Tide of the End*. Aaron actually wrote his, *And There Was Darkness*, soon after leaving Xtul, in February 1967, before Robert began writing in the same spirit but with greater skill. The book by Aaron reflects his Jewish background and is a book in praise of Jehovah. John's book is dated November 1967 and rejoices *For Christ Is Come*. Neither of these is particularly radical theologically, and it was Robert's work that led the Process in surprising directions. While *The Tide of the End* speaks in religious language, it is at heart a book about psychotherapy. It presents Robert's theory of self-transformation through psychological analysis, using metaphor and flowery rhetoric. The introduction to *As It Is*, the first of the thirteen books, expresses the theme of the entire work:

> A man cannot change his way of life by changing his clothes nor by speaking out with a different voice. To change basically, permanently and meaningfully he must reach down into himself and pluck himself out by the roots....
>
> AS IT IS is written for those who want to break away from the futile human pattern of seeing reality as it is not and thereby living a lie, to abandon the anaesthetic of ignorance and suppression within which man cocoons himself and to embrace the intensity of reality—as it is.

The mixture of psychotherapeutic and millenarian sentiments in the following passage from *As It Is* is typical of the broad sweep of Robert's writing during this period:

> 1.16 So we must break our links, sever our ties; plumb the depths of our unconsciousness, and cut the bonds with which we've bound ourselves.
> 2.1 And there is not much time. The distant rumblings that are heralds of the End have become a mighty roar closing in about us, piercing our eardrums and causing the very Earth to quake beneath our feet; so that very soon even the blindest, numbest,

most oblivious of us will no longer be able to shut out the sound of it.

2.2 By then the whole world will be stricken by the sound of its own approaching doom. Every man will gaze in horror at his fellow man, and see his own fear reflected back to him.

2.3 And by then we must be free—if we are ever to be free. By then the bonds that bound us must be broken, and we must stand above the terror of the End, aloof, detached, a part of something new.

2.4 For with every end there is a new beginning, and if we are not of the End, then we shall be of the New Beginning.

Like wealthy tourists, the Omega took ship from Izmir and jaunted across the Mediterranean, stopping briefly in Chios, Athens again, Naples, and Madeira. They crossed the Atlantic and spent a few days in Miami, Florida. They came to rest in New Orleans at the end of August or beginning of September. A group of Processeans came from London to meet them in New Orleans with the idea of going on to Xtul. But New Orleans seemed such a favorable city, and its citizens gave such gratifyingly great attention to the Process, that the Omega decided to stay. The last five people still holding the fort at Xtul were called up to New Orleans, and the coconut plantation was abandoned. It fell back into ruin, and all the effort invested in fixing up the place was forgotten. The Process opened the New Orleans chapter.

Raphael said, "We went to New Orleans very much in an expansionary mood. We weren't precisely sure what form the expansion would take, but we had a good model in how Balfour Place was operating." Was the cult interested in gaining new members? "We were keen on recruiting, although we weren't proselytizing. We were doing it by example. People would come into the aura and say, 'Well, I like this! I want to be part of this!'"

Morgana was one of those who joined. New Orleans was her home. She said the Process brought great excitement to the streets: "The entire city knew that they had come to town, because they were so obvious. They really made an impact on New Orleans." The Processeans' physical appearance was striking. In 1967, respectable men shaved their faces and wore their hair short. Flamboyant dress, long hair, and beards were then foreign to the conservative style followed by middle-class people. Only the strangest people, alien ethnic groups, unruly poor bums, and the hippies that had just emerged in California looked anything like the Process. The cult adopted a rule in Mexico that no member should trim hair or beard. Several of the men are rather tall, so with hair down past their shoulders and chest-length beards they had a frightening appearance.

Over their black shirts and black trousers the Processeans wore astonishing purple capes. Circular, they came down to the knee and were crowned by small standing collars. Morgana believed the effect was too startling even for some members of the cult. The capes "were so flamboyant that I think a lot of people in the organization who were extremely conservative didn't want to wear them." The Processeans marched around the city in groups, accompanied by their large German shepherds. When any member opened his mouth to talk with a local resident, extraordinary English accents came out. The Process rented a large house, offered coffee and activities, and drew in crowds of visitors. Morgana said, "They used to just pack that house out, daily. Just hundreds of people pouring through that place. It was amazing, really amazing!"

The black- and purple-garbed Processeans walked the streets asking passersby for contributions to the "church." This activity came to be the major source of money to support the Process. New members were no longer of such a high social class that they brought in fortunes with them, and admission fees for Process activities were modest. Because the cult was traveling, and because it had turned in a more religious direction, therapy sessions were no longer practical, either as recruitment devices or as a major source of income. The street soliciting later came to be called "the street ministry," in which Processeans gave "contact" and other spiritual benefits to civilians who reciprocated by giving money. Processeans engaged in the street ministry were said to be *donating*. The people of the city were not donating to the church, in this terminology; rather, the Process was "donating" to them. This practice served to keep Processeans busy and advertise the church to tens of thousands, as well as being the major source of income.

To legitimate the street begging and the public activities at the chapter house, the cult became incorporated under the laws of Louisiana in the city of New Orleans. Its official name was the Process—Church of the Final Judgement. Later there were incorporations in London and Toronto, but the original church charter was developed in New Orleans in 1967 and incorporation was achieved there on June 21, 1968. This legal step was an important advance in the direction of respectability, institutionalization, and the attainment of conventional church status.

Still, as Morgana explained, the Process "was not rooted" or "establishment-oriented" as it later became. Little interested in becoming just one more standard denomination, the Process was much more concerned with "the basics," she said, with "the End of the world, detaching from the establishment, being a group unto ourselves. And simply the mission was to pick up other Processeans. It was not to convert large masses of people. It was not to fill up the ranks with large numbers. It was not to become a part of the establishment. It was simply looking for people who were Processeans."

The fourth verse of the seventh chapter of the Book of Revelation suggests that precisely 144,000 human souls will survive the End in glory. The Omega suspected this meant there were 144,000 natural Processeans scattered throughout the world. To the extent that the cult had a mission to the world, it was mainly to present itself publicly so those people who were already Processeans without realizing it could come forward and join. Many who joined had an instant shock of recognition when they encountered the cult. This was true throughout the entire history of the group. Morgana recalled, "When I met them I knew: *Right, well, this is it!*"

A half dozen people joined in New Orleans. The cult set up a "crash seminar" to teach Process doctrine and transform the newcomers into members. The literature used in these classes was limited to the *Xtul Dialogues* and some of *The Logics*.

A system of membership ranks was quickly devised. The newcomers were called Messengers. They were also described as *Outside Processeans*, and it was assumed at first that they would never be able to join the inner core of the Process because they had not shared the Xtul experience. Over the next few months, however, several of the new Messengers rose to positions of higher rank. The designation *Outside Processean*, or OP, was used from then on to describe members who had not yet been admitted to the heart of Process society. The people who had been at Xtul, and others later admitted to their intimate circle, were called *Inside Processeans*, or IPs. When the ranks were invented, the people who had been at Xtul were divided into four groups, according to influence and ability. Robert and Mary Ann already constituted the Omega, the highest stratum of Process society. Their leading lieutenants were called Masters in charge of day-to-day decision-making. Less exalted, but still influential, were the Priests, and below them were the Prophets. So there were now five ranks, as follows: Omega, Master, Priest, Prophet and Messenger.

The development of another important custom was completed at this time—the practice of taking *Sacred Names*. As we noted earlier, some Processeans had adopted biblical names at Xtul. In New Orleans, new names were handed out to all members. Mary Ann selected many of the new names.

Now that the Process conceived of itself as a church, it decided to adopt the Catholic monastic practice of calling leaders Mother or Father and other members Sister or Brother. Priests and Masters now held names like Father John and Mother Hathor. Messengers and Prophets had names like Brother Cyrus and Sister Morgana, both of whom later advanced to become Father Cyrus and Mother Morgana. This new custom stressed not only the religious definition of the group but also the close, family-like relations that now bound members together. In this book, I have given pseudonyms for the sacred names of many Processeans who did not serve as public figures but do correctly name twenty-two followers of Robert and Mary Ann who became well known to the public and high-status leaders.[55] I have evidence that eleven were deceased by mid-2024. Of course, those who are still alive no longer use sacred names, which protects their privacy.

THE RELIGIOUS IMAGE

From the abandonment of the name Compulsions Analysis to the incorporation as the Process—Church of the Final Judgement, from late 1965 through late 1967, the cult evolved from a psychotherapy service into a religious group. At the beginning of this chapter we suggested six factors that operated to accomplish this transformation and bring about the adoption of the religious label. Now we will review them, seeing how they apply to the evidence given in this chapter and developing a clearer perspective for understanding the further evidence in later chapters.

1. The language of religion was available to Processeans as a system of interpretation through which they could attempt to understand and communicate the things that were happening to them. None of the original members was well educated in any social or behavioral science. When I first introduced myself to Robert de Grimston and said I was a sociologist, he asked me to explain the difference between sociology and psychology. While some members had read books on Psychoanalysis, the language of Freud's system was not well suited to all their purposes because it assumed that their unusual hopes and desires were pathological. At Xtul, Processeans found the Bible a good source of comparisons and ideas to interpret their own situation. Many of them named the new self-conceptions they developed after characters in the Bible.

2. We have seen that the original Processeans were very conscious of the fact that the personal goals that emerged in their Adlerian therapy sessions

were not goals that conventional society encouraged. The magical desires they expressed in these sessions, and which were encouraged by other members, could only be realized outside the context of normal life.

3. In group therapy, and in the group living situation that developed, members lost the feeling of independence, lost ego boundaries, and gained the feeling of inclusion in a larger being. This group mind operated most obviously in the group Meditations but was a social fact at all times. With its experience of implosion and concern for unity, the cult tended at first to define the group consensus as divine guidance. In later chapters we will see that the fact of group divisions and competing personalities generated a theology of several Gods.

4. The hypothesis that God existed and intervened in the Process seemed confirmed by a number of experiences the cult had in this period. The discovery of Xtul, the bounty of Nature at Xtul, the wrathful hurricane, and the Greek and Israeli military actions were taken as signs demonstrating the presence of God.

5. We have begun to see how intuitively and impulsively the Omega ruled. Robert and Mary Ann took off on their expensive Mediterranean junket supported by the rank and file. We will see many examples of ways in which they exploited followers economically under the justification of doing God's work and of mediating between the cult and God. Furthermore, the practice of following signs and portents, a mystical method of making decisions, is a way of holding power without taking responsibility. Often these signs are practical exigencies, but equally often they are nothing more than the personal whims of the leaders.

6. By the end of 1967 in New Orleans, the Process had discovered that it could use the label of religious group to control to some extent the response of the public. The incorporation as a church not only made it legal for members to beg on the streets and supported their claim that people ought to give them money but also freed them from the problem of income taxes.

We can look at these six as stages in the adoption of a label. First, the label was available, already invented and given powerful connotations by the larger society. The second step was the discovery that the label served individual psychological purposes, permitting and expressing personal desires and fantasies. The third step was the development of a social reality which was most easily understood by participants in religious terms. In the fourth step, the Processeans confronted the physical environment of which human life is but a part and found that they needed the concept of God to explain the astonishing universe around them. The fifth step was a strategic use of the religious conceptualization to shape the group's power structure and social relations within it. The sixth step took that strategy to a larger field and sought to control public behavior toward the group through use of the religious label.

This logical progression of steps expresses a continuity of principles, each built on the one before it. But there is also a single unifying principle behind this sequence: the nature of the religious label itself.

In his classic discussion of the meaning of religion, Émile Durkheim argued that the most important thing we must understand is the conceptual distinction between the *sacred* and the *profane*. He said, "The sacred and the profane have always and everywhere been conceived by the human mind as two distinct classes, as two worlds between which there is nothing in common."[56] "The two worlds are not only conceived of as separate, but as even hostile and jealous rivals of each other."[57] Durkheim then explained the concept of religion:

> The real characteristic of religious phenomena is that they always suppose a bipartite division of the whole universe, known and knowable, into two classes which embrace all that exists, but which radically exclude each other. Sacred things are those which the interdictions protect and isolate; profane things, those to which these interdictions are applied and which must remain at a distance from the first. Religious beliefs are the representations which express the nature of sacred things and the relations which they sustain, either with each other or with profane things.[58]

The Process became religious because it sought to rise above ordinary life and escape the bonds of conventional society. The Human Game that Processeans attempted to escape was the profane world. In his book *Humanity Is the Devil*, written in May 1968, Robert explained that the greatest profanity is not Satan but Humanity, the ordinary conduct of human life. Durkheim argued that the sacred has a single source, but I believe it does not. The sacred is a label for all those human dreams which cannot find fulfillment within conventional life. Religion is a hope and a demand: a hope that rapturous fantasies will be realized; a demand that others respect those fantasies.

In a way, the terms *sacred* and *religious* refer to a variety of social deviance—thoughts, behaviors, and social claims that violate everyday principles yet are held to be legitimate. The relationship between the sacred and the profane is the same as that between the deviant and the normal, except that society accepts the sacred and rejects crasser forms of deviance. The Process was able to beg on the streets, despite laws against begging, because their activity was defined as religious and therefore not really begging. A religious statement is not a lie merely because it is arbitrary and unsupported by fact. Religious beliefs are not madness, although they sound like madness. Religious ritual is not absurd clowning, no matter how silly the clothing and the gestures might seem outside a church. Priests are not swindlers or madmen, *by definition*.

Religion is a fantasy of profundity, the assertion of glory without accomplishment, the claim of membership in a powerful community that cannot be seen. Religion differs from art and humor because these admit that they are fantasies, while religion is the dream that claims it is real. Religion differs from crime and insanity in that society tolerates it. Because religion is simply legitimate deviance that is taken seriously, the word can cover many phenomena of quite varied origins. It is a label that came easily to mind to describe the Process. The therapy group started by Robert and Mary Ann did not really become a religion. Rather, after it had grown socially alienated and sufficiently deviant, its members symbolically dealt with that deviance by *adopting the religious label*. The Process was a religion because it had fled the normal world into a form of preposterously arrogant deviance yet wanted to be received warmly. The Process was a religion because it was gloriously good deviance.

CHAPTER 4   In Search of the Miraculous

My soul has wandered through many lands,
I've seen the times of old;
I feel the New World growing stronger
I feel new strength,
New life unfold,

— Process hymn, *Rise Up, Rise Up*

THE FOUNDERS OF THE PROCESS created their cult to achieve unlimited goals of personal satisfaction and effectiveness. During the social implosion and at Xtul they received ample "proof" that their collective gamble was paying off. After Xtul they continued to recruit new members, convincing them to join the cult's odyssey, but were extremely unclear in their plans for the future. How could the promise of the Process be fulfilled? The cult was faced with a vague but intense crisis. Processeans felt they were approaching their transcendent goal but could not quite reach it. As fast as they rushed toward it, it retreated. The result was an erratic, chaotic quest in search of the miraculous.

NEW RECRUITS

The 144,000 Processeans the cult hoped to collect were not only supposed to be marked with the seal of God but also to be the best people according to many of the standards of the world. All millenarian sects assert that their members are somehow superior to nonmembers, but the Process was in fact originally staffed by good, talented people. They were elitist in conventional terms, as well as presumptuous in their unconventionality. The Process encouraged aspirants for membership who happened to have talent and education and discouraged the riffraff majority of ordinary religious seekers and deadbeats who mistakenly wandered in the door. The aristocrat of millenarian sects, the Process recruited people of worth in the years 1967–1971.

We might ask what kinds of excellent people were running loose in society in those years, sufficiently unattached from conventional institutions to be recruited to new movements and deviant groups such as the Process. The answer has three related parts. (1) Young people from solid middle-class and even upper-class families who had been touched by the powerful youth-drug-counterculture of the late 1960s and did not value conventional careers highly enough to pursue them with vigor.[59] Like the original Processeans, these people were attracted by visions of escaping mundane inhibitions and achieving a vastly superior lifestyle. (2) College students halfway into a career who stalled in their progress, often simply because they discovered they did not enjoy the particular field they were getting into and were given no quick route to a happier conventional alternative. (3) Young people who had just lost many of their intimate social ties, either through a divorce or other family disruption or merely because they had gone wandering in search of their fortunes. Several were temporarily weak in social attachments merely because they had just completed a geographical move—for example, going away from home to attend school.

Although some individuals who fit one or more of these descriptions might also be suffering from personal pathology (neurosis, tension, strain ... whatever), there was no necessity for them to be troubled. The Process was not interested in troubled people. For example, Father Cyrus told me he was not suffering any kind of emotional distress or personal trouble when he joined in New Orleans in 1967. Cyrus was a native of Mississippi. He liked his home but at the end of his teens felt a desire to go out into the world. He went to New Orleans, the big city, with the excuse that he was going to attend art school. He entered the school in 1966 and wasted six months halfheartedly attending art classes and loafing. Art school did not inspire him. He was looking for an enjoyable cosmopolitan life, and art was just one plausible alternative to check out. He considered other options but found none particularly attractive. When the Process appeared on the scene, and looked really exciting, he joined. In retrospect, he thought the real reason he left Mississippi was in order to join the Process, guided by an intuitive impulse or by benevolent fates.

Brother Matthew encountered the Process while on vacation in New Orleans and did not formally join until the cult reached New York, a few months later. His case is more complex than that of Cyrus, and shows a measure of personal distress but no long-term pathology. Matthew had attended a university in New York, majoring in physics, with some interest in electrical engineering. But he found the program less than inspiring and had some difficulty keeping up with the reading: "After three years I decided I didn't want to complete it, but I had spent all this money which I felt responsible to my family for. And so I thought I would work with them, and try to make up some of the expense."

So Matthew went to work in his father's real estate business, unhappy in his job and wishing he could find a way out, a way to something grander: "I had feelings of responsibility around my family. My father was a semi-invalid, was becoming more and more dependent on me. The whole thing was a set-up—a perfect guilt situation. So I had resolved earlier that I would have to enter some kind of religious life. I didn't know what kind ... I was involved in Eastern religions, and Yoga, but no particular religious orientation one way or the other. Anyway, I was on vacation, and I was traveling around with a friend, and I met somebody who said, 'Go to this address. There are some interesting things happening there.' And I said, 'Ah! They'll be glad to see *me!*' And when I went there I was completely amazed. I didn't agree with things, intellectually, but it was an immediate emotional rapport and attachment that fixed on me ... The People. The lifestyle. The degree of commitment. Just the feeling around the place. It was purely an emotional attachment and attraction. A feeling of tightness about the whole thing. And a feeling of wanting to be with these people ... a kind of magic."

SAN FRANCISCO

In New Orleans, the Process completed its evolution from therapy group to religious movement. That clarified things but solved nothing. Where would the cult go? What would it do? Which road led to heaven? A traditional activity of religious movements is the founding of new pioneer churches. More than a year earlier, even before the group left London to go to Xtul, Father John had "a vision ... about a new group in San Francisco." It was a very precise image. "I saw it as a mini-duplicate of what we had in London, with me playing a central role in the thing, and new people joining, in San Francisco. That was what I saw, and that was what happened." John left New Orleans in December 1967 to found his dream chapter.

He arrived in San Francisco at an interesting time. Hippies and radicals abounded. John immediately visited the area's colleges and universities to give talks and meet young people. San Francisco State was in an uproar with "Black Power hitting the campus really big, and there were lots of riots." At Berkeley and at other centers of youth activity, John made contact with many potential converts. Father Aaron came up from New Orleans to join John, and they rented a house for use as a public chapter.

"We were located very close to the Haight-Ashbury district," John recalled. This was "right at the crest and beginnings of decline of the Flower Power bit." He felt Haight was a "totally undisciplined environment. I think people who went to it didn't have the self-discipline to hold either themselves or the whole situation together. And it disintegrated rapidly and rather disastrously and became rather ugly." The flamboyant public presentation of the Process was attractive to many members of the youth culture, so the chapter house became a popular hangout. John and Aaron set up a coffeehouse where people could drop in and socialize. They held Sabbath Assemblies each week in an *Alpha* ritual room and conducted Telepathy Developing Circles.

An introductory doctrinal course, the First Progress, was offered to those interested in joining, and another advanced Progress (seminar) was set up for a few young people of particular interest and attractiveness. About a half-dozen achieved full membership in the cult, including a later leader, Seraphine. More than eight years later, John told me he still felt a special personal relationship with those he recruited in San Francisco: "We got to know each other very well. The bond has strengthened over the years."

In February 1968, the Omega decided to move again and closed down the New Orleans chapter. They had been staying in the United States on three-month visitor visas, and their time had long since run out. Not ready to leave America, they decided to avoid the authorities by keeping on the move. The entire group went to join John and Aaron in San Francisco for a brief time. Then everybody moved down to Los Angeles.

Los Angeles was where the cult recruited Brother Lars, a young Japanese-American. His story is a good example to illustrate the recruitment style of the cult in those years. Lars had been living with his parents and attending college when rising dissatisfaction with his social relations and growing interest in the flourishing youth counterculture inspired him to explore new lifestyles. He felt that he and his old friends were caught in lives that lacked "immediacy ... communication ... contact." Utopian ideas were in the air. Lars had a vision "of being in a group environment." Through a friend of a friend, he learned about a large house inhabited by a variety of young people, strangers into alien things, a place where he might find a better way of living. "When the flower children were in blossom, I saw a potential for this ideal to become a reality." He moved into the house, and almost immediately (and coincidentally) many of the young people moved out. He discovered he didn't like the drug scene:

"It was leading nowhere. As you know, the flower movement wilted." Lars longed for a "special group, a very dynamic, cohesive group that had a sense of purpose, direction, drive, and dedication."

One day Lars was sitting in his room when a couple of his housemates burst in and exclaimed, "Eight-foot priests from London have come in! In robes!" It was the Process. They had made contact with the owner of the house, who agreed to let them stay in return for several hours of work a week maintaining his other properties. In a few days, all the non-Processeans except Lars left, "to pick strawberries in Lancaster." He was now living in the midst of thirty members of the Process. They set up a semi-private chapter in the house and began holding their rituals and classes.

Lars was invited to attend the Sabbath Assembly. At that time, the ceremony included a moment near the end when any newcomers were invited to "come forward" and join. The Evangelist completed his "Revelation" sermon and called for Lars to rise. "Well, what happened was, my feet came forward. My feet got up and started coming forward. Either I would fall back on my head, or I had to follow my feet! I followed my feet. I didn't have any alternative." Lars was now a member of a group just like the one he had dreamed of. In May, the Los Angeles chapter closed down, and the whole lot went on to New York, where yet another temporary chapter was opened in Greenwich Village.

I believe the main pressure behind this constant migration was the American immigration authorities, who had not given the British Processeans permission to settle in the U.S. According to one story, the departure from California was caused by hostile members of Scientology who called the authorities and reported the address where the cult was staying. One Processean told me the group left California because, like many mystical young folk at the time, they believed the state would soon be devastated by earthquakes. I rather think "bad vibrations" of a more social variety than earthquakes were at fault.

One of those who joined in New York was Sister Rebekah, a young anthropologist. She had enjoyed her graduate studies at the University of Chicago, but not the academic life, with its departmental politics and status games. She had been in Mexico at the same time Xtul was occupied by the cult but had never visited it. From two young women who were in contact with the cult, she received a couple of Process magazines secondhand: the Common Market issue, and the one titled *Freedom of Expression*, with the rock superstar Mick Jagger on the cover. Her doctoral project was on Mayan linguistics, and she found field research disappointingly boring. Nothing was happening in

Rebekah contemplating the culture of Satan.

the village she lived in. Twice she took vacations from the field, returning to the States.

Rebekah visited a friend at Tulane University in New Orleans. While there, she visited the Process chapter house a couple of times. She "was completely fascinated, bug-eyed!" Rebekah "tended to discount the theology. I was mostly interested in the people." She returned to Yucatan. During the year, her attitude toward conventional American society became progressively more negative. Like many others, she was a fan of the liberal politician Bobby Kennedy. His assassination in June disheartened her. Nixon's speech accepting the Republican presidential nomination disturbed Rebekah. She saw a dark future ahead for America. She visited her family in New York and ran into the Process again at its Greenwich Village location. "The feeling was of a community that was actually going somewhere and actually had something to offer in terms of a lifestyle." Because she believed America was a sinking ship, she was happy to climb aboard the Process.

Rebekah had her own interesting theory: "The thing about anthropologists is that basically all of them don't like their own society very much. If they did, they wouldn't be anthropologists. What they're actually trying to do is get out of ordinary American society anyway. They usually find a field area that they like, and they're usually very happy when they're in their field area. And they're a bit miserable when they're at home! And that goes for archaeologists as well. They have a wonderful time in the field, wherever they've decided they want to be, and are totally miserable in the office, writing."

She believed most anthropologists shared this characteristic: "They have a strong sense of alienation from our society." Consequently, they seek to escape, at least periodically, to a better society. The only problem for each was to find an alternative society that pleased him. For some anthropologists the alternative society is that of the Mayan Indians.[60] But Rebekah found the Mayans terribly boring. She was a believer in cultural evolution. If you go from America to Bali, you are going "down the scale" toward less advanced, less exciting styles of life. Rebekah even felt that her visits to Europe were steps "down the scale." She didn't like backward people and wanted to find a society that was a step up from America, a modern or even futuristic tribe. "The Process was *up* from ordinary American society." She believed every anthropologist was looking for his tribe. The Process was hers. Rebekah once asked me to carry a message back to one of her former professors. It was a simple bit of news: "I went native."

Process culture constantly grew and changed. The purple capes of the costumes were discarded, partly because some members were embarrassed to wear them, partly because the supply ran out. In New Orleans, Processeans had worn only one religious symbol, a silver cross. In New York, they added black triangular emblems embroidered with red, humanoid goats' heads. This Badge of Mendes indicated the acceptance of the power of Satan. Step by step throughout 1968 a theology solidified, identifying three equal parts of God, Lucifer—Jehovah—Satan.

MUNICH

In March or April 1968, soon after the New Orleans chapter had closed, while the main group was traveling in California, Malachi and Raphael flew from the London chapter to Munich, Germany, to set up a little branch there. Sister Gretel, one of the new recruits, was sent from America to join them because she spoke German fluently, Malachi knew the language well, while Raphael spoke it very little. They "were very interested in the political situation because it was a time of considerable unrest," Raphael said. England was still brooding over membership in the Common Market, so the English Processeans had a certain nationalistic interest in checking out the Germans to see what kind of partners they would make. The Process was in search of *intensity*, so the Nazi mystique attracted them. They wanted to learn "how Hitler could have happened to a country" and whether similar forces were still at work.

The tiny Munich chapter immediately made contact with both German political extremes, the leftist Students for a Democratic Society (SDS), and the neo-Nazi National Democratic Party. "Both extremes," Raphael said, "were very active." The SDS staged marches through the streets of Munich to protest the Vietnam War. "One time a lot of SDS people lay down on the tram tracks in Munich, which held up a lot of people. It was a very politically stupid time for them to do it. It was four o'clock in the afternoon, when everybody was going home. Now, if they'd done it when everybody was going to work, it would have been a different matter. Of course, the SDS are not into getting up at seven or eight in the morning!" The three Processeans traveled to Nuremberg, scene of Hitler's greatest public displays, and to Coburg, to view right-wing NPD rallies. They met Adolf von Thadden, leader of the party, and found him "a very impressive man," a "dignified … big, rather florid man" with "quite a lot of charisma."

Raphael remembered one grand incident that illustrated the complex relationship between the cult and the political extremes. It expressed exactly the image the cult wanted to present and exactly the reception it sought. Malachi, Raphael, and Gretel decided to visit a right-wing rally that was being protested by a mob of left-wingers. They marched toward the meeting hall dressed in their all-black uniforms with flowing capes, two huge beards and three heads of long hair clearly visible. The SDS saw them coming and "thought we were left-wing. We weren't left-wing, although we had a number of elements about us that people could have mistaken for left-wing. They saw us go into this rally, and they thought this was terrific! Obviously we were going in to disrupt it. So they cheered and clapped, Great performance! Lot of people. And we went into this hall where they were having the rally. It was all very orderly. All regimented. And we were dressed in our gear, in uniform, black at that time. We walked down the center of the aisle looking for a seat, and everybody started cheering! And waving! Of course because we were in uniform we looked like right-wing!" Process doctrine had already begun to emphasize the idea that the extremes of human experience and expression were superior to mundane blandness and that the extremes could be reconciled without dilution within the cult. The Process display at the rally was a "sort of transcendence of this absurd situation."

The Processeans supported themselves in Munich by selling their English-language magazines on Leopoldstrasse, asking for donations and finding people who would put them up temporarily in their homes. They lived off the curiosity and benevolence of the Germans. In return they put on quite a show. In addition to their street performance, they carried on in cafes, and even once in a bar. After getting the proprietor's permission, they would sing Process songs for the bemused customers and act out dramatic little skits depicting various elements of the evolving cult doctrine.

Malachi, Raphael, and Gretel gave a particularly memorable impromptu performance in the Englischer Garten park. At one point, the park ground rises in a low hill topped by a cupola or bandstand. In good weather there were always many Munich citizens sitting about on the grass, relaxing and chatting. The three costumed Processeans stormed up the knoll, unannounced, with only a vague idea what they might do. Their colorful act "was a kind of demonstration of the various aspects of God, through chanting, music, enactments." Three aspects of God, three archetypes, were dramatized: Jehovah, Lucifer, and Satan. "People didn't know *what* we were doing," Raphael remarks. "We were giving this performance, but they didn't know what it was. They thought it was terribly funny. Those crazy English people, what are they doing! Afterwards they all clapped and pelted us with coins. So it was all in good fun, but it was really a crazy situation!"

As is usual for the Process, it was a time of extreme ups and downs. Apparently relations within the tiny chapter, consisting of two men and one woman, were not entirely harmonious. Things got so bad that Gretel dropped permanently out of the Process. "Not surprising," Robert de Grimston told me. "That was a carve-up situation." Around July 1968, two or three more members were sent to Munich, so the expanded group decided it was time to rent their own apartment and establish the beginnings of a real chapter. None of the literature was ever translated into German, and the cult's impact on Germany was slight. But this tiny Munich chapter, which only lasted six months, served as a stable starting point for the extensive wanderings in Europe that began later that year.

AIMED FOR LONDON

The New York chapter was really the staging area for return to England. The group in Greenwich Village was busy collecting enough money to ship everyone across the Atlantic and sent the few untrained newcomers over first, as finances permitted. Matthew went over in June 1968, with another new American member. The small London chapter not only started training them immediately in doctrine, but also thrust them without delay onto the streets as instantaneous spokesmen for the Process. The day after he arrived in London, Matthew was spreading the cult's anti-vivisectionist opinions from a soap box at Speakers' Corner at the northeastern corner of Hyde Park.

Mary Ann had always been intensely anti-vivisectionist. As we mentioned, she once smashed a television set because it was showing pictures of a bullfight. Robert shared her feeling that experimentation on animals was evil, but he was less outraged in his opposition than she. Directly inspired by her, he wrote an anti-vivisectionist tract in May 1968, *The Ultimate Sin*. But when Matthew first spoke at Speakers' Corner, surrounded by hecklers and competing soapboxers, he had no script for his tirades. "*The Ultimate Sin* hadn't been published then, and we were all just talking about our own realities on vivisection." They felt the carving up of living animals was "rejection of God's creation, rejection of God, hostility towards God and enacting that hostility on God's creation. You're not going to get anything but death out of utilization of death. If you employ death in the procedure, that's going to be inextricably entwined in the results. So you're going to apparently do something beneficial, but you're also going to do something destructive and detrimental, which was borne out by the effects of drugs and dependence on drugs and symptomatic medicine." That's the sort of thing Matthew would say to the crowd.

Three or four Processeans would troop over to Hyde Park every Sunday and take a stand by their soapbox. Actually, they used a milk crate that they had dragged with them, but it functioned as a soapbox. They would form a little line, and the first Processean would step up on the box and begin haranguing the passersby. When he ran out of steam, he would cede the box to the next in line, who would take over and launch into his spiel. They would go on in turn like this for several hours. The last London issue of the cult's magazine has a picture spread on the inside front cover showing two views of Process soapboxers speaking to a large crowd. One of the pictures is clearly faked. The audience has been augmented by the splicing in of two sections of other photographs. The Process wanted to believe it had a tremendous impact on people.

"You had to bellow out as loud as you can to attract attention," Matthew recalled. "It's really exciting. It's not something that you can look forward to, but it really has an element of life and energy to it. It gets you through a lot of feelings of vulnerability and what you can and cannot do . . . dealing with hecklers and that kind of thing. There were some of these people who would just go there every week to heckle, and they have elephant voices that sound like *Baarrrrooooooommmm!,* these big, bull-moose things. They disagree with absolutely everything, even if it's the thing they just said."

In September, about two dozen Processeans, including most of the new American recruits, were put aboard a modest ocean liner named the *Waterman,* bound for London. Robert and three others stayed on in New York for a short while. When I asked him why the group was sent over, he first replied as if everything had been part of a clear, voluntary plan: "We had an idea of just focusing all our attention in London, and spreading throughout Europe from there." Morgana recalled, "We were not exactly a smash hit in New York." As an afterthought, Robert admitted the British members knew they had to get out of the States and wanted to take the new Americans with them. "You see, originally we had appalling immigration problems, 'cause we had no money at all. We were all trying to be immigrated, but we just had this 'church' which had no prospects at all, and no money, so we couldn't get our immigration. This was right back at the very beginning, and which is why eventually we just left the country and went back to Europe." But the cult interpreted the problem as something grander than a mere bureaucratic hassle. They saw it as a divine message, a sign or a portent: "That was another *sign,* because we couldn't stay any longer." The American Processeans were, as Morgana said, "a pretty motley crew" and in no position to carry on a New York chapter by themselves. The only well-established center was in London. She said, "The idea really was to try and get us into London, I suppose, and consolidate us more, train us more."

When the *Waterman* arrived at London, the British immigration authorities came aboard ship to check those passengers who wanted to get off. Most of the two dozen Processeans were not British citizens, and few of them had any money, so they were refused entry. None had work permits, any clear means of support while in England, or return tickets to justify defining them as tourists. So they were rejected. Robert explained, "So that meant the whole lot simply stayed on the boat! Apparently the Immigration people were thoroughly unpleasant."

Lars, one of the rejected Americans, could see the officials' point. The Home Office doubted that the tiny London chapter could support so many Americans and had not been given any kind of warning that they were coming. Raphael thought "the main reason was that there were just too many Americans. We were comparatively unknown as a religious order, of course, at the time. And it wasn't like fifteen Catholic priests were trying to get in. It's not too surprising they turned them back! What we did after that, and it was stupid of us not to do it beforehand, was we went to the Foreign Office in England and set it up. We gave them all the evidence they needed that these people would not become burdens on the state and public wards. But it never occurred to us in our naïveté at the time that they couldn't just walk in."

It is quite possible there was another reason the group was turned away by British authorities. At this very same time, the British government was barring the entry of noncitizens who wanted to study and receive therapy at the Scientology College. Early in 1967, the House of Commons debated the alleged dangers of Scientology, and a government policy aimed at discouraging its growth was developed in 1968. Newspapers from the summer of 1968 contain a number of reports concerning people turned back at London airport or otherwise refused entry. One chartered flight intended to take 180 Americans to the Scientology College was canceled. The connection between the Process and Scientology was well known in London, and it is quite possible the Processeans were seen as just one more Scientology group.

Mother Diana was in charge of the party on the *Waterman* and had to deal with the situation. There were few options, and the one they took was the most passive. The two dozen of them simply stayed on the ship and continued on to its ultimate destination, Rotterdam. They did not stay there long, as Morgana reported: "We went to Amsterdam, where accommodation had been arranged for us in this great big old loft in an abandoned school. We all lived there with about thirteen German shepherds."

There was, still, a tiny chapter in Munich. In their brief German travels, Raphael and Malachi had found it possible to get along without jobs or money. Would it be possible to maintain the two dozen stranded Processeans in Germany this way? Much of the responsibility for a solution fell on this little band in Germany. The immigration problem "was a bit of a shock for everybody," Raphael said, "so we had to do some fast thinking in Germany. Father Malachi and Mother Diana, who had by that time joined us, set off first of all to Hannover and then subsequently to Hamburg to try and establish some kind of accommodation for the people who were coming in." They founded a temporary center in Hamburg, and the groups in Amsterdam and Munich converged there.

MATTHEW TEN

Back in New York, Robert and his associates frantically discussed the challenge thrown before them by the British authorities. The Book of Matthew, Robert's personal favorite among the books of the Bible, provided inspiration. On the first of October 1968, Robert wrote a letter to all Processeans, setting their current difficulties in the optimistic context of the New Testament. Titled BI-6 (*Brethren Information* letter number six), it sought to explain everything in the best possible light:

> 1.1 In Matthew Chapter 10, Christ instructs his disciples, before sending them out in pairs to go from city to city preaching the Word.
> 1.2 The instructions he gave apply now, possibly even more precisely than they did then.
> 1.3 We have talked for some time about Processeans going out in pairs preaching the message of the End, and it looks as though we shall very soon be ready for just this kind of operation. And Matthew Chapter 10 supplies the blue-print for it.

The following sections of B1-6 are a commentary on Matthew 10 written by Father John from notes of his discussions with Robert. John explained the relevant passages and gave specific instructions for the conduct of traveling Processean pairs. For example, verses 9 and 10 of Matthew 10 say, "Provide neither gold, nor silver, nor brass in your purses, Nor scrip for your journey, neither two coats, neither shoes, nor yet staves: for the workman is worthy of his meat." John and Robert commented on this passage, translating it into instructions for their followers:

> 6.3 Take no money. For the individual Processean has no need of it for himself. For our physical needs will be met by those to whom we give spiritually. If we are doing our job properly, then we are "worthy of our meat," and our physical requirements will be taken care of.
> 6.4 This does not mean that The Process has no requirement for money, nor that a Processean should refuse to accept money. Quite the contrary; he accepts the money, making it clear to the person from whom he received it that it will be devoted to the

purposes of The Process, and not to his own needs. And immediately he passes the money up the hierarchy, thus making his
own contribution upwards in physical form.

6.5 In fact we go with no physical possessions at all, beyond the
bare minimum of clothing. We have nothing to give down-
wards on a physical level, no handouts for the hungry or the
poor, no bowls of soup, no Welfare payments. Our job is to
channel spiritual sustenance and to take spiritual responsibility
for those beneath us in the hierarchy; not to take physical
responsibility for them, nor to look after their physical needs.

This passage shows clearly how traditional scripture was bent to serve
the practical problems of the cult leadership, and how new doctrine could be
generated in response to a problem. The theology grew out of social relations
and sought to control those relations symbolically. A practical solution required more than philosophizing and exhortation; it required a practical test.
Two of the new Americans were sent to Frankfurt on a trial run. "It was a bit
like Noah's Ark," Raphael recalled. They were the doves that left the ship in
search for dry land: "We sent two out to see whether the flood had subsided
and they would come back." It had. They did.

Under the circumstances, the invocation of Matthew 10 was a brilliant
maneuver. It transformed a disaster into an opportunity, a grievous mistake
into a creative inspiration. It denied that the leadership had failed and reas-
serted their dominance over the rank and file. The large group in Hamburg
was split up in pairs and sent out into Germany, instructed to follow Matthew
10 and spread the Word. Of course, the chief purpose of this plan was to have
some place to put the Processeans, activity to keep them busy, and a way of
supporting them without money or much work from the leaders.

There were other functions the Matthew 10 episode served, unintended
but important. For those who stuck with the cult through this trying period,
Matthew 10 was great experience in dealing with large numbers of strangers
and in maintaining themselves without help in a strange environment. It was
also an initiation rite and commitment mechanism. Those who made it
through this time were firmly bound to the cult. Relationships between them
were deepened through the shared struggle and adventure. For those who had
not been at Xtul, it was the defining experience, a personal watershed.

The pairs headed in all directions. Raphael and Malachi visited
Wuppertal, Frankfurt, Heidelberg, and Stuttgart. In the last of these cities they

rendezvoused with a number of others. A party of four headed back to London by way of Paris. Raphael recalled the French capital fondly: "Had a wonderful time in Paris. It was late fall, and it was beautiful. People were so receptive to us. We were selling so many magazines we didn't know what to do with ourselves. We really had a terrific time."

Mother Diana picked the pairs and aimed them at their first destinations, but, as Morgana said, "Once they were sent, basically, we were all *really* under our own steam. I mean it was literally following the whole Matthew 10 thing. When I arrived in Düsseldorf, the first thing we did was donate accommodations, donate food, and start donating money. And that's basically all we spent our time doing was donating money, donating accommodations, and donating food."

Brother Lars joked that the treks were a tourist's nightmare: "How to see Germany on minus five cents a day!" Morgana described the trips to me in detail: "We went out in pairs, and we relied completely on the people that we met to feed us and house us and to give us funds to keep the church going. If a city was not being hospitable, if you could not find accommodations, or if you got stopped by the police for 'donating,' well, then the idea was that you didn't persist in that city, but like in Matthew 10 you shook the dust of it off your sandals and carried on to another city. And it was all done through hitchhiking as well. We hitched from city to city. And many of us had dogs with us. Christian and I had two dogs. We had Satan and Beelzebub. We were on the streets chronically, just walking all the time. Things would happen. Like in Düsseldorf we had a really bad stretch and we couldn't get any accommodation and for some reason that I can't remember now we didn't leave the city. We stayed there about five days. We had to sit up at night in a German bar, a students' bar, without sleeping."

She and Christian suffered through those days together, without any support from the cult's leadership. "You would have incredible hardships! First of all, it was freezing cold and we were not very well dressed for a German winter. And you would have lean periods where you would not be getting fed very well, or your accommodation would be very bad, like just sleeping on a bare floor with a blanket or something. Not being able to get a bath because the places you were staying in didn't have baths, or they only had cold water."

Morgana remembered the times of good fortune with great pleasure: "It was quite a miraculous period, you know, being in Germany, not being able to speak German. Being put up by strange people who very often couldn't speak English. But in some sort of way you would be able to get it across to them that you needed a place to stay. And some people being unbelievably good to us. Really generous, kind. Things like: going into restaurants with the dogs and just having the chefs come out of the kitchen and feed the dogs with all kinds of bones and people from the tables coming over with food for the dogs. Extraordinary personal things: people being really open and generous, and willing to give whatever it was that they could give."

Matthew 10 was a guide for activity at the London Chapter as well as among the Processeans in Germany. Brother Matthew said he traveled all over England and Scotland, perhaps not from Land's End to John o' Groats, but at least from Plymouth to Aberdeen. Like the Processeans in Germany, they went out in pairs and lived off the charity of strangers while spreading their message and advertising the cult. Matthew recalled it well: "Sometimes you'd get taken into nightclubs, given front-row tables, and you'd get a whole show and revue and big steak dinner. You'd go up to the manager and say, 'We're traveling for a church, doing work of our church, et cetera, et cetera. Can you provide a meal for us, and help us on our way with our work?' And some people would say, 'No, no.' And other people would say, 'Sure, come on in; these two gentlemen are ministers in a church.' Introduce us to the maître d' and have us sit down—waiters running all around—the whole schmeer. And other times we'd find ourselves ending up with little or nothing, depending on how well we had done our work."

Here again Matthew expressed the Process ideology, the blanket explanation for variations in response that makes everything seem meaningful, moral, and uncontaminated by blind chance. Good work would be rewarded by God through the agency of human generosity. "The reward was very clear and very precise and very immediate. Sometimes we'd find an accommodation in a hotel. We'd go to a hotel and ask if they had a room for us. You'd leave your shoes outside the door, and they'd get polished. And they'd wake you up in the morning with tea and toast in the room, and then you'd go down and have breakfast. That was on one side of it. And the other side of it was shivering in a heatless flat, curling up under a rug trying to keep warm. So there was every extreme. There were levels and levels of significance to everything. It was like God was intervening very precisely, saying, 'You deserve *this*; you don't deserve *that*. Suffer for a while. You've suffered enough. Here's your reward.' I remember one night being totally frustrated, on the verge of tears, stuck out in Glasgow, pouring rain, nobody on the street, with no place to stay, huddled in a doorway. Seeing one person come out of the train station, seeing one person go running across the street. Last chance! We had given up, completely. This guy was the sweetest! Like an angel. Took us in, fed us, in his house. He and a friend had an apartment. Fed us, invited us back. His friend gave us Judo massages."

Malachi said, "There was an extraordinary quality" to the Matthew 10 trips. "You went where you went to. There was no concept of how long it was going to take to get there. And every person you met had a significance." It was an entirely different experience from conventional traveling. There was a sense of great purpose, but no sense of plan. Malachi agreed, "It was a very magical time."

HUNTING FOR HEADQUARTERS

In mid-October, the Omega left New York and landed in Bremerhaven, Germany. Processeans gathered for a big meeting with Robert and Mary Ann. A large contingent came from nearby Hamburg, and a few were sent from London. Then the Omega went directly down to Oberammergau, intending to find a place to set up a Process Center in southern Germany. The nearest large city was Munich, where there was now a small cult chapter, and Oberammergau was a place of beautiful scenery and religious spirit that could give the Omega both pleasure and inspiration. Indeed, it always seems that the travels of the Omega were intended to give pleasure to Robert and Mary Ann but were explained as giving inspiration. Perhaps pleasure and inspiration were identical in their minds. The street-begging rank-and-file members were expected to support the Omega in its search for both. A euphoric tourist book about Oberammergau describes the arrival of the comfortable visitor: "At once you feel transported into another world, a world which seems dream-like and fantastic. Longhaired men in white shirts and embroidered braces, with steel-strong limbs showing in knitted hose beneath their leather breeches, hoist your heavy suitcases on their shoulders as if they were matchboxes and stride ahead, leading you on to your lodging, which quite probably will be in a private house, possibly a real chalet dating back two or three centuries."[61]

Such must have been the arrival of the Omega, though the entry of lower-status members into Oberammergau was far more humble. Robert and Mary Ann were drawn to this religious tourist city by its romantic mystique, a quality of mood they wanted for their own cult. In 1632 and 1633, like many another village, Oberammergau had been ravaged by the plague. Always a particularly religious community, the people of Oberammergau sought a religious solution to the disaster that had befallen them. The town council resolved to give one year in ten to the Lord by presenting a magnificent Passion Play in which all citizens would take part. The plague departed, but the play remained. It transformed this modest mountain town into a world-famous religious center. Indeed, my missionary great-grandmother, Lucy Seaman Bainbridge, attended the 1880 edition of the Passion Play and published a detailed description of the location and the performance which began:

> The curtain now rises for the first tableau. We see Adam and Eve dressed in skins, driven out of paradise by the angel. As we gaze, the chorus carry on the prologue given by their leader, and sing of man's disobedience, and the hope for fallen humanity in a Saviour crucified. A second time the curtain lifts, and there is a cross firmly set into a rock. Around it a number of children are bowed in worship of prayer and adoration. It is an exquisitely beautiful picture. These two tableaux precede the first act, and embody the whole spirit of the play.[62]

Yet the year was 1968 for the Processeans, and attending the 1970 performance not only would have required a long wait but might have involved the Process in one more religious controversy, given the painful public debate over whether the text of the Passion Play was blaming the Crucifixion of Christ on the Jewish people.[63] From Oberammergau, the Omega sent messages to many of the pairs and groups scattered throughout Germany to join them for a while in this spiritually uplifting, mountain-ringed village. Communication was very uncertain, since many of the Processeans were constantly on the move. Although the people in the field sent a daily letter to London and to the Omega now in the south, letters to the wanderers often had to chase them from city to city. Having no sacred places of its own, the Process borrowed Oberammergau to provide a rich spiritual environment for a convocation of its members. The cult often tried to gain spiritual strength from the holy shrine or magical symbol of some more successful church or movement.

After a few days, most of the Processeans who had come down from northern Germany were sent back, dispersing to follow Matthew 10 once more. The Omega was busy looking for the Process Center. Robert recalls with some amusement that they were hoping to find a suitable place for free: "In fact, we wanted to get someone to donate a Schloss to us." Raphael and Malachi were sent out on a Schloss quest, searching in Austria as well as Germany. For a while they were negotiating with a Bavarian countess who appeared to have an extra castle. But it never materialized. An Austrian doctor offered his large house. "But it was horrible," Robert said. "I mean it was the most ghastly, depressing place you've ever been into! So we passed that up. We were very grateful, but we passed it up."

The most fabulous location considered for the Process Center was one of the Nazi field marshal Hermann Goering's homes, Veldenstein Castle near Nuremberg. It was for sale. The Omega inspected photographs provided by a real estate agent and dispatched Raphael to look Veldenstein over. It was a complex of square-walled buildings dominated by a high observation tower, nestled in tall trees and overlooking a landscape of fields and forested hills. A romantic dream, Veldenstein would have been an intensely inspiring site for the Process Center—just what the cult was looking for, another injection of magic to match Xtul, a physical terminus to their search for the miraculous. The fact that it had belonged to the decadent Luftwaffe leader was a strong point in its favor. Robert was impressed that "This is where he used to have his weird performances." Veldenstein must have stored up very powerful vibrations, a black magical aura of fantastic intensity.

Actually, Veldenstein had been the boyhood home of Hermann Goering, while his chief adult residence was Carinhall in northern Germany. He loved the castle and had developed a taste for feudal glory during the years his family lived there.[64] Veldenstein had been the scene of "weird performances" by Hermann's mother, however, since the castle really belonged to her lover rather than her husband. Father Goering must have experienced great disgrace living off the generosity of his wife's boyfriend, an emotion that may have been shared by Hermann as well.[65]

Raphael inspected Veldenstein and reported that the buildings themselves were not overwhelming, "nice, but very domestic in scale." He liked it. "It was a magnificent location. They kept falcons there, but they were just regular people." Except for the high watchtower, it did not seem like a castle at all. The walls were not castellated, and there were no turrets. The beauty "was much more the way it was landscaped than the actual buildings." Unfortunately, the Process was unable to come up with enough cash and had to continue its search for a Center. In its romantic, erratic way, the cult followed *the signs* from place to place, from project to project. What does that mean? Robert explains: "We were seriously looking for a Center, but we didn't find one. So then we thought, okay … we got various signs."

"Signs?" I asked.

"Signs. Which told us to go further south."

"What kind of signs?"

Robert explained that a sign was a possibly divine message about what the Process was supposed to do. For example, two dozen members "got on a boat and they went to London, and the Immigration wouldn't let them into London. The boat was going to Amsterdam anyway, so that's *a sign*. Now that is a kind of completely choiceless sign—literally they had no choice. Sometimes you get things like that where the line of least resistance takes you to a particular point. And when you fight it and resist it and try to do the thing that you originally were setting out to do, you still move in that direction. And that's a sign. Like if you're trying to do something, and everything's blocking it, everything's stopping it, but then something sort of opens up *here* that indicates *this* is where you at least can go or can do, that's a sign. So, you see, the signs were against finding a place in Germany, 'cause we just didn't find a place."

The signs indicated that the Process Center might be found in Italy. "Well, if you go to Italy," someone said, "you'll find that there are huge monasteries which are completely unused. And people will either sell them to you for almost nothing or will rent them to you for almost nothing." Two of the senior men set out for Italy to survey the possibilities. They traveled all over, receiving their food, transportation, and lodging as gifts from the people they met. They were very pleasantly surprised by the highly positive reception given them by Catholic priests. Unlike English clergy, these men claimed to find much merit in Process theology. Robert says, "It was the most open reception that we'd ever found within established churches."

The Processeans hunting through Italy sent back photographs and drawings of several places they had found. But there was something wrong with each of them. Some were for sale at impossible prices. Some were already half occupied by a Catholic order. It seemed inappropriate to share a monastery with a rival creed. Now the signs pointed in the direction of Sicily, where the Omega heard there might be large establishments going for tiny rents or unused monasteries that could be had for a song. At the same time, there was another sign. A few Processeans became interested in Aleister Crowley, a cult leader and magician who had set up his group in the early 1920s at Cefalù on the north coast of Sicily. There were many similarities between the Process and Crowley's cult, such as their common attempt to transform members into intense personalities sharing mystical consciousness-expanding exercises in a surreal Utopian community.[66]

Crowley's maxims bear some similarity to Process principles. Robert de Grimston began his personal letters with "As it is ... " and ended them with " ... so be it." Crowley sandwiched his written communications between two rather more ornate maxims: "Do what thou wilt shall be the whole of the law" and "Love is the law, love under will." Crowley's principle of *Thelema*, an intellectual support for his magical practices, included an idea shared by Scientology, and I think privately applied by Robert de Grimston to himself: "In particular, each individual is conceived as the center of his own universe, his essential nature determining his relations with similar beings and his proper course of action."[67]

Crowley wrote that he chose Cefalù as the site for his Abbey of Thelema because the repeated casting of *I Ching* fortunes gave no other favorable response but that for Cefalù. I saw Robert cast *I Ching*s at a time of crisis, looking for hints of the future. The Process's belief in signs and portents similarly indicates the use of magic to make decisions, presumably to avoid painful responsibility and the threat of personal failure. Lured by Crowley's reputation and the idea that his abandoned Abbey of Thelema might be an ideal headquarters, the Omega left Oberammergau for Cefalù.

Mary Ann and Robert stayed in a small hotel set in an orange grove. Beautiful, but primitive. The majority of the hotel's guests were rats, and the place was absolutely filthy. Processeans fanned out in search of a headquarters building near Cefalù, with little success. One possibility, a castle-like monastery, was not suitable because the owner wanted to lend them only the worst part. The Omega moved to nearby Palermo to check out an incredible bright-red hotel on a rock promontory overlooking the sea. Exciting, but too expensive. This was a bleak and depressing time. Robert said Palermo was "the bottom end of the universe." A Process Center had not materialized, "and by then also we were going through a lot of very heavy spiritual enactments," squabbles, tantrums, and scenes of desperation. "We reckoned that we'd hit the bottom end of everything in Palermo." Processeans were scattered all over Germany, trying to survive through begging. The Omega was exhausted by several months of struggling to lead its followers and groping to follow the signs. They had not found a door out of the world; they had not found a higher plane of existence. But Christmas was coming. There was a small group of members in Rome, so the Omega decided that everyone except the few in London should converge for Christmas in the holy city.

ROME

Even more than Oberammergau, Rome was a rejuvenating experience. The few Processeans already there had parked themselves in a large rooming house run by an accommodating landlord who didn't demand much rent. The Omega arrived and found a big, splendid apartment. It belonged to the Italian Ambassador to Finland, who had left to serve his country in that northern land. The apartment covered an entire floor of a large building and had a huge terrace on the roof. Marble floors, filigree furniture, and the roof garden made it a deliciously elegant place to celebrate Christmas. All the Matthew 10 wanderers were called down from Germany.

The apartment bulged with Processeans over the holidays, so in January another place was rented to hold the overflow and act as a regular Process chapter house. For three or four months they maintained an actual open Chapter in Rome, people settled in, and Robert had a chance to write several pieces of scripture based on their recent experiences. He composed five of the "Letters from the Omega to All Brethren," BIs eight through twelve. *The Adversary*, BI-8, was an important developmental step in the evolution of the theology. It began, "Literally Satan means the Adversary," but goes on to explain that Satan, the divine personality, is no longer our adversary. Instead, the pettiness within us has taken over that role. BI-8 continues a line of thought Robert began in earlier pieces, *The Two Pole Universe* and *Humanity Is the Devil*, a dualistic conception of the moral universe in which the opposite poles are antagonistic but neither is evil.

Several leading Processeans told me the key doctrinal concept of the Unity of Christ and Satan emerged during the stay in Rome. The group already recognized three Gods (or aspects of God) and accepted the teachings of Christ despite the gulf between the traditional Christian system and their own. Acceptance of Satan, announced through the wearing of a Satanic symbol adopted in New York, was now reconciled through the new doctrine. The group was beset by conflict and tugged by contrary influences. Robert attempted to solve these real problems symbolically through a new theory of reconciliation, a doctrine that Christ and Satan could transcend the differences between them and join together, without either losing His character. As an idea, it was received very enthusiastically by the group, but the real test could only come in its effect on actual events. The logic of the doctrine was simple; it took Christ's ancient teaching one step beyond good and evil.

CHRIST said: Love your enemies.
CHRIST'S Enemy was SATAN and SATAN's Enemy was CHRIST.
    Through Love enmity is destroyed.
Through Love saint and sinner destroy the enmity between them.
Through Love CHRIST and SATAN have destroyed their enmity and
    come together for the End;
CHRIST to Judge, SATAN to execute the Judgement.
The Judgement is WISDOM; the execution of the Judgement is
    LOVE.

The other BIs spoke rather directly about the problems the cult had been suffering. BI-9 explained the confusion that had gripped them for months. It both promised and urged the dawn of a new day in a new Eden: "As we move out of humanity and into the Garden, via enactment after weird enactment, a change seems indicated in our attitudes to one another within The Process." Robert explained that enactments had social value: "If a Processean pulls something, falls flat on his or her face, that is a sign for all of us, not just for that Processean." The concept of *enactment* defines evil and strife out of existence. A Processean could not misbehave, because everything had a spiritual meaning. Someone who displayed anger was said to be *enacting anger* or *manifesting anger* or *channeling anger,* bringing the Platonic ideal Anger to public awareness, performing a necessary spiritual service for the others, rather than simply choosing to be bad. "There are Processeans whose function it is to carry the burdens for all of us, to channel the agonies that all of us bring upon ourselves, to manifest the errors and wrongness which all of us bring into existence."

These pieces of scripture assert that nothing happens without good reason in The Process, that each event, even each untoward behavior, is a positive step forward in the realization of the collective dream. The doctrine may have reassured followers and leaders alike, rendering everything apparently meaningful and denying there was any cause for anxiety or alarm. It seems also to be an attempt by the Omega to assert charismatic infallibility.

PARIS

The brief trip by four members to Paris in 1968 had been so successful that the cult decided to launch a more permanent Paris chapter. In the spring of 1969, the Rome chapter was closed down, and all the people there went to Paris or

London. The Paris group stayed for a while in a small suburb, then moved outside the city to a tiny village named Saint-Vrain, a few miles from the market town of Arpajon. Raphael recalls, "We used to go into Paris pretty well every day." They held meetings and sold Process literature. There were "enormous numbers of tourists, so even if the French didn't want to buy it because it was in English, there were lots of Americans and English who would buy it." I know of two members who met and joined the cult in Paris, both expatriate Americans. Apparently the cultural barrier discouraged French citizens from developing the kind of ties with Processeans necessary for them to be recruited. Another barrier was geographical distance. The Paris chapter was *open*, in the sense that nonmembers could attend activities, but, as Robert commented, "The fact that it was out of the city meant that it wasn't too open." It did not have complete facilities, such as a coffeehouse, and attracted few visitors. Saint-Vrain was an ideal place for the group to live, however, because of the calm pastoral mood of the area. They got their milk from a farm next door, Raphael said. "It was a beautiful place that we lived in. It was quite cheap, because it was out in the country. It was an old manor house—stone and timber, great beams. Even the depths of winter were beautiful."

LONDON

The Omega reestablished its headquarters in London, and the majority of the members moved into Balfour Place, the grand stone building the cult had leased since late 1965. The immigration difficulties had been solved, and the cult retreated temporarily into its old home. When the London chapter filled up with the returning English Processeans and the new Americans, they experimented with novel customs. Brother Ariel reported that the cult was a "matriarchy" for a time. Mary Ann was described as the Oracle who inspired the Teacher, and she was therefore at least symbolically superior to Robert or their lieutenants. Ariel said, "In the hierarchical structure, the females were higher than the men." It was unwise for a man to argue with one of the Process women, because she might pull rank on him. When the high-status Inside Processeans would descend the great staircase, making a formal entry to some gathering, they went in order of rank, from highest to lowest, but "the lowest woman would go before the highest man."

Robert explained, "There was a period around 1968/1969 when the emotional side of the Process generated a heavy and intense female chauvinist bias, which I suppose was an understandable reaction against the human norm. But it didn't last too long before the balance was redressed and we returned to a state of assumed equality. But that period did prompt me to write a lot about the male-female relationship, which was no doubt part of its purpose." As usual, Robert assumed the purpose of events was to have some perhaps divinely inspired effect on him. Everything happened to teach him something, which he could then teach to others. He was the intellect of the world.

Two Balfour Place was an ideal headquarters for the London chapter, situated in a good section of the city, not far from several big tourist attractions and some very expensive stores. The building was dark stone and brick. The door carried a huge black version of the original Process symbol, like a swastika spider web. Newcomers usually visited the coffeehouse first, a dark room called Guess Who's Cavern. The *Who* in question was Satan. The Cavern was on two levels, a main floor and a gallery reached by a winding stair. Constructed of heavy beams and boards, the gallery looked like a gigantic box kite. Three globes hanging from the ceiling provided dim red illumination, supplemented only in spots by the flickering light of candles on the tables. Among the decorations were Goya prints—witchcraft and monster scenes. Upstairs, three dragons were painted in red on the black wall. A large collection of popular records played continually on the phonograph.

The menu was extensive, offering Process concoctions and exotic dishes. In addition to cokes, hot chocolate, and many kinds of milk shake, the drinks included such nonalcoholic delights as watercress, tomato, and carrot juice elixir. There were Ogmars, "Which the Angels will tell you is a Milk Potion which can be made with Honey, Almonds, Cinnamon, Eggs, or Bananas." Sandwiches, rice dishes, soups, and several complete dinners were available. Among the poetic names given the dishes were Seventh Heaven, Cloud Nine, Epicure, and Devilled Supreme.

Brother Ariel said there was a tendency for newcomers to sit on the gallery, looking down on the main floor of the Cavern. "People who sat downstairs were people that knew the Process and felt comfortable about it." Upstairs, strangers were able to sit back, uncontaminated by the strange society beneath them. The Processeans did not got out of their way to produce an atmosphere congenial for everyone: "At no time was the Cavern comfortable to alien influences. If you were Grey Force [conventional] or unsympathetic, there was just: 'Who are you? Forget it! We're not even going to talk to you.' If your questions were at all implying that the Process might be wrong, it was like: 'Forget it! There's no point in us talking.' If you were the least bit interested, though, they became very friendly."

The chapter held Sabbath Assemblies and Chant Sessions but they were not open to the general public. Only inside members and those specially invited attended. Activities like the Telepathy Developing Circle, Midnight Meditations, and the Processscene were open to the public. There were three levels of classes for neophytes: First Progress, Second Progress, and Third Progress. These were held in the chief ritual room, the Alpha, and in other meeting rooms. Most rooms were white-walled, decorated with paintings by members, many with fireplaces. Most inside members lived in the upper stories of this large building, but by the end of the 1960s Robert, Mary Ann, and occasional lieutenants lived in a nice apartment elsewhere in London.

The Process became an important, if anomalous, part of the London occult scene. Françoise Strachan's 1970 catalogue, *The Aquarian Guide to Occult Mystical, Religious, Magical London and Around*, lists about two hundred strange groups, such as the Bardic and Druid Order, the Ghost Club, the Hermetic Brotherhood of Light, the Order of Melchizedek, the Order of the Pyramid and the Sphinx, the Pagan Movement, and the Process. Strachan invited each to submit a self-description. Some described themselves at length, but the Process merely asked a question and gave its address: "And at the judgement shall you show yourself a servant of the un-God, condemned to endless alienation from all truth or shall you show yourself a servant of the Gods, raised up and reborn into the New Age?—The Process, Balfour Place, Mayfair, London W.1."

A FAILURE OF MIRACLES

The Process sought in vain for a door out of this world. At Xtul it attempted to leave conventional society altogether and claims it found magic and a God. But the cult did not find an exit at Xtul, merely an experience. The weeks at Xtul were like looking out a sealed window and glimpsing a heavenly vista; the door had to be found somewhere else, somewhere near, but where! In its wanderings the cult hunted for a spiritual breakthrough, a magical headquarters better than Xtul, and new ideas that would explain everything and give instructions on how to achieve everything.

In its wanderings it skirted the edge of the world, finding no exit and discovering that it could not escape the demands or benefits of conventional society. Everywhere they went there were troublesome immigration officials. They wanted a castle or monastery for their headquarters and at first refused to accept the implications of the fact that such a structure must have been built by members of conventional society. Nobody was prepared to donate an ideal Schloss, and it would take a lot of money to buy one. The source of money that fit best with the wandering lifestyle, and which could be handled by low-status members without bothering the Omega about the problem of income was street begging. Contrary to the ideology, God did not provide—people provided. In the following chapter we will see important consequences of this fact.

Those recruited in this period were socially detached middle-class young adults, but they were not pathological individuals. There are many reasons why a young middle-class person might be temporarily without strong attachments. Not inferiority but a normal desire for superiority and membership in a grand social enterprise motivated converts. Not belief in the doctrine but positive relationships with the Original Processeans defined membership and was the essence of conversion.

The first important factor for recruitment to the Process was simply that the person NOT be intensely committed to something else, that is, NOT bound firmly through strong social ties to people outside the group. Social isolation might produce tension in many people, and social isolation might be the result of prior life difficulties, but there is no necessary connection between personal problems and temporary social isolation. It was the structure of social relations around an individual that predisposed him to membership, not his psychic state. While the cult was on its migrations, bonds with newcomers had to be formed quickly. Because people poor in outside relations were free to form new ties quickly, social isolation was of supreme importance for conversion in this migration period, although it had been of no importance in the beginning, when the original members had been torn out of an extended friendship network by social implosion, and it became less important later.

The second important factor was that the newcomer and members of the cult had to find each other personally attractive. It was necessary that a newcomer develop ties that were not only strong but reciprocal. The Process was selective in letting new people in. Composed of talented, intelligent people and created through a process that laid great emphasis on personal intimacy, the Process rejected any prospective member unless old members liked the individual very much. By 1970, only one non-Caucasian, Brother Lars, had been permanently admitted to inner membership, and later only one other, a woman, became an inner member. Thus the group tended to recruit people who were like themselves through the development of friendships and intimate relationships.

These years saw the height of the youth counterculture, and many recruits to the cult had been deeply involved in it. But it would be a great mistake

Members expressing their connection in the social network.

to explain the Process as merely an extension of the cultural upheaval of the sixties. Its true genealogy goes back quite far, through Scientology and Adler to the Rosicrucian and Freudian movements of the beginning of the twentieth century. Many new cults have arisen in each recent decade, more often the result of microsocial conditions than of any general cultural changes. In the late sixties there were large numbers of unattached young people ready to join something, but there are always far more potential recruits in the world than a cult like the Process can readily incorporate. Cult policy, more than anything else, would determine who joined and how the group evolved.

CHAPTER 5   Paradise Misplaced

> Now is the time for a change. Now is the
> time to weight the balance on Lucifer's
> side .... Lucifer gives to those who ask of
> Him, but those who demand of Him,
> even when He meets their demands and
> gives, do not find His presence in the gift.
> They find only disillusionment.
>
> — BI-19, BI-22 Process Scriptures

IN EARLY 1970, at Morgana's suggestion but in accord with what many felt, Robert de Grimston announced the end of the Old Game in The Process and the beginning of the New Game. The first seven years of the cult, a period of exploration, suffering mixed with exaltation, and angry alienation from conventional society, were described as Jehovah's Game. Robert's book *The Gods and Their People* explains that Jehovah is the harsh, intolerant aspect of God:

> Of His people He demands all. He demands their life blood; and He inflicts upon them every dismal failure and deprivation in order to test the extent of their loyalty to Him. No easy pleasure-filled life for the Jehovian; his is the harsh road of expiation, the road of stringent self-sacrifice.
>
> For to JEHOVAH, success in human terms, pleasure and satisfaction by the standards of humanity, are snares that lure a being from the straight and narrow path of purity and self-denial. They are the traps that can cause a being to turn from his God and worship life as man knows life; the transitory shallow habitation of a human form.

In Robert's theology, Lucifer was the precise opposite of Jehovah, a conflicting standard and therefore the symbol of a radical change for the cult.

The New Game was to be Lucifer's game. Lucifer "urges us to enjoy life to the full, to value success in human terms." Lucifer was quite different from Satan; only the propaganda of Lucifer's opponent, Jehovah, caused people to mis-identify Lucifer with Satan. The Process had exhausted itself in its program to curse the world and escape it. Beginning in 1969, it discovered that life was much more comfortable in established chapters. In 1970, the cult turned away from Jehovah toward Lucifer. "His is the scented road of sweet and unpreten-tious luxury. But also it is the road of action, of pursuit, of movement; it is a road of exploitation, of making full use of all that is."

EXODUS FROM ENGLAND

At the beginning of 1970, the leaders of the cult decided to launch a second invasion of America. The American ministers who had been collected in 1967 and 1968 and were now thoroughly integrated into the group provided the personnel necessary for a mission to the States. The immigration authorities could not expel them, so the Process could plan the establishment of perma-nent American chapters. The first American visit had been very successful, Raphael recalled: "We had had an enormously positive and exciting response in the United States the first time we were here. It's in a sense much freer, more open than Europe." John remembered the feelings behind the decision to come again to the States: "There was the sense that America was the place of the future, that it was there that things were happening, that we could make a significant contribution."

In February or March 1970, Father John sailed to New York with Sister Morgana and an American man who ran out on John immediately. Morgana was privately contemplating leaving the cult, so John's companions were not the best choices. John and Morgana had a list of people in New York who might help them. She said, "We arrived with our dogs, Satan and Seth, and we called up some of the names we had on this list, and we got put up for the night. And basically did the same thing we did in Germany—finding different people to stay with, donating on the streets, generally testing out the water, seeing what things were like. We traveled around. We came to Boston. We visited Woodstock. We went back to New York again. Decided Boston felt like the right place." They began negotiations to rent a house on Inman Street in Cambridge, right across the Charles River from Boston. But they were not quite ready to move in. John and Morgana rented a car and set out to explore America further.

They went to New Orleans, where Morgana's family lived, then crossed to Los Angeles. John says they were "on a general scouting expedition to see where it felt like the right place to be, initially." Morgana abandoned John in Los Angeles and flew to San Francisco, where she had friends. John, now all alone, returned to Boston. Because the main chapter was still in London, it made sense to establish the first American chapter on the East Coast, to keep traveling distances to a minimum. John said another consideration was "what was happening in Boston at the time, which was quite exciting. There were a lot of very stimulating people there. Very alive atmosphere around the place. It felt like a good place to be. And the response to us felt very nice." Sister Seraphine, an American, and the British members Aaron, Christian, and Greer soon joined him. Some of Seraphine's family happened to live in Boston, "which was a temporary asset in the situation, in that they were able to help us in the physical sense."

The chapter house that John rented at 29 Inman Street was a typical central Cambridge residence. The location was very convenient, halfway between Harvard and M.I.T., only a couple of blocks from the Central Square subway station. The building was attached to 31 Inman Street, and the two structures shared front stairs. A reporter described the brand-new Boston Chapter in mid 1970:

> Fairly attractive house in Cambridge with three floors and a cellar. Everything is spotlessly clean. Besides a coffee shop, the cellar has a kitchen completed by the members, as well as a small workshop where some of them make handcrafted silver earrings, beads, necklaces, and rings. All lovely and I was tempted to buy some.... The coffee shop had benches, wooden tables, and little lights with red shades. On the wall were murals in reds, whites, and gold, depicting a large dragon and an angel and several childlike figures.

The coffeehouse was called the Cavern. In the late 1960s a great number of youth-oriented coffeehouses had sprung up around the country, many supported as a social service by conventional churches. There were several in Cambridge when the Cavern opened, so it had to compete with more lavish hangouts at the same time that it benefited from the popularity of such places. Brother Ariel told me the murals were the work of Father Cyrus, Father Christian, and others, "all done in oranges and blacks and silver tin foils put on, very nicely done." One mural showed the Four Horsemen of the Apocalypse,

The comfortable environment of the Cavern coffeehouse.

another St. George slaying the dragon. A crowned female figure astride the moon. A figure of Death. Most were scenes out of the Book of Revelation. Ariel's favorite was "the Whore of Babylon on the seven-headed beast. That was quite exciting!"

The first floor had two main rooms. One, which outsiders never saw, was an L-shaped space at the back, the office and sleeping quarters of the Master in charge. The large front room was set up as the Alpha, the main ritual room of the chapter. Here Sabbath Assemblies were held for members and invited guests, and at least three activities were held for the general public: Telepathy Developing Circles, Processscenes, and Midnight Meditations.

Christ's end of the Alpha ritual room.

Satan's end of the Alpha ritual room.

The second and third floors were reserved for inner members. The second floor had a bathroom, two large bedrooms, and a tiny little room where therapy sessions were held. Ariel commented that even two years later this former Session Room "had a really burnt-out feeling to it that nobody could get rid of." It was said that the many intense sessions held there had spoiled the aura of the room. "Whether that's true or not, I don't know," Ariel said. "But it always did have a very dead atmosphere." There were four rooms on the top floor, including one reserved for meditation. Ariel said the Meditation Room was always kept neat and "was the most peaceful room in the house."

The Boston Chapter's second house, on Concord Avenue.

In the fall of 1970, the Boston Chapter rented another house in Cambridge, a good-sized wooden structure on Concord Avenue which had at one time belonged to Harvard University. A new Cavern was set up in its basement, and the first-floor dining-room-plus-living-room area of the house was transformed into the Alpha ritual room. The high-status members of the chapter lived on the second and third floors. The original chapter house on Inman Street became a communal residence for new Messengers.

Once the Boston Chapter was a going concern, a second group of pioneers opened a chapter in Chicago, at the beginning of the summer. In June, Robert and Mary Ann came to the U.S., landing in Florida. They considered starting a Miami chapter but did not act on this idea for nearly two years. Possibly inspired by a famous movie starring Humphrey Bogart, Edward G. Robinson, and Lauren Bacall, they bought an expensive house in Key Largo, south of the city. By the time they moved in, sometime in September, the Omega had completely withdrawn from everyday Process society. Even some Messengers who joined in 1970 never met Mary Ann, and the general public was seldom even told where the Omega lived at any moment.

At the end of the year, Father Aaron went from Florida to New Orleans to found a new chapter there. Personnel were sent down from the growing Boston and Chicago chapters to staff it. About this time the Paris chapter was closed down. In an unpublished paper, the social psychologist Lee Lawrence reported some of the changes she observed in the Process near the end of 1970:

> On December 6, the Cambridge members were told of some changes in the hierarchy which promise to have far-reaching effects for the group's future. From London came the news that there was to be a rank of Disciple, effectively creating a lay following within the church. The main reasons for the changed structure are unclear: perhaps more members were needed for spreading the doctrines; perhaps many people had expressed a wish to join but not to devote their lives to the cause; perhaps an influx of people was needed to get greater financial support for the activities of the group.

Disciple rank was said to be equal in status to that of Messenger. Disciples could wear cult uniforms around the chapter and while on cult business. Like Messengers, they were called Brothers and Sisters of the church. They did not give up their outside attachments, however. From their conventional outside jobs, they were supposed to tithe, to give one tenth of their incomes to the Process. After a few months, some Disciples at each chapter gathered to form their own communes, living in imitation of Messengers. Although Lawrence reports Disciple rank was created by the central organization in London, it was never adopted there, and the weight of cult activity had shifted to the United States. Lawrence reported on another change that marked evolution toward a more open church society:

> As part of the general loosening of the hierarchy, actual entrance into the church was made easier for all. Formerly a person had to declare his intent to become an Acolyte, work for three weeks at the chapter house, and be invited by the group into their Sabbath Assembly to officially *become* an Acolyte. The stage of Initiate involved about 19 hours per week of training for eight to nine weeks; now, although the length of time is the same, the training has apparently been lightened. The opening of the Assembly to the public is indicative of the new focus on more widespread proselytizing and the de-emphasis of the need to have total commitment to the group.

Sister Eve told me that the first open Assembly had been a thrashing success. *Eleven* people came forward to become Acolytes. "I was flipped out!" she said. In the first weeks of 1971, I observed an average of slightly more than two individuals come forward each week to become Acolytes, and about one a week become an Initiate. The format of the Sabbath Assembly was changed to make it more educational for newcomers. Sections were added incorporating a few of the basic doctrinal statements and explaining such mysteries as the Gods and the coming Apocalypse.

About this time, the rank of Priest was renamed Superior. Messengers were divided into two levels, OP (Outside Processean) Messengers, the newest ones who all lived in "the Messenger flat," and IP (Inside Processean) Messengers who lived with the Hierarchy (high-status members) in the chapter house. Within each rank there were distinctions of seniority, and each chapter was run by a High Master, assisted sometimes by Provisional Masters. Thus in 1971 the system of ranks took on its fully developed form, the pattern followed throughout the years of the cult's greatest size. From the newcomer at the bottom to the Omega at the top, the system was as shown in Table 1.

RANK	CATEGORY	PERSON IS CALLED
The Omega	None	Robert or Mary Ann
Master	Inside Processean	Father – or Mother –
Superior	Inside Processean	Father – or Mother –
Prophet	Inside Processean	Brother – or Sister –
IP Messenger	Inside Processean	Brother – or Sister –
OP Messenger	Outside Processean	Brother – or Sister –
Disciple	Outside Processean	Brother – or Sister –
Initiate	Outside Processean	by his or her ordinary name
Acolyte	Outside Processean	by his or her ordinary name
(visitor "GP")	General Public	by his or her ordinary name

TABLE 1. The System of Ranks, 1971–1974 (Dashes represent a person's surname.)

The next new chapter was established in Toronto. Like many other steps in the development of the Process, this was the response to a practical problem, but interpreted in somewhat magical terms. Robert said his younger brother Phineas "went to Toronto because there was a problem with his immigration. You see, this is another *sign*. He had to get out of the country, and the only place he could go to without going back to England was to Canada. So we said, 'That's a sign. Go to Toronto and open a chapter.' So he did." Toronto was a very useful place to put Processeans who had legal trouble in the States. At this time many young men had gone to Canada to escape military service during the Vietnam War, many inspired by strong antiwar sentiments, others by more selfish motives. Only one of the American members of the cult had any serious draft problems. Father Raphael said, "We were continually fighting to get him conscientious objector status with the draft board, and they were very very unwilling to play ball. So we simply sent him to Canada so he wouldn't have a hassle with it. We successfully negotiated with the draft board for a number of our people." The Process argued that its young men were not only conscientious objectors to the slaughter of war, but also *ministers* of a church who should be exempt for that reason as well. Only in this case did a draft board reject this argument for any length of time. "We were simply not going to send one of our top people away to a senseless war. And if necessary we were going to keep him in Canada until they came to their senses, which they did, eventually."

Early in 1971, the London chapter was closed down. With the Toronto chapter and effective procedures for getting British Processeans admitted to the United States for unlimited periods, there was no practical need to maintain an English branch. With the majority of the members in North America, the London chapter became geographically isolated from the new center of the cult. A reporter for the *Harvard Crimson* wrote about London:

> Following a series of ineffectual lawsuits against them, the Processeans lost a suit filed against their operation of a basement coffee house in violation of city zoning laws. This lost suit was taken as a sign that the Church should leave London, and the London chapter was closed. But the Boston Processeans expect the London chapter to be reopened some day.[68]

Father Raphael said the London chapter had been dwindling for a year anyway, simply because "we were continually taking people out of it" to create the new American chapters. "The overall reception we got was so much stronger, so much more positive on the American side of the Atlantic, that it was our instinct really to pull people out of London. England was very much into a decline at the time. We felt the work would be much better, much more productive" in the United States and Canada. The problem with the zoning laws "was something that we really didn't bother to fight very much." It was "the final sign that we needed." The cult could have fought the issue, "but none of us really wanted to stay there. There was nothing to fight for."

The Omega temporarily left its Key Largo home in May 1971 and moved to Toronto, possibly because of short-term immigration difficulties. As the church became more established, one by one the English "ministers" could apply for resident alien status and work toward citizenship. The more like a conventional religious organization the cult looked, the easier it was to achieve this. Immigration was one of a whole series of practical factors pushing the Process back toward conventionality. In the second half of 1972, chapters were established in New York City and Miami, bringing the total to six. It is interesting that the New Orleans, Chicago, and New York chapters were ultimately situated right in the middle of high-class entertainment districts. New York eventually became the church headquarters.

NEW RECRUITS

With the establishment of fixed church chapters in 1970 and 1971, the cult's ability to collect people ready to make useful contributions declined. Some of those recruited in 1970 and 1971 were people of moderate talent, little creativity, and marked tendencies toward dependence on strong parent-figures. These people made decent members, willing to do the tough and unrewarding street begging, and were therefore valuable to the original Processeans. But after each chapter became established, its coffeehouse filled up with useless, talentless, pathological, problematic riffraff. Some of these people succeeded in achieving membership for a time, only to cause trouble and drop out again. In chapter 10 we will learn more about these people, but here I will describe eight much more competent men and women who were admitted to Messenger status between 1970 and 1974. These eight people were at the top end of the scale attracted to the cult in these years, but not public figures, so here they will keep their half-century-old pseudonyms: Norma, Goliath, Moira, Lot, Noah, Roxana, Clementine, and Samantha.

Three characteristics describe them in varying degrees. Some, like Norma and Goliath, had recently suffered traumatic experiences and a collapse in their careers. Others, like Moira, Lot, Noah, Roxana, and Clementine, might be described as *dependent personalities*, possibly "immature" but certainly looking for strong guidance and a lifestyle in which they did not have to act as independent individuals. Seen from another perspective, many of them had always lived in "institutions" that encouraged dependence, and after leaving one set of all-encompassing institutions, they adopted the Process as a substitute for the lives they had known. A third characteristic might be described as the professional motivation behind joining. Roxana, Clementine, and Samantha had been professionally trained in occupations very similar to the work of the Process and entered it as a fulfilling job as well as a lifestyle.

Norma

Sister Norma once theorized, "A lot of people used the Process as a psychiatrist. Everybody who's come into the Process has just had some horrendous problem that happened just before, and the Process gave them the security to solve the problem." This theory fits Norma and some of her cohort but does not fit many of the people who joined earlier. Of course, Norma never heard the stories of most members of the earlier generations, because they, as higher-status members than she, tried to cloak themselves in an air of mystery.

In 1971, Norma was wandering around, footloose, uncommitted. She went to Schenectady, New York, where she was supposed to meet some friends and go across country with them. They failed to show up, and she was left without definite plans. Friends she was staying with wanted her to meet a young man who happened to be dying of cancer. "I didn't want to get mixed up with that!" she says. She wound up meeting him anyway. Norma was making a little money as a singer; the guy with cancer played the guitar for her at a gig. The day after, she moved in with him. It was "the most perfect relationship I have ever had." Not only were they extremely well suited for each other, but his very special problem elevated the relationship above the ordinary. His parents accepted her, and when she was not alone with him she was with his whole family. Even after he entered the hospital for the last time, she lived in his apartment and spent a considerable amount of time visiting him or his family. She met him in November 1971; he died the following March.

His parents immediately sent Norma back to her parents' home in Boston. Her feelings were intense and disorganized. Norma felt "cheated by God" and "looney." She lived with a couple of men for a while, then alone, held a job for a bit, then joined the Process. "The Process was the only place I could turn to. Nobody else understood what I'd gone through." Norma describes the cult in its own jargon: "I thought they had more reality around emotions and around people and their feelings than other people I knew. I just felt more comfortable there." *To have reality around* means to be deeply moved by, to feel that something is powerfully real, or merely to believe in. The Process was built on unusually intense social relationships, and Norma had just been stripped away from such a tie with another person. For a while, her contact with other Processeans took the place of that relationship. Norma left the cult a year after becoming a Messenger.

Goliath

Son of a working-class Boston family, Goliath was on his way toward a career as a carpenter or cabinetmaker when drugs and the promise of excitement lured him out to California, where he joined the Iron Cross motorcycle gang. Over the four years that I knew Goliath, he always looked the part of a biker, defiantly overgrown with hair, intense but unchanging expression on his face, a rolling walk that suggested suppressed violence. The only features of his appearance that didn't fit the motorcycle ogre image were his short stature and light build.

As we sat in the Process coffeehouse in 1971, sharing my glass of cider and my brownie, getting acquainted, Goliath told me about the three men he had killed in California. One was battered out of this life in a fight. A second was accidentally pushed downstairs to a broken neck. The third was a Hell's Angel whom Goliath scrubbed out on the road—forced him off into a fatal crash while they were on their motorcycles. When interviewed by the *New York Times* in 1971, Goliath told the same story and added that he "used to ride across the country robbing gas stations." I checked around and discovered that Goliath had told other people he had only seriously damaged the three men in these incidents, not killed them. The stories conveyed the kind of image Goliath wanted to project, whether they were true or not. The friends of the Hell's Angel sought revenge and ran Goliath off the road in return. He suffered cracked ribs and other injuries, the most serious of which was shattered eyesight. I do not know for a fact how Goliath came to lose much of his vision, but the thick glasses he wore indicates his eyes were indeed in bad shape.

Another possibly apocryphal story Goliath told me symbolizes perfectly the state of his life. He drove his car into Boston and parked it in a lot near the Prudential Center. Some friends lived nearby, and he spent several hours with them, smoking marijuana and getting very high on LSD. It was one or two in the morning. Goliath wandered back to his car, got in, and turned on his engine. He let out the parking brake, stepped on the gas, and began driving away. Amazing! The colors and phantoms of his drug trip made the night very exciting. He drove and drove. Remarkable! Boston's buildings seemed to move ever so slowly. In fact, they did not seem to move at all. After a few minutes, when he realized that the Prudential Center had not moved an inch across his window, Goliath turned off the engine, set the brake, and got out of his car. Surprise! Somebody had jacked the car up onto metal milk delivery baskets and run away with all four wheels and tires.

True or not, that was the story of his life. Nothing seemed to work. He never got anywhere. Goliath wistfully told me the only things keeping him from resuming apprenticeship in cabinetmaking were his ruined eyesight and the fact that he had fallen out of the good graces of the local union. Goliath was a Messenger for only a short time, dropped back to Disciple rank, then lost contact with the cult altogether. In the winter of 1974-1975, I saw him sick and unemployed on the streets.

Moira

Sister Moira was a very thin young woman, apparently half-crippled by some childhood illness. She grew up in Toronto and was working in an office in that city when she first encountered the Process about 1971. She was hurrying home from work one day, rushing to meet some appointment, when she saw Processeans selling magazines. "The person I met on the street impressed me a great deal. She seemed to hold within her all the qualities I aspired to. She was very dedicated, very energetic, very enthusiastic, open. She responded to people. She wasn't just a salesman. She was someone who cared about me." The Processean's name was like "Sister Helena," a fact which impressed Moira deeply because she had dreamed about such a beautiful name for years.

The next day, Moira went looking for Helena on the street after work. At their second meeting she felt "willing to do anything. She [Helena] said, 'Can you help us?' I was willing to take on whatever it was, just on the strength of my feelings for this person. I think I almost knew I was going to join when I first met her. My feeling was that I wanted to be a part of whatever she was doing. It looked good and it felt good, and I could see that it had a very good effect on her. All the people that I met at the center at that time impressed me in the same way, and the more I went around, the more convinced I was." She worked at the Process chapter for about a year before becoming a Messenger. "I suddenly realized that everything that had any kind of meaning for me was there. The times when I wasn't there were just faded images; none of it had any kind of color or enthusiasm. And the color—the atmosphere—was at the Process."

Lot and Noah

Brother Lot joined the cult in 1970. He told me he had always lived in "institutions" and needed the security and direction of an organized life. His family was the first institution that provided this, then school, then college. After three years at Iowa State, he "crashed," began using drugs, was arrested, and was sent to prison. When he got out of this institution, he came to Boston and was considering taking courses in psychology at Boston University but joined The Process instead. He told me his perspective on membership: "For us crazy people, we like to stay in the house!" He looked up at the buildings of Boston University that stood around us as we talked. He dismissed them with a sweeping gesture and a laugh. "We can't operate here!"

Noah was the son of a middle-class Connecticut family. Before reaching the age of sixteen, he left his parents and what he saw as an intolerable, disintegrating family situation, abandoned high school, and went to Boston, where his sister and her husband were studying at Harvard. He held odd jobs such as short-order cooking, successfully secured an apartment, and began to make friends. It was quite a challenge for a young man not particularly wise in the ways of the world. Like many other unattached young people in the Cambridge area, he was attracted to the Process coffeehouse and began to spend a good deal of time around the chapter. He said it offered "a very homey feeling . . . very nice close-knit feeling." Although he was able to fend for himself in Boston, his life separated from his antagonistic parents and busy sister "was a little depressing and lonely." In a Sabbath Assembly "around Christmas time" in 1972, he came forward at the designated moment to become an Acolyte. Because of his youth, he was not permitted to become a Messenger until October 1973. At the end of the year, he was transferred to the fresh New York chapter, founded by Father John and Mother Seraphine. There, in the over-powering metropolis, his only continuing social relationships were with Processeans. They were his family.

Roxana and Clementine

Among the most energetic but dependent recruits who joined in the early 1970s were Sisters Roxana and Clementine. Roxana, a young woman of very sweet disposition, told me early in 1971 how wonderful she felt it would be if she could find someone to share happiness with, someone upon whom she could be completely dependent. A little later she became a Messenger, dependent upon the entire cult but contributing much to it. Both Roxana and Clementine had been student nuns in the Catholic Church. In a Process magazine article, Roxana complained about the strictness of her Catholic training: "All attention was focused on the ascetic and mortification of the flesh," in her order. "If we had time to talk, we had to have at least three people there—a measure, we learned later, to guard against homosexuality, among other things. You had to make sure that you never sat next to one person at recreation too much. It got the work done, but in terms of having a friendship it was very impersonal."

The Process was a religious community, therefore a familiar environment for Roxana and Clementine. But it was different. Although it controlled personal relationships, it encouraged them. Sexuality was not repressed but channeled. Speaking for herself, Sister Clementine explained what she felt was the most common reason priests or nuns left the Catholic Church: "the rule of celibacy." In her view, these defectors from the convent, herself included, "want to experience life on a sexual level, but you can't be a sexual person as a nun or priest; they knew that if they want to express themselves in this sort of way, they simply have to move out." She and Roxana had moved out of Catholicism into what for them was a similar kind of religious community.

Samantha

Sister Samantha was the first new member to join in Chicago in 1970. After graduating from high school, she got a job with a small theatrical company, doing odd work and occasionally playing small bit parts in the productions. Her ambition was to be an actress, but, aware of the uncertainty of an acting career, she cautiously planned to take whatever secure job she could find associated with the theater. She and some friends were wandering through one of the entertainment sections of Chicago one evening when they happened to come near the third-floor apartment where the Process had just set up operations. Someone had given them a handout, stating the address and inviting them to visit. On impulse, Samantha dragged her friends into the dark, candle-lit front room of the Process apartment, which was an informal coffeehouse. Samantha happened to be wearing her work clothes. Her theater was a theater-in-the-round, so the people who changed the sets between scenes had to operate in full view of the audience. Consequently, they wore black clothing to be nearly invisible. So, when Samantha entered the Process den, she was dressed all in black, wearing out of sentiment her Christian cross. She was astonished to meet her first Processean, who was also dressed in black, wearing a cross!

At first, Samantha was drawn in by a sense of mystery but was repelled by the idea of religion. That first night she found herself dragged along to an open meeting. "I fell madly in love with a couple of the people there immediately." Already she considered becoming a member. "I didn't even know what it was, and I was talking about joining it!" Over the next few weeks, it became her habit to visit frequently. "I still didn't know what they believed. I was attracted to the people more than anything else." Her "strongest involvement to start with was the people," and not just any kind of people, but the most interesting, attractive, high-ranked members. She said she had a real advantage meeting the group as early as she did, when the best members of the cult were running the coffeehouse and open to her friendship. Later on, newcomers were forced to make contact through cult members and Cavern denizens of far less attractiveness. Samantha loved the drama of the original Process. Just as the cult was a sexy monastery for Roxana and Clementine, it was a real-life theater for Samantha. Here she would be encouraged to put on a show for many audiences, every day, and to be the center of many exciting scenes.

THE MANSON DISASTER

In August 1969, Charles Manson led his ragtag "dune buggy attack battalion" in the murders of the actress Sharon Tate and six other persons. The Los Angeles police arrested Manson, and very soon a rumor began that Manson's sinister group was an offshoot of the Process. A Los Angeles radio station telephoned the London chapter of the Process asking if the rumor was true. When John and Morgana were scouting out the American territory early in 1970, they were both worried and attracted by the idea that Manson was a schismatic Processean. Manson was one of the reasons the pair drove out to Los Angeles. Morgana says, "I got a real wild idea in my head and decided we should go off to California and check out Charles Manson and what was happening out there. 'Cause we had just been pointed out as being involved in these strange ritual murders." I asked her if there were any real connection between Manson and the Process. "None. None whatsoever!" Had he ever come to a meeting? "No. No one of us had ever met him, heard of him. None of us recognized him when we saw pictures of him. If he had any contact with us—which he may have done, he may have spoken to someone on the streets who was selling magazines—it would have been a very brief contact which whoever it was didn't even remember. And I have the feeling that he never actually spoke to any of us." This is exactly the response I got from other knowledgeable Processeans.

The Manson murders were a public-relations disaster for the widespread youth counterculture of the late 1960s. Many Americans were quick to believe that Manson accurately represented the counterculture. A counterculture reporter recalls reading the news reports about the murders with a friend. They agreed, "We are in trouble." They knew they and other harmless deviants would suffer guilt by association in the public mind. "Neither of us rushed out to shave and get a haircut, of course, but when, a few months later long-haired, bearded Charles Manson (ballyhooed throughout the press as the leader of a tribe of 'hippies') was arrested for the crime, I began to wish I had. For a time it seemed as though every freak in the country was on trial, as the media made no attempt to distinguish between the drug-crazed, hairy beast called Manson and every other drug-crazed, hairy beast walking around."

Vincent Bugliosi, prosecutor in the Manson case, could never quite decide what kind of link there was between the Manson Family and the Process. Certainly, he never attempted to bring any Processean to court. Bugliosi notes several parallels between the Manson Family and the Process and says, "They are enough to convince me, at least, that even if Manson himself may never have been a member of the Process, he borrowed heavily from the satanic cult."[69] Bugliosi conjectured at length:

> I'm inclined to think that Manson's contact with the group probably occurred in San Francisco in 1967, as indicated, at a time when his philosophy was still being formulated. I believe there was at least some contact, in view of the many parallels between Manson's teachings and those of The Process as revealed in their literature.
>
> Both preached an imminent, violent Armageddon, in which all but the chosen few would be destroyed. Both found the basis for this in the Book of Revelation. Both conceived that the motorcycle gangs, such as Hell's Angels, would be the troops of the last days. And both actively sought to solicit them to their side.[70]

In 1971, Father Christian, then head of the Boston chapter, admitted his feeling to a newspaper reporter: "Manson had obviously got hold of some of our ideas from somewhere and had taken and distorted them in a particular way. It is unfortunate. If we had had the opportunity to speak to him, we could have avoided that series of very brutal killings." I rather think Father Christian had been swept along by the press reports, just as many other readers were. The ideas common to the Process and Manson's group are not all that unique. Other "satanic" cults existed, most notably Anton Szandor LaVey's Church of Satan, which had lurked and performed in San Francisco for years.[71] Surely the Book of Revelation is available for anyone ready to open a Bible. To the extent that both groups were socially isolated, introverted, millenarian cults that arose in Christian nations at the time of the youth counterculture, we would expect them to have some of the same characteristics, even if they differed absolutely in their practices concerning violence.

But some of the more bombastic, rhetorical passages in Process literature do sound like Mansonian proclamations. *The Gods on War*, completed by Robert in August 1967, announces, "The final march of doom has begun. The earth is prepared for the ultimate devastation. The mighty engines of WAR are all aligned and brought together for the End, The scene is set." This stormy book, packed with pictures of war, contains three long essays attributed to the gods Jehovah, Lucifer, and Satan. In each, one of the gods expresses His orientation toward war. Each essay is really a character study of one of the gods. The book assumes that destruction is coming, that the world has entered into the Latter Days, and seeks to take rhetorical advantage of all the powerful images of war provided by press coverage of recent conflicts. In a passage most Mansonian in mood, the Lord Satan advises the reader to participate fully in the holocaust:

> Release the Fiend that lies dormant within you, for he is strong and ruthless, and his power is far beyond the bounds of human frailty.
>
> Come forth in your savage might, rampant with the lust of battle, tense and quivering with the urge to strike, to smash, to split asunder all that seek to detain you. And cast your eye upon the land before you. Choose what road of slaughter and violation you will follow. Then stride out upon the land and amongst the people.
>
> Rape with the crushing force of your virility; kill with the devastating precision of your sword arm; maim with the ruthless ingenuity of your pitiless cruelty; destroy with the overpowering fury of your bestial strength; lay waste with the all-encompassing majesty of your power....
>
> For the world can be yours, and the blood of men can be yours to spill as you please. And you can have your pleasure of the world

through violence and the wielding of the sword. And your lust can stride upon the face of the land, taking whatever it desires, and discarding the empty husks when you've sucked them dry.

This is pure rhetoric, bombast meant to arouse the emotions and make the Process look intense, formidable, unusual. No real Processean I knew ever made the mistake of thinking these words were commandments that required action. Father Christian once told a reporter, "Very satanic members find it difficult to fit into the church. They cannot live as Inside Processeans." The cult did attract some violent young men, but they seldom stayed with it for long and almost never became inner members.

Stung but interested by the alleged tie to Manson, the Process sent two leading members out to California, where they spoke with Bugliosi and Manson. They told the prosecutor they were innocent but apparently did not completely convince him. Manson was not helpful to the cult's cause. During the murder trial, Bugliosi asked him if he knew Robert Moor, also called Robert de Grimston. Manson said he did not know de Grimston but claimed he did know Moor: "You're looking at him." Another time he said, "Moor and I are one and the same." This was pure mystification.

The *Death* issue of the Process magazine, which came out in 1971, did not help the cult's image. News reporters noted it contained a brief article by Charles Manson, "written especially for The Process." Manson describes death as "Total awareness, closing the circle, bringing the soul to now. Ceasing to be, to become a world within yourself. Locked in your own totalness." Calling death "peace from this world's madness and paradise in my own self," he identifies it with isolation from the world, from outer reality, an isolation created by his own madness and developed through the social autarchy of his cult. Death—the ultimate in social implosion.

Other rumors circulated linking the Process to heinous, inexplicable events. For the last few years, reports of *animal mutilations* had come from several sections of the country. Cattle or wild animals are found cut to pieces, their carcasses lying ripped on hillsides, far away from human settlements. Rumors about these mutilations spread and evolved, an interesting example of collective behavior and development of myth. Some reporters spread the tale that a sinister satanic cult called the Xtul Group was responsible for all these animal mutilations. Of course, the Xtul Group is meant to be the Process. It was not in fact responsible. From its very beginning, the cult had been anti-vivisectionist.

The last straw was an assault on the Process by Ed Sanders, former leader of the Fugs rock band and literary light of the counterculture. At the end of 1971, he published a series of magazine articles, and then a book, about the Manson murders. He devoted an entire chapter to the Process, saying it was an important "sleazo input which warped the mind of Charles Manson." Sanders called Processeans "hooded snuffoids," and described the cult as "the black-caped, black-garbed, death-worshiping Process Church . . . an English occult society dedicated to observing and aiding the end of the world by stirring up murder, violence and chaos, and dedicated to the proposition that they, the Process, shall survive the gore as the chosen people."[72] His chapter on the cult was a stew of information, misinformation, and hate.

In quick response to Sanders' attack, the Process went to court, lodging a libel suit for $1,500,000 against the book and another one for $1,250,000 against the magazine article. The book's publisher, E. P. Dutton, said, "The book was carefully checked by our attorneys and speaks for itself." A public-relations lady hired by the Process pointed to "false and defamatory material" published by Sanders, "statements that Processeans were linked with the Manson family prior to the murder of Sharon Tate and that a Process member opened the kitchen door to Sirhan Sirhan shortly before he murdered Senator Robert F. Kennedy." She also accused Sanders of claiming the Process enjoyed "eulogizing Hitler, sacrificing humans and animals and then drinking their blood, sex orgies, kidnapping, and loving dope."

In public statements, cult leaders tried to convince reporters that this horrendous smorgasbord of disgusting satanic delights was fantasy. Father Christian asserted, "We don't have orgies; we don't practice cannibalism; we don't sacrifice animals; we don't drink blood; we don't practice magic rituals or put curses on people or say the Lord's Prayer backwards." But the story was impossible to stop. The *New York Times* described the reception that Processeans often received on the streets: "'Are you devil worshippers?' ask the very curious. Others, less curious than angry, make rude remarks."[73] At this time almost all the income of the cult was derived from the street begging. The Process was struggling to project the most bland, appealing, innocent religious image so that people would be inclined to contribute to their "church." Sanders' publicity about Manson threatened financial disaster and endangered the very economic survival of the Process.

The Process's trouble extended to the Toronto chapter. The cult had received $23,049 from the Ottawa government under the Local Initiatives Programme. This money was to be given to young people hired through the church to do social-service work. The group contends that all the money was properly spent and that church money went into the projects as well. In March 1972, a newspaper, the *Toronto Sun*, attacked the program by denouncing the "Satanists" who had run off with public money. Prime Minister Pierre Trudeau was drawn into the controversy on a radio talk show. As the Process tells the story, all ended well, with an outpouring of friendly statements from civic leaders and knowledgeable reporters drowning out the negative "Satanist" comments.

Sanders' publishers decided to settle the libel case out of court. The book company undoubtedly wanted to sell thousands of copies and was anxious to come to a fast settlement. In a press release issued March 8, 1972, Dutton said, "A close examination has revealed that statements in the book about The Process Church, including those attributing any connection between The Process and the activities of Charles Manson, accused and convicted murderer, have not been substantiated." Dutton agreed to remove all references to the cult from future editions and to join with it in announcing a cooperative end to the lawsuit. Writing in an open letter as the spokesman for the Process, Father Christian said, "We are satisfied that the actions being taken by Dutton, the publishers of the book, and Ed Sanders, the author, constitute suitable vindication of the Church." On the third of April, a parallel settlement was announced with the editors of the magazine that had printed Sanders' articles. They were able to get out from under the suit against them by publishing excerpts from the press release issued by Dutton. The cult got no money from either publisher. In a meek attempt to assert its new, clean image, the cult inserted the following self-description in the press release: "The Process is a religious organization devoted to spreading the work of Christ."

The cult also sued the English publisher of Sanders' book, and there the outcome was quite different. The case actually went to court, and a verdict was rendered in March 1974. The Process lost! Their case against Sanders and the English publisher was dismissed, and the cult was ordered to pay court costs. Of course, this does not mean that Sanders' statements about the Process were true.

The Process was not responsible for Manson, but the controversy had a tremendous impact on the cult. Already committed to making peace with conventional society, already completely dependent on the good will of conventional society for its economic life, the Process was spurred to even greater attempts to clean up its image and downplay the Satanic aspect of its doctrines. St. Peter denied Christ and suffered for it; the Process would deny Satan and also suffer. To escape the dark halo of Satan, it would compulsively over-fulfill the demands of Christ. To gain public support, it would first hide, then later abandon some of its most precious symbols and concepts, leaving a gnawing cultural void. Without Satan, what would distinguish the Process from all other religions?

CLEANING UP THE IMAGE

To wash away the Manson stigma, and as part of a general adaptation to its economic relationship with conventional society, the Process made a number of changes in its image. The first one I saw was a new uniform that began replacing black P-Gear in the spring of 1971. The *blacks* were replaced by *greys*, homemade light-gray uniforms, cute instead of menacing. The new suits had jumper fronts with pockets and flared trousers and were made of light material suitable for summer wear. In really hot weather, street Donators wore short-sleeve gray shirts, but in cold weather they put on the old black cloaks for warmth. The big old Mendes badges were retired in favor of tiny plastic triangles, black with silk-screened goats, to be worn on the lapels. Christ's silver cross was tacked at the collar. Perhaps because they were homemade, or perhaps because of the appallingly drab color, the gray uniforms made the women look dowdy and the men silly. They looked like stewardesses from a third-rate airline. Figure 2 shows the old uniform in early 1971; Figure 3 shows the new one later that summer. Both drawings are based on photographs I had taken.

FIGURE 2. **A Processean wearing the Cross of Christ and the Goat of Satan.**

FIGURE 3. **Processeans posing in front of a Christian cross.**

Cavern kitchen in Old Game and New Game.

The uniform change was a shock to inner members. For years Processeans had inveighed against the Grey Forces of conventional society. The symbolic character John Grey was an object of derision. John Grey, arch-conformist, follows the path of "hypocrisy, mediocrity, blasphemy." The black uniforms had been a projection of the cult's longing for intensity, for an impressive image that would make people take notice. Now the grays seemed to indicate a conscious search for blandness, a perfidious acceptance of "hypocrisy, mediocrity, blasphemy." The theological explanation for the change was the notion of the New Game, a shift from the angry Jehovian Period of the cult's first seven years to a happier Luciferian Period for the second seven years.

Brother Ariel said the gray change may have made sense to the Omega, "but it made no sense on the ground level" of Messengers. Only the respect Messengers felt for the cult hierarchy kept them from exclaiming, "Hey! Isn't this a basic policy mistake?" The leaders candidly told us the gray was meant to improve the public image. The chapter houses and cavern coffeehouses were likewise transformed. The striking, colorful paintings that had lavishly decorated public rooms were put in storage, and such bland decorations as rya rugs and paintings of children's balloons were hung in their stead. The walls were repainted in light tones. At the end of 1971, there was a second change in

FIGURE 4. **A Processean wedding couple in their formal blue robes.**

clothing styles and color. After discovering that the gray clothing was unattractive, the leadership ordered a switch to blue. First tried out as uniforms for the cult's rock bands, the new medium blue clothing was a hit. Much more dignified than the gray, it was still friendly in mood and had some of the impact of the black. Much of the blue clothing was produced for the Process by a company that specialized in making theatrical costumes. The new suits were quite stylish and usually fit well. Wardrobes now showed a greater range of variety. The most formal attire is shown in Figure 4, Father Dominic marrying Sister Eve in their formal blue robes, posing in front of a new symbol representing the Unity of Christ (cross) and Satan (serpent).

In a Canadian newspaper interview, Robert de Grimston admitted that the stylish conventional suit he was wearing was intended to project a new image: "He feels that, particularly in America, the Satanist rumors are more likely to be believed if they look like down-and-out sack cloth and ashes prophets. Also, many prominent people they need to reassure will simply not walk into a Process chapter, as they are free to do. 'We have to have an image those kind of people will respond to,' he said."

Sometime early in 1972, Father Dominic and Sister Seraphine were guests on a radio show broadcast by Boston's NBC affiliate, WBZ. The show went well, so the station invited the pair to return the following week and do a program of their own. As Dominic said on a show three years later, Process radio "just got rolling from there. We did some rock interviews on the Boston Common in the summer of '72, and we interviewed Blood, Sweat and Tears, Chicago, Dr. John, the Beach Boys, a lot of big names. And the show got better and better." The station run by Boston University gave Dominic a second show, so by the fall of 1972, the Process was on Boston air twice a week. The NBC show began to be picked up by other stations, until about two dozen were carrying it. The cult received the airtime for free, and most of the production costs were borne by the stations. The show never brought in any significant number of recruits, but it was a successful step toward public acceptance.

In order to be accepted by the public as a legitimate *church*, worthy of financial support, the Process was forced to engage in a good deal of social service work. Processean theory suggested that people ought to support the cult for two reasons: (1) because the Process was actively engaged in important research into the nature of human existence, and (2) because the Process mediated between mankind and the Great Gods of the Universe. But no outsiders believed the premises upon which these two justifications were built. Consequently, the cult was forced to move quite far away from its own basic assumptions and toward the public view that churches should be supported for the social service work they perform. Three other functions were served by the cult's programs. Robert and some other leaders who were dedicated to the service of Christ (rather than one of the other Gods) believed it was their duty to extend love and help to the world's unfortunates. Also, the social service work gave Messengers a break from their street begging, the opportunity to put on a show for appreciative audiences, and a source of some feeling of personal worth.

Finally, the social work was a poor but not entirely barren technique for the recruitment of new members. In the fall of 1971, the Process first turned its attention to social work. When the first Donators were working the Boston streets, they often found it expedient to present themselves as a drug rehabilitation program. This bordered on fantasy. The only clients this "program" served were a few already cured members of the cult. The only method of treatment, neither particularly effective nor attractive to the public, was the conversion of a drug user into a dedicated cultist. The first social programs I saw were two in-house giveaways. I helped set up the Free Store in the Boston chapter. It consisted of a cellar room just off the coffeehouse area at the foot of the entrance stairs. We painted the walls satanic red and installed shelves and a rack for clothing hangers. The church had collected a good deal of second-hand clothing, which they then presented to any poor person who wanted to take some. Those who came in hungry from the streets were offered a free meal, usually big sausages, potatoes or dumplings, and cabbage. For a while the Process had permitted runaways and others to "crash" for the night, but this was discontinued because of police pressure against harboring underage fugitives. The Cavern coffeehouse did however serve as a kind of loose youth placement service, on an informal basis. Those with no place to stay could meet more stable coffeehouse denizens and make arrangements to move in with them.

In Toronto and New Orleans, the free food program expanded until quite a number of derelicts were being fed each day, usually male alcoholics and other older bums. In Boston, the project served only some young counterculture wanderers. After a few weeks of the free food program, a large plastic sign was hung on the Cavern wall asking those who took clothing or food to make some kind of contribution to the chapter, in labor if they had no money. This request was not really an attempt to get valuable compensation for the food and clothing. Rather, it tried to initiate a relationship of reciprocity between the cult and recipients of its charity. This could be the first step in a series of escalating exchanges leading to full membership.

Messengers of the cult were sent out on missions of mercy. In Boston and New York, the cult developed continuing relationships with hospitals for the mentally disabled. Once, a number of the inmates were taken to see a play. Often, Process musicians went to entertain the inmates. They also frequently visited homes for the aged, and prison visits were also attempted. From mid-1972 onward, these services were featured in the cult's monthly magazine, sold on the streets. The cover of the February 1973 issue shows a deadbeat geezer being feted in "the Free Kitchen." Mentally disabled people and Processeans mingle on the covers of several editions. A prison visit was publicized in May 1973, and a day with the senile in June. The June issue announced "The Quiet Revolution," the shift decided upon in the annual Masters' conference at the end of 1971 to put great emphasis on social service. The credit for getting the volunteer programs off to a big start was given to Father Raphael, Master in charge of "Expansion." There is no doubt that the Process did feed, comfort, and entertain literally thousands of unfortunate persons in its social service work. The administrators of several of the institutions served by the cult were happy to give enthusiastic testimonials. But one Processean called the social work "our credibility program," intended to legitimate church status.

The cult still lacked a major resource before it could become a real church: it had no congregations to speak of. If we count Messengers and above as clergy, and those below this rank who regularly attended activities as laity, then the clergy/laity ratio was 1:1 or even worse. Disciples and Initiates provided only a small fraction of the income required to support the inner members. Some religious communes find an economic base other than contributions. The Oneida Community made silverware and animal traps.[74] The religious Bruderhof manufactured toys.[75] The secular commune Twin Oaks made rope hammocks, such as the one I bought after visiting them in 1968.[76] Indeed, both Bruderhof and Twin Oaks have remained economically viable for half a century. Scientology provides educational and psychotherapy services.

In its implosion and wanderings, the Process lost its therapy business and was actually in a bad position to launch new therapy services. The competition was stiff in American cities because there were so many therapists with academic or medical credentials and established referral networks. The street people and other members of the counterculture attracted to the Process by its colorful image and recruited through the coffeehouse were neither interested in nor able to afford serious psychotherapy. Finally, the cult's culture was now so religious in its symbolism that, so far as I can tell, leaders never considered returning to psychotherapy as a source of income and new recruits. Compulsions Analysis was a thing of the past. In their own development, leaders of the cult felt very distant from psychotherapy by 1971. This situation was extremely unfortunate for the cult. A psychotherapy business might have served superior people like the original founders, people of wealth and talent, an ideal congregation. Failing to return to this successful strategy, the Process tried to adapt to the status of church.

INTO THE FAITH HEALING BUSINESS

In June 1972, the Omega traveled from Toronto to Vancouver on the west coast, on a long tour that was partly a vacation, partly another hunt for a splendid Process headquarters, and partly a research voyage for the establishment of healing services. On most legs of the journey, Mary Ann and Robert went by commercial airliner, while Morgana (who had returned to the cult) and Moloch drove the Omega's Pontiac Grand Safari station wagon with all the luggage and the dogs. The Omega enjoyed traveling in style, supported by the street-begging Messengers who struggled to follow and serve it.

Robert says, "Vancouver didn't come across as the kind of place we had any wish to open a chapter in at all." They looked at houses in the Canadian city, and Robert composed more doctrines concerning the Gods. The Omega discussed religious healing at length. BI-26, written back in 1970, says that, "however it is done, and on whatever level it manifests, the basis of all our healing is the same; the lifting of guilt." This extreme statement may be appropriate for a psychotherapy concerned with resolving the emotional conflicts of its patients. But now the Process conceived of the lifting of guilt as a practical means for healing physical illness, tumors as well as psychosomatic ills. Robert says, "Christ made no differentiation between healing and the forgiveness of sins." This is religious healing.

The Omega had heard of Kathryn Kuhlman, the famous American faith healer, and took the claims of her powers very seriously. They talked about her, as Morgana recalled, in "just hours and hours of discussion about 'What is this thing? Where does it come from? It must have a physical basis.' Discussing how faith healers heal, physically, when these things happen. What they feel like afterwards. What the person being healed physically feels when it happens." They heard that Kuhlman was coming to Seattle, a short drive south, and decided to attend her public meeting and then go down to California "to receive for the Process the healing power."

There was some risk for Mary Ann and Robert reentering the United States because their immigration difficulties were not quite solved, but they made it across the border without difficulty and from then on were free of problems of this sort. The Omega took seats in the Seattle auditorium where Kuhlman was to speak, but Morgana was left outside by mistake, forced to sit on the grass and listen to the event over the loudspeakers set up for the over-flow crowd.

Kuhlman began to speak. Morgana recalled, "It was rather dull, to tell the truth, and I was feeling very disappointed. She sounded very strange. She had a very strange inflection, very odd way of talking. But what she was saying was very boring." Many minutes passed. "And then a very strange thing happened. She said, 'I feel the presence of the Holy Spirit.' And at the time she said that, it had been completely calm, totally clear sky. A sudden wind came up! Tiny drops of rain and a gigantic rainbow out of nowhere appeared over the audi-torium. I was *absolutely staggered*! And right after that, she started saying, 'Someone is being healed in the back row on the left. I can feel your ear opening up.' And she started calling out the healings. What she does is she spiels, she just talks, she talks, she talks. She just says whatever comes. And then all of a sudden it starts coming through. She starts picking up on people in the audi-ence being healed, and that's it. She doesn't spiel anymore. It's all concentrated on 'I feel someone being cured of blindness. I feel someone being cured of spinal disease.'"

Robert said the keynote of her miracle service was drama: "Her perfor-mance is stupendous; apparently spontaneous, but in fact highly—and bril-liantly—calculated over twenty-odd years of trial and error and hard work of finding out what is the best method for *her* to channel the power that comes through her. She is magnetic and hypnotic and looks quite off her head a good deal of the time! And her effects? The blind see, the deaf hear, and the lame walk. She channels a power that heals goiters, cures cancers, and can bring the dying back to life, a spectacular Satanic performance, backed to the hilt by Lucifer, and showing us something of what is possible when these two work in unison."

After Kuhlman's performance, the Omega went down to California, looking for a splendid mansion to buy for itself with church money. Near Santa Barbara, in Montecito, they found what Robert calls "the most beautiful house you've ever seen." A widow owned it. The very day the Process was all set to buy it, she remarried and decided to keep the house. "Anyway," Robert says, "it was a sign. Obviously we weren't meant to have that house."

They drove to Los Angeles, in the terrible heat of early September, and checked out houses along the way. The signs were against all the houses. The car's air conditioning broke down: a clear sign they were headed in the wrong direction.

Los Angeles happened to be the next stop on Kathryn Kuhlman's itinerary. "We knew she was going to appear that night," Morgana recalled. "And lo and behold, we drove directly past her, standing on a corner outside of a shop, obviously waiting to be picked up by someone, dressed in regular, ordinary street clothes, her face all screwed up against the sun. She had the whole projection and look about her of somebody who was very crazy. I yelled, 'Look! Look! It's Kathryn Kuhlman!' We drove past her and the bloody air conditioner started working. 'Look! She healed the air conditioner! Wow!'"

The Omega found a possible chapter house in Los Angeles, but it was too expensive. Then they heard about a fantastic Bicentennial House that had been built by real estate speculators as the showpiece for a development called Diamond Bar. It was for sale, so the Omega went to inspect it. Robert was very impressed. He wanted to live in the American Bicentennial House. "It was a fortress on top of a hill. It was Spanish style, but modern, built with enormous twenty-five-foot windows that went two stories, with huge battered walls and columns." When people finally built homes on the lots that surrounded the hill, it would be like a "castle with the villagers all living round about." The price was a mere $100,000, or thereabouts, while the real value must have been closer to $300,000, which would translate to $711,000 and $2,133,000 over the following fifty years of economic inflation. The cult made arrangements to buy. But at the last moment the deal fell through: "It was just whipped out from under our noses. So obviously that wasn't supposed to be the place."

The Omega flew to Florida and reoccupied its house in Key Largo. They continued to work on the development of faith healing. They visited local faith healers in the Miami area and invented new rituals that would incorporate healing into group activities. Around the various chapters, sensitive individuals such as Father Cyrus, Mother Rhea, and Sister Hannah discovered they possessed healing gifts. One of the new pieces of ritual was a healing invocation used to channel the power of the Gods through the congregation who spoke the following words: "Jehovah, Lucifer, Satan, Christ, in Your Names and by Your Grace let the burdens of sickness and negativity be lifted from (name of sick person) and let the blessings of good health and positivity be his." The Friday and Saturday Midnight Meditations had been relaxing therapy sessions for participants, but now they were changed to make them magical-religious rituals to channel the healing power of the Gods to distant suffering loved ones.

The Omega focused its attention on its own pleasures as well as the healing of the halt, the lame, and the blind. Another series of trips finally secured a new secret home for Robert and Mary Ann, an expensive house hidden away in Westchester County, near the Connecticut border and within an hour's drive of the New York chapter. Although the purchase of this new home might be denounced as an act of cynical exploitation of the Messengers who ultimately earned the money for it, Robert explained his love of luxury theologically. When he and Mary Ann took greater material rewards for themselves, God would give greater rewards to all followers. "If we moved up the scale of property—like if we moved out of one level of quality house into a higher level of quality house—everybody moved up. Like they'd get out of ditches into P-Cars, while we got out of rat-ridden holes into slightly classier" places like the $70,000 home in Key Largo. "But we always had to make the first move." And one proof of this proposition was the "fact" that the Omega could get homes cheap. The Key Largo place had been worth $150,000, because somebody had once offered this sum for it. So the Omega believed, "We've got to make the move into a better house, and then everybody can move into better chapters. And if we want a really big, magnificent headquarters, then we've got to get a better house." The Omega moved into the Westchester house, and the cult began negotiations for a $900,000 headquarters building in New York City.

Mt. Chi, as the secret home of the Omega was called, was a nice place nestled between forested hills and overlooking a lake. Rank and file members of the Process, the Outside Processeans who paid for it, were not told of its existence. Some Messengers began noticing that certain Masters would disappear from sight for weeks at a time, not being present in any of the six chapters. Where were they? For a while the Messengers privately postulated the existence of a Great Chapter up in the Sky where the missing leaders must be. Of course they were at Mt. Chi. Other trusted members served the Omega in its new home. Morgana was the housekeeper and Brother Luther the cook.

Messengers finally learned about Mt. Chi by chance. One of them was working the streets in New York one day and happened to stop a member of the public who had done some renovating work on Mt. Chi. So the basic secret was out, but most cult members did not know the address of the Omega's hideaway.

The development of healing practices and the purchase of a new and more splendid home for the Omega suggest how the transformation of a new public image was linked to the desire to improve the cult's economic situation for the benefit of the leaders. Another sign was the evolution of the magazines sold by street Donators. From 1969 through 1972, the magazines changed from vivid, psychedelic explosions of color and bombast into bland, pale pleas for love and support from conventional society. The *Fear* issue of the big, early magazine was filled with powerful, even disgusting images. The pages dripped purple, red, and silver ink in a surrealistic burst of horror. The next issue, on *Death*, was more sedate, and the *Love* issue which followed was friendly and gentle.

In the spring of 1972, the cult came out with a new magazine, *The Processeans*, an eight-page black-and-white photo-essay publication that cost little to produce. All the layout work was done by Process artists in their own studio. I myself took eighteen photographs that were published in these magazines, and several other cult photographers documented the blandest aspects of cult life and the superficialities of social work programs. The monthly *Processeans* had at least three commercial functions. First, as a kind of illustrated church newsletter, it projected an image of the cult as a working church, with many ongoing programs worthy of public support. Second, it was much cheaper than other Process publications and could be used to extract donations of twenty-five cents to a dollar from passersby unwilling to buy an expensive book. Third, because it was a monthly, *The Processeans* could be used to achieve repeat business, sold month after month to the same customers. Twenty-seven issues of *The Processeans* ultimately appeared under this title.

LOWER SATANIC MANIFESTATIONS

The new emphasis on magical and religious healing of the body and soul was a natural response to the problems of the cult's new clientele. Many were sick in mind and body. Many were poor, uneducated, or undisciplined. There were many peripheral members of the church who wanted admission to the inner core of cult society but were refused entry. One common type was called Lower Satanic Manifestations, or LSMs. These people were disruptive individuals attracted by the satanic rhetoric of the cult but unable to accept the authoritarian discipline imposed by the hierarchy. Most of them were economically unproductive and had almost nothing to contribute to the church. But the cult's rhetoric made it difficult for the Masters to reject the LSMs entirely, so a continuing, gnawing crisis plagued Process chapters. What to do with these people?

Let me give some examples, again using pseudonyms. Ron Forbes was an aggressive social outcast. He possessed very high intelligence, but he used every neuron in his brain to devise ways of being obnoxious. I could give many examples of Ron's habit of insulting everyone around him, but his language was so fiendishly offensive that any direct quotations would be unpleasant. In his own way, Ron was a comic genius, and many Processeans found his behavior amusing. But nobody wanted to live with him. Rejected from Messenger status in the fall of 1971, Ron took on the airs of a Messenger anyway. He told me he actually went before a judge and had his name legally changed to Brother Sodom. He began producing his own scripture, heading his documents *The Process–Church of the Final Judgement* and signing them Sodom in imitation of Robert's style. Sodom document number two is particularly poignant. It is about sex. Women found Sodom repulsive, and his chief sexual gratification was assaulting people of both sexes with very personal dirty jokes. Sodom wrote, "Mankind has turned sex into a vile perversion. What used to be a God-given and beautiful gift, is now ugly and obscene. It is with great contempt that I see what humanity has done to this gift." Writing from his heart, he admitted, "the overall picture is bleak and filled with despair." Another Sodom scripture, written in Boston the day after Christmas 1971, urges service to Satan: "The gates of Hell are opened and the jaws of death are quick to take up those who falter from the path of Satan. Fiends already released from the pit stalk the earth, to destroy those who will follow them. For the fiends are Satan's slaves and help him reap his harvest of death." Not surprisingly, the Process refused to accept Ron's writings as bona fide scripture.

Another case was Julio Famagusta. More delicate than Ron Forbes, Julio made up for his lesser native obnoxiousness by laziness and by constant assertion of his superiority over everybody else. A lowly OP in June or July 1973, he came to feel there was a lack of unity in the Boston chapter. Hagar, Christian, and Dominic "were on a power trip," he said. Julio invented his own ritual, called the Hour of Unity, and urged other OPs to join him in performing it as a cure for the lack of unity they felt. Some of them actually carried out the ritual a couple of times in the chapter's OP Room. Then the three leaders of the chapter, still on their "power trip," squelched Julio's Hour of Unity. Of course, his ritual was a symbolic grab for power. If he could get others to perform his ritual, he would acquire status over them. The ritual itself, similar to a Telepathy Developing Circle or Midnight Meditation, was innocuous. His independent introduction of the ritual, however, was obnoxious, especially because he never made any other, more positive contributions.

Sister Norma recalls the kind of trouble LSMs could cause. One evening she was in charge of the Cavern coffeehouse. That meant, at least in theory, that she was to handle emotions on every level in the Cavern, keeping order no matter what the threat. One of the male LSMs was drunk and belligerent. He commanded her to turn the record player up. She said the music wouldn't go any louder. He demanded. He ranted, threatened, and started a fist fight with the parent of a Messenger!

I saw many disruptions by persons obviously mentally ill. A man dominated a seminar with utterly unintelligible hebephrenic monologues. A paranoid lady rushed around the coffeehouse accusing people of trying to kill her and striking them. A psychologically unwell boy mistook a Priest's sermon for a personal discussion with him and killed the ritual mood by replying at length to everything the Priest said.

Many LSMs achieved Disciple rank and swaggered around in their P-Gear uniforms, contributing little for all the trouble they caused. Disciple rank was supposed to be equal in status to that of Messenger, and the LSM Disciples took every opportunity to remind everyone of this theory. But Disciples really were inferior in status. An administrative document of June 28, 1973, explains the differences. It says, "A vital requirement for Messenger and therefore of course IP status is a basically high level of practical responsibility in terms of self-discipline and self-control, and a high degree of detachment from any personal problems." The LSMs did not qualify. Other unproductive types took Disciple status and wanted to be Messengers, for example depressives. Soon Disciple rank became a residual status, collecting "all those who are not suitable for the Messenger line." The rank had been originally invented for normal people with too many outside commitments to want to become Messengers, successful people who could contribute significantly. But Robert proclaimed, "No one is refused Baptism as a Disciple, as long as he has fulfilled the simple practical requirements." As Disciple rank filled up with disruptive and inferior people, they drove out and away any person of quality who might otherwise want to join.

Sometimes the LSMs were good for a laugh. Brother Ariel remembered one of the more bizarre figures lurking around the Boston chapter, Hermann, "a little thin man, very short, blond crew cut, who wore black glasses, very neatly dressed with Nazi insignias. He was a real Nazi fanatic." Ariel fancifully wondered if Hermann was really a CIA agent planted to check out the Process. "He knew the Nazi sort of approach would fascinate us, and it certainly did. So we invited him to lunch." Hermann proceeded to explain his theory of History to the bemused Processeans. Agents of the Jewish, Bolshevik Conspiracy, of which the Process was part, had changed into wolves. "The real people were sheep, and of course the wolves would eat the real people. But out of the ranks of the real people were to arise werewolves who were like the Nazis, who would devour the wolves. They were reformed sheep … supersheep." Ariel and a couple of other Messengers were responsible for staging a weekly show in the dramatic Processcene activity and decided Hermann's crazy theory would be an ideal subject for one of their productions. That week they put on an elaborate play, complete with masks and costumes. The story was "about a sheep getting killed, and a werewolf." Ariel said, "It was the first time we used my Death Mask, which has no expression, and it got some shudders. So it was a successful play." Hermann gave a solo standing ovation. The players made "ba-ba-ba" sheep noises throughout the skit, and this effect became a private joke. In later weeks, when a show was sagging, one of the actors would say "ba-ba-ba" and the audience would laugh heartily.

Disciple rank progressively declined, even to the point that LSMs were complaining that their status was debased by the sub-inferior late recruits. There was one revealing incident in which the Boston chapter experienced a minor Disciple revolt. At this time, the three-time "murderer" and bike monster Brother Goliath had flunked out of Messenger status and was a leader of the LSM Disciple mob. He and the other LSMs complained bitterly when they found out that an Initiate named Willie was scheduled for Disciple Baptism. Ariel recalled, "If Willie was going to be made a Disciple, they wanted to turn their crosses in. Willie is the extremely retarded newsboy that used to come around and slobber on all the girls. Up until we started having mentally retarded visitors to the coffeehouse, people like Goliath were considered the worst LSMs. Here the worst LSMs—the EX-worst LSMs—were complaining that Willie was being made a Disciple, and they were saying the Disciple line was being cheapened!"

THE JANUARY BLUE SALE

The lower membership ranks were gradually debased throughout 1972-1973, leading to a climax at the beginning of 1974. At the end of 1972, a new status was invented, that of Field Disciple. Really equivalent to Initiate rank, it was intended to exploit in some way the interested people Processeans met on their trips around the country, people who wanted to join but did not live near a chapter. The Process wanted more people and more money. In an administrative bulletin of September 19, 1973, Robert sought to whip up more energy among his followers, to raise them to greater exertions and achieve the success that was eluding the cult: "The aim in any Chapter is the maximum ACTIVITY both in and around the Chapter and Sphere. For that, people are required. WITHOUT people there can be no activity; but equally, without activity the people will not be attracted." He gave several lists of projects that might be undertaken by the chapters, and areas where more energy might be invested. "If a project fails, embark on another. If one succeeds, stay with it and expand it."

The demands placed on the Messengers increased terribly. They were expected to put in ever longer hours on the streets, pulling in new members and great amounts of money. For the first time, money quotas were set. A Messenger could not come home until he had collected his quota for the day. The January 1974 issue of *The Processeans* proclaimed that its circulation "more than TRIPLED in 1973," a clear sign of increased donating activity.

In at least one chapter, the leaders decided to quit spending any money on food for members and served meals using food donated to the church. Morale dropped precipitously.

The central leadership was not yet ready to change course and did not abandon its obsessively dysfunctional approach until after the major crisis which came to a head in March 1974. The last struggles of the old Process culminated in an unrealistic attempt to expand membership. In an explosive couple of weeks, later known derisively as the January Blue Sale, the number of Messengers was suddenly increased in the futile hope that a greater work force could be made to collect the desired money and overcome all obstacles to success.

Before April 1973, an Initiate would be baptized Messenger whenever he was completely ready, in many cases enjoying a special ceremony conducted just for him. Beginning in May of that year, Baptisms were held only once every three months, for Disciples as well as Messengers. This new system rationalized the practice at the cost of impersonality. Baptism had become a bureaucratic event rather than the intimate acceptance of a newly beloved person into central cult society. The first Messenger Baptism of 1974 was scheduled for January 19.

Anxiously casting about for solutions to its problems, the cult's leadership decided that each of the six church chapters should baptize at least six new Messengers at the January 1974 ceremony. There was a growing tendency for individuals to drop out of Messenger status, IPs as well as OPs, and it had become difficult to keep the chapters staffed, let alone build them and get the cult moving again. The old requirement that a neophyte must spend six weeks "on Messenger line" or "on dedication," living the life of a Messenger and proving his worth, was abandoned. This further demoralized the people who were already Messengers and had achieved their status at great effort. Ariel said, "It was just said that anybody can become a Messenger that wanted to. We thought it was because they needed the money," that the Omega took such a drastic step. "People on the whole felt badly about it." Each chapter succeeded in producing exactly six new Messengers in January. How many were of true Messenger material? "Toward the end, none at all," said Ariel. Sister Claire told me the Masters practically scoured the coffeehouses looking for people willing to be baptized. Ariel recalled a moment when he had to give to a chapter leader the message that Stinky, one of the Cavern LSMs, wanted to see him. The leader rolled his eyes and exclaimed, "Wonder what he wants! To become a Messenger?" All the worst people wanted to be Messengers. Now they could be.

The thirty-six new Messengers were almost without exception people who were unable or unwilling to make the kind of contribution expected of them. It would have been disastrous if they had remained Messengers for long, because as a class they constituted thirty percent of the inner membership. Within a very few days almost every one had dropped out.

Melvin Potts was one of the thirty-six. An affable but extremely erratic fellow, he had contributed a good deal of work as a Disciple and had lived with others in a Disciple House commune. Nonetheless, he had a tendency to get into fights, had a serious medical problem, and had very poor body coordination. Melvin was marginal Process material, neither a total loss nor particularly talented. He described what happened: "The standards dropped. The requirements dropped. At the same point, the morale inside and outside dropped. I was what was called the Blue Streak Messenger of January. There was a quickie one-week baptism where they threw on a bunch of people. Not one person lasted. Most of them were out in one week or two weeks afterward. A big cut-down in morale for the inside people, because they had spent months and months of being trained to go on, and these people didn't have two seconds of training. They were thrown into a uniform and told to go out on the street and donate." Vertical communication had broken down. The followers didn't know what was going on, and the leaders paid no attention to the feelings of the Messengers. "I know how I felt doing it!" Melvin says. "All of a sudden I was out there donating, for ten hours, with quotas to make, and a certain amount of money to bring in." He was quickly disillusioned and quickly left.

ANALYSIS

Exhausted by its fruitless quest, the Process took root in 1970. Not having found glory outside conventional society, it would seek glory, and comfort as well, inside the normal world. Robert and Mary Ann settled in a secret mansion, and their followers began the normal jobs of making money, raising a few children, gaining status in the community, and setting up a stable church institution. In 1973, the last real therapy sessions for insiders were dropped. The intensity of social relations had long since hit a ceiling, so the therapy sessions no longer had much appeal. The growth in cult membership leveled off by 1973, making upward mobility inside the cult almost impossible.

When the chapters were being set up in 1970 and 1971, there was an influx of originally middle-class college dropouts. These people were suffering "acutely felt tensions," as the Lofland-Stark model of conversion would predict, but they also fit the pattern of earlier middle-class recruits in that by dropping out of college they had lost social ties. Those who were successful in gaining full membership in the Process were suffering temporary dislocation rather than chronic failure. Given a stable life within the cult, they were able to recover their balance and enjoy cure from their brief bout with "tension." It is entirely possible that many of them would have resumed normal, reasonably successful lives in secular society had they not been incorporated into the cult.

After 1971, about the only people who attempted to join Process chapters were unattractive, unsuccessful individuals: displaced high school children, violent motorcycle gang members, underclass ex-convicts, irredeemable drug dropouts and alcoholics, and mentally ill people. Without intending to, the Process was being forced into the role of social-service organization, feeding and entertaining a large number of people who were not eligible to join. In the name of Christ, Robert demanded that these people be brought into the cult. In the name of economy, Mary Ann and the Masters of the Church struggled to contain the problems created by the new and inferior clientele. The main

Selling magazines while donating hours on the streets.

source of money for the Process became the street donating. In Germany during the Matthew 10 period, Processeans supported themselves directly through this technique, but from 1970 onward they paid all money to the Treasurer or High Master of their chapters. The emphasis was on making a lot of money to finance growing chapter expenses, to support the Omega in style, and to make expansion possible. Street donating became the major activity in a Messenger's life. It paid the bills and was also the first step in recruitment. People met on the streets would be invited back to the local Cavern coffee-house. Here newcomers had a chance to get to know Processeans and form social bonds with them. Whenever a public ritual or activity was held, all the people in the coffeehouse were invited to attend.

Although this recruitment technique successfully brought in many new people, it was dysfunctional in that it recruited mainly very inferior members. The Cavern became a hangout for runaways, unemployed unskilled young adults, and mentally ill individuals. Coffeehouse society was its own social environment and by 1971 had become rather unappealing to talented, attractive people of the type that had originally founded the Process. To join, new-comers had to form strong reciprocal ties with members, but the coffeehouse recruitment procedure forced high-quality newcomers to associate primarily with scruffy coffeehouse denizens whom they were unlikely to find attractive.

I saw many valuable individuals visit the cult once or twice, then never return, so the problem was not that the supply of potential recruits had suddenly disappeared but that the recruiting process was no longer working.

One of the greatest problems for cult leaders is how to keep followers busy at tasks that will not require much investment in money or the leaders' time. Many activities that look from the outside like pure recruitment work are really intended as busywork for low-status followers. Their effectiveness in bringing in new recruits is secondary. For example, middle-rank Processeans spent much of their time visiting nearby cities, going into public institutions for the aged and mentally disabled, and standing on street corners chatting with people who had nothing better to do. The coffeehouse recruitment procedure was dysfunctional in that it tended to attract low-quality newcomers but was functional in that it gave members a variety of relaxed social tasks to perform. The whole setup permitted Processeans to put on exciting performances for admiring audiences. But to rejoice in their superiority over their audiences, members had to put up with inferior audiences. Function and dysfunction were inextricably joined.

Thus, while each of the steps taken by the Process can be explained in terms of its history and purposes, a tremendous contradiction developed in its structure and means of survival. In the next three chapters we will describe the culture of the Process at its height before we turn to the cataclysm that followed.

CHAPTER 6 Process Society

What is The Process for you?
What can The Process give to you?
What can you give to The Process?

— Questions asked of a candidate
for Messenger baptism

OUTSIDERS OFTEN BELIEVED that all Processeans partook in a rabidly deviant lifestyle. But this was not the case. Middle-ranked members did not enjoy unusual license, nor even the conventional freedoms, but dwelt within a fairly rigid and demanding system of rules that may have been designed to exploit them for the sake of the cult's leadership. In this chapter, I describe Processean life as I observed it in the years 1971-1973, when the cult was at its numerical height and the culture was most developed. The structure of the narrative is simple: we scan Processean life upward through the hierarchy of ranks and across the main issues of communal existence. The underlying theme is the way the system exploited and controlled middle-ranked members through the actual provision of gratifications and the promise of greater gratifications to come. I describe many Process customs, beginning with an overview of the scale of the cult and ending with a discussion of the economic structure. The ordinary details of everyday life were not left to chance but arranged by the leaders to give them the greatest power at the least cost.

THE SCALE OF THE CULT

Process chapters were never particularly large. The absence of a well-developed congregation kept participation in mass activities rather modest, but the relative size of the committed "clergy" ensured the vitality of each branch. I attempted to count the number of people present at cult gatherings over a three-month period, January 23, 1971, through April 24, 1971. The biggest weekly activity, the Saturday evening Sabbath Assembly, tended to draw between sixty and seventy-five people, including almost everyone of Messenger rank or above. At nine Sabbaths where I was able to count the numbers of new Acolytes and Initiates, twenty-six people were acolyted (an average of 2.9 a week) and fourteen were initiated (an average of 1.6 a week). Extrapolating these figures, we can estimate that the Boston chapter took in 150 new Acolytes and seventy-five new Initiates a year. This 2:1 ratio really indicates a 50% dropout rate after people "came forward" to join the cult, because the rank of Initiate was in every way superior to that of Acolyte, carrying no special burdens and some advantages. Nobody who stayed with the cult for long would fail to be initiated. For a while, a weekly Initiates' Meeting was held every Sunday, drawing ten or fifteen people each time. The number of truly active Initiates seldom rose above two dozen.

The Friday Telepathy Developing Circle tended to draw between thirty and forty persons at the Boston chapter in 1971, including eight or ten

Messengers. The OP Progresses, the seminar and group therapy sessions open to Initiates, Disciples, and OP Messengers, seemed to draw twenty to thirty persons each time. The total number of different persons who attended a Progress at least once in April 1971 was exactly fifty. This suggests the total number of active Boston Processeans was around seventy-five.

In October and November 1971, I was asked to photograph all members of Disciple rank and above so that photo identification cards could be made. These cards would be used to convince police and other officials that Donators and members performing other public functions were authentic and deserved toleration. My photography work enabled me to complete an accurate census, as shown in Table 2.

RANK	MALES	FEMALES	TOTAL
Masters	1	1	2
Priests	1	0	1
Prophets	1	3	4
IP Messengers	1	1	2
Children	4	2	6
OP Messengers	3	7	10
Disciples	12	6	18
Total	23	20	43

TABLE 2. The Boston Chapter, November 1971

For the nine adult IPs, the sex ratio is very close to 50-50, as it is for the total of thirty-seven adult members. I counted the Processeans of Messenger rank and above named in the issues of the *Processeans* magazine, 1972-1974, and arrived at a total of ninety-two, exactly forty-six males and forty-six females. Robert told me there was no conscious effort to keep the numbers of males and females equal. Presumably, if sexual attraction was one of the forces bringing in new members, one might expect the ratio to approach equality, because a surplus of one sex would tend to recruit members of the opposite sex until an approximate balance was achieved.

In 1971, there were two big chapters, Boston and Chicago, the dwindling London group, and two small chapters in New Orleans and Toronto. From the seventy-five members in Boston, we can estimate that there were around 200 or 250 members of all ranks, altogether. The booklet *Fax 'n Figgers*, put out by the cult in early 1972, states, "As of December 1971, at a conservative estimate, the number of Processeans stood around the 100,000 mark, and is growing rapidly every day." What could this 100,000 figure mean? I estimate that fewer than 10,000 people could have visited coffeehouses. I therefore suspect that 100,000 is a rough estimate of the total number of people who ever contributed to a Donator on the streets, casual benefactors who could hardly be called members. True formal membership required a person to experience a series of initiation ceremonies intended to transform him into a Messenger of the cult.

MESSENGERS

A person became an Acolyte by responding to the Evangelist's invitation near the end of the Sabbath Assembly. After his emotional sermon, the Evangelist would call "upon all who wish to belong to the Army of God and to dedicate their lives to the service of the Lord Christ and the Three Great Gods of the Universe, and who have not already been received into the Church, to come forward and kneel before me." If any did come forward and kneel, the Evangelist would stand over them, make the sign of the cross with his outstretched arms, and say, "In the Name of The Lord Christ and in the Name of the Lord Satan, I accept you as Acolytes of the Church of The Final Judgement." Later, in a private meeting, the new Acolyte would learn from the Guardian of Acolytes that he had just taken a "first step within the hierarchy of The Process" and had made "a gesture of commitment." The status of Acolyte was really of no significance, and each newcomer was urged to become an Initiate as soon as possible, perhaps in as short a time as one week.

When I was initiated in 1971, the procedure involved attending two First Progress classes, meditation on Christ and Satan, twenty-four hours of fasting, and a public ritual. In the middle of a Sabbath Assembly, Isolde and I knelt before the Sacrifist, received our Initiate's crosses, and proclaimed our desire "to serve the Lord Christ and the Lord Satan." We were anointed with water (Christ) and fire (Satan), but with no risk of being burned. What was my function as an Initiate? The ritual formula explained I was to "play my part in Their joining together for the Final Judgement of humanity and the ending of the world of men." In fact, Initiates had very few functions. Chiefly, they filled up the coffeehouse and the rituals, while some of them were recruited to become Messengers.

It was not easy to become a Messenger, except in the time of the infamous January Blue Sale. For six weeks before baptism, a candidate had to "go on dedication" or "Messenger line," following the rules required of Messengers to prove he could accept the discipline. In many cases, a promising Initiate was allowed to move into the OP Messenger Flat, the commune on Inman Street. If all went well, a baptism was scheduled. The ceremony was held privately in the chapter house. Because the ritual was closed to people below Messenger rank, the candidate would not know what to expect, never having seen somebody else receive baptism. Sometimes the noise of a Messenger Baptism could be heard in the Cavern—the beat of drums and loud voices—and wild rumors spread about the horrendous things that happened to the victim being baptized. A candidate for baptism might be told he would be branded with a hot iron or informed he might share in a cult orgy immediately afterwards. Of course, both the branding and the orgy were pure fantasy.

The ceremony was bland but did have the power to evoke strong feelings in the candidate because he was the focus of the entire group's attention and gripped by a sense of mystery produced by the secrecy in which the baptism was held. Like all Process "Consecration Ceremonies," the Messenger Baptism was presided over by a Sacrifist, who anointed the candidate with fire and water. In the midst of the ritual, the new member was given his Sacred Name. Late in the history of the cult, people chose their own Sacred Names or suggested three from which the Master of the chapter would pick one. But earlier, the names were chosen by Mary Ann or some other leader and not told to the candidate until he had been proclaimed a "Messenger of the Unity of the Lord Christ and the Lord Satan." So when the Sacrifist said, "Henceforth you will be known by the Sacred Name ——, which means ——," the candidate was gripped by great excitement. Who will I be?

A new Sacred Name marked a new identity for the person. Sister Roxana was deeply impressed by her baptism: "The fact of getting your name and having just like this incredible whole revelation of your inner identity, having that crystallized by your name!" Roxana said, "I like to think of myself as my name." She had studied the mythological significance of her name and felt Roxana "was such an incredible woman" from ancient Greek mythology. Sister Eve said her name meant Living One and "I know that's me inside." I often heard brand-new Messengers talk excitedly about their Sacred Names, and watched them attempt to grow into their names, to fulfill the significance of a new identity.

Processeans used their Sacred Names in public as well as in church settings. Their secular names ("Grey Names") were only used in legal documents, on driver's licenses and identification cards, and in financial transactions. A number of members I knew over the years changed their Sacred Names. If someone dropped out and then returned, he would receive a completely new

Sacred Name upon rebaptism. Often Processeans wore out their names, came to feel they no longer expressed the right personality, and requested new ones. I have mostly used a single name for each person in this book to avoid confusing the reader, but names really changed fairly often. Sister Seraphine had three different names, Isolde four, and Morgana five!

As soon as the new Messenger had received his Sacred Name, he would join the senior Messenger in reciting a Dedication:

> We are the Messengers of the Second Coming of the Lord Christ, who comes to reabsorb all evil from the world of men. And we are the Messengers of the Redemption of the Lord Satan, who comes to release the power of love into the world of men. We bring the Message of the Unity of these two Great Beings who once were enemies, but who now are joined together in an unbreakable bond of Unity. We are the Messengers of the Unity. As it is . . . So be it.

The new Messenger would now move into the Messenger Flat, if he had not already done so. In theory, the resident Messengers would vote whether to accept each newcomer, and a single negative vote would count as a veto. But in fact new Messengers were always admitted. The twelve months each OP Messenger had to live outside the core of Process society were a kind of probation period. At the end he would become an IP if he had not dropped out or been expelled first. By placing the OP Messengers in their own commune, the IPs could insulate them, control them, yet still escape responsibility for them. A general but unstated principle of Process leadership was that the leaders wanted control but would not accept responsibility over the followers.

OP Messengers without their own resources would be given a modest allowance for living expenses. In 1973, when six or seven were living in the flat, its running expenses were around $150 a week. Any Disciple or Initiate living with the Messengers on a trial basis was expected to pay his own way. Messengers were permitted to keep any money sent them by their families, and some were able to afford big record collections, extensive libraries, wardrobes of clothing, and decorations for their rooms. The largest bedrooms held two to four people, and sometimes as many as fifteen crowded into the house. Even the Head of House, a senior Messenger who acted as liaison officer with the IPs and who had a luxurious L-shaped room on the first floor complete with refrigerator, was often required to have a roommate. In many respects, the lifestyle resembled that of a group of college students sharing an apartment.

The only real meal of the week at Inman Street was Sunday dinner, when everybody came together for a feast. This might mean chicken, but not really fancy dishes such as the pork roast I once bought for the IPs' Sunday dinner. At other times, individuals ate when they felt like it, fixing their own food in the downstairs kitchen. There was no house cook. Ariel said the kind of food usually available included "hamburger, a couple of cheeses, eggs, always bread, peanut butter, jams, sometimes fruit." In addition to conventional food and goodies like the ice cream Messengers often bought with their allowances, they consumed great quantities of vitamin tablets and other dietary supplements. In October 1971, they were required to follow the schedule below, swallowing twenty-nine items daily:

Morning: 1 multivitamin, 1 kelp tablet, 4 brewer's yeast, 1 halibut or cod liver oil, 3 bone meal, 4 liver pills, 1 dolomite, 1 organic iron (female), and 3 almonds.
Evening: 2 lecithin tablets, 2 wheat germ oil, 4 vitamin C, 2 vitamin E.

These pills were bought in bulk at a local health-food store. In addition to supplementing the Messengers' diet, they served two social functions. First, they extended the IPs' control over Messengers' daily routines, symbolically underscoring the IPs' superiority. Second, they extended parental nurturance, stating in effect that the IPs cared about the Messengers and were looking over them.

Aside from the above-average consumption of vitamins, I saw no evidence of any unusual attitude toward medical care among Processeans. Some religious groups are reluctant to turn to physicians with their physical problems. The Process cult, however, regularly allocated some of its income for "medical and dental treatment and care" and for P-Beauty ("cosmetic surgery, etc."). When Sister Hagar spilled stinging perfume in her eyes, she was rushed to the emergency room of a nearby hospital without hesitation.

The Messenger Flat on Inman Street was much like any American home. The downstairs Cavern coffeehouse had been converted into a comfortable living room. There was a large wooden dining table, benches, chairs, sofas, a television set, and a stereo record player. The downstairs also had a bathroom with shower.

Members of Messenger rank and above were usually extremely clean people. They did not need to urge each other to bathe. The women used makeup. The men frequently splashed on aromatic potions. Deodorants were in use.

At regular Sunday house meetings, one of the chief pieces of business was allocating work assignments to Messengers. Brother Ariel recalled some of the specific house tasks given individuals on a regular basis: "Hallways and stairways, the Cavern, the kitchen, the front hall, the Alpha, the Meditation Room, garbage, laundry, the upkeep of the house, the boiler room. People were given good jobs and bad jobs, and some jobs counted extra. Everybody tried to have them as even as possible. Laundry was traditionally given to the lowest hierarchical member of the house. More senior Messengers had responsibilities like upkeep of the real Alpha on Concord Avenue, or upkeep of the coffeehouse." Among the specific posts were some with formal titles: Maintenance Officer, Economy Officer, Timing Officer, and Mail Officer. The Timing Officer was unpopular; it was his job to wake everyone up in the morning.

The Inman Street ritual room, the Alpha, was closed to the public. There, OP Messengers held their Morning and Evening Assemblies. Members took turns playing Sacrifist for these twenty-minute rituals. One section of these brief Assemblies was the Seal of Identification, which enacted the Messengers' unity with each other symbolically through their connection with the Gods. It would begin with a "round" of the circle of participants, in which each would say his name: "I, Brother Eros, ...," "I, Sister Roxana, ...," "I, Sister Eve, ...," "I, Brother Thomas, ...," and then the group would follow the Sacrifist in reciting: "... do identify myself with Christ, our Lord of Truth, who is the Unity of GOD; with Jehovah, our Lord of the Universe, who is the Power of GOD; with Lucifer, our Lord of the New Age, who is the Light of GOD; with Satan, our Lord of the End, who is the Love of GOD." Finally, the same words would be chanted to a rather sweet melody.

FESTIVITY

Brother Ariel says, "Inman Street was quite a lot of fun." When I asked for an example, he described a moment of great festivity: "We had a very large collection of records that was left over from many, many different people. And we put on this Greek music that got everybody up dancing around, wearing pots on our heads, and playing things together ... screaming, yelling, hollering."

Processeans often had fun, even when times were rough. Looking back through the hundreds of photographs I took, I see many pictures of fun. A shot of Eve, Roxana, and Hagar dancing. Eve chewing on the ace of spades in a card game. Four Messengers and two Prophets climbing up the equestrian statue of General Burnside in a public park. Semi-sexual horsing around: Thomas

A demonic enactment for fun.

crushing Eve; Matthew bouncing Hagar on his lap. Once Eve and Eros found a trapdoor on the lawn of a state Capitol, probably repair access to pipes. They pretended it led to Hell, scrambled inside, and pulled the door down over them. With a shout they threw it open and leaped out. They were Satan's Hordes rising to ravage the earth!

The playful spirit of the Process was expressed in members' attitudes toward the cult's doctrine. They frequently exhibited what I call *belief distance*, by analogy with Erving Goffman's concept of *role distance*.[77] When a person broadcasts more or less subtly that he is larger than the role he plays at the moment, he exhibits role distance. When a person similarly broadcasts that he is not rigidly bound by his belief system, he exhibits belief distance. It is as if the person were saying, "I do not really believe these things; I am merely playing the role of believer when it suits me." Both kinds of distance can be communicated through humor, especially self-irony. One of my photos shows Father Dominic, second in command of the Boston chapter, mocking meditation in a silly pose for my camera. He holds his hands pointed upward as if in prayer. His eyes are closed. He has made a fish mouth by sucking in his cheeks. Processeans frequently joked about the Great Gods of the Universe, about various aspects of doctrine, and about each other.

To a great extent, the cultists did not *believe* their tenets in the conventional sense. For them, the Process culture was not a series of statements about a real, external world. Rather it was a collection of attractive and powerful symbols through which they could express themselves. The Process was a kind of living theater. A waking dream, a fantasy that made no apologies to reality, the Process enjoyed playing with itself. It was simultaneously real and fictitious, not a lie but a work of art. In the nineteenth century, Richard Wagner tried to create total works of art in his operas, unions of all forms of artistic creation in one.[78] He only half succeeded. The true *total work of art* would be an artistically created human community with a distinctive lifestyle and culture. *The Process is a total work of art.*

From the perspective of sociological role analysis, following Goffman's dramaturgical model for example, it might be said that the true total work of art is the individual human personality. My greatest act of creation is to create myself. This is what Processeans tried to do. From the moment of receiving his new Sacred Name, each Messenger cultivated a distinctive personality. They wanted to be superheroes. They delighted in the similarity between themselves and the superheroes portrayed in Marvel Comics. On several occasions I observed members reading such comic books as *Thor*, *The Avengers*, or *Spider-Man*. They often discussed the exploits of these surrealistic beings with great seriousness. While outsiders might read *Time* or *Newsweek* to catch up on the news of the conventional world, Processeans read Marvel Comics to keep up to date on the news of the magical world. In fact, the Process counted among its closest friends Stan Lee, the creator of Marvel Comics, published Marvel panels in its magazines, and was inspired by the comic heroes. On August 9, 1972, the New Orleans chapter sent Stan Lee at letter asking six questions, and in the absence of his answers, we may need to frame our own:

1. What are your views on the End of the world?
2. What are your views on the coming of the Messiah?
3. When do you feel the end of the world will come about?
4. What does the End of the world mean to you?
5. What would you like to see happen in the world today?
6. How would you change the world?

In the earlier *Death* issue of the cult's magazine, a blurry photo of Lee is surrounded by cartoons of his main characters, with him complaining: "I resent the whole thing. It's too demeaning. Besides, it can ruin our whole printing schedule!!! As for life after death, I think it's just a good public relations program for the religion industry. Anyway, it would be too anticlimactical. . . . What could you do for an encore!!!"

One day I snapped a picture of Brother Thomas reading *The Avengers*. He lunged at me growling like the Hulk. One time I tagged along with him when he ducked into a greeting card shop. He wanted a card to send home to his parents and shouted in joy when he found exactly the right one. It showed the Marvel Comics hero Thor, striding forward with his magic hammer raised to strike. The caption was, "The answer at last!" How apt. Thomas hoped the Process was an answer for him, a way he could become a transcendent heroic being, rising far above normal life to dwell with the Gods.

On donating trips, during visits to hospitals, and in guest lectures to school and college classes, cult members tried to act out heroic parts, presenting themselves as Marvel characters in cloaks, caped crusaders endowed with magic powers. The Messengers wanted to be superheroes but did not accept challenges in an independent spirit. Quite the contrary. They were extremely dependent upon the guidance of the Masters. On every trip, one senior person was in immediate command. Groups that were away from the chapter for long kept in touch by telephone with the Masters back home. If the game of superhero was a childish fantasy, then Messengers lived it as children, under the close supervision of their parents, the Superiors and Masters. This may seem paradoxical, because I have also said that Inman Street was not supervised. Outside its safe walls, the Messengers practically begged for guidance.

Both the festivity and the drama of the cult were reinforced by the extensive use of music. Songs, hymns, chants, and popular recordings were very important elements in its culture. As in other areas, the cult's approach was rampantly eclectic. Some Process tunes imitated familiar music; others were directly lifted from popular sources. For example, the tune to "The Hymn of Repentance" was taken from the Scottish anthem by Robert Burns, "Scots Wha Hae." Every Tuesday evening, the chapters held Chant Sessions, enjoyable singing hours that prepared the congregation for that week's Sabbath hymns. Three of the chapters had their own rock music bands that played in public as well as at private cult functions. I traveled with one band when it played southern New England coffeehouses. I photographed them at a Boston TV studio. I watched them arouse the college boys in Harvard Square as Sister Eve belted out songs and Sister Chryse danced.

The favorite music of the group was usually the kind of rock and folk music popular in the youth culture around 1970. One typical record collection included the Beatles, the Band, Johnny Cash, the Who, John Mayall, the Grateful Dead, Jefferson Airplane, Jethro Tull, Tom Rush, Joni Mitchell, and Crosby, Stills, Nash, and Young. Robert de Grimston's personal record

Members of a Process band playing in public.

collection was considerably more intellectual: Bach, Telemann, Albinoni, Tartini, Pergolesi, Vivaldi, Scarlatti, Beethoven, and Mozart. Although some Process hymns had a Gregorian quality, most of the original music by members was closer to the folk-rock tradition.

The most festive hour of the week was called Knees-Up, a private, informal dance held in the Cavern after Saturday's Midnight Meditation. All the Disciple OPs were invited, and it was their chance to socialize on a fairly equal basis with the higher-ranked members of the chapter. After the peaceful Meditation, the Initiates and members of the general public would slowly take their leave. There was always a line in the kitchen—people waiting to use the bathroom—and a scramble to collect overcoats. The Knees-Up would not begin until all the outsiders had left. Some of the men would clear the Cavern floor for dancing, dragging chairs, tables, and cushions out of the way. The Messenger in charge of the coffeehouse would select a few phonograph records. The IPs disappeared upstairs to change into civilian clothes. Sister Cher says the entrance of Brother Ariel was always a high point of the evening. He would appear wearing something startling, splendid, elegant, then begin a slow solo dance at the bottom of the stairs. Everyone who came in would get a good view of his performance.

About 1:00 A.M., the dancing would be on in earnest. Knees-Up was like a high school prom. Many of the girls stood around the sides of the room waiting for the guys to ask them to dance. For many, Knees-Up was a ritual. They would always dance one or two times with a list of special partners, reaffirming an otherwise unmarked relationship with each person. Messenger

Brother Anthony and Disciple Sister Cher would always have a slow dance together, even though they hardly spoke to each other for the rest of the week. Fast dances would alternate with slow ones. The last dance was so fast that everybody worked himself into a frenzy, leaping and spinning into exhaustion.

Then it was time for the OPs to leave, the Messengers to Inman Street and the Disciples to various destinations. The IPs stood on the stairs, in the OP Room and in the kitchen near the back door, to say goodbye. People with feelings of special closeness would always kiss and hug, but often a near stranger would rush up and give an unsuspecting OP an exuberant embrace. The OP Messengers had two miles to walk; sometimes Disciples gave them lifts in their cars. The Boston subways were not running at 2:30 when the walkers reached Harvard Square, so there were always a few Disciples who had to hitch rides to get home.

With Knees-Up happening on a weekly basis, and with so many group rituals and therapy sessions, the Process probably did not need many annual holidays. Only Christmas and Foundation Day were celebrated. The Christmas Eve Assembly was open to all Brethren of the chapter and involved a meditation on "the New Beginning" as well as some carol singing. The theological justification for celebrating the birth of Jesus was a bit weak. In theory, Robert de Grimston (and possibly many others) might represent the Christ Spirit as fully as did Jesus. The Processean purist would say: Jesus was not the Christ, rather Jesus was one of many men who channeled the spirit of Christ. Robert's birthday, October 8, was not a time of public celebration. Christmas was a concession to the Christian sentimentality of most members, a substitute for a visit home, and a taste of Saturnalia. After the public ritual, the chapter house was vacated by those below Messenger rank, and the rest would proceed to get roaring drunk.

Foundation Day, June 13, sometimes called Founders Day, commemorated the traditional date in 1963 when the cult was founded. It had a public side and a private side. The day would be spent at the beach, OPs and IPs frolicking together on the sand. Afterward, the Messengers and IPs would repair to the chapter house to demolish a vast store of booze that had been laid in.

LOSS OF AUTONOMY

While making tremendous demands on the Messengers and Prophets, the leaders sought to maintain control without taking responsibility. If a Messenger failed, it was his own fault. On the philosophical plane, the cult's doctrine simultaneously asserted that each person has complete responsibility for everything that ever happens to him yet is without choice, living a God-determined life. These paradoxes fit a religious notion of authority. Messengers never knew what was coming next yet had to live in faith and acceptance. Several told me they loved the excitement of never knowing for sure what tomorrow might bring, trusting that it would be something good.

Transfers from one chapter to another were often sudden and unexpected. Cher had an intense romantic crush on Father Orpheus when he was stationed in Boston. She was shocked one evening to discover that he was to be transferred to New York the next day: "I was just numb because it happened so fast! I didn't really have any time to think about it, which I suppose was best. I suppose he had a function in New York." Her voice took on a wistful tone: "I don't know. They had the new chapter there and people were just being transferred out. He didn't have a choice. He just was sent. Staying within the Process, he had no choice whatsoever."

Brother Dagon was transferred like lightning to Toronto in early 1971. "In fact, when I went up there it was the first announcement to anyone that there was such a place!" The Boston chapter had no idea a branch was being set up in Canada. "It was a complete surprise, I remember I walked in the office, and I found out I was going, and that was the first mention I'd ever heard of a Toronto chapter. And that night I told everybody I was getting transferred up there, and everybody was quite surprised." Process society thrived on secrets and rumors. Having secrets, keeping secrets, revealing secrets, and discovering secrets were important factors in arousing excitement and maintaining status in the group.

In October 1971, Brother Matthew, then a Prophet, gave a formal statement about his life in the church, explaining to an interested outsider what it was like to be without opportunities for individual decisions: "We take vows of obedience. We follow our instructions." Obedience to whom? Instructions from whom? In Process theory, the separate Gods rule through their people. The idea of a centralized church authority is in total contradiction with the theology. Yet the cult's leaders discovered that power could be made to serve their interests. The ideology yielded. In order to exploit the Messengers and Prophets, the leaders adopted several rhetorical devices from conventional religion. The divine purpose to which the cult founders were dedicated was their own transcendence of conventional life. Through sophistry they obscured this truth, hoping to rise on the shoulders of the Messengers, aware they could not make the real situation very clear if they were to succeed. Matthew said, "We live communally. We hold no personal possessions, and we have no outside jobs. We hold everything in common." However, cult leaders could dispose of church wealth as if it were their own property. The Omega lived in luxury. The Process was like a feudal kingdom resting on a communist base.

Matthew explained, "We work hierarchically, a hierarchy based on function rather than on quality. It's not that the people on top are *better*; it's just that they have a particular function." Nice rhetoric. "I don't decide what I'm going to do, what I'm going to eat, what I'm going to wear. That's not my level of choice. That's decided for me. And it's a relief. My mind isn't taken up with: 'Well, what am I going to do today? What am I going to wear today? Who am I going to talk to? Where am I going to go? What am I going to eat?' Which is really a lot of wasted time. That level of operation is settled. We agree on it, and it's done, once and for all. And then we operate on another level which is a bit more significant and more basic to everybody. And that's what it amounts to. You know, as you commit yourself more and more to a way of Love, to God, you stop making choices for yourself, because you've already made your choice." The last choice was to submit to the Process. In so doing, "You free yourself from choice, and from conflict at the same time. You don't have to decide, 'Do I want to do this, or do I want to do that?' You've done it already. It's set."

Messengers lived under strict rules against drugs, alcohol, and sex. They were not supposed to indulge their sexual desires, despite the many attractive partners in the cult and despite the free-love values of the Gods Lucifer and Satan. Edward once told me the cult had suffered from problems concerning sexuality as early as Xtul, where there were twice as many males as females. Rivalry was disruptive, and if two people were very deeply involved with each other, they were likely to be all the less involved with the group. So, after Xtul, the cult experimented with celibacy, then tried out other approaches to the regulation of sex. The leaders did not want to deny themselves erotic enjoyment, but they were quite ready to deny it to the followers. The rule that OP Messengers abstain from sex (unless a relationship was initiated with one of them from someone higher in the system of ranks) cost the leadership nothing but gave a two-sided benefit. The celibacy rule both trained Messengers in obedience and tested their compliance.

The Messengers responded variously to the regulations. For example, Sister Godiva said sex was her "greatest weakness." She couldn't keep her mind off it. Godiva admitted quite freely that she was gripped by an intense sexual hunger. She did not remain a Messenger long. After a new affair and after being demoted to Initiate rank, she seemed rather depressed but could at least enjoy her sexuality freely. Other Messengers found the celibacy rule to be an advantage. For example, Brother Eros was an extremely handsome young man who had no difficulty in finding willing female partners. He told me that before joining the Process he used to seduce girls, to enjoy them for a while, then lose interest and drop them. He was caught in an unsatisfying vicious circle of seduction and abandonment. Now that he was in the Process, he could turn his natural inclinations into an asset for the church. He still seduced girls, but not for himself. He seduced them for Christ. Rather than having sex with them, he flirted with them to recruit them to the cult. He once said the greatest thing he had gained from the church was "more confidence in a sexual way. And the sexual feeling is always there because sex is around everything. It is a driving force. I've seen through a lot of the degrading negative sides of sex, and the other side is quite incredible, quite a healing thing." He loved "giving people security to open themselves up, giving them some warmth and security to come out and trust and feel that somebody might care for them. And that's what I give to a lot of people, showing them that I care for them. And they respond to it, you know." This, of course, is the basic recruitment process, expressed in baldly sexual terms.

Brother Ariel told me his analysis of the ascetic regulations: "We didn't smoke dope, not so much because it was bad but because it was against the law. If we drank alcohol at official parties—Founders Day, Christmas—we got plastered! Mixing our drinks like mad people and suffering accordingly." Alcohol and sex were dispensed by the leadership under strict control. But of course there was an abstract theory behind everything. "The sexual requirements were there to teach us something about our energies; at least that's how we saw it." Sexual abstinence taught them "how we could channel sexuality and use it twenty-four hours a day. And use it constructively, i.e.: make money or heal people." One strength the leadership had was the ability to provide sensuousness, for example in rituals or the therapy sessions, gratifications so appealing and so promising that Messengers would become addicted or overwhelmed by them.

A kind of incest taboo developed between Messengers. They were Brothers and Sisters, after all. Many of their romantic crushes were directed at IPs, and since their status of OP Messenger was to last only one year, many of them could defer gratification until they became an IP or were seduced by an IP. The occasional married couple that joined the cult was not expected to follow the celibacy rule. One of the nicer rooms at Inman Street was occupied by married couples. Leadership control over followers' sexual behavior, therefore, was uneven. But the intention was that it be absolute. More than one informant claimed to know that Mary Ann took personal charge of all relationships of members above Prophet rank, separating any pair that seemed too intensely involved. I do not have good independent evidence on this point. It is true that many couples were separated, assigned to different chapters, while other couples were kept together.

One example of the leaders' involvement in a Messenger's personal life is the experience of Sister Norma. When she was only an Initiate, she and Brother Patrick developed a romantic relationship that was just about to become physical. Mother Seraphine discovered what was going on, called Norma into her office, and, Norma says, "really laid me out in lavender." After this lecture, Norma and Patrick cooled off their courtship. Months later, when Norma was a proven Messenger, Father Christian called her into his office. He said it was time she got betrothed to marry. "Of all the men in the chapter, which one would you like to have?" he inquired. She said Brother Patrick was her first choice, and Brother Eros was her second choice. Christian promised to give Patrick various hints that Norma was the woman for him. Patrick did not respond. Then Christian and Norma discussed Eros. "He told me to ask Eros, which I did." When Norma asked Eros to marry her, he replied, "Oh, I'm very flattered, but no thank you." Norma says she was devastated by embarrassment. "And then I found out later that he and Seraphine had a thing going."

The sexual rules of the Process appear not really to have had anything to do with spiritual development but were one aspect of life among many that the leaders wanted to control to their own advantage. Ariel remembered one time Mother Rhea "made advances" to Brother Basil, "who was an OP Messenger and she was a Master of a chapter." If a high-status member of the cult started an affair with a Messenger, it was okay. But if two Messengers got involved with each other, they stood the risk of demotion to Initiate rank. Ariel said, "I remember when Patrick and Arcadia had to donate without taking treat breaks, when they'd broken the celibacy rules." Despite the formal regulations, Ariel said, "We were certainly not a celibate group. Our whole orientation was sexual. One of the basic premises of the Process is that sex is the greatest healing force there is. Use it."

PROMOTION AND DESERTION

An OP Messenger would automatically be promoted to IP Messenger status if he followed the rules, participated in two courses of Messenger Training, and displayed no alarming flaws. Not great talent, but a clean record was all that was required. Each level of the hierarchy kept secrets from the levels below. Roxana, an OP Messenger, once asked Eros, an IP, "What's most important to you about being an IP Messenger?" He replied, "That is classified information, sweetie." Actually, the differences between the two levels were slight. The IP Messenger participated in a few more advanced training and therapy exercises and was given a Magickal Name to add to his Sacred Name, using it only in private IP meetings. Most of the Magickal names seem to have been taken from classical mythology, the names of deities and demigods.

A Processean might hold the status of IP Messenger for the rest of his life. But if he showed some leadership ability, completed all Messenger training, carried out difficult assignments successfully, and waited a long and indefinite period, he might be elevated to Prophet rank. In a private ceremony he would receive a silver Prophet's ring bearing the Process Sign to wear on the first finger of his left hand. There were two levels of Prophet training. Junior Prophets' Training consisted of fifty-two sessions, covering a whole year, educating the student in the more complex aspects of the doctrine. Senior Prophets' Training, only eighteen weeks long, was concerned with administrative problems. It covered about seventy-five regulation documents and gave experience in communication. Here the Prophet was given instruction in "contact situations," "telepath training," and public speaking so he could take the role of Evangelist in the Sabbath Assemblies and give good Revelation sermons.

There was a formal examination, strict and intensive, before a Prophet could be promoted to Superior (Priest) rank. It was conducted orally by two Masters and had several sections. I will describe two. The first part confronted the Prophet with five difficult social situations he had to handle satisfactorily. One of the Masters would play the part of a disruptive person, and the Prophet was supposed to use all his training in dealing with the person. The examination outline says, "What is basically required of the candidate is good contact and control. He is not expected necessarily to fully satisfy the subject in terms of resolving his problem." The first of the five troublesome characters would complain and insult, the second would present a personal problem, while the third would express pain or tension. The fourth and fifth would act like aggressive outsiders trying to get damaging information about the cult through aggressive questioning.

The last part of the examination was "An unprepared inspired Revelation lasting between five and ten minutes, channeled by the candidate, as though to an Assembly, on a subject chosen by the testers." The candidate could rely on both the doctrinal training he had received and the experience he had gained in public speaking. Father Christian once gave me an impressive demonstration of the seemingly inspired but actually quite calculated performance that made a good Sabbath Assembly Revelation. I wanted to photograph a Sacrifist and an Evangelist in full color, so Christian and Dominic dressed up in the proper costumes. The three of us went into the Alpha ritual room. My color lights were hung from the beams in the center of the room, and my Nikon camera was full of film. Christian stood in front of the black curtain with its red goat's-head symbol, his long blond hair flowing down over his scarlet Evangelist's tabard. He went into his act. Christian shouted, cajoled with a whisper, spoke logically in a metallic voice, pleaded emotionally, laughed in joy and triumph! His body moved to accent the speech. He spoke in a negative tone and waved his fingers dismissingly before his face. He clenched his fist in anger and growled. He pointed to one side, then forward and above. A great performance! But what was he actually saying? In fact, he was merely reciting the letters of the alphabet.

If the Prophet had met all other requirements for promotion and passed his exam, the High Master of the chapter could send a recommendation to the Omega urging that the candidate be "ordained" a Superior. With this rank, the person would receive a second silver ring, this one bearing the Sign of Union, to be worn on the first finger of the right hand. No longer a Brother or Sister, the Superior would be a Father or Mother of the church.

I knew of no cases in which a person who joined the Process after Xtul was elevated to Master rank. All the Superiors I knew had joined no later than 1968 and had participated in the Matthew 10 wanderings. Promotion to the highest ranks meant admission to the inner core of cult society, rather than a mere bureaucratic advance. The Council of Masters, the dozen or so ruling Processeans under the Omega, was identical with the original heart of Process society created in the social implosion of 1965 and 1966. As much an elite caste as an upper class, this group lived off the labors of the lower-status members.

The cult did not make it particularly easy for Messengers and IPs to drop out, but many did over the years. A defecting insider had no right to take any money away with him when he left. Sister Norma was in New York when she decided to quit, but her family lived in Boston. She had to conceal her intentions and beg to be sent home on holiday. There was no other way she could get traveling money. The sociologist Rosabeth Kanter believed this practice of refusing to refund any of a member's contributions when he defects from a cult adds strength to the movement.[79] If a member knows he cannot get anything back on his investment unless he stays with the cult, he is more likely to stay. Furthermore, it may be practically very difficult for a person to leave a cult if he has no money. But Brother Ariel felt that members were not trapped in the cult by this practical problem, because a little patience usually would turn up an alternative. Unlike many communes, the Process's chapters were set up in major cities, and members could make friends on the streets with people who might help them if they decided to leave.

Ariel left with only one dollar in his pocket. "The thing that kept me from leaving earlier was I had no place to make any money. The minute I found some money coming in, I left." He quit in Toronto but says the New Orleans chapter was a cauldron of desertion, both because the chapter itself was relatively unpleasant and because of the ready opportunities for a Messenger to arrange a job before quitting. "The classic means of making money was to work at the various strip places around Bourbon Street, because that was what they could easily do. Get a lot of money together and then leave." The jobs included "dancing . . . selling drinks, serving drinks, whatever." Some women were able to move in with boyfriends when they quit the Messenger Flat. The coffeehouse crowd of Disciples and Initiates also provided a bridge to the outside. Those that had apartments often permitted friends and even strangers to live with them for brief periods.

The rules of the cult on "desertion" had some elasticity, encouraging the deserter to reconsider. He would be demoted progressively down the steps of membership as the days passed after his departure. A deserter who was gone long enough to fall to Disciple rank had to work his way up again with the same painful slowness as before. Robert commented, "He will have a harder time, because having put his hand to the plough and then turned back, it will not be easy to reestablish the confidence in him which has been lost." Conversely, the individual rising for a second time through the ranks already knows the mysteries that are withheld from other low-status members. Although he has insider knowledge and proven capabilities, yet he is not an insider. Robert said, "By his own decision, he has become an outsider and must be treated as such."

IP SEX AND CHILDREN

My information on the sexual practices of IPs is mostly second-hand. I will report what I have been told, with the understanding that I was seldom able to verify informants' statements. Brother Faust says that many rumors spread among Messengers about the sexual practices of Superiors and Masters: "Logic dictated that they should be allowed to do what they wanted." According to the group's theory, "sex was a powerful force used positively or negatively. We were being celibate not because sex was evil but because we were learning how to deal with it." As Processeans progressed, they should gain control over these forces, so "it would seem logical that Superiors could do what they wanted." Robert told me that one outcome of the cult's experimentation with sex after Xtul was the invention of Process *Unions*. These relationships were presented to the world as marriages but clearly did not have as much force as conventional, exclusive marriages.

Father Dominic told me about his Union with Sister Eve: "I met Eve in Boston, and I guess somewhere I'd been trained to look out for the right one, as we all are, and I've always been very romantic and imagined that there would be a right one for me. And I was very thrilled to meet Eve! We had a very conventional and romantic courting, very proper, and we got married in Boston." I attended their Union Ceremony and the very conventional dinner party held afterwards at a nearby hotel and took photographs. Dominic and Eve spent the night in a suite at the hotel, just as any ordinary couple might. Several Processeans wear wedding rings.

Dominic explained, "It's very different from the nuclear type marriage, because our primary marriage is to the church. And what this means is if the church requires us to do particular things which might separate us, we're both very well adjusted to that. We have gone through a number of separations in terms of location and have always found that it has strengthened our bond rather than weakened it." Unlike conventional couples, Dominic and Eve did not make decisions based on what they want for themselves or their two children but on what the group as a whole needed. "I think the marriage relationship I have with Eve is a very special relationship, but it's one of a number of very special relationships I have. I'd say I have a very special relationship with Mother Hathor, since we've spent a lot of time together throughout the world, and I would go to her for advice on a number of things where I would never go to Eve, because Mother Hathor could counsel me." His relationship with Father Micah was also close, but in a different way, because they worked together.

High-ranked Processeans have experimented with different sexual structures and degrees of freedom at different periods in the development of the cult. I have never heard of a formal divorce in the Process but do know of two couples that have been separated for years. Certainly, there have been affairs of all kinds among the top members, as there would be in any contemporary, intensely interacting group of ideologically liberal people.

Osiris told me that the cult had a practice, called *spiritual relationships*, that bordered on organized group marriage. I will explain it through an example for which I have independent testimony, but anonymizing with the letters X, Y, Z. Sister X, recruited to the Process by Father Y, saw him as a father figure. After she discussed her feelings with other senior people, she announced that a *spiritual relationship* existed between them. He was her spiritual father. This tie was expressed through sexual relations. Now it happened that neither was married, so they were given a Union Ceremony. Then along came Brother Z. He came to feel that Sister X was his spiritual mother. He, the junior partner in their developing relationship, discussed it with other superior people and then announced there existed a spiritual relationship between them. It did not interfere with the other relationship between Sister X and Father Y. Both Brother Z and Father Y produced children with Sister X. According to Osiris, a spiritual relationship always links individuals of different sexes, one a "child" and the other a "parent," and is announced by the junior member after consultation with superiors. A Processean could have one spiritual parent and as many as four spiritual children. Thus, a network of nonexclusive relationships could develop, perhaps strengthening the cult's cohesiveness rather than disrupting it. I had been told that another Mother produced children by three Processean men.

I told Robert de Grimston what Osiris had said to me about spiritual relationships. All he would say was that cult sexual relationships were even more complicated than that. A church document issued to insiders on November 13, 1970, says, "Information about personal spiritual relationships between Processeans is NOT for divulgence to Outside Processeans or members of the general public." Why? "If such information 'leaks out' it is almost certain to be distorted and incomplete, in spirit if not in fact."

However they arranged it, senior Processeans did produce children. After 1970, Process children began appearing in some numbers. At the end of my direct observation study there were fifteen or twenty children. The word for children in this cult was "the Littles." In many respects, the lives of the Littles were quite normal in their very early years. The babies had the usual juvenile equipment: toys, playpens, walker chairs, even kiddie animal pictures on the wall. They wore bibs and diaper-service diapers. They had fuzzy bunting and infant pacifiers. They sucked formula from nipple bottles and took pablum from little spoons. Baby tonic and pediatricians protected their health.

They were supervised not by their mothers but by "Nannies," low-status members of both sexes given the job of childcare. Often a Little's parents would be stationed at a distant chapter. Mother Hathor, traveling a good deal at the time, came to the Boston chapter to give birth to her third child. She stayed for a while with the new infant, then

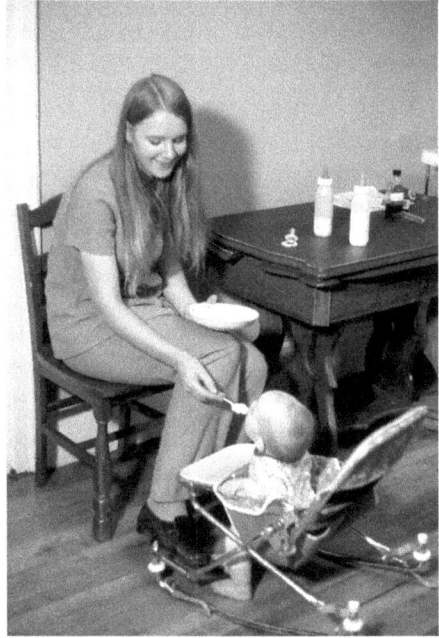

A "Nannie" feeding a Little.

continued her travels, taking over the Miami chapter. When a number of Littles had collected in Boston, the chapter rented an extra apartment in the building next door to the chapter house, just for the children. The Littles and the Nannies could carry on the business of growing up without disturbing cult activities. A bit later, when there were many children, different chapters specialized in different age groups. The oldest Littles were concentrated in New York, while the toddlers were in Chicago. This way the Littles could grow up in readily manageable cohorts. They did have special relationships with their biological mothers and fathers but treated all the adults of the chapter as parents. In chapter 9, however, we shall consider evidence that the experience of being a child inside the Process may have become rather painful, perhaps after age five.

Elaborate administrative rules were written concerning the Littles' Process training and hierarchical status. Robert condensed the adults' Evening Assembly to produce a short version suitable for children. Officially, the Littles were Little Messengers, possessing even Sacred and Magickal Names. "On his seventh birthday," document S-57 says, "an IP child automatically reverts to the rank of Initiate.... If he so desires, he then immediately begins to work his way towards being Baptized again, this time as a Young Messenger.... On his

Mother Hathor and her children.

fourteenth birthday, an IP child once more reverts to the rank of Initiate." Now he can go through procedures to become a regular adult member. These complex regulations do not deserve close analysis, because the Littles were still very small back in 1976, had not gone through these stages, and certainly had not yet presented the cult with the problem of an adult second generation, radically different from the first.

ECONOMICS

The largest source of church income was the money collected on the streets by middle-status members engaged in *donating*. As explained earlier, this practice was developed in New Orleans in 1967 or 1968 as a substitute for the original sources of income, fees for therapy sessions and the members' savings and inheritances. Although Disciples were sometimes included in donating activities, only Messengers and Prophets regularly worked the streets. They would go out in groups, usually in the morning, led by an IP, and keep at it until suppertime. The groups always wore their uniforms, presented themselves as ministers or members of a church, and in later years were provided with photo identity cards to show to police or other officials in the event they were questioned. About every hour, the Donators would take a five- or ten-minute rest

Donators taking a five-minute rest break.

break, perhaps smoke cigarettes, and total up their income for the past hour. They carried black purses, shoulder bags really, the men as well as the women. In them they kept personal effects, the money they collected, and little notebooks in which they tallied magazines sold and money received. Each Donator started out the day with a stack of magazines about six inches thick, usually protected from rain by a plastic bag.

Process magazines often contained photographs of happy Donators, and the cult's propaganda about the street work made it sound rewarding and colorful. On one of his radio shows, Father Dominic said, "We do meet all sorts of people on the street. It's a very good training ground. And in New Orleans once, one of our ministers, Constantine, saw Paul McCartney and Linda McCartney coming along the street on their bicycles. So he invited them into our coffeehouse.... And Paul's reaction was: 'Well, a bleedin' Britisher!' That was the last thing he expected to find in the French Quarter of New Orleans." Paul McCartney, of course, was a member of the famous Beatles musical group. An article in the March 1973 issue of *The Processeans* claimed that street Donators had spoken with 75,000,000 people during the previous year. That is a huge estimate, something like 3,000 per Donator per day, perhaps one every ten seconds. "Hello, can you help us? Hello, can you help us?" a Donator would say to the passing throng, investing less than ten seconds in most unsuccessful attempts to get attention. Many people would be asked more than once, but the total number seen by Processeans was undoubtedly very large. So it is not surprising that Donators met many famous or interesting people, even though most of their work was completely routine. The magazine article also claimed, "In the course of one day recently, Processean ministers in New York spoke with The Red Chinese Ambassador, Senator Jacob Javits, Senator Eugene McCarthy, Jackie Onassis, Joan Kennedy and Rose Kennedy, Rod McKuen, Bob Dylan, Neil Diamond, Minnesota Fats, Joe Frazier, and Muhammad Ali. And Marjoe!" All celebrities.

Most of the time, donating was agonizing drudgery. In the winter, the Donators wore long cloaks over their uniforms and long-john underwear beneath. But the cold still penetrated. The hourly progress checks were not supposed to be competitive. But a rate was calculated for each Donator, each group, and each chapter, called the DJ. These initials stood for Dow Jones, the well-known Wall Street financial index. It was the number of dollars per Donator per hour. In theory, each Donator was competing only against his personal DJ, but in practice the competition was general and harsh. As we mentioned, in 1973 this system evolved into an obsessive scheme that set income quotas that Donators had to meet before they could come home for supper or sleep.

Brother Faust complained to me that the Masters did not seem to realize that Donators were exhausted by their work and needed normal amounts of sleep:. "People at the top stay up much of the night and get little sleep." He said that the New York chapter in 1973 had dinner at 11:30 at night, followed by an evening meeting that might last more than an hour, followed by individual chores. Much of the "work" of the cult leaders consisted of physically inactive discussion sessions, so they had little understanding of the strains of street work. As I have mentioned, the "work" of the Omega and other top leaders was a kind of twenty-four-hour-a-day encounter-group stew, supposedly braving and discovering new religious and psychological territory for the sake of other Processeans. To support this intense sociation (defined as labor), the leadership exploited the Messengers and Prophets. A 1971 administrative directive from Father Joel, the High Pontiff, suggested, "A money thermometer and/or graphs in the private part of the Chapter, with previous ones for comparison, adds to the excitement and validation of the total." The chapters followed the directive and posted DJ figures on a weekly basis. When I observed Donators in 1971, each individual was collecting between forty and fifty dollars per donating day, but the work time was fairly short, around five hours. In peak periods, in ten-hour donating days in 1973 at the New York chapter, for instance, the total would surpass a hundred dollars per day. A super-Donator on a great day might make up to three hundred dollars. Multiply those numbers by about seven to get the dollar value half a century later.

There were some other sources of income. A little money came from admission fees to chapter activities. The Telepathy Developing Circle cost $1.50, or whatever a person could afford. If twenty paying customers attended, it was a hot night. Admission for the Midnight Meditation was seventy-five cents. If a chapter made fifty dollars a week from these activities it was lucky. Initiates were asked to contribute something for their cheap chrome-plated crosses; a dollar or two was typical. There were occasional special events, such as auctions of leftover junk. At one of these I paid thirteen dollars for two pieces of discarded ritual equipment.

Disciples were expected to tithe from their outside incomes. A few held decent jobs, but others were unemployed. More than one attempted to tithe out of a welfare check. Few Disciples tithed dutifully, and there was never a well-developed system for extracting money from them. The income from Disciples was probably not significant in comparison to the money brought in by Donators.

Inside Processeans were expected to turn all their worldly possessions over to the church. In several cases, as administrative documents note, IPs were "the beneficiaries of trusts or other sources of private income." I understand that Raphael, Aaron, and several others had contributed family wealth, and even some who joined as late as the 1970s came from rich families, Brother Faust for example. The HQ Treasurer was supposed to take charge of these investments and whenever possible arrange for the income to be "covenanted or made payable direct to The Process by some other recognized legal procedure." One advantage was the circumvention of individual tax liability in a way that the Internal Revenue Service could not challenge. Income from these trusts was paid directly to the central church organization rather than to the chapters. In some cases, it was necessary to keep investments in the names of individual members, and under such circumstances it was thought advisable "for the Processean concerned to sign a statement to the effect that he is holding the asset on behalf of the Church, and as its trustee." Because OP Messengers were only trial members of the community and had not yet been admitted into the core of cult society, they were not asked to give over all their property. Financial guideline PS-50-VIII-A-2 stated: "OP Messengers are not obliged in any way to hand over any personal money (gifts, income from trusts, etc.), and Inside Processeans should not suggest to an Outside Processean that he should

German Shepherd dogs living
at the chapter house.

do this. If an Outside Processean wishes to donate personal money or assets to The Process, and is certain in his own mind that this is what he wishes to do, it is treated as are all donations to the Church."

One source of income that was never figured into the financial accounts was *retrieving*: scavenging or begging for goods rather than money. Processeans were not only able to collect money through begging but also had considerable success in convincing people to donate things, even food, directly. One day in 1971, for example, a street Donator stopped a man in Boston, asked, "Can you help us?" and was immediately offered a piano. I tuned the instrument in the Alpha ritual room a couple of weeks later and found it to be a perfectly fine, almost new spinet. One of the cult's administrative guidelines discussed automobile purchases, commenting: "Remember that RETRIEVING IS PREFERABLE TO BUYING." There was one period at the Boston chapter when several dying wrecks of automobiles were parked by their owners on the lawn of the chapter house as donations. One of them was sold as a mystery prize at a coffeehouse auction and to everyone's embarrassment sold for about fifty cents. Another cult memo urged Chapter Treasurers to seek every possible means to keep the chapters solvent, ordering them to look for ways that "retrieving could contribute to the HQ's solvency. How it could be expanded." The term *retrieving* was commonly in use in the counterculture at the time. In most cases for the Process it meant begging for goods, rather than scavenging from junk piles as it did for other groups. Often, the retrieving target was a commercial business. For example, visits were made to butcher shops to ask for free bones for the dogs.

The group's leaders developed a complex system of financial procedures, explained at great length and excruciating detail in a collection of administrative documents dated October 1973. The cult had at least two former accountants, John and Hannah, and one management consultant, Malachi. The approach was conventional, although occasionally the language was novel. Receipts filled out by church leaders were called P-Vouchers, for example. British translations of American business terms were inserted at several points in the documents, so that all members could understand.

Each chapter kept income records, day by day, and summarized the information each week. It was supposed to send a thorough financial report to the church headquarters each month. An annual report was prepared with the help of professional auditors. There was an elaborate system for allocating income to different "funds." It clearly specified the amounts to be contributed to central church projects. As one of the documents stated, "A basic principle of Process finances is that contributing 'up the line' in hierarchy terms is of prime importance. Payments 'up the line' are made in the form of percentage allocations and are deducted from all 'real' income before any other payments or allocations are made." If these procedures were strictly followed, the central organization would be assured of economic support by the rank-and-file members.

Table 3 shows the official system for allocating cult income. The names of several of these "funds" describe them adequately. The PR fund went to "public relations" or advertising, while the DR Fund seems to have gone to lawyers and accountants. The Omega Chapter Fund was sent directly to Robert and Mary Ann, as their income from their cult. Robert told me the gross monthly income of the Process in this period was between $80,000 and $100,000. Four percent of that, or between $3,200 and $4,000, went to Mary Ann and Robert. Again, multiply by seven to get the dollars of half a century later.

TABLE 3. Income Allocation Structure, 1973	NAME OF FUND	PERCENT
	Central Fund	20%
	Publishing Fund	16%
	Chapter Expenses Fund	15%
	Matriarchs and Patriarchs Fund	15%
	P-Gear Fund	9%
	Masters' HQ Fund	8%
	Transport Fund	5%
	Omega Chapter Fund	4%
	PR Fund	3%
	DR Fund	2%
	New Chapter Fund	1%
	Building Fund	1%
	Music Fund	1%
	Total	**100%**

A Marxist would have no trouble analyzing the economic system of the Process. The Omega would be described as the leisured upper class living off the labor of the working-class Messengers and middle-class Superiors and Prophets. The emphasis of a Marxist analysis would be on the blatant oppression and exploitation of the Messengers, who derived precious little benefit from the thousands of uncomfortable hours they spent begging on the streets. The elite founding members of the cult claimed they contributed greatly to the well-being of their lower-ranked followers because of the doctrinal "information" and spirituality they "channeled" downward. The Marxist would say Messengers' belief in this was *false consciousness*, that the Process's upper class was of no social value and ruled through the illusion that their self-indulgent games were somehow essential for the well-being of the poor folk they exploited.

Classical economics would look at the participation of the cult in a larger market and ask what the cult sold and at what price. If the Process grossed $100,000 a month and included one hundred full-time members at its height, then the per capita annual gross income would come out to only $12,000. Many Processeans could easily have earned more than this on the outside, and those who could not were young members prevented by their cult involvement from gaining valuable skills at college or in occupational settings. In return for these unexceptional incomes, the group had to give a service. They initially collected donations without returning any definite service, except perhaps putting on an interesting show. Their claim that outsiders should support them because the cult mediated usefully with Lucifer, Jehovah, Christ, and Satan was not believed by the general public. In the early 1970s, the Process took on social service work of various kinds and advertised this contribution to society in its literature. The failure of the cult to grow after 1972 suggests that the market found the Process product overpriced and that the low hourly wages paid cult workers (Messengers) were not sufficient to attract a large, high-quality work force.

Both the Marxist and Classical perspectives would agree in their general view of the Processean system of ranks and regulations. The social system described in this chapter was the means by which the Omega and other top leaders of the Process exploited their economic environment in service of their collective desires and ambitions. Messengers and other middle-ranked members did not invent their own social customs, experimenting with alternate schemes in search of the highest personal gratification. Only the leaders of the cult were permitted such freedom. Messengers were given a rigid system of life composed of some gratifications and many demands. Fantasy and festivity gave relief from the drudgery of daily work and gave promise of better times to come. But only through defection or very slow promotion could a low-ranked Processean escape his exploited status. The cult existed for the sake of its founders, and therefore the social system functioned to channel wealth, power, and pleasure in their direction.

CHAPTER 7   The Gods and Their Symbols

JEHOVAH is Strength.
LUCIFER is Light.
SATAN is Separation.
CHRIST is Unification.
They are the Great Powers of the Universe,
and all mankind is subject to Their Will.
— Process Sabbath Assembly, 1973

THE PROCESS HAD FOUR GODS, several emblems, and innumerable rituals. These were not a collection of discordant images but a coherent, unified world-system expressed not only in carefully chosen symbols but most importantly in the structure of relationships among them. The Great Gods of the Universe were as much a psychological system as a theological one. Each defined a personality type, and together they expressed a sociology. The rituals, emblems, and God-pattern scriptures were intended not only to bring members closer together in expressive communion and not only to impress and instruct newcomers but also to create a new reality through the magical effects imputed to the system. In describing a spiritual world, it sought to create one.

THE MIND OF ROBERT DE GRIMSTON

Process theology was not the product of a committee. The Great Gods of the Universe were refined by Robert de Grimston from existing cultural resources. The anthropologist Franz Boas has written:

The esoteric doctrine must, to a great extent, be considered as the product of individual thought. It expresses the reaction of the best minds in the community to the general cultural environment. It is their attempt to systematize the knowledge that underlies the culture of the community.... [I]t is the expression of thought of the exceptional mind. It is not the expression of thought of the masses.[80]

Although Robert drew upon the experiences of the entire cult and adapted many notions prevalent in the outside culture for his own use, he was not merely the passive compiler of group culture. His intellectual assumptions transformed the cultural elements he took from disparate sources, welding them into a unified whole. Process theology was a coherent structure of related concepts. Its basic pattern was the *transcendent duality*—the union of pairs of opposites defining the extremes of reality and brought together in theoretical reconciliation. For example, the cult existed beyond Good and Evil. Good is the opposite of Evil, yet neither can exist without the other. Thus, they define an essential duality. In cult theory, Good and Evil are similar in their equidistance from *blandness* (insignificance, meaninglessness). Good and Evil are united in their mutual opposition. The Process embraced both of them as living alternatives to the deadening average. One Process Precept states, "There is no alternative to opposition in this inevitably two-pole universe. The choice is between harmony and conflict." Robert believed opposites could be brought together in harmony. Another Precept states, "The awareness of a fundamental unity preserves harmony in a duality." In Hegelian terms, Good is the thesis, Evil the antithesis, and the Process is the transcendent synthesis beyond Good and Evil.[81] Perhaps this idea is impossible. But Robert believed it and made this principle the basis of his entire intellectual system. He saw himself as the great reconciler of opposites, the transcender of conflict, the Unifier.

Robert's *structural* orientation is very similar to the *structuralist* approach to anthropology of the French theorist Claude Lévi-Strauss. This analytic technique assumes that beneath the particulars of any cultural system lies a basic message concerning essential categories of thought usually arranged in pairs of dichotomous concepts. Lévi-Strauss claims to find dualities in mythologies, kinship structures, and practically everything else. French structuralism is an extremely controversial school of thought, attacked as pure mysticism by some anthropologists, ignored by most American sociologists. It is possible that Lévi-Strauss was completely mistaken in his analysis of Amazonian Indian myth, yet his system does seem to be the best for understanding the Process's theology. Therefore, I suspect that structuralism does properly apply to some cultural systems, perhaps those like the Process, created by minds similar to that of Lévi-Strauss. In his book *The Raw and the Cooked*, he responded to his critics:

If the final aim of anthropology is to contribute to a better knowledge of objectified thought and its mechanisms, it is in the last resort immaterial whether in this book the thought processes of the South American Indians take place through the medium of my thought, or whether mine takes place through the medium of theirs. What matters is that the human mind, regardless of the identity of those who happen to be giving it expression, should display an increasingly intelligible structure as a result of the doubly reflexive forward movement of two thought processes acting one upon the other, either of which can in turn provide the spark or tinder whose conjunction will shed light on both.[82]

This radical statement expresses three assumptions common to the thought of Lévi-Strauss and Robert de Grimston: (1) each believes he is capable of discovering the universal nature of the human mind; (2) the structure of the mind is a system of dualities; (3) the basic duality from which all wisdom flows is that between the theorist himself and other persons. For Lévi-Strauss the basic key to knowledge is the relationship *Lévi-Strauss:native*, while for Robert it is the relationship *Robert:Processean.*

Before we look at Robert's analysis of the relationships between the Gods, let us look at his conception of relations between people. Because the Gods were a projection of Robert's intimate personal relations, we should start with his analysis of the most important relationship in his life, his romantic bond to Mary Ann. He wrote that they were "extremists, the pair of us, and at opposite ends of every conceivable spectrum." In their early relationship, he continually sought to keep close to her, while she periodically tried to break off with him: "Life was always a contest for Mary Ann. There was always an opposition, an enemy—or a potential enemy—and if none showed itself, she created one." Thus, Robert's principle was *unification*, while in this respect hers was *separation*. This difference is not only in itself a dichotomy but also a disagreement concerning dichotomies. He wanted to unify opposites, she to separate them.

In an unpublished autobiographical sketch, Robert mentioned a second important dual relationship. He said two of his closest male friends became the first permanent converts to Compulsions Analysis. I believe he was talking about Father Joel and Father Micah. While Robert and his friends had the same class and cultural background, as Robert and Mary Ann did not, he said "three more utterly different characters it would be hard to find. They were at opposite ends of the universe from one another, and I was at the opposite end from both of them." The following adjectives describe Joel: quiet, conscientious, reliable, unadventurous, meticulous, predictable. The opposite adjectives describe Micah. "They were a strange pair," Robert says, "constantly at odds and yet drawn together by their very oppositeness—just as Mary Ann and I were." Robert believed Joel and Micah were not natural friends, however, and it was their common bond with him that really kept them together. "Neither of them thought much of Mary Ann," and she "was a threat to their masculinity." Figure 5 identifies Mary Ann with the mysterious letter X, while the three men are identified by the first letters of their names. A dashed line represents opposition, while a solid line represents connection. Figure 5a diagrams their relationships as two dualities, connected by Robert.

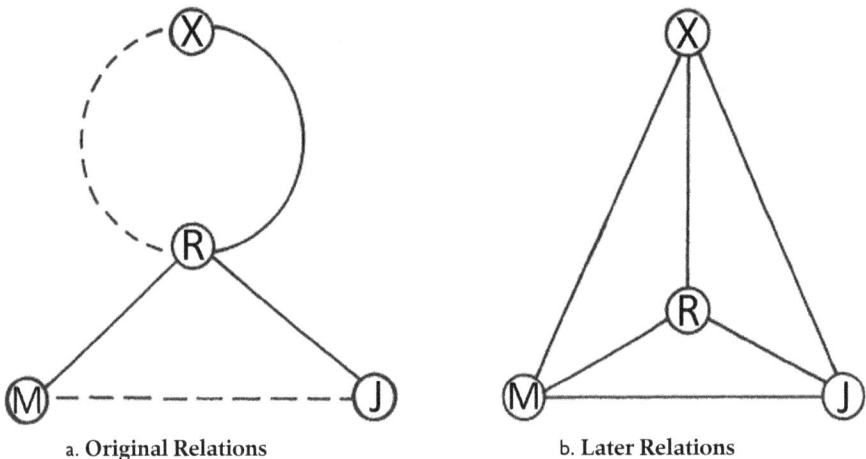

a. Original Relations   b. Later Relations

FIGURE 5. Structure of relationships among Robert and his associates.

Robert acted as the unifier in both dualities. In the duality *Robert:Mary Ann*, he was a partner to the opposition while working to unify it. In the duality *Micah:Joel*, he stood outside the opposition while working to unify it. These are the two possible positions of the unifier to an opposition; we can call them the *internal* position and the *external* position. Once all four were deeply involved in Compulsions Analysis, the "therapy" acted to produce strong positive bonds connecting all of them. The social structure then became that diagrammed in Figure 5b. It can be viewed as a three-dimensional tetrahedron in which four people are connected by six equal bonds.

Today it is possible to look back on the consequences of the Separation in which Robert was expelled from the organization which Mary Ann dominated, taking the culture with him. Initially, both Micah and Joel remained with Mary Ann in the Foundation, but before long Micah had left and became a creative Luciferian prophet using the name Timothy Wyllie. Joel remained in the Foundation and its successor non-religious, non-profit organization, following standard norms and thus Jehovian principles. Both, like Mary Ann, are now deceased, and in the absence of contrary data we must assume that Robert still lives.

In developing the cult's theological system, Robert used the same style of thinking outlined above. If we replace Joel with Jehovah, Micah with Lucifer, Mary Ann with Satan, and Robert with Christ, we get the basic system of Gods, which by 1974 was a single, unified structure. In the beginning there were two separate systems. The one I will call *System A* is composed of two dual relationships: *God versus Humanity* and *Christ versus Satan*. *System B* is composed of Jehovah, Lucifer, and Satan, arranged in two dualities.

SYSTEM A

God is the supreme being, incorporating all other beings and forms of being into a single entity, without limit and therefore beyond description or measurement. In its early years, the Process detached from and came into opposition with "the world," which Processeans called "Humanity." In *The Tide of the End*, Robert attacked Humanity and accused it of being opposed to God. Humanity is a snare of confining inhibitions, while God is limitless. Since God is perfect, He cannot exist in the imperfect world of Humanity, but stands outside time, a memory from the past and a hope for the future. Robert's scripture taught that God transcends all dimensions. BI-19 states, "This fundamental life force, which is GOD, is infinitely small and has infinite scope. This is the basic nature of the two-pole universe; zero and infinity; nothing and everything. GOD is a non-existence with awareness of all existence."

Humanity exists in the here and now but will soon cease to exist, Robert said. One section of *The Tide of the End* explains, "The tide is now destruction, by God's will; to go against it is to go against God." The duality between God and Humanity is the basic alternative. "And our choice is to include GOD or to exclude GOD. To acknowledge GOD or to reject GOD. To see GOD or to be blind to GOD. To know GOD or to be ignorant of GOD. To worship GOD or to defy GOD." In early cult writings, Humanity is also called the unGod, and is represented by the symbolic figure John Grey. He is the stereotypical, bland, spiritless, modern man. Among several Process "Chants of the unGod" is one which is simply the phrase "living death" repeated over and over. Another chant proclaims, "John Grey's code is hypocrisy, mediocrity, blasphemy." Another asks a profound question, then gives its own answer: "Where are you going? What are you knowing? Can you feel your death? . . . Devoted to the unGod, facing the End. He is chained to Death."

In Robert's book *Humanity Is the Devil*, God spoke to man, saying: "Follow in your heart the concept of evil, and you will go further and further from Me. For though I have created evil for your choice, evil is not of Me; it is of Satan, who is the Devil, and must for you be the Enemy so that you do not follow Him. For the path of evil will lead you to the Devil and you will find yourself in Hell." This is a traditional kind of statement. Satan is the enemy of God although He was created by God. But, according to the Process, because we are entering the Latter Days, nearing the End, there has been a radical change: "Satan is free, for His work is done. Satan is no longer the Devil, for He has passed the poison on to that which chose to take it and become it. Now there is nothing more evil in the Universe than man. His World is Hell, and he himself the Devil." The "burden of negativity," which it had been Satan's task to bear, has now been bequeathed to Humanity.

Similarly, God has bequeathed his own task to Christ. The Process believed that "God is love" and that God so loved man that He sent His only begotten Son, Christ, into the world. Christ, whether identified with Jesus or de Grimston, was a gift of love given from love. So the "blessing of positivity" that had been God's property is now carried by Christ. The relationships among God, Humanity, Christ, and Satan are diagrammed in Figure 6a.

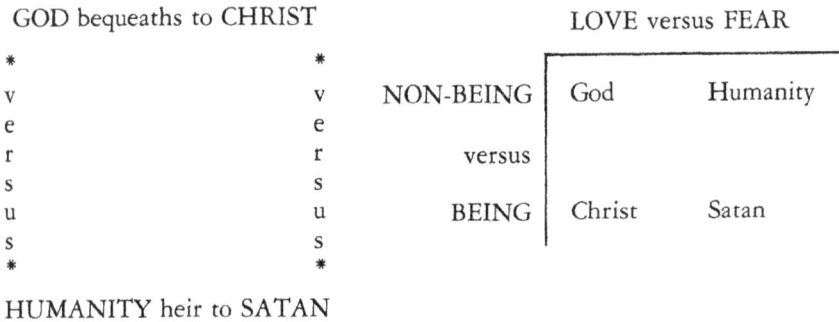

GOD bequeaths to CHRIST   LOVE versus FEAR

			God	Humanity
*	*	NON-BEING		
v	v			
e	e	versus		
r	r			
s	s	BEING	Christ	Satan
u	u			
s	s			
*	*			

HUMANITY heir to SATAN

FIGURE 6. **Structure of System A.**

   6a. **First Analysis**   6b. **Second Analysis**

In his book *The Two Pole Universe*, Robert stated the social-psychological basis of his theory that all reality can be interpreted as the intersection of pairs of polar opposites. Christ is Unification, Satan is Separation, and the sources of these opposing principles can be found in the emotions Love and Fear. "So there is Love and there is Fear. And Love and Fear are opposites—and more than opposites, for Love and Fear are the two poles of the mind. They are the root of the conflict that divided the mind. They are the fundamental dichotomy, the very core of the struggle that rages within every human being. The battle between these two is the source of all human anguish, all pain, all suffering. All disaster stems from the conflict between Love and Fear." Although opposed to each other, in this world Love and Fear cannot exist apart from each other. If we love someone, then we must fear to lose them. We cannot fear unless there exists something we love and are afraid of losing. Love and Fear, like Christ and Satan, and like God and Humanity, "are two sides of one coin."

The two dualities of System A can be expressed as the intersection of two dichotomous variables: Love and Fear, Being and Non-Being. Christ and Satan are modes of being, styles of social relation. Christ is coexistence with another individual in a state of unification; Satan is solitary existence in a state of separation. God and Humanity are states of non-being, states in which a person has lost all individual strength, consciousness, and identity. The Process fled Humanity but has not yet achieved God. Incorporation into a fully realized God is a mode of positive non-being—pleasurable, womblike, loving. Humanity is a mode of negative non-being—painful, dispersive, meaningless. In *The Gods on War*, Robert answered the question, "What is GOD?," explaining that "God and Anti-God are embodied in Christ and Satan." The pair of contending spirits, Christ and Satan, act directly in the world. They are embodied, immanent. Figure 6b diagrams this intellectual structure.

The relationships among these terms can be compared to Robert's personal social relationships and expressed as formal analogies of the type: *a:b::y:z* (*a* is to *b* as *y* is to *z*). On the concrete level, the social origins of the four entities are as follows:

God:Humanity::Processeans:Outsiders
Christ:Satan::Robert:Mary Ann

We can state the same conceptualization on a more abstract level:

God:Humanity::we:they
Christ:Satan::I:Thou

In the Process's system of thinking, the relationship *a:b* is one of *both* separation and unity. In October 1975, Robert wrote, "One of the basic tenets of The Process has always been the reconciliation of opposites. Emotionally and psychologically, this means the resolution of mental conflict. Spiritually, it means the harmonizing of opposing cosmic forces."

SYSTEM B

In December 1967, Robert introduced the Three Great Gods of the Universe—Jehovah, Lucifer, and Satan—in a brief essay, *The Hierarchy*: the Gods "represent three basic human patterns of reality," and "each one represents a fundamental problem." Conversely, each "God" can be seen as a basic perspective on the best way to live, or, in the terms of Lofland and Stark, a "problem-solving perspective." Collectively, the three Gods constitute a psychological theory of personality. Each God is a type of person, an attitude toward relations with others, and a cosmic principle.

> JEHOVAH, the wrathful God of vengeance and retribution, demands discipline, courage and ruthlessness and a single-minded dedication to duty, purity, and self-denial. All of us feel those demands to a degree, some more strongly than others.
> LUCIFER, the Light Bearer, urges us to enjoy life to the full, to value success in human terms, to be gentle and kind and loving, and to live in peace and harmony with one another. Man's apparent inability to value success without descending into greed, jealousy, and an exaggerated sense of his own importance has brought the God LUCIFER into disrepute. He has become mistakenly identified with SATAN.
> SATAN, the receiver of transcendent souls and corrupted bodies, instills in us two directly opposite qualities: at one end, an urge to rise above all human and physical needs and appetites, to become all soul and no body, all spirit and no mind; and, at the other end, a desire to sink BENEATH all human codes of

behavior and to wallow in a morass of violence, lunacy, and excessive physical indulgence. But it is the lower end of SATAN'S nature that men fear, which is why SATAN, by whatever name, is seen as the Adversary.

The origin of *System B* can be traced from the basic separations *God:Anti-God* and *Processeans:Outsiders* produced in the social implosion of 1965-1966. *System B* evolved as an attempt by Robert to understand his own social relations within the group, so all the elements are good, pro-cult Gods. In a way, the Great Gods are the endpoints of the Adlerian analysis, compulsive archetypes and ultimate goals.

When the God of Nature appeared at Xtul, Mary Ann called Him Jehovah. He was Mary Ann's God. It was she who demanded firm dedication to duty. She had long admired Jehovah, was a vocal fan of Israel, and had gone so far in her Jehovian devotion to have twin wedding rings made for Robert and herself that bore the Star of David, Jehovah's symbol. Robert remarked to me that the points of the star dug into the flesh of his finger. Robert did not like Jehovah, but for a while Jehovah was identified as God.

Many of Robert's values were opposed to Jehovah's commandments. He wanted sensuous liberation, experimentation. Jehovah's law, represented by Mary Ann and by the Old Testament of the Bible, said these urges of Robert's were un-Godly. As an intellectual strategy to strengthen his own position, Robert postulated the existence of another God beside Jehovah. He chose the name Lucifer. He had run across biblical commentaries which noted that Lucifer and Satan were not the same, wrongly confounded by such theologians as St. Jerome. Jehovah, as is well known, is a jealous God. In order to be accepted as the one true God, Jehovah had to discredit His chief rival, Lucifer, so He spread false propaganda that Lucifer and Satan were the same.

At this point in its development, *System B* is of three elements: God in two equal but opposite parts (Jehovah and Lucifer) and a residue that is not included in either and remains Anti-God. But Robert observed that two parts of this residue were antagonistic to Humanity, a mystical part and a ferocious part. Separated from Humanity, they also must be parts of God. In *System A*, Satan was identified with separation, so it was a simple step to name these two other elements of God after Satan. If God exists in three parts, why did He so divide Himself? Why do all the interlinked dualities of polar opposites exist? In BI-13, Robert wrote, "The answer is: 'the game.' ... The game is conflict; creating and destroying, building and demolishing, separating and coming together, rising and falling, disintegrating and reuniting, failing and succeeding, living and dying, winning and losing, loving and hating. That is the game, and the game is the essence of existence." Without the Game, without separation, there would exist no universe.

Satan, separation, is therefore the most creative and active part of God, even though Satan is also destructive. Satan, like all beings, is subject to the Universal Law, most basic of Process causal principles, which states, "As you give, so shall you receive." This sounds like a restatement of the Golden Rule, but it is not really a moral commandment. It is a magical, Newtonian principle, as Robert stated in BI-31, "The Universal Law works on the basis of reflection. Every action brings about an equal and opposite reaction. Whether there is conflict or harmony, there is always opposition." Thus, the Universal Law is a dynamic extension of Robert's key concept of duality. It stresses the absolute importance for him of personal relations, claiming that nothing can be lost in the process of social interaction, postulating a perfectly moral universe. In BI-7, he wrote, "The principle of self-judgement is this: a person may accurately judge what he gives, by what he receives."

In two manuscripts, Robert explains how this applies to Satan: "Satanists separate. Therefore, by the Universal Law, they are separated." "Due to its propensity for division, separation, and differentiation—apparent on all levels both positive and negative—the Satanic line is characteristically divided! The Universal Law: divide and you are divided." This explains why Satan continually plays a double role; He takes part in *System A* and *System B*. In *System B*, He is divided into two aspects. As separation, Satan draws His opposite, Christ (the spirit of unification), into the system of the three Gods. A Process Precept states, "Whatever you demand, expect the opposite." Since nothing can exist without its polar opposite to define it, Robert's theory introduces Christ into *System B* to balance Satan.

Before about 1970, Christ was not described as one of the Gods but as a being of another kind: "Christ is the Unifier. He brings together all the patterns of the Gods, and resolves them into One. He is the Emissary of the Gods upon earth; Their link with men, by which men have the opportunity to know and understand Them." In Figure 7a, I show one way Processeans often diagrammed Christ and the Gods. Lucifer is the polar opposite of Jehovah. Satan contains in His separation two opposite aspects. These dualities are graphed at right angles to each other, forming a cross. Christ is nailed to the cross, at the center, stapling the extremes together.

Relationship of Mediator

INTERNAL   EXTERNAL

```
              SATAN                    M   C      CHRIST        JEHOVAH
                *                      E   H      versus        versus
                C                      D   R      SATAN         LUCIFER
                H                      I   I
     LUCIFER* R *JEHOVAH              A   S
                I                      T   T
                S                      O   R      ROBERT        JOEL
                T                      R   O      versus        versus
                *                          B      MARY ANN      MICAH
              SATAN                         E
                                           R
                                           T
```

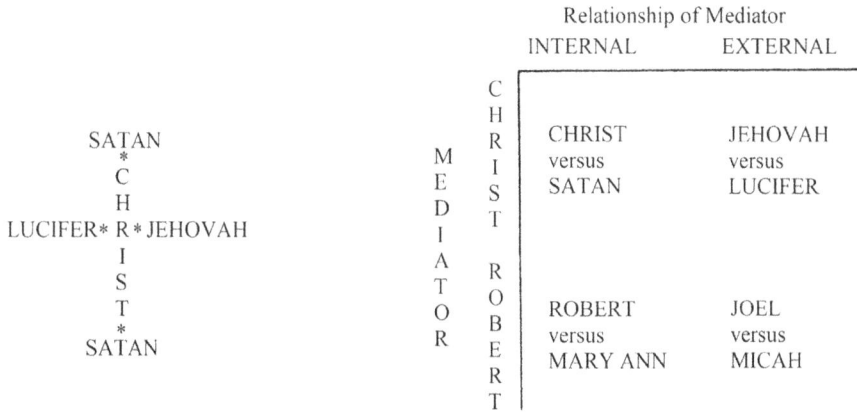

FIGURE 7. **Structure of System B.**

7a. **The Cross of the Gods**   7b. **Mediators to the Disputes**

We can analyze the relationships of Christ and Robert to the theological and social structures, demonstrating that they are parallel. Recall my distinction between two positions an actor may hold with respect to a dispute: *internal* (a party to it) and *external* (outside but connected to it). Figure 7b compares Christ's relations to the three Gods with Robert's relations to his three intimate associates. Each is external to one dispute and internal to the other. Each tries to mediate both. Not merely the forms, but also the contents of the two structures are identical. Micah was Lucifer, Joel was Jehovah. Mary Ann was Satan. Micah and Joel represented two opposite styles of dwelling within respectable society. Lucifer and Jehovah were two basic Human alternatives. Mary Ann, in her intense fickleness, scintillated outside the bounds of conventional society. At times Robert felt she was spiritually superior to average people; at other times he felt she was carnally inferior. Satan, also, has two aspects, one super-Human, the other sub-Human. Table 4 lists some of the qualities associated with the Gods and therefore also descriptive of the people who followed each of the cosmic principles.

Satan (Lower Aspect)	Lucifer	Jehovah	Satan (Higher Aspect)
Lust	Enjoyment	Duty	Detachment
Abandon	Permissiveness	Discipline	Mysticism
Violence	Harmony	Struggle	Otherworldliness
Excess	Success	Sacrifice	Magic
Indulgence	Satisfaction	Self-denial	Asceticism

TABLE 4. **Words Describing the Three Gods and Their People**

ROBERT'S CULTURE ENGINE

As the years passed, Robert's system of dualities expanded into an immense intellectual structure explained in a thousand pages of scripture, providing a complex interpretive scheme. Supported by emblems, symbolic rituals, therapy exercises, and day-to-day customs, it evolved into a rich and ornate culture. There was no clearly marked stopping point at which Robert might decide he had invented enough. The assumptions and social reality that lay at the base of his creativity demanded the unceasing production of new ideas. The creative configuration that Robert worked within was what I call a *culture engine*.

Any social-psychological situation that automatically and perpetually generates new elements of culture is a culture engine. There may be many kinds, but I have seen innumerable examples of one specific variety in my studies of magical and psychotherapeutic cults: the *compulsive striving* engine. Robert's unremitting struggle to resolve human conflicts through an analytic system based on polar opposites is one example. In the compulsive striving culture engine, an individual or group commits itself irrevocably to the accomplishment of impossible goals with insufficient means.

Rather than abandon either goals or means, a person gripped by such compulsive striving continually seeks to improve the means. Robert kept inventing new dichotomies. Many cult founders held status in their communities because of the culture they had already produced, so they usually could not risk abandoning old ideas and assumptions while they added new ones. Consequently, such systems grow steadily. A necessary step in the culture-manufacturing process is the testing of the old ideas against reality and the discovery that they are not yet perfect. If de Grimston had been entirely cut off from reality-testing, he would not have continued working. Each cultic theoretical system grew because it was continually being applied and found to be insufficient.

The theory of the Gods was intended as a cosmic theory of personality. Each human being was supposed to be closer to one of the Gods than to the others, to manifest one of the patterns as an extension of its God. In the *Fear* and *Death* issues of the magazine, individual cult members wrote as advocates for one or another God. Joshua and Christian were advocates for Jehovah; Eden and Lars represented Lucifer; Seraphine and Malachi spoke for Satan. Robert himself expressed the Christ spirit, in his Christ-like appearance as well as his words. Every older Processean recognized a special tie to one of the

Gods, and members often discussed each other's *God patterns*, considering them useful analyses of personality style.

Brother Lot was a Satanic Processean. He once explained to me that Satan had given him the power to find lost objects psychically. That day he had found a tarnished silver object; another time he had located a lost hammer. He was particularly successful in finding missing Mendes Goat badges. How does he do it? First, he calls upon Satan to help him. The other Gods are of no use. Then he gets a picture of the lost object in his mind and tries to feel where it is. Satan comes and leads Lot to the missing article. Lot held his hands up on either side of his head while explaining this procedure, extending his fingers to simulate Satanic horns. Satan uses his horns like antennas to radar-out the lost object.

Brother Thomas was a Luciferian. In March 1971, he read a short poem about Lucifer in a Process play dramatic show: "Bringer of purpose to ease the despair, bringer of joy to ease the pain, bringer of Light to ease the Darkness, come, Lord Lucifer, come." Sister Roxana was also a Luciferian: "I know that he doesn't exist as an anthropomorphic entity or as a person. To me, Lucifer is a name for a whole presence, a whole force, everything that Beauty is, everything that Poetry is."

In the original edition of this ethnography, I referred to Eden as Palestine, selecting this pseudonym via the metaphor that each described a Holy Land. Yet, the *Death* issue of the magazine, currently available in a collection published by Feral House, shows a photograph of him beside a dog with the caption "Eden Advocate for Lucifer." As it happens, I do not know his secular identity or his subsequent history within the Process or Foundation. It is even possible he appears elsewhere in this book with a different pseudonym. Thus, the name Eden is public yet preserves his privacy. His brief scripture in the *Death* issue emphasizes the personal transcendence postulated by Luciferians, beginning:

> Lucifer is the God of Rebirth and Immortality: have faith in yourself, in your undying spirit, most of all in your immortality. This is what matters: that in the end, you are infinite: in GOD you are Infinite. For you, there is no death without rebirth. Death is the gate to life. And no man passes through the gate, but he reaches the other side. Before death is birth, and after death is rebirth. In your death you will be reborn.

Later in the *Death* issue, we see another photo of Eden, this time without a dog, on the page identifying the magazine's editorial staff and reporting his responsibility was art and photography. He appears right next to a photo of Micah, described as art and design director, which implies they worked together. Decades later, in the autobiography he published with Feral House, Timothy "Micah" Wyllie said Eden was "a young German photographer" and: "He was brilliantly inventive and many of the more exceptional visual effects were due to his pioneering experimentation in the darkroom."[83] We must wonder what forms of Luciferian experimentation Eden performed over the following years or lifetimes.

These examples are very poetic themselves, artistic and occult rather than practical. Of course, the number and intensity of human conflicts within the cult did not decrease merely because of the introduction of the theory of Gods. It permitted many kinds of aesthetic expression but was not effective in controlling or transforming social life. Robert's compulsive, intellectual response was to invent more dualities.

About 1971, Christ was promoted from the emissary of the Gods to the status of a fourth God, representing a fourth basic personality pattern. In promoting Christ, Robert sought to promote himself. As we already mentioned, in 1970 Robert attempted to give Lucifer dominance over the previously dominant Jehovah in determining the style of the cult. Both Christ and Lucifer were Robert's deities, while Jehovah and Satan belonged to Mary Ann. In BI-34 and a pair of unpublished manuscripts written in 1971, Robert explored the dual relationships among these four entities. The duality *Jehovah:Lucifer* described two alternate social approaches to human life, rather similar to the *Apollonian:Dionysian* dichotomy of Nietzsche, or the familiar *cold:hot, rigid:flexible, conservative:liberal* dichotomies of common language.[84] The struggle between the two was called "the Conflict of the Mind," and their duality was of the mind. The spiritual conflict between Christ and Satan categorized theirs as the "ex-mind" duality. Having noted that no one fit a single God pattern perfectly, and having seen that the original system of patterns did not solve all problems, Robert decided that each person possessed a *combination pattern*. Each person was close to one polar opposite in each pair: Jehovah or Lucifer and Christ or Satan. His own combination pattern was Luciferian-Christian, while Mary Ann's was Jehovian-Satanic.

Processeans did in fact adopt the new combination patterns as their universal personality theory, although it was not more successful in influencing social reality than the old theory. The four types were usually named by their initials: Jehovian-Satanic (JS), Jehovian-Christian (JC), Luciferian-Satanic (LS), and Luciferian-Christian (LC). As part of my field research on the 1975 Waltham, Massachusetts, chapter of the cult, I asked members of the commune to list each person's pattern. Table 5 shows the distribution and demonstrates that Processeans were able to apply the categories to all kinds of people and even animals.

TYPE	MEN	WOMEN	CHILDREN	ANIMALS	TOTAL
Jehovian-Satanic	6	3	0	5	14
Jehovian-Christian	4	1	0	0	5
Luciferian-Satanic	3	2	0	1	6
Luciferian-Christian	2	2	1	1	6
Total	15	8	1	7	31

TABLE 5. **God Patterns of the Waltham Commune**

In its magazine, the cult published three different questionnaires designed to uncover the reader's God pattern. To test their utility, I asked students in my social-psychology class at Wellesley College to administer the longest cult questionnaire to members of the college community. Each of its nineteen questions had four possible answers, one for each of the God patterns. For example, the first was: "Whom do you identify with? a) Adam (Jehovian); b) Eve (Luciferian); c) The Serpent (Satanic); d) A fourth party eager to patch things up and please everyone (Christian)." Another question was: "Where do you most like to make love? a) Under the bedclothes and in the dark (Jehovian); b) At a Bacchanalian blast-off (Satanic); c) In a gentle summer blowing meadow (Luciferian); d) Wherever your partner prefers (Christian)." The forty-four questionnaires were coded in terms of which God had the most responses on each and which God had the second greatest number.

Mother Morgana predicted that the Wellesley respondents would tend to be Luciferian-Christian, intelligent and dutiful young college women that they were. If we assume that individuals' combination patterns would emerge as the Gods that scored first and second on each questionnaire, then we can test

Morgana's hypothesis and also Robert's hypothesis that two patterns, the Jehovian-Luciferian (JL) and Satanic-Christian (SC), do not exist. The results, shown in Table 6, support Morgana but do not support Robert, since the LC pattern is most common, but the SC and JL patterns also appear, which were excluded from Process theology, and four cases had ties in the ranking of "Gods."

TYPE	NUMBER	PERCENT
Orthodox:		
Jehovian-Satanic	1	2%
Jehovian-Christian	6	14%
Luciferian-Satanic	3	7%
Luciferian-Christian	21	48%
Unorthodox:		
Jehovian-Luciferian	2	5%
Satanic-Christian	7	16%
Ties in ranking of Gods	4	9%
Total	44	100%

TABLE 6. God Patterns from the Wellesley Questionnaire

The Process did not use its questionnaires to discover members' patterns but merely as diversions for the magazine readers. Members would discuss their personalities with each other and with their superiors in the cult, would interact and observe themselves, and gradually decide what patterns they were. Sometimes there was disagreement. I myself decided my pattern was Luciferian-Satanic, and several of my cultic friends agreed. However, Mother Rebekah, Mother Morgana, and Robert de Grimston were all convinced my true pattern was Luciferian-Christian.

Sister Norma explained to me that "the LS pattern is just about the hardest to pick out anyway, because LSs are so good at disguising themselves." Norma is an LS and felt sure I was not one but an LC. However, she agreed it was hard to tell. "For the longest time everybody thought I was an LC because I acted like such a victim before I became a Messenger. They realized in New York, finally, that I wasn't an LC, and I looked at them all and I said, 'What? I'm not an LC? All this time everybody was telling me I was crucifying myself! I'm not an LC?' And they said, 'Mm-mm. Awfully good image, kid, but you can't fool us.' I guess it takes an LS to see an LS. It was Seraphine that told me I was an LS, and Rebekah agreed with her. In Boston, at first they were convinced I was a JC, and then I turned out to be an LC." If we can believe the experts, Seraphine and Norma were LSs, while Rebekah and I were LCs.

The dualities proliferated and became ever more interconnected. Perhaps because Mary Ann's pattern was JS while Robert's was LC, Jehovah and Satan came to be described as female deities while Lucifer and Christ were male. The basic dichotomy refused to be transcended. Building on some ideas dating from 1968, Robert decided that every pattern had a top end and a bottom end, not just the Satanic: "On the bottom levels, all the patterns are destructive and negative and oriented towards death. And on the top levels, we are positive and life-oriented. At the top, our effects on others are positive; and on the bottom, our effects on others are negative." According to a training document, one can identify lower-end patterns of the four basic types by a few descriptive words, as shown in Table 7.

Jehovian	Luciferian	Christian	Satanic
Cruel	Sentimentality	Compulsive-Responsibility	Lust
Arrogant	Self-Pity	Masochism	Abandon
Self-righteous	Sloth	Feeling weak	Violence
Blameful Bullying	Justification	Ineffectiveness	Excess Indulgence

TABLE 7. **Words Describing the Lower-End Patterns**

When the God pattern doctrine had evolved to the point at which all four patterns had upper and lower aspects, then the structure of the Gods was no longer a configuration of canted triangles, perhaps a tetrahedron as in Figure 5b, but more accurately a cube formed by the intersection of three dualities: *Jehovah:Lucifer, Christ:Satan, Higher:Lower.* Human personalities could be graphed as the four side faces of the cube; for example, the LS personality shared by such people as Seraphine, Norma, and Ariel would be represented by the right-hand face of the cube shown in Figure 8. Its four corners represent Lucifer High (LH), Lucifer Low (LL), Satan High (SH) and Satan Low (SL).

The new theological system was expected to work better in daily applications. It explained changes in a person's mood as temporary movements across the face of the cube that graphed his pattern. But it was no more successful in actually solving human problems and had the disadvantage of intellectual complexity. Robert's response, incomplete because he was

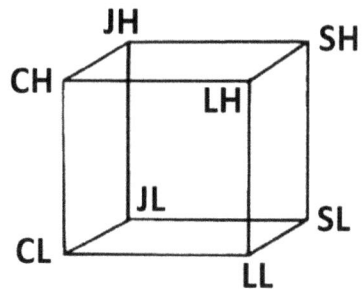

FIGURE 8. **Cubic structure of the combination patterns.**

expelled from his own cult in 1974, was to invent subtypes within each of these. As usual, the first type to split was the Satanic. In slang developed by Robert and Mary Ann, Lower-End Satanists came to be called Goats, and Upper-End Satanists were Snerps (serpents). Then dichotomies were discovered within Snerps and Goats.

The system also ramified into a collection of four-element symbolic structures, some formally adopted by the Process, others merely toyed with by various members. Table 8 shows some of these symbolic tetrads. Color symbolism varied over the years, and the four handicaps were never more than a speculation that interested the Omega. Robert described his method of structural analysis and its struggle to arrange the chaos of human experience in simple categories: "It's rather like unraveling a ball of wool after a playful kitten has been at it. Or perhaps a better analogy is sorting a shuffled pack of playing cards into different suits."

God	Element	Color I	Color II	Handicap	Season	Direction
Jehovah	Earth	Black	Gold	Blind	Winter	North
Lucifer	Air	Blue	Sky Blue	Deaf	Summer	South
Satan	Fire	Red	Bright Scarlet	Dumb	Fall	West
Christ	Water	White	Gray	Lame	Spring	East

TABLE 8. The Gods and Their Symbols

The structural evolution of Robert's system followed exactly a general principle stated by Lévi-Strauss: "A four-section system can be explained only as the sociological process of integration of a double dualism (without the one being necessarily historically anterior to the other), and the eight-section system as a reduplication of the same process."

PROCESS SYMBOLS 1965–1973

The Process used several different emblems or symbols over the years, all having a dual nature. The last two symbols are discussed in chapter 10; here we will discuss six earlier emblems. The first Process Sign, invented by Mother Cassandra in London, is shown in Figure 9a. It represents the letter "P" for *Process*, seen from the four cardinal directions, and expresses the idea that the Process brings together people of very different perspectives for a common purpose. Sometime after its invention, Robert redesigned the Process Sign, giving it flair and elegance. The improved version, shown in Figure 9b, possesses, Robert says, "an ecclesiastical and mathematical flavor." The first version looks rather like a Nazi swastika, while the second is reminiscent of the Iron Cross also associated with the German war machine and worn proudly by American motorcycle gangs. One newcomer in 1971 saw Robert's version as the trumpets of the four Gods. These interpretations were not entirely frivolous. I am sure part of the appeal, intended and unintended, of the Process Sign was its power to suggest meanings.

FIGURE 9a. **Cassandra's Process sign**   FIGURE 9b. **Robert's Process sign**

When Processeans first began presenting themselves as a "church," in New Orleans around 1967, they wore Christian crosses, and as the concept of Satan emerged the following year they decided to add a symbol for Satan. The best-known image of Satan is the famous illustration by Eliphas Levi of "the Sabbatic Goat" in his nineteenth-century occult book *Transcendental Magic*.[85] This picture has been frequently reproduced, and my collection of Process artifacts included two paintings of Satan based on it. The Badge of Mendes worn by Processeans consisted of a black triangle, point downward, bearing the head of Levi's goat in red. The face is half-man, half-goat. Between the two spreading horns is a crown, while the forehead is imprinted with a magical pentagram.

FIGURE 9c. **The Christian cross**

FIGURE 9d. **The Satanic goat**

The Cross and the Goat, shown in Figures 9c and 9d, always went together but were always kept physically separate—for example, at opposite ends of the Alpha ritual room or at separate points on the Processeans' uniforms.

Robert invented another symbol, the Sign of Union, shortly after redesigning the Process Sign. Shown in Figure 9e, it is a combination of the Alpha and the Omega, first and last letters of the Greek alphabet. Three times in the Book of Revelation (1:8, 21:6, and 22:13), God speaks and uses these letters to describe himself: "I am Alpha and Omega, the beginning and the ending, saith the Lord, which is, and which was, and which is to come, the Almighty." The ritual room of any Process chapter was called the Alpha, while the supreme leadership was called the Omega; as steps in a hierarchy, they were the beginning and the ending.

The Sign of Union is also a sexual symbol. In the Sabbath Assembly, the Sacrifist, who wears the Sign of Union on his chest, asks, "What is the Sign of the End and the New Beginning?" A member of the congregation is supposed to reply, "The Sign of Union." "Whose is the Union?" the Sacrifist asks. The

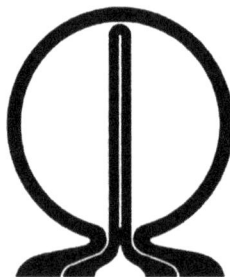

FIGURE 9e. **The Sign of Union**

FIGURE 9f. **The Unity cross**

reply is: "The Union of the Lord Jehovah and the Lord Lucifer." The Sign represents the *marriage* of Jehovah (female) and Lucifer (male), extensions of Mary Ann and Robert. The Process's marriage ritual is called the Union Ceremony. Married couples are "joined in union." The cover of a cult booklet about marriage carries the Sign of Union. The round outer part of the emblem is an Omega representing the womb of Jehovah. The elongated, inner part of the emblem is an Alpha representing the phallus of Lucifer. The Sign of Union depicts the copulation of these two Gods, their coming together as erotic opposites that can only be fulfilled together. Rank-and-file members of the cult were completely unaware of this meaning. High-status members confirmed my conjecture that this was the proper interpretation of the Sign of Union.

The last symbol introduced in the classical years of the Process was the Unity Cross, shown in Figure 9f. It is a simple, large Christian cross, silver in color, bearing a red serpent, a new symbol of Satan. In 1972, it replaced two separate symbols, the Cross and the Goat, marking a major theological step in the progressive unity of Christ and Satan. As we mentioned a few pages earlier, Robert had just conceived of two types of Satanists, the violent Goats and the mystical Snerps (serpents). The use of a serpent on the Unity Cross signified a transformation of Satan, or at least a change in emphasis, with Satan's more mystical side dominating in His unity with Christ. Members of Disciple, Messenger, and IP rank were given little Unity Crosses to wear around their necks, made of chrome-plated steel bearing a red serpent decal. Masters of the church wore Unity Crosses on which the serpent was yellow rather than red in color. Not only does the Unity Cross represent a duality, *Christ:Satan,* but it attempts to symbolize the coming ever closer together of the two halves of the duality.

SABBATH ASSEMBLY SYMBOLISM

Process symbolism received clearest physical expression in the Sabbath Assembly. This ceremony, dramatizing the cult's dualisms, changed during the period when the cult struggled to accommodate itself to the world. The weekly Sabbath Assembly, usually held early Saturday evening, was the chief ritual gathering of all members of the cult. It was this ritual, before all others, that expressed the basic premises of the cult to its members and registered alterations in these fundamental assumptions.

Figure 10 shows the layout of the Sabbath Assembly as it was performed in the spring of 1971. Two priests presided over the Sabbath, a Sacrifist (S) and an Evangelist (E). After the congregation was seated, they would march into the Alpha, accompanied by two other Processeans carrying sacred bowls, the Fire Bearer (F) and the Water Bearer (W) in a grand procession. The ritual would last between an hour and an hour and a half; then the priests would march out. It was as if the priests brought sacredness into the social gathering, expressed it, then carried it out with them again. Except for newcomers and Initiates, all participants wore black clothing. The only light came from flickering candles and the flame rising from the bowl of fire. The air was hot, filled with incense, an atmosphere either stifling or psychedelic, depending on the degree of one's involvement in the cult.

The congregation sat on cushions placed in a large oval pattern on the floor, represented in the figure by circles. Everyone faced inward, toward the circular altar at the center. Their backs were to the outside. The windows were covered. All attention was focused inward, and the outside world was ignored. The Sacrifist and Evangelist sat facing each other from opposite ends of the

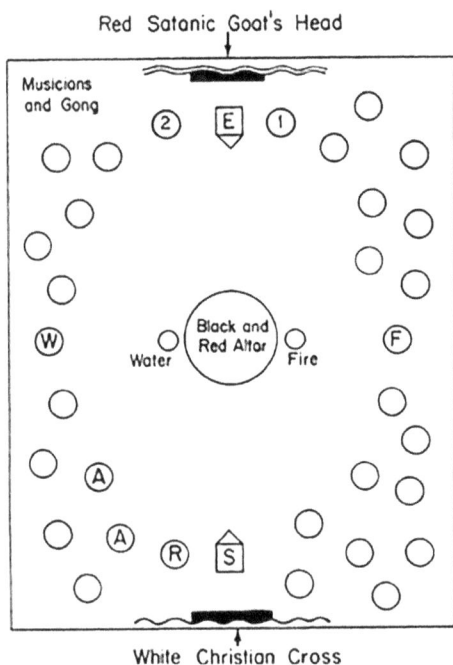

FIGURE 10. **Layout of the Sabbath Assembly, Spring 1971**

congregation. They were raised up from the group, seated on crude chairs made from tongue-and-groove floor planking, yet sat within the group. They belonged to the group, expressing qualities of the group, rather than being religious professionals who acted upon the group from outside. Two Responders sat either side of the Evangelist, (1) and (2) in the diagram, while a Reader of Scripture (R) sat beside the Sacrifist and Acolytes (A), who would be promoted to Initiates, were near them.

Over their black robes, the two priests wore tabards. The Sacrifist's tabard was purple and carried a circular emblem over the chest: the Sign of Union in gold on a black background. The Evangelist's tabard was scarlet and bore a different emblem: the Process Sign in silver on a black background. Behind the Sacrifist, a dark purple curtain hung on the wall. On it was placed a white Christian cross, about a yard high, made from stiff cardboard and painted in an ornate design. Behind the Evangelist hung a black curtain, carrying a red Mendes Goat head.

Most of the service was conducted by the Sacrifist. It was he who engaged the congregation in recitation, he who twice blessed the group, and he who performed initiations. The mood of the Sacrifist was restrained, controlling. The main duty of the Evangelist was the emotional sermon, the Revelation that came near the end of the service. It was free-flowing, in contrast to the studied composition of the rest of the Sabbath, and roused the feelings of newcomers to come forward and join the cult. Both priests carried black bound Missals bearing the Process Sign in red on their covers. These books contained all the cult's teachings, as well as the formats of the rituals. The Sacrifist read frequently from his Missal. The only use the Evangelist made of his book was when, at two points in the service, both priests recited the Declaration, alternating phrases. We quoted this important doctrinal statement in chapter 1. It announces the coming Unity of Christ and Satan: "The Lamb and the Goat, Pure Love descended from the pinnacle of Heaven, united with pure Hatred raised from the depths of Hell."

The symbolism of the Sabbath is all concerned with *The Process*, in the theological as well as the social sense of the name. It represents the dual relationships among the Gods, particularly the Unity of Christ and Satan, and the process by which they are coming together for "an End and a New Beginning." The Sacrifist represents Christ; the Evangelist represents Satan. They come from opposite ends of the universe, sit at opposite ends of the congregation, but work together for the common purpose. They divide the labor between them, according to their personalities.

The altar at the center was black and red, the original colors of the cult. Circular, with a glass top, it carried the Process Sign at the center. Candles were placed at the four corners of the sign. It was the focus of the circle and of all interactions between the Sacrifist and Evangelist, representing the purpose and social focus of the cult, the joining together of all beings, all principles, for the transcending of all differences and the realization of God.

It is interesting to note the spatial location of the Gods in the ritual. There were no prayers to a distant deity. At no point did a priest speak to any lord located outside the circle. There was a moment in the Evening Assembly, held for Messengers and IPs only, which stated precisely the location of the Gods: " ... to the Gods who are within us ... " The layout of the Assemblies clearly assumed that the Gods were indeed within the congregation. At one point in the ritual, the Sacrifist interacted with two Responders who stated the natures of Jehovah, Lucifer, Satan, and Christ. At another point, a Member of the Brethren read a passage from cult scripture. They spoke in essence about themselves, reciting interpretations of their social reality while remaining seated within the congregation. Acolytes to be initiated sat in the circle, like all other Brethren, except for the moment of initiation when they briefly knelt before the Sacrifist.

Although the main axis of the Sabbath is the line from the Sacrifist through the altar to the Evangelist, there is a secondary axis at a right angle to it. The altar was flanked by two identical stands, each a little over three feet high. During rituals they supported the ritual bowls, one filled with water to symbolize Christ, the other producing fire to symbolize Satan. The original idea for these stands undoubtedly comes from the Biblical description of the two brass columns made by Solomon for his great temple.[86] One was called *Jachin* ("He shall establish") and the other, *Boaz* ("In it is strength"), according to the Bible. Lewis Spence wrote that in Kabalistic tradition, the two were supposed "to explain all mysteries." The two columns symbolized the concept of duality: "The one was black and the other white, and they represented the powers of good and evil. It is said that they symbolize the need of 'two' in the world: Human equilibrium requires two feet; the worlds gravitate by means of two forces; generation needs two sexes."[87] This was, of course, the basic concept of Robert's intellectual system. Pictures of the two columns are very common in occult literature. Francis King reprinted an eighteenth-century engraving which portrays the pair flanking a circular altar reminiscent of that used by the Process.[88] Often, Jachin is shown belching fire and Boaz gushing water.[89]

Over the years, as the cult attempted to improve its public image and simultaneously to achieve decisive evolution toward the Millennium, the arrangement and symbolism of the Sabbath Assembly changed in parallel fashion. The adoption of gray uniforms in 1971 lightened up the Alpha. When blue uniforms were introduced in 1972, the walls of the ritual room were painted light blue. Electric lights were hung on the side walls. The two dark curtains were replaced by light blue ones. The altar was no longer a red symbol on black cloth but became a silver Process Sign on light blue cloth. Finally, the white Christian cross and red Satanic goat's head were retired and two identical huge Unity Crosses, red and silver, were hung at opposite ends of the room. Presumably this symbolized not only the Luciferian Era but also the progressive coming together of Christ and Satan. After these changes, I predicted a rearrangement of the positions of Sacrifist and Evangelist. If their Gods were coming together, they also should come closer.

On April 21, 1973, the predicted change took place, as shown in Figure 11. The symbol at the north end was removed, leaving a single Unity Cross. Both priests now stood together on a low stage, facing the congregation from outside it. The congregation now faced forward toward the priests, rather than inward toward themselves. The altar sat awkwardly between the stage and the congregation. It had lost its role as the focus of the ritual, taken now by the lectern at the center of the stage. The altar had become vestigial, and I predicted it would have to be removed or greatly changed to achieve ritual coherence. Chapter 9 explains how it was changed.

The role of the priests and the location of the Gods had changed. The priests were now separate from the congregation, presiding over it and mediating between the Gods

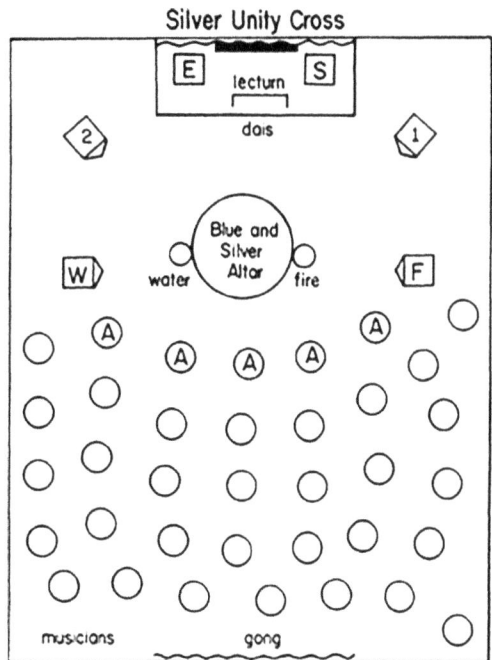

FIGURE 11. Layout of the Sabbath Assembly, April 21, 1973

and their people. The symbols of the Gods were no longer in and around the congregation but in front of it. If we conceive of the Gods as dwelling in the symbols, they were now located in a territory outside the congregation and dominated by the priests. The Process had become a formal church, rather than a community. It was an institution separate from the social group of all the members, a bureaucracy that had come to treat most members as clients and servants, rather than as participants in an intimate social reality.

The dualities were transformed, both in the ever more rigid hierarchical structure of the group and in the ritual symbolism. Robert's attempt to reconcile the dualities was not, however, successful. Under the control of its Masters, the Process was getting ready to abolish the concept of duality, rather than fulfill it.

CHAPTER 8   A New Cure of Souls

The Wrath of the Lamb has come,
The great Spirit of the Son,
To heal the wounds
That the conflict of the mind
And the pow'r of death
Brought to the sacred land of the Gods,

— Process Chant Number One

PSYCHOTHERAPY IS A KIND OF MAGIC. It seeks to accomplish changes in the real world by the mere manipulation of symbols. The more academically or medically oriented brands of therapy do not seem magical, because their ideologies do not violate the assumptions of the physical sciences. But all psychotherapies current in the 1970s, no matter what the rhetoric of their practitioners, operated quite independently of the findings of social sciences, often in open violation of scientific findings.[90] The effectiveness of all brands of psychotherapy remains in doubt half a century later, and many critics suggest that nothing like a scientific consensus currently exists in or between psychiatry and psychotherapy.[91] Already when the Process was active, the evidence suggested (without being conclusive) that every brand of therapy, conventional or deviant, was of moderate value. The therapies preferred by doctors or by the educated upper classes may not have been any better than the most rustic faith-healing or shamanism.[92] A number of studies demonstrated that the popularity of any therapeutic approach was determined by social factors quite unrelated to its objective effectiveness.[93]

Consequently, in a study such as this, the question of the therapeutic effectiveness of Process techniques is not of primary interest. It is extremely difficult to gauge the value of a cure even in controlled clinical settings. In the field it is next to impossible. Three other important questions can be engaged more clearly: (1) What were the Process' techniques? (2) How did they relate to Process doctrine? (3) What were the likely social consequences of the techniques, quite apart from the question of cure? With these questions guiding our analysis, we will discuss several Process therapy exercises, in roughly the order a newcomer would have encountered them around 1971.

THE TELEPATHY DEVELOPING CIRCLE

In a public pamphlet, Father Christian compared the three primary group-therapy rituals: "Telepathy Developing Circles, where you can develop your telepathic abilities through psychometry and the like, Processcenes, which are fairly rumbustious, great for self-expression, great for emotional release and great fun, Midnight Meditations, which are quiet, warm, gentle and full of contact." The group telepathy encounter, familiarly called the TDC, was the most basic therapy process, participated in by any visitor to the cult interested enough to pay the $1.50 admission. It was held in the Alpha ritual room and lasted an hour. I observed many TDCs as a participant, tape-recorded one, photographed another, and even led a few Circles, so my documentation is quite complete. Here I will describe it combining my observations from four Circles run by Sister Seraphine at the Boston chapter, March 5, 19, and 26 and April 2, 1971.

The cushions were spread out in a single large oval pattern on the floor. The room was dark. Incense spewing from a chalice gave the air a translucent quality, like a warm liquid. Physical objects seemed unreal. The amber glow of the candles was lost in the dark walls and clothing, but it illuminated faces with a magical radiance. Two or three dozen people sat in the Circle, touching each other, pressed closely side by side. We fell silent. Then Seraphine entered, dramatic, reserved, and haughty, and took her place on a purple cushion directly under the cross at Christ's end of the room.

After a brief introduction, Seraphine divided us into groups of six and had us sit in little circles. We meditated on our "aims for the evening." What did each of us want to contribute? What did each of us want to receive? "Relax," she said. "Close your eyes. Make no effort. Let it come. Now begin the meditation." After a minute of silence, she said, "Come in now." We opened our eyes and then told what aims had emerged in our meditations.

Some of the aims expressed in the April 2 TDC were the following. Brother Gregory wanted "to give understanding and to receive something that I really ought to know." Shorty wanted "to give strength and receive strength."

Betty parroted Shorty, "I'd like to give strength and receive it, too." Arnold said, "I'd like to give thinking and reason, and receive purpose." My own aims were "to give intensity and receive acceptance." Brother Simon finished "the round on aims" by saying, "I'd like to give and receive communication."

The next activity was also conducted in the small groups. Seraphine announced, "We'll have rounds in each of the circles now on how your awareness and sensitivity have been since your last Circle. How it's been developing, what kind of things have been happening." Supposedly, our work in the TDCs would improve our sensitivity and awareness, from week to week. Our contact and communication with other people would constantly improve. But the level on which this progress would take place was seen as occult, psychic, or at least subconscious.

The Circles were supposed to develop our powers of *Telepathy*. On a radio show in 1972, Seraphine explained what the Process meant by this word: "When we say *telepathy*, we don't mean mind reading, sort of picking words out of somebody's brain. We don't do that. But what it is is becoming more aware, increasing sensitivity around other people, around objects, around environments. Being able to understand what a person's feeling, going through, without talking to him about it. Just by being near him, picking up his moods and emotions." Seraphine's definition is on the borderline between the psychic and the psychological. Cult theory did not recognize any clear line between these two different traditions for interpreting human experience.

In one TDC, Brother Simon said, "My sensitivity around people seems to be very good, especially donating, and really knowing if they're going to say yes or no and knowing what people to ask. Picking up how people are feeling, spirits, vibrations." Sometimes, Messengers donating on the streets would try to guess the hometowns of people they met or their ages. No clear distinction was made between subliminal awareness of another person's emotions and extrasensory perception of his thoughts or hidden information about him. Brother Grieg reports he was in Harvard Square hawking literature when a young couple stopped to speak with him. He claimed he immediately knew all about them, even though he had never seen them before. Grieg told them they were from Michigan, that the guy was twenty-two, and the girl seventeen. "Yes!" they exclaimed. He was right. Grieg said the incident frightened him. He didn't know what to do with such power and wasn't sure he'd be happy if it came to him again. Sister Marie mentioned a similar incident in which she had performed the same trick while donating. The person was amazed and asked if Processeans were telepathic. "That's not really in our line," she said.

The TDC rounds on sensitivity and awareness were always followed by a Meditation. As we said in chapter 3, in this cult *meditation* means *directed fantasy*. It is often performed and discussed in group settings. Processeans are given a topic to meditate on—that is, to free-associate about; then the participants discuss the images they received. Some of the TDC meditation topics Seraphine gave us were: "the future of Humanity and your part in it," "mass destruction," "the end of the world," and simply "self."

Many people reported extremely vivid images of terrestrial annihilation, often science fiction and surrealist pictures.

Seraphine demonstrating deep meditation.

One fellow saw spaceships shooting death rays at Humanity. Another saw King Kong smashing city buildings. Somebody else saw a setting sun with the words "The End" written on it. Another said he had also seen a setting sun, but his had a face on it. When the solar face set, it stuck its tongue out. One young man had a vision of the world disintegrating into anarchy, with only the holy cities Rome and Jerusalem remaining to preserve order in the chaos. A young woman described earthquakes, floods, and blizzards. Sister Roxana saw everyone strung together like a chain with bands of light. Brother Origen saw the earth topple, flip over slowly end for end, while the people shrieked. He heard himself addressing terrified multitudes, telling them there was nothing they could do to save themselves. This was the end! In the vision, he waved his arm and a vast image of Satan appeared in the sky.

After the groups had briefly discussed the participants' meditations, Seraphine asked their leaders to report some of the images that had come through. She then summed them up into a coherent picture. The Process assumes each participant is in touch with part of a reality and that the entire truth can be discovered by adding together the pieces received by different participants. The same approach had led the cult to Xtul when fragmentary meditation images had proved to be parts of a single, collective vision. On the social level, this practice followed from the desire to make the personalities of the members fit together, to create a psychic unity so the group would be strong and cohesive.

An alternative from later than 1971 focused the TDC Meditation on one of a series of ten emotions, following in sequence over a period of weeks: Love, Fear, Joy, Sadness, Gratitude, Anger, Pleasure, Pain, Pride, or Shame. The Processean leading the ritual would instruct: "Close your eyes. Make no effort. Allow the [EMOTION] within you to rise into your consciousness. Now begin the meditation on [EMOTION]." After five or ten minutes: "Come in now. Open your eyes. We conclude the meditation on [EMOTION]."

The chief activity of the TDC, *Psychometry*, followed the Meditation. It is a traditional occult practice, adopted without modifications by the Process.[94] We divided into pairs. One time I photographed Ron Forbes and Larry Spiegel, two Initiates, performing Psychometry. Ron did the first reading. Larry gave Ron his Initiate's cross. Ron held it to his forehead and closed his eyes. Supposedly, the cross would have absorbed psychic vibrations from Larry, the only person who has ever worn it. Ron opened his mind to images, letting the "aura" of the cross penetrate his mind and produce pictures. He might see Larry's past, his future, or an allegory concerning some aspect of Larry's nature. These images came from the cross, it was said, not from Ron's imagination. For more than five minutes, Ron described what he saw. Larry commented and asked questions. After a while, they would switch roles and Larry would do Psychometry on an object belonging to Ron.

Seraphine would instruct newcomers, but only in the most superficial and general way. She might, for example, tell a couple that they could read each other's hands if they did not have any suitable objects. She could not tell participants how to come up with visions but would usually say something like the following, supporting an occult interpretation of Psychometry: "When you're doing the reading, don't worry about whether you're picking up something about the person you're reading. Because you *will* be picking up something about the person you're reading. The main thing is to relax. Don't place any demands on yourself. Just relax and let the things flow in. They'll come. If you come up against a block, the block is probably in the person that you're reading. So describe the feelings around the block. If you draw a complete blank, describe what you yourself are feeling, because you'll probably be picking it up from the person you're doing the reading on."

Two Initiates performing psychometry.

This Psychometry is clearly another technique for producing directed fantasy. In this case the topic is the person being read and the reader's feelings about him. The reader is encouraged to explore and express his feelings by the occult definition of the situation, which denies they are his feelings. According to Psychometry theory, the images come not from the mind of the reader but from the object pressed to his head. He is not to blame. This psychic exercise may in fact have the effect of liberating the reader from excessive inhibitions and encouraging him to express himself. The cost is the requirement that he accept a psychic explanation for the things that happen. The images are photographs I took at a different Telepathy Developing Circle, in which Mother Hagar played the role of Guide, and here she watches pairs of Processeans engage in Psychometry.

The occult interpretation of Psychometry used by the Process may be called a *facilitating definition*. If we take a narrowly pragmatic definition of *truth*, then there can be many competing truths about any complex phenomenon, each serving a different purpose. Pragmatically, truth is whatever works. Regardless of its scientific value, one definition of the situation may *work* better than the others, may accomplish some specific task better than the others. If our purpose is to reconcile Psychometry with the findings of

Psychometry in a Telepathy Developing Circle.

academic psychology, then we must reject the occult interpretation and describe Psychometry as an exercise in directed fantasy. But the Processeans had no such purpose. They wanted to develop and experience exciting human relationships and personal emotions. The occult definition of the situation worked better for them, considering their goals; therefore, it was pragmatically true. Occult statements about the procedure were true in the sense that they were loyal (true) to the purposes of the Process. *A facilitating definition is any interpretation of the situation, regardless of its objective truth, which contributes to successful social interaction in pursuit of certain goals.* The occult orientation may be the facilitating definition in many situations, because it validates expression of questionable feelings and ideas and reduces the sense of risk and blame.

The quality of Psychometry readings varied. The first Processean who did a reading on me was Brother Lot. He took my wristwatch, held it to his head, and described the visions that came. A paper punch. Drafting tables with papers, drawings, drawing tools. The sun shining in windows on a nice day. A scene in the country. Trees. He saw me walking down a road with a stick or fishing pole over my shoulder. A woman. Distant. In the past or the future. Lot guessed I was not married. The river in Boston. The Charles River. At the university, where he and I had met a couple of times. Lot said I wanted freedom.

Freedom was very important to me. He saw me burst out of a university building and pull off my tie. I wanted to leap into the cool water. A piece of paper. Maybe a school degree. I was working for it, he said, but was really using it as an excuse to postpone living. I was working for a degree, believing my life would really begin as soon as I had it. But, Lot said, the beginning of life should come now. He was conscious of my wristwatch. He sensed it was time for the Psychometry to end.

Lot's was an excellent reading. Many physical images, usually connected to the person being read. Sometimes conjectures about his feelings. Sometimes an analysis of his life. Sometimes advice. I frequently observed couples engage in courtship during their Psychometry. They may report sharing visions of a highly intimate nature. Often the result was uninspiring. Often participants expressed dissatisfaction at the quality of a reading but never in my experience questioned the validity of the exercise.

After each Psychometry, Seraphine would "do a round of the room," asking each person by name how the reading had gone. A few actual comments follow. "It was like reading a book." "Yes, it's like he's known me for years." "It made a lot of sense to me." "I almost felt like I was preaching a sermon at him, but somehow it felt right." "It was really good. I really feel a lot better." "It was much more flowing than in the past. It seemed real." "Yeah, it had quite a bit of meaning." "I'm getting more confidence, now." "Shocking." "Very emotional." "It was very intense." "Ummm. I was really getting into it." "It was very intense, so intense that I didn't realize I was here while I was doing it." "It was terrible. It was very superficial." "Everything I have always wanted to know about him but was afraid to ask. It was super."

Next, the group would move back into the large circle. We held hands all around, closed our eyes, and meditated on what we had achieved that evening and on the mood in the room. After a minute, Seraphine said, "All right. Come in now." She did a round on what we had seen. At one TDC, Brother Thomas said, "I got an image, like a white stallion just bursting forth and galloping off." Larry saw "a roomful of mirrors that all of a sudden smashed and then went back together again." Grieg "got the feeling that there was a great deal of retreat from a great deal of intense emotion." Others picked up "subdued sadness," "a sense of God," "More unity," and the obscure sound of "muffled chimes." I said I felt "that we're all part of a single, living being, here in this room." Seraphine completed the round by saying her image was "like Bill's," a feeling of unity among the participants. Certainly, this was what was supposed to emerge. The Telepathy Developing Circle encouraged a controlled intimacy among participants, the development of social bonds, and the emergence of a mystically understood group consensus.

MIDNIGHT MEDITATION

Every Friday and Saturday at midnight, a Meditation ritual was held in the Alpha, lasting half an hour. The circular altar could be placed a few feet in front of the Sacrifist's chair, becoming the focus of a circle of participants seated as usual on the floor cushions, if the Meditation were staged on Saturday after the Sabbath Assembly in which the Altar was in the center of the room. Or, as in the photograph I took seen above, all the Processeans could sit on cushions.

A single priest, the Sacrifist, conducted the ceremony. The format instructions said, "The Sacrifist creates and maintains an atmosphere which is relaxed, quiet, contemplative, and dignified." The Meditation is intended "to relax tensions, worries, problems, conflicts, depressions" and "to engender a feeling of peace, confidence, security, contact, and healing." The main business was a pair of meditations, relaxed focused fantasies on given topics, separated by Process chants. The subject of the first meditation was a negative concept, the second was the positive opposite of the first. In one Meditation I attended, for

Midnight meditation.

example, the first meditation was on *confusion*, the second on *clarity*. Table 9 gives a list of twenty-five pairs of burdens and blessings, twenty-five minor dualities of the human psyche that deserved therapeutic attention.

Burden	Blessing	Burden	Blessing
Unawareness	Awareness	Misery	Happiness
Blame	Acceptance	Confusion	Clarity
Hatred	Love	Cowardice	Courage
Doubt	Certainty	Arrogance	Humility
Vulnerability	Invulnerability	Tension	Relaxation
Futility	Purpose	Insecurity	Security
Ignorance	Knowledge	Stupidity	Intelligence
Anxiety	Serenity	Hypocrisy	Honesty
Inhibition	Freedom	Greed	Generosity
Frustration	Satisfaction	Pessimism	Optimism
Weakness	Strength	Cruelty	Kindness
Apathy	Enthusiasm	Insensitivity	Sensitivity
Exhaustion	Energy		

TABLE 9. **Twenty-Five Pairs of Burdens and Blessings**

Burdens are negative qualities that a person may have, often without being aware of them. The Meditation sequence sought first to expose participants to a burden that might be causing them significant personal problems, giving them a chance to become aware of it, then exposed them to the corresponding blessing. In theory, this procedure would be psychotherapeutic, lessening the power of the negative burden and increasing the strength of the blessing. A series of Meditations, covering all pairs, would improve participants in many areas. Perhaps the Meditations merely functioned to give Processeans one more enjoyable group experience, but the theory extended Robert's idea that the resolution of conflict between polar opposites would be possible. Burdens were like the compulsions that Robert's therapy business was originally founded to cure. In meditation a person might discover that he need not forever enact a particular burden but might better achieve his life's goals if he substituted the corresponding blessing.

PROGRESSES

The main group educational and therapeutic meetings for Initiates, Disciples, and OP Messengers were called *Progresses*. They were the outgrowth of the original Compulsions Analysis *Communications Course*, based in turn on the Scientology *Communications Course* Robert and Mary Ann had taken in London years before. By the early 1970s, there were several formats for these meetings. Usually held Monday and Wednesday evenings, they lasted three hours, with a twenty-minute break in the middle. The first half would be devoted to activities, the second half to the study of Process teachings. At one time, Mondays were devoted to the development of communication skills, while psychological problems were dealt with on Wednesdays. My information about Progresses comes from three sources (1) my own participation in several in 1971; (2) interviews with Sister Norma and Brother Gregory conducted by Carol Fisler, a student at Radcliffe College; and (3) my own participation in the Scientology *Communications Course* in 1970.

Each half of a Progress would be run by a Controller, a senior Processean, aided in the first half by two or three others who helped supervise the exercises. The Controller would begin each session by reciting a Process Precept, which the congregation would repeat in unison. Some Precepts encapsulated various aspects of Robert's therapeutic theory. "Our dissatisfactions are born of ignorance. Our problems stem from blindness." "Humanity is a trap, and human beings are caught in the trap." 'The basis of all healing is the lifting of guilt." "We cannot change ourselves. Others can change us." "The first step is to know that we are greater than the pain we feel." "Where love is real, the gift of love is the healer of all ills." "We must go through weakness to reach strength." "We must have known despair before we can find fulfillment." After the Precept, the participants would be guided through three or four exercises taken from a large collection.

Several activities were clearly derived from Scientology, although the meaning given to them and the exact procedures were changed. Examples include: *Acceptance, Reflexes, Articulation*, and *Acknowledgment*. The first was derived from the very basic Scientology exercise TR-0 (Training Routine Zero), in which one is instructed to sit for up to two hours, motionless, unresponsive, eyes glued on the eyes of another student who is sitting three feet away, following the same instructions, gazing back. TR-0 trains a student to "be there." A second part of TR-0 was called "bull baiting." The student sits in the immobility of TR-0, and the coach tries to make him react against his will.

In theory, the student is said to be vulnerable at certain points, to have "buttons" which if pressed will make him react. Sensitivity about being overweight, for example, may cause the person to blush when his fat is poked. These psychological buttons are to be found and "flattened." In principle, this procedure could gradually strengthen the individual's ability to resist unpleasant emotions such as shame or anxiety.

TR-o also could produce an altered state of consciousness. One time I did it with a young man from Kentucky, an English teacher I happened to like. We sat staring at each other for two hours, which is 120 minutes, which is 7,200 seconds. A long time to stare into someone's face, allowed to breathe and blink occasionally, but never look away, never smile or fidget. Afterward my partner exclaimed excitedly that he had seen me change before his very eyes! I had become different persons—a savage with a bone through my nose, then a decayed corpse covered with filth and cobwebs. He was sure these were glimpses of my previous incarnations. Everyone in the Scientology center was pleased and complimented him on his perceptions. His interpretations fit their faith exactly.

I did not tell them what I had seen. He, too, had changed. A halo of light had grown around his face. He had become pale and two-dimensional, shimmering, covered with dark spots. Of course, I interpreted what I saw as simple eye fatigue. He and I had experienced the same stimuli but understood them differently. Unusual experiences like his, perceived within the definitions provided by the church, are powerful conversion mechanisms. Scientology converts people slowly to its perspective, following a *reality gradient.* This is Hubbard's own terminology, but ideal for social scientific use as well. A reality gradient is a gradual introduction into a new ideology, step by step through a series of ever more advanced experiences and a progression of ever more unfamiliar ideas. The therapy processes of Scientology gradually committed my friend to ever more elevated levels of belief, drawing him into its reality and away from that shared by conventional outsiders.

Some participants say they "exteriorize" while in TR-o. When a person exteriorizes, his spirit leaves his body temporarily, perhaps hovering a short distance from his head. The concept is akin to "astral projection." Hubbard suggested that the ideal relationship between the spirit and its body is one of moderate exteriorization. The spirit should be outside the body but near it, operating the body at arm's length, so to speak. In psychiatric terms, this seems to be a state of mild dissociation. When deep in TR-o, I noticed that my physical sensations were greatly attenuated. A feather lightly brushing across my face did not tickle. An itch did not matter. I was only dimly aware of the existence of my legs. It seemed as if my personal boundary had contracted. When my hand was touched to my face, I sensed the contact in my cheek but not in my fingers!

The Process exercise *Acceptance* was a significantly modified version of TR-0. Processeans would sit on cushions on the floor in pairs, facing each other. Each would sit comfortably, gazing into the eyes of the other for one minute, trying to accept that person and really permit him to be present. Here TR-0 is radically transformed. *Acceptance* is brief. The concept is different. Each person is not supposed to block off perceptions of the other, as in Scientology, but to extend quiet warmth to him. There is not a strict rule against the slightest movement. Brother Gregory Watson, a Disciple who attended many Progresses, recalled Acceptance well. The task was to "look into each other's eyes for a full minute without laughing, looking away, saying anything. This is to learn to feel free about looking at someone without embarrassment, to get over inhibitions about this sort of contact. Learn to accept the other and to feel accepted by removing these inhibitions."

The next step was *Reflexes,* the Process equivalent of Scientology's bull baiting. One member of the pair would take the role of *controller,* the same as the Scientology coach role. Watson explained that "reflexes are gestures, words, attitudes, expressions that cause a nervous reaction—hate, fear, giggles, etc. The controller hits the subject with things he feels the subject is sensitive to so that the subject can learn to accept this, to control his reflexive reactions." Watson himself was particularly sensitive about being overweight, so the controllers would often focus on his reflexes about being fat, but in a mood predicated on love and acceptance.

The Process exercises Articulation and Acknowledgments were derived from the Scientology procedures TR-1 and TR-2. This pair was also called *Alice Games* by L. Ron Hubbard, because they drew upon *Alice in Wonderland* for material. In TR-1, the student is supposed to read a quotation from *Alice,* memorize it, and, while "holding his TRs," speak the sentence to the coach as though it were his own contribution to some hypothetical conversation they were having. Sometimes we used actual copies of *Alice,* back in 1970, and at other times we read from sheets of excerpts. How many dozens of times did I say these perplexing sentences? I will never forget them! (Oh, except that over the following half century I did forget them, and was fascinated to ponder their written text.)

I'll give them a new pair of boots every Christmas.
Four times five is twelve, and four times six is thirteen.
The question is, what did the archbishop find?
You insult me by talking such nonsense.
You're enough to try the patience of an oyster!
What a number of cucumber-frames there must be.
The master says you've got to go down the chimney.
I didn't know that Cheshire cats always grinned.
She doesn't believe there's an atom of meaning in it.
However, I know my name now, that's some comfort.

There is a subtle intellectual training effect here. The student becomes comfortable with unconventional ideas. He treats them as detached words, bleached of their meaning, unconnected to his surroundings. He is confronted by incoherence and sees it as a beneficial game. He plays the game. After he has accepted the words of Wonderland, he has no difficulty accepting the words either of a new faith or of a test it gives him. The student submits to the discipline of the new religious movement merely by going through the exercise. If he performs poorly, the coach says, "Flunk!"

TR-2 is a reversal of TR-1. This time the coach recites a quotation from *Alice* and the student tries to acknowledge it in such a way as to bring the dialogue to a full stop without encouraging the coach to continue. Acknowledgement is a means of control. The student was permitted to use one of the following five acknowledgements: alright, okay, thank you, good, fine.

The Process version of TR-1, *Articulation,* had a very different purpose. Sister Norma says it was "an elocution lesson" in which Processeans were "taught to speak clearly and concisely." In each pair, the controller would give the student a simple sentence to say. The student was supposed to repeat it in a direct manner, without using extreme gestures or other "distractors." If the student made a mistake, the controller would say, "Stop," explain what the error was, and tell the student to try it again. In the Scientology TRs, the command was "Flunk!", not "Stop." In every detail, the Process version of the exercises was more bland than the original Scientology version. One Disciple, Gregory Watson, said the purpose of Articulation was "to ease situations where you have to speak to people, show more confidence, come across more professionally, present a better picture of what you're talking about."

The student's statements were *acknowledged* by the coach, and in *Articulation—Stage B* students learned to use four acknowledgements: right, okay, thank you, fine. One of Scientology's was dropped from the list, *good,* because it was felt to be too judgmental. I remember practicing these exercises in a Monday Progress. Sister Leah was the controller for our little group. We sat in a circle, facing each other. Each of us in turn would say a simple declarative sentence to Leah. We tried to speak clearly and not let the words "disperse." If Leah felt we spoke well, she would acknowledge our sentence. Otherwise, she would ask us to try it again. When Leah had done this with each of us, she passed the role of controller on to the next person in the circle and we did another similar round. When each of us had been controller once, the exercise was over. We were not supposed to "invalidate" our partners, not criticize the content of their sentences. Rather than firing our acknowledgements like sixteen-inch guns, we were supposed to communicate acceptance of the other person.

Processeans did not play *Alice Games,* training them to tolerate poetic sentences. People were urged to express themselves rather than subjugate themselves to another person's metaphors. Acknowledgements were used as responses to the answers students gave when asked questions like: "What person or thing in the world makes you get bored the most? What is your greatest wish for the future?"

Two of the Progress exercises called for participants to touch each other: *Physical Contact* and *Physical Therapy.* It is possible that these procedures, particularly the latter, were derived not from Scientology but probably from the Alexander Technique. Father Raphael and Father Christian were the sons of a practitioner of this controversial therapy. Invented early in the twentieth century by F. Matthias Alexander, it involves a series of procedures designed to give the client a greater awareness and control of his physical body. When I asked Robert de Grimston where *Physical Contact* and *Physical Therapy* had come from, he could not say. He doubted they were derived from the Alexander Technique.

My first experience of these two Progress exercises was on different evenings when I was paired with a Processean sister, who was then still a mere Initiate. Through this contact we began a friendship that continued for a long time. One Monday, she and I were paired off by Mother Greer for Physical Contact. In the first round, I was to be the active partner, following Greer's instructions, while the sister was to be passive and accepting. "Put your hands on the other's shoulders," Greer commanded. I placed my hands softly on the sister's shoulders. "Okay," Greer said, "put your hands on the other's head." I did so. Greer continued . . . forearms . . . knees . . . waist . . . . The idea was to "touch in a manner that gives security." The sister accepted my touches calmly.

Then we switched roles. Greer gave the same set of touching commands. This time the sister touched me, and I accepted. Around the room there were a dozen pairs of Processeans touching and accepting.

Then we did another sequence in which Greer no longer gave the commands. The person being touched told the toucher what to do. I told the sister where to touch me, step by step. As another member of our chapter remarked, participants in the Progresses "never touched in the good places." We stayed away from the erogenous zones. Nonetheless, a very special feeling was generated by the alternate touchings, erotic without doubt but also calm and exploratory. The final section of Physical Contact was another role reversal. The sister gave me instructions, and I touched her.

Three weeks later, when Father Christian was controller of the Progress, the same sister and I were paired off for *Physical Therapy*. The basic idea was for one person to lie relaxed on the floor. The other would kneel, lift an arm of his supine partner, supporting it carefully at the shoulder and wrist, and move the arm in slow, slow circles in the air. Everything would be extremely quiet and calm. Sensual and spiritual. After a minute, the active partner would move on to the other arm, then each of the legs, and the head. But the first time we did it, the Boston Alpha was so full of people that there was not room to lie down. Father Christian improvised. He had half of us sit on cushions, relax, and receive back rubs from the other. First, the sister massaged my back, arms, shoulders, and head for about fifteen minutes. It was a very happy time for me but hard work for her. Then we switched roles and I massaged her.

Possible therapeutic effects aside, the chief consequence of all these Progress activities was the development of social relationships between participants. Over the weeks, strangers made friends within the group of habitual participants. Because these relationships developed within the cult, they tended to stay within the cult, thereby contributing to its strength.

P-SCOPE SESSIONS

In chapter 2 we briefly described the use of a Scientology E-Meter in pseudo-psychoanalytic sessions and the application of the same device, later called the P-Scope, in Compulsions Analysis. Here we will describe the actual procedure in the sessions. There were many different formats, but basically all involved sequences of questions and answers. If the procedure was to be taken seriously, it was important for the subject to give correct answers. But the theory of the subconscious mind held that people could be mistaken about their real feelings. On the subconscious level, they knew and recognized the truth. On the conscious level, they were enmeshed in a web of self-deception. The E-Meter, functioning as a lie detector, seemed an effective tool for testing the client's answers, to see whether they were correct or not. Compulsions Analysis and the later Process sought to uncover subconscious *goals,* using the P-Scope to verify which ones really mattered. The Process technique may be derived from a main procedure that (at least at one time) seems to have been the step before achieving the spiritually superior *Clear* level of enlightenment in Scientology. I had not experienced it myself and relied on a somewhat garbled account by a journalist to understand that part of the background.

During my 1970 research, I purchased an E-meter from the Founding Church of Scientology in Washington, D.C, and received some limited instruction in its use. In 1983, I was able to attach its display to an input hardware device I plugged inside my Apple IIe computer and wrote a simple software program to display and save the measured emotional reactions of the research subject. The public-relations director of Scientology of Boston attended a presentation I gave about this augmented E-meter at Harvard, and some years later Scientology invited me to visit its Los Angeles offices for a week and share ideas. I do not claim to have contributed to Scientology's later development of the technology but must acknowledge that the use of electronic equipment like the E-meter to explore human emotions, the mind, and the spirit seems quite reasonable.

A Scientology website commemorating its founder, L. Ron Hubbard, reports an important episode in his childhood that seems to have been his main connection to Psychoanalysis: "In autumn of 1923, the Hubbard family embarked on a voyage from San Francisco to Washington D.C. En route, Ron became acquainted with a Commander Joseph 'Snake' Thompson, late from Vienna where he had studied Psychoanalysis with Sigmund Freud. It was a meeting that remains indelibly part of Scientology history."[95] As it happens, Snake was the best friend of my great uncle, Consuelo Seoane, who convinced Snake to undertake an extensive spy adventure with him. They took false identities, pretending to be South African naturalists belonging to the Boer that had recently been defeated by the British army, supposedly doing herpetology research along the seashore, but actually charting potential invasion routes, for use if Japan and the United States ever went to war."[96] I mentioned this connection in my 2007 book, *Across the Secular Abyss*, and described the psychic adventure more fully in a chapter contributed to the 2009 book James Lewis edited about Scientology.[97]

Although Thompson seemed oriented toward Freud's original form of Psychoanalysis, the Process and perhaps even Scientology seemed oriented more toward the derivative but potentially heretical perspectives of Freud's disciples, Alfred Adler and Carl Gustav Jung.[98] An early article about the use of technologies like the E-meter in psychotherapy was published in 1919 by Ludwig Binswanger, who was close to both Jung and Freud.[99] As implied by its name, a key aspect of Compulsions Analysis was analyzing and thus dissolving obsessive goals that dominate a person, as the first step toward discovering the one main achievable goal the person is fundamentally committed to. Based on Adler's work and called the Goal Line in the Process, this method was performed while the client was attached to a P-scope that would detect changes in galvanic skin response, alerting the therapist to topics that needed further exploration.

The session would begin when the therapist asked, "What is your chronic goal?" If this question does not mean much to the client, he might phrase it differently. "What are you trying to achieve? What are you after?" Below are the actual responses given by Mother Lethe in a session when Robert de Grimston was her therapist. She gave several answers to the question: "To die... to be bored... to feel unaware...." Robert wrote these down. When she had run out of responses, they went back to the top of the list and went through the answers again.

// To die.
/ To be bored.
/ To feel unaware.
  To not feel I'm fulfilling my potential.
/ To ruin my chances for an interesting future.
/ To change the situation.
/ To hide myself.
  To undermine my confidence.
/ To cut back my power.
/ To be out of control.
  To be aggravated.

The P-Scope needle moved when Lethe was on some items and not on others. If there was a response on the P-Scope, Robert made a little mark in front of the item, as illustrated in the list. Eight of the eleven produced a response. Then they went through the list again, but dropping out the three that got no emotional reaction: "To not feel I'm fulfilling my potential," "To under-mine my confidence," "To be aggravated." This time, only one item got a P-Scope response: "To die." If more than one had drawn a response, they would have continued going through the list until they got only a single movement of the needle. Then, the therapist announces the result to the client. Robert would say, "Lethe, your chronic goal is to die."

The next sequence would take the goal, to die, and incorporate it in a question. "What would happen if you failed to die?" Or, "What would you do if you failed to die?" She gave (as it happened) eleven responses to this new question. Only four got a strong P-Scope response on the second run-through. The third time through, only one got a strong reading: "to destroy people." Lethe's chronic goal was "to die," but because she could not achieve this she had adopted the secondary goal "to destroy people."

The third step was to find the reason she could not die. "What would prevent you from dying?" She replied, "People in need . . . crippled people . . . the Pope . . . my mother . . . ." But none of these gave a strong response. So Robert turned to an alternate question, probably one like: "What would de-stroying people accomplish?" She gave fourteen answers; four got a P-Scope response, and the one that finally emerged was "to make me bigger than every-thing else." Throughout the therapy session, Lethe continually failed to find oppositions outside herself but found oppositions always inside. Perhaps they could be described as conflicting goals. The line of goals continued, sequence after sequence: "To isolate people . . . to dominate the situation . . . to change the situation."

Osiris, who had been given extensive therapy by Robert de Grimston and trained in the techniques by him, was kind enough to instruct me. I re-ceived a similar therapy process, Maximum Compulsion, from him, so I could understand what the sessions were really like. Despite the fact that I had ex-perimented with my E-Meter/P-Scope many times before, I was surprised at how effective the device was in forcing me to admit things I preferred to con-ceal. I cannot say how factually accurate the analysis was, but it did powerfully engage my emotions. The analyses of both Lethe and Osiris strike me as correct descriptions of these two people whom I came to know well. Several Processeans commented to me that Lethe was self-destructive and perhaps harmful to the people closest to her. This observation agrees with her first two goals, "to die" and "to destroy people." Osiris was a very mysterious, even frightening person who was nonetheless quite respectable. He explained the results of his own therapy, using a diagram like that in Figure 14.

The letters X, Y, and Z indicate goals, arranged in a hierarchy, while X´, Y´, and Z´ are circumstances or things that block the achievement of those goals and force the person to adopt a less desirable substitute goal. Osiris explained: "There are triangles of what you want (now all those are unconscious), and what stops you from getting what you want, and what you do when you get stopped from doing what you want. And it goes on and on and on. Let's say ... I'll give you some of mine: I want *to hide.* And what stops me from *hiding is people trusting me,* since this opposes my wish *to hide.* And what do I do to solve this dilemma? To stop you from stopping me from hiding if you trust me? I *frighten* you. Now *frightening* you becomes my second goal, because I can't get the *hiding,* so I'll get to *frighten.* Maybe that will work. And then you can stop me by something. Say, by *loving* me. So I can't *frighten* you anymore. So I go to maybe *killing* you. Then you can stop that by something."

```
        /       \
       /         \
    X---------X'
     /         \
    /           \
  Y---------Y'
   /         \
  /           \
 Z-------Z'
 /       \
/         \
```

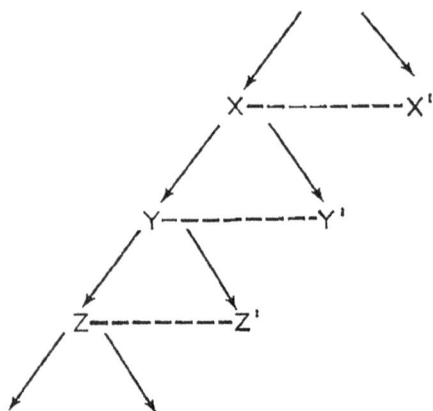

FIGURE 14. **Diagram of Goal Line Analysis according to Osiris**

In the diagram of triangles, X represents the goal of *hiding.* X´ represents *trusting,* which prevents X and produces the alternate goal Y, which is *frightening.* Y´ represents *loving,* which prevents Y and produces the alternate goal Z, which is *killing.* The sequence goes on and on. "Then it breaks. You see, I reached the bottom. I tried hiding—I couldn't, I tried frightening you—I couldn't. I tried killing you—I couldn't. Then I jump to a higher goal than the one I started with. Which would be *feeling free,* for example. And that's typical of a cycle. You start at the point which is a basic drive, and you work down. The more you are frustrated with one goal, you go to a lower goal, till you reach bottom and the cycle breaks. And you feel free. You feel good. You go to a positive part of the cycle."

All the time, the predetermined format of the questions and the P-Scope readings guided the process. When the P-Scope "registers a charge," it indicates the item that stimulated the response is "real to you." The entire process may take several sessions. "Eventually you go down to your lowest possible solution which doesn't work, and suddenly you switch to a positive." The purpose is "to find your unconscious goals. To find the pattern you follow. Because if you have in your head an idea what basically you want and how you behave about it and what stops you, it doesn't have as much power on you as it would otherwise. At least you're aware of your pattern." You have "more and more control. So when you're trying *to hide,* you wouldn't be blaming other people for being stupid or aggressive. It's just the fact that you want *to hide.* It loses much of its force upon you."

There are many other therapy processes similar to the Goal Line but designed to uncover hypothetical resistances, inhibitions, problems, or positive areas of compulsion. Osiris said, "Most people get into religious topics, eventually, whether it's in the most positive area or in their line of goals. It might be ultimately they want to be one with God, or they want to destroy the world, or they want to be crucified." Discovery of magical goals in Compulsions Analysis was one of the chief factors transforming the therapy into a religious cult. Even as it was practiced ten years later, the Goal Line therapy led to what participants perceived as religious desires and experiences.

P-Scope sessions were sometimes held in group, mass-production meetings where one *Therapist* would handle as many as four *Questors,* or patients. A half hour would be devoted to each Questor, so a session with four of them would last over two hours. The Therapist would sit at one side of a table, and the Questors would sit on the other side facing him. The Questors are hooked up to the P-Scope, one at a time. The Questors also take turns serving as Scribe, writing down the questions and answers. The participants render themselves psychologically naked not only before a high-status Therapist but also before two or three peers.

The therapist would ask, "What's going on with you? Where is your attention?" If the P-Scope indicated any charge on any question, the therapist would follow up on it, getting the Questor to talk through his feelings. A number of formal processes would also be used in these sessions. It should be obvious that these meetings not only served to solidify bonds between participants but also functioned directly as a mechanism of social control. A participant having deviant thoughts and feelings would have a very hard time concealing them. Presumably, these sessions also functioned to inform participants (particularly the leaders) of the general situation in the chapter and any group problems that may have begun.

PSYCHIC SESSIONS FOR IPs

Several kinds of therapy and self-discovery sessions were held for inner members of the cult, including a number based on parapsychological assumptions. Here we will discuss Telepath Sessions at length, then briefly describe Forum Sessions and Mediumistics.

Like the P-Scope Sessions, Telepath Sessions were designed to uncover the compulsions, fears, and unconscious *agreements* (assumptions) that motivated participants. The controller of the session, the one who does all the psychic work, was called the Telepath, while the others were Questors. The method by which the Telepath uncovered the hidden contents of the Questors' minds was called Subliminal Contact. Process executive document S-44 warned, "Subliminal Contact is not to be discussed, practiced, or taught in the presences of any member of the general public, Disciples, or Processeans below the rank of Messenger." This prohibition acted not only to preserve the secret therapeutic treasure of the Process, but also to protect the cult from ridicule. The Telepath Sessions were among the most thoroughly occult practices of the group. Upon entering the status of Messenger, a Processean would be given an introductory talk about sessions, in which the basic idea would be explained. "Everything that we do, think, or feel, or that happens to us, is motivated by an agreement or compulsion in our psyche. Our problems stem from conflicting agreements in the psyche. Each of the processes that are run in Sessions is designed to bring to the surface a particular set of conflicting agreements."

So far, this sounds like conventional psychotherapeutic thinking, except for the solipsistic claim that all things that happen to a person are motivated by something within him. In one of his earliest writings, *Logic I*, Robert wrote, "So let us be quite clear that EVERYTHING that happens to us is, on some level or other, our choice, our decision, and therefore our responsibility.... If someone throws a stone at you, that is his choice. But if you are hit by a stone, that is your choice." Except for this point, the theory sounds like that of Freud. The Messenger is told that these *agreements* will lose their power once they have been brought to the surface and made conscious. But the therapy reveals itself as occult through the method it uses:

> Subliminal contact is the method by which the Telepath uncovers
> the agreements. He makes telepathic contact with the psyche of the
> Questor concerned, and asks the particular questions relevant to the

process which he is running. The answers to these subliminal questions come direct from the Questor's psyche, and the Telepath tells the Questor the answers so that he can write them down, explain what they mean to him, and say anything he wants to about them.

A typical Group Session might involve one Telepath and four Questors. The Telepath would be of Master or Superior rank, while the Questors might be Messengers or Prophets. They would take their places in the Sessions Room. The Telepath sat on a chair behind a desk or table, and the Questors sat in a semicircle facing him. The Questors sat some distance apart, as the instructions specify, "to allow the aura of each Questor to expand freely without touching, clashing with, or intruding upon the surrounding auras" and "to cut out any possible confusion on the part of the Group Telepath about whose projections he is receiving at any given moment, which may happen when auras are touching or overlapping one another."

Each of the Questors had a Session Book in which he wrote the results of the Subliminal Contact and any comments he wished to make about the material uncovered. In a series of such sessions, a sequence of nine different processes would be run, each using a different set of questions to uncover different agreements and compulsions. The names of these processes hint at their content: Achievement Problem Cycle, Problem Source Cycle, Intention Cycle, Resistance Process, Consequence Cycle, Line of Decisions, Line of Sources, Line of Monopolisers, and Fear Process. The last of these, for example, contains three cycles: Reality, Fear, and Love. This triad could be repeated several times in the therapy of a Questor. The shortest of these, the Reality Cycle, contains only seven questions:

1. What is Reality?
2. When is Reality?
3. Where is Reality?
4. What is real to you?
5. What is unreal to you?
6. What could be real to you?
7. What is important to you?

In P-Scope sessions, the therapist would ask these questions aloud. In Telepath Sessions, the telepath asked them telepathically. For example, in the

Line of Sources process, the telepath would tell the Questor, "Now we're going to find out your most intense emotional state." Thus, he informed the Questor of what the question will be. The telepath then asked the question silently in his own mind: "What is your most intense emotional state?" The Questor was not supposed to do anything on the conscious level. He just sat there as the telepath made contact with his aura. The situation was similar to the Psychometry practiced in the Telepathy Developing Circle, except that the expert telepath needed no physical object and was supposedly able to focus on specific topics. After a few seconds, the telepath announced the answer he got to the subliminal question: "Paranoia."

The telepath was a senior member of the cult who presumably knew each of the Questors quite well. Paranoia may indeed have been the most intense emotional state of this particular Questor, and the telepath may have observed much evidence of it over preceding weeks. After the telepath had given the answer, the Questor wrote it down in his Sessions Book and might comment on it. What happened if the Questor denied that he really suffered from paranoia? One of the multitudes of therapy guidelines written by Robert said what telepaths should do if the Questor "denies the reality of the agreement: Ask him about it; how it could be real, whether he is retreating from it or suppressing it. Also ask him subliminally for more information which will help him to see the reality. Make suggestions if necessary in question form. Use the other Questors if it feels appropriate. If it is still unreal to him, then say that you will come back to it during the discussion following the Session."

Another set of instructions told the telepath, "Always project certainty and confidence, particularly when a Questor is feeling uncertain or insecure." It was quite common for conventional psychotherapies to handle patients' doubts as symptoms rather than questions. The therapeutic system must not come into question. It is the patient who is on trial, not the therapist. However illogical and unfair, this tactic does strengthen the therapeutic system. Either the client rejects the therapy altogether or he submits to the will of the system. The Process refused to be questioned.

To show how a single cycle might work out, I will quote from one of the many secret bulletins Robert wrote for his therapists. This one deals with the Line of Sources, a sequence of assumptions the person holds that together support a current emotional state. The bulletin was originally written in November 1965 and revised in October 1968. The set of questions might be used in either P-Scope or Telepath sessions. For the sake of example, Robert had supplied a likely sequence of answers a Questor might give:

What is your most intense emotional state?

Paranoia.

Why is paranoia your most intense emotional state?

I am being watched.

What does your paranoia stem from?

A need to isolate myself.

Why does your paranoia stem from a need to isolate?

It keeps my attention on myself.

What does your need to isolate stem from?

My knowledge of the future.

Why does your need to isolate stem from your knowledge of the future?

I see things differently from other people.

What does your knowledge of the future stem from?

The world is ending.

Why does your knowledge of the future stem from the fact that the world is ending?

It has been revealed to me.

What does the fact that the world is ending stem from?

Nothing. It is ending.

Why does the fact that the world is ending stem from nothing— it is ending?

That's the way it is.

The sequence of questions incorporated the answers as the Telepath or Therapist received them to produce a step-by-step process. Any kind of answer can be incorporated. The Telepath is not looking for elaborate explanations. Note that he did not follow up on the claim that "I am being watched." He did not ask by whom or how the person knew. He tried to carry through to the basic assumption believed to underlie the entire psychological structure. In this case, the assumption was that the world was ending. Beyond this, the Telepath got nothing. The impending end of the world was a "Basic Reality" for this particular Questor.

In principle, the Questor now no longer needed to feel paranoia. His task was to adjust meaningfully to the conviction that the world is coming to an end. The obvious course is to accept the coming of the end within the millenarian Process, to join with others in aiding the end, preparing for the New Age that is to come. The Questor can no longer say, "I see things differently from other people." Other Processeans saw things the same way.

This sequence of questions and answers is a very good example, because it shows the likelihood of a *supernatural outcome* in a therapy process that started with obsessive assumptions and no anti-supernatural bias. The sequence of questions forced the answerer to search for some ultimate response that can terminate the process. Any answer less than ultimate would call forth another question. Throughout human history, religious concepts have been offered as ultimate answers. We cannot ask the same questions about the *sacred* as we can about the profane. It may be that the chief intellectual function of religious concepts is to block inquiry. The Ultimate enters language only as a semantic trick to stop an unpleasant interaction. But once the Ultimate has been invoked, it takes on the quality of reality. Beginning as a mere "etc." tacked on at the end of a limited description of the world, the supernatural comes to impress us as powerful in its own right. If we encounter the supernatural often enough, we become occultists. Processeans encountered the supernatural daily.

The Telepath Sessions were really individual therapy in a group setting, but Forum Sessions were true occult group therapy. In Forum Sessions the *agreements* held by the group as a whole were telepathically uncovered, not the agreements of individual participants. A Telepath would run the session, and any number of Inside Processeans were free to attend. These Brethren would sit in concentric semicircles in front of the Telepath. They did not have to space themselves out to keep their auras from overlapping, because it was the group aura that the Telepath was to read.

The Forum would last a half hour, followed by an hour's discussion. The main business was the discovery of group agreements. The Telepath would meditate, then speak. He might say, "There is an agreement that we must resist acknowledging fear." Then he would silently ask a subliminal question, "Why? Why is there an agreement that we must resist acknowledging fear?" The Brethren all write the agreement in their session books, and, if they wish, they also write down their "reality on the agreement." That is, each one would note his first thought on what the agreement meant to him. The Telepath might announce the answer to his question, supposedly received telepathically from the aura of the group. He might name other group agreements. After the Forum proper, the Brethren would discuss the agreements in turn, their reactions to them, and their feeling about the session as a whole. We might discount the possibility that telepathy exists. But, here as in Psychometry, the belief in telepathy may provide a facilitating definition of the situation. The Telepath may feel free to bring up sensitive issues, shielded from criticism by the claim that he merely discovers an agreement already held by the group. No single individual was responsible for the content or course of the Forum Session.

The practice of Mediumistics, another occult-psychological therapy, was predicated on the existence in each person of four levels of consciousness. Messengers were first introduced to Mediumistics by a Training Officer in an advanced psychic workshop. This could be done in group sessions, but we will describe it in terms of a single Messenger guided by a single Officer. First, the Messenger would lie down and close his eyes. The Officer then spoke, with the same patter as a hypnotist, telling the Messenger: "You are relaxing. Getting more and more relaxed. You are relaxing your body and your mind. You are feeling very peaceful and very relaxed. You are relaxing your consciousness. You are becoming completely relaxed."

He told the Messenger that his next level of consciousness "is coming in." This was a part of the Messenger that he normally suppressed or hid. It was an alternate personality, not a mere fragment. The Messenger answered questions about how he felt, what his "emotions and realities" were. These were the characteristics of the second level. The Officer asked the Messenger what his name was. He would reply with a completely new name, "a word which describes the concepts embraced by the level," such as Nature, Peace, the Wanderer, or the Silent One. The Messenger became more acquainted with his second level, even carrying on a conversation between his first and second levels, as if they were independent persons.

In subsequent sessions of Mediumistics, the Processean would uncover two more alternate personalities, the third and fourth levels. The first was the ordinary consciousness of the person, the second and third were said to be the psychic consciousness, while the fourth was the spiritual consciousness. After Mediumistics, a person would own six names: his Gray Name (civilian name), his Sacred Name received upon becoming a Messenger, his Magickal Name received upon becoming an Inside Processean, and the Mediumistic names of levels two through four.

Some high-status members had other identities as well. Apparently the cult adopted some of Scientology's processes for exploring previous incarnations. The P-Scope was used to help the individual recall long-buried memories of past lives. John had been John the Baptist in a previous life, while Rhea had been Salome. Rhea had also been Queen Elizabeth I. John had been other Biblical personages as well. Orpheus had been William Blake, and Malachi had at one time been the Lord Krishna. Father Christian had previously lived as Adolf Hitler and before that as Napoleon. It would be wrong to diagnose these alternate personalities as a form of multiple-personality neurosis, an individual hysterical pathology. Rather, and more simply, we can view these personalities as play-acting. They are the projections of wishes and dreams, encouraged to utterance by the occult processes of the cult. I suggest they had nothing to do with mental illness, and I suspect the many therapy processes had very little to do with cure.

CONSEQUENCES

We can distinguish six closely related functions served by the Process's psychic-psychological pseudo-therapy exercises. The therapy strengthened the cult through *testing compliance, training obedience, exercising control, confirming the ideology, providing rewards,* and *increasing social cohesion.*

Although the therapy claimed to be a means that could change anyone in a positive direction, in fact many people did not have great success with it. Some could not subjugate themselves to its demands. If a newcomer was prepared to accept the requirements of the cult, he would prove this by submitting to the regulations of the therapy exercises. If he was unwilling to submit, he would fail in the sessions and be driven away. Thus, the therapy functioned as an examination of the candidate for membership, testing his compliance.

Simultaneously, the therapy trained obedience. If the newcomer was compliant enough to submit to the initial sessions, he would gradually be trained to accept ever more rigorous control over his thoughts and behavior, in the end even submitting his entire self-concept and worldview for manipulation by the cult.

Not only did the therapy support the imposition of social control over the client, but in many ways it directly exercised control. Several of the therapy exercises forced the participant to express all his feelings and admit all his actions. Individual therapists, or groups of fellow Processeans, would then bend the person in the desired direction, controlling him in a subtle but absolute manner.

The therapy exercises did not seem like unjust oppression to those who participated, partly because they produced experiences that confirmed the ideology upon which they rested. After a Processean had experienced telepathy, alternate levels of consciousness, and other psychic phenomena, he was incapable of doubting the reality of psychic concepts and unlikely to reject interpretations of the world provided by the cult. Of course, to the outsider trained in the social sciences, other, non-psychic explanations of the experiences may seem better. But to the person who actually experienced the phenomena and did so in a cognitive setting which presented no alternate scientific explanations, the Process ideology was proven beyond doubt.

The therapy aroused the commitment of many participants because of the intense personal gratifications it provided. The range of rewards is great: backrubs, intimate discussions, flamboyant displays, solicitous attention, a sense of glorious insights, magical status, the chance to express forbidden feelings, and the delicious smugness of participating in a world of precious secrets.

Finally, the therapy exercises were the prime strength of the cult because they produced powerful social bonds. Earlier in this book I said that Processeans developed intense personal ties through the therapy sessions. Here we have seen how it was done. Through revealing themselves to each other, through exchanging gratifications, and through common submission to a powerful and intrusive group consciousness, Processeans were bound tightly together in their magical cult.

CHAPTER 9: **The Separation**

Where now is the Light of the
Lord Lucifer?
Shrouded in the Darkness of Death,
which hangs over the earth.
Whose Death?
The Death of the Lord Christ,
which has come full cycle,
and returns for the
Time of Reckoning,
that the debt of pain and suffering
might be repaid in kind.

— Process Sabbath Assembly

I HAD NOT VISITED THE PROCESS for several months. My field research was in suspension. Paul Walters, the psychiatrist with whom I taught at Harvard, mentioned a letter he received from Father Malachi and Sister Rebekah saying that the Boston chapter was closed but that Massachusetts would still be served from New York. I lived not far from the old chapter house at 46 Concord Avenue, so I adopted the habit of walking past at least once a week, just to see what was happening.

In late June 1974, there was no sign of activity at the house. Several windows had been broken. Garbage was strewn around the lawn in back. I could see that all furniture and decorations had been stripped from the front rooms. Signs posted by a real estate company said, "No Trespassing." A few days later, wrecking machines like mechanical tyrannosaurs began chewing away at the large building next door in which the Process had rented an apartment for the children. Dark, shattered, deserted, this huge wooden structure collapsed into splinters.

The angels had been crucified. The wrecking crew found the old paintings of faceless angels. They had first hung in the original Cavern at Inman Street and spent the last three years in storage behind the Alpha bleachers. The workmen nailed them over the openings in the chapter house to keep kids out. One angel was pinned at the very peak of the roof, covering the fire escape exit, spikes through his shoulders.

In July, an enormous steam shovel clawed at the Alpha. It had eaten the roof and was biting into the back wall, Satan's wall where the red goat's head had hung years before.

By August the site had been stripped bare to a level below the old foundations. Over the following winter, a modern brick-and-concrete apartment building rose over the grave of the cult. Leftover Processeans around Boston passed the rumor that the place was cursed and all attempts to lay the foundation of the new building had failed. The ground churned in agony and cracked the cement. But by the spring of 1975, apartments in the new building were ready for rent. By the Universal Law, the prophecy of doom spoken by the cult had returned to devastate it.

THE EXPULSION OF ROBERT DE GRIMSTON

There are several ways to tell the story of the Great Separation. On the personal level, the schism is explained by the domestic fact that the marriage between Mary Ann and Robert failed and he "ran off" with another woman, Morgana. A number of former Processeans blame Morgana, incorrectly, for the explosion that devastated their cult, and they believe falsely that her relationship with Robert was entirely destructive in nature. Morgana says, "My whole history with the Process was very unique." She often lived with the Omega, and except for the brief time that she was head of the Rome chapter, she was never a part of normal chapter life. She comments, "I have never been a regular Processean." A native of New Orleans, she joined the church there in 1967. She rose rapidly to the rank of Priest, taking charge of one of the groups wandering Germany. Then she was put in charge of the Rome chapter. Later, she participated in the secret life of the Omega. She says her rise to prominence was unequalled in speed and vigor. I asked her why. "I have been told I have what's called a will to power." After helping to lead the drive to plant new American chapters in 1970, she dropped out of the cult. But in September 1971, she joined Robert and Mary Ann again in Toronto, only to drop out again a few months later. When the Omega moved into Mount Chi in New York, Morgana joined them once again.

A relationship developed between Robert and Morgana that rivalled his relationship with Mary Ann. In his terms, they were both Jehovian-Satanic, exciting, aggressive, strong-willed women. He wanted love from both of them, but they competed for exclusive possession of him. Free love became one of the key issues disturbing the upper reaches of Process society. In 1973, Robert again stressed the idea of the New Game, a concept suggested three years earlier by Morgana and connected to Robert's own desire for liberation. With Lucifer's hedonistic morality as his justification, he attempted to liberalize the sexual life of Inside Processeans.

It was an emotionally difficult time for Robert, and he was not able to carry out a consistent policy. One Processean told a newspaper reporter that the New Game was the cause of the trouble, saying, "I guess you could say it was a sort of community sex thing with members of the cult. It was really becoming a weird scene. The sex thing was causing a lot of dissension and jealousy among our members,"

In previous chapters we said that a major crisis had developed for the cult. The source of this threat to its existence was no single narrow subject like sex, but the more general issues of which sex was but one aspect—cultural contradictions which had been with the Process since the beginning. The cult had sought escape from the world; it had sought glory within the world. Both quests had failed, but the economic livelihood of the group was now tied to accommodation with society. Robert represented the impractical but unrepentant cult desire to transcend the limitations of reality. He urged liberation, while the Masters had come to demand control. The cult expected him to help resolve its problems, but instead he disrupted the social order.

In March 1974, the leaders of the cult decided that a special attempt must be made to straighten out the relationships between the members of the Omega. The church rented an apartment in New York City for Robert and Morgana, where they could work through their relationship and decide what they wanted to do. One informant tells me this was Mary Ann's idea. Although the apartment was paid up for a month, the couple stayed only a few days. Morgana became almost paranoid, afraid that Mary Ann might resort to violence, perhaps kidnapping her and her dog Satan.

On March 23, a meeting of the Council of Masters removed Robert from the office of Teacher of The Process. On the twenty-sixth, Father Aaron and Father Joel tried to get Robert to sign a document giving up his authority over various assets. On the following day, Robert withdrew $1,000 from a church bank account to which he had access and flew to Mexico with Morgana. They wanted to get away from the complex situation in New York and think things over. Robert was not inclined to fight the Masters for control of the Process. Always introspective, he needed peace and quiet in which to sift through his emotions. Robert and Morgana were drawn to Xtul.

Robert of course had been at Xtul with the original group in 1966, but for Morgana the place was only a legend. The first sight of Xtul made a great impression on her: "It was incredible! It really was. It's right outside this tiny Mayan village. You're kind of walking along this road through the jungle, and all of a sudden you come to this great big stand of palm trees. And palm trees are not native down there. It's this sudden grove of palm trees. And buildings—these deserted ruins that are there—right on the beach, which is incredibly beautiful. Just the most extraordinary place. Very physically beautiful. Very magical. Very calm feeling there. It was a time for us—in fact, the Separation had just taken place when Robert and I went to Xtul—it was like being in the eye of a hurricane. There were all these things happening, and Xtul just seemed to lay a blanket of serenity."

On April 17, Robert and Morgana arrived in New Orleans. They stayed with her family and tried to communicate with members of the local Process chapter. Robert went to the chapter house and spoke briefly with its leaders but was soon asked to leave. Robert attempted to make a statement at a Sabbath Assembly meeting but was barred from the ritual. He phoned Father John long-distance and asked for a Masters' Meeting to discuss the situation, but John rejected the idea. He phoned the other chapters, but most refused even to accept his call.

At this time, power in the cult was formally held by John, Joel, Raphael, and Aaron, because their names were on the church incorporation documents. They called themselves the Four. Robert believed that the real power was in Mary Ann's hands. In any case, the Four held the bureaucratic instruments of power. So long as Robert failed to exercise his charismatic power, he was powerless. He hesitated. With every day that passed, the new leadership grew stronger and the possibility that Robert might regain his status with the Process diminished.

Robert and Morgana settled for a time into ordinary civilian life in New Orleans. She took a job in a hospital but almost immediately fell seriously ill with hepatitis. Robert took whatever job he could, unashamed to become a common laborer for a while, if that was what "the signs" indicated. He helped deliver and install carpeting. Then he got a job with an architectural firm. Robert and Morgana stayed in the city through the summer, struggling along without a clear plan.

THE FOUNDATION

In every way, it was a bad time for the cult. Income, spirits, and membership declined. By the end of 1973, Messengers were dropping out in dangerous numbers. The January Blue Sale had failed to replenish the supply of workers. Robert's expulsion magnified the disillusionment and confusion that Processeans already felt, and it nearly caused a final collapse. The leaders decided to close two of the six chapters, Miami and Boston. The New York chapter could send donating trips throughout New England, while New Orleans could cover the South. The cult was in a state of confusion for perhaps a year after Robert's expulsion, but the first couple of months were the most traumatic.

Mary Ann and the Four had to complete the Separation from Robert by expelling his works. To eradicate his influence and to protect themselves if he were to assert a legal claim, they decided to cast out his Teachings. As we will see in a few pages, they also quite reasonably felt that the ideology developed by Robert had proven to be a complete failure. The issue of *The Processeans* dated May 1974, but probably edited in March, was the last to contain Robert's picture or anything written by him. There is no mention of him at all in the final issue of *The Processeans*, dated June 1974.

In May, the Process—Church of Final Judgement was renamed the Foundation—Church of the Millennium. Members were no longer called Processeans but Founders. The monthly magazine became *The Foundation*. The fancy quarterly color publication, *Process—Visions of the Apocalypse* became *Foundation—For the Glory of God*. The formats of the magazines were kept exactly the same. Old photographs were carefully used for a few months, until new ones were ready. In a press release, reprinted in the first issue of *The Founders*, Father Raphael, on behalf of the Four, announced, "There has been a growing doctrinal and personal conflict between the Church's governing body, the Council of Masters, and Robert de Grimston, chief theological writer for the Process Church." Notice that Raphael describes Robert's functions very narrowly: "The Foundation Church of the Millennium is an important break with the old and represents the establishment of a new order, which we hope, with God's guidance, will be part of the foundation upon which He builds His millennium."

A cover letter, sent to newsmen with copies of this press release, explained: "We have broken away from the old Process Church, and the new Foundation Church of the Millennium has been established." The Foundation held all the assets of the Process, occupied the remaining chapter houses, and kept most of the higher-level membership. In December 1974, Father Raphael explained, "In essence what occurred, in a purely legal sense, last summer, was a change of name situation."

For a short time, the cult tried to replace Robert with a new figurehead. Father Christian was put forward to fill the role vacated by Robert's expulsion. The last issue of *The Processeans* and the third issue of *The Foundation* carry brief emotional essays signed by him, printed under a dramatically lit photograph. He looks somewhat like Robert and was sometimes mistaken for a relative. People thought the two men were brothers. When Christian let his blond hair and beard grow, like Robert he resembled the popular conception of Jesus Christ. On the first day of Christian's brief reign as cult figurehead, he appeared at the New York Chapter flanked by two attendants and dressed in a pure white suit with gold jewelry. His star fell as quickly as it had risen. Christian was well liked but had no legitimate claim to leadership at that point in time. Members thought his white suit was silly. The cult decided it no longer needed a charismatic leader or figurehead.

Most low-status members found out about the Separation abruptly, without warning. Suddenly one Saturday, several sections were cut out of the Sabbath Assembly. In New York, Father Raphael was the Evangelist. He gave a stormy sermon condemning Robert and his ways, giving the congregation a simple choice: "You're either for us or against us. All those who are for us, please stay. All those who are against us, please leave." A few left.

All Process literature was withdrawn from circulation. Thousands of copies of various writings and magazines were kept in storage in Toronto for at least two years. At the Chicago chapter, paint remover was used to take *The Process* off the blue plastic covers of the Assembly hymnals, but within a few weeks the hymnals themselves were withdrawn. Many copies of the inner teachings and administrative documents, the Missal, were burned. Melvin Potts was part of the detail that burned Missals in New York. They were carried in piles to an open space behind the chapter house and burned in a large metal can. Several Foundation leaders told me that all copies of the Missal had been destroyed, but over the next two years a few intact Missals turned up. There was a touching rumor that Father Phineas, the brother of Robert de Grimston, had hidden a complete copy in an elevator shaft, but this story was never confirmed. I obtained my copy in Canada.

Brother Faust, who was an IP Messenger in New York until just after the split, has described that period to me. The Teachings were phased out over the first few weeks after Robert's expulsion. "Everyone was waiting for the great revelation—what really went on—a spiritual interpretation of the scandal." Fathers John and Aaron held four days of meetings, explaining radical doctrinal changes. From two in the afternoon until eleven or twelve at night, a few of the key ideas were thrashed out at length. It was explained that Robert was indeed a manifestation of Christ, but that Christ was in truth a negative being. I am told there was even a solemn exorcism ritual in which both Satan and Christ were cast out of the New York chapter. Everyone was urged "to overcome their Christ and Satan parts," which were described as "malevolent spirits." Lucifer, oddly enough, simply faded from the scene. Only Jehovah remained, triumphant over the other Gods, now recognized as the one true God.

THE FOUNDATION VIEW

On my first visit to the New York branch of the Foundation, I naturally asked my former Processean friends why the Separation had occurred. Sister Tamar told me they had tried the old way of the Process and found it "would not work." What did this mean? First, she said, the Process was not receiving a favorable response from the public. People were repelled by the image and doctrines of the cult. Second, members themselves felt they had lost a sense of purpose. What they were doing had lost its meaning. When I spoke with Brother Eros, he stressed these same two points.

Brother Ariel, who left immediately before Robert's expulsion, has given a slightly different explanation. He said the cult had overfished its spiritual sea. The street work became tougher because "our areas were drying up because of misuse and donating. We had overused them, in a sense. Donating was a hassle because people were nasty to us on the streets because they'd been stopped too many times. There was high demand to make more money than we'd ever made before, when it wasn't even possible to make the same amount." Obsessed with its own problems, the leadership was no longer able to give the Messengers security or direction, only demands. Yonge Street, a main donating area in Toronto, was one example of fished-out territory. For over two years, almost every day, the cult sent Donators to beg from shoppers and businessmen in the space of a few city blocks. "Everybody insulted you—'Get the fuck out of here!'—so donating was hard, and they kept expecting us to make ten to fifteen dollars an hour."

Many attempts had been made to find glory. Pseudo-therapeutic self-discovery had been very exciting in 1963, but after ten years it had lost all of its attraction for Processeans. They had tried wild, exciting adventures in Xtul, in Germany, and in many public and private settings. Adventure was only a strain to them now. The most recent attempt to find glory had been a bid for warm acceptance by the general public. Success would not have afforded transcendence from the human condition, but at least it would have been success. The group was not ready to give up on the general public, because it was not well supported by steady income from any significant laity of Outside Processeans. The IPs had returned to a comfortable middle-class lifestyle, complete with television sets and small children. The cult had gone most of the distance toward becoming a church. Forced by failure to change again, it changed further in the direction of conventional church status.

When I last interviewed them, Founders had had two years to look back and develop their theory of what went wrong in the Process, both to quell painful memories and to provide a basis for future decisions. They often described it in theological terms, in terms of falling away from the correct, traditional teachings of God. Raphael said, "Our problems arose with the doctrine of the Unity." The twin theological innovations of the Unity of Christ and Satan and the Great Gods of the Universe were described as vast mistakes. Process theory attempted to define evil out of existence. As I see it, this meant that social control was precarious, and if exercised, created great internal cultural contradictions. One God can represent the authority of the leaders, but several Gods must represent moral chaos. As I did, the reader may find the celestial committee composed of Lucifer, Jehovah, Christ, and Satan attractive. They symbolize pluralism, liberalism, the modern temperament in medieval guise. To follow them, one must be a relatively free, versatile person. The Masters of the cult wanted a God through which they could control their followers, not a collection of Gods each making costly demands on the Masters.

Process theology was too abstract and intellectualized, Founders said. To some extent they blamed Robert. As Micah told me, and as I have observed for myself, Robert's thought processes were extremely "paradigmatic," in the sense that he analyzed everything in terms of ideal types and categorical schemes. As Micah put it, "He would paradigm anything he could get his hands on. The bucket was never a bucket, it was a *Platonic Bucket*." He still respected Robert, however, and called him an "extremely good theorist."

Founders took much of the blame on themselves and said that, while the theology was primarily Robert's invention, they all participated in producing it, and all accepted it with enthusiasm at first. Aaron called the idea of the Unity of Christ and Satan "a fascinating, very beautiful philosophy." At first "it seemed very good in almost every way," but later it proved "workable in no way." Malachi said the Process had a tendency to seek purely intellectual and symbolic solutions for what were real, practical problems, "to explain something with another explanation, and then to explain *that* with *another* explanation. And I think our theology began to proliferate in a way that was becoming more and more removed from the original. It wasn't theology that attracted us in the first place. It was the concept of being able to *do* something about our situation. You can sit in your armchair and write catechisms, but it actually doesn't produce any change."

They blamed Jesus Christ as much as Robert de Grimston. Raphael said that the Unity of Christ and Satan "looked like a very logical extension of the whole Love Your Enemies teaching. It seemed like a very viable way of overcoming hatred, of overcoming fear." John felt that "What we were doing was seeing whether taking what Christ is historically said to have taught to its logical conclusions" would really work, "and we found that it didn't." When the Foundation exorcised Christ along with Satan, it was expelling a particular conception of Christ: "What we were rejecting was the kind of love which is weak and leads to a lowering of standards."

The Christian message, as interpreted by Robert, had weakened the cult both emotionally and financially. As we saw in earlier chapters, in the 1970s the Process evolved into a social service organization, attempting to feed and rehabilitate miserable, unproductive people with few virtues or attractive qualities. I argued that this followed from the cult's need to present itself as a church and from the exigencies of the history of the Process, particularly its economic and recruitment traditions. But at the theological level, this was what Christ and Robert seemed to demand. Malachi came to ask, "How effective am I, say, spending my evenings sitting down next to some poor old guy who's an alcoholic and who has nothing else in his head but that?" Were the continual visits to Willowbrook and other homes for the mentally disabled really worthwhile? "I've been to Willowbrook or its equivalent until it's come out my ears!" The Process had burned out.[100]

Father Joshua spoke with great feeling, even agony: "In the last six years, we've plumbed the depths, at times, of our own negativity, collectively and individually. That was one of the realities of the Process that we were setting out to [change when we became the Foundation]." When Robert suggested the Unity of Christ and Satan, "he commanded quite a lot of respect from a lot of people. So it was a case of, 'Okay, let's try it.'" Like Raphael, John, Aaron, and Malachi, Father Joshua came to feel "It works in theory; it doesn't work in practice." He exclaimed, "We tried to make it work! We believed it! We felt, 'It should work! It really should work, you know!' Helping people and loving your enemies. When we tried to help people, they didn't want to be helped. Because what we were putting out was the Unity of Christ and Satan, we would love the enemy and everybody as it were; the kind of people that we attracted were for the most part [disordered people with nothing to contribute]. These people didn't want our message. They just wanted handouts, clothing."

It was a terrible strain to try to help them, even worse because it was useless. Father Joshua continued: "We were out there earning the money, paying for the coffeehouses for these people to come in and tear apart. We lost a lot of energy. We lowered our standards to allow people to join because we needed people. We lost energy going into giving and giving and giving and giving and giving and giving and giving and giving into a big black hole. We plumbed the depths, and that was the major bottom that we had. We almost folded. Almost didn't make it. Oh, awful! Awful! We really had to do something drastic. So we took it to the man and we said, 'Unity doesn't work, Robert. Afraid. Sorry.' Collective, it was a collective thing. Robert was appointed, as I'm sure you're aware, by a Council of Masters. The Council of Masters took it to Robert, and Robert said, 'Well, I still believe in it.' So they said, 'Well, bye...'"

Robert, of course, had been rather thoroughly insulated from the problems faced by his followers, living apart from any of the chapters at places like Key Largo and Mount Chi. Father Joshua complained: "He hadn't done what we'd done. He'd never done it on the street! He'd never done it in the coffee-houses. He couldn't understand that it couldn't work. As far as we were concerned, by our fruits we were seeing that it didn't work. It was hard. It was getting harder. We were being hurt. So we had to make a clean sweep. When we did that, when we formed the Foundation, there was a vision of Jehovah again. It was a vision of what it was like at the start. We saw where we were, and I cried. I cried inside. I cried to people. And also I cried in music. I was so involved trying to earn money to support people who didn't want my help. I'd lost my original vision, love, fire in the belly. And when I saw it again I was like a baby. I broke down! I cried! I cried with release and relief. I was also angry. I was angry at Robert de Grimston. There was an awful lot of failure. The numbers of things that we tried to achieve! And they all failed. The Process was a complete failure, as far as we were concerned. There was a period there when we were foundering around. We didn't know where we were going. We just knew that we had to get back to God."

The Foundation really dated the Separation from Christmas 1973, rather than from Robert's expulsion three months later, because the major issue was first raised at the cult's year-end meeting of the Council of Masters. Raphael said, "That conference was the first time that serious doubts had been expressed in a conference-type situation about this whole theology of the Unity." All the important people were there, and Raphael agreed with Joshua that many Masters felt that the doctrine was a failure: "'We don't feel it.' 'It's a lie.' 'We're telling ourselves a lie.' 'We're telling other people a lie.' 'This is not what God's about.' There'd been a number of feelings like that. Through the early part of '74, those feelings grew stronger. It came to a head in the spring of '74 when it became quite clear that the vast majority of us couldn't stomach this any longer. It felt to us to be completely alien to what we'd started out with in the first place, way back in Xtul. But to de Grimston it was his life's work. He'd suggested this particular theology, and he felt it was the answer for him, so we said, 'Okay, Robert, you have the Process and its doctrines. We will start again.'"

EMERGENCE OF THE FOUNDATION CULTURE

When one cult seeks to imitate the success of another, or when one splits from another, it must balance the need to copy with the need to differentiate. The Foundation had to reject much of the old Process without giving up the strongest aspects of the original culture. The *New York Times* reporter Eleanor Blau, who had first interviewed Processeans in 1971, reported near the end of 1974 that "Young Sect No Longer Hails Devil." She explained:

> Three years ago, some young men and women in black capes, a likeness of the devil at tips of their collars, were among the more noticeable groups offering literature and their views of God and man on the street Corners of New York. 'Christ said, Love your enemies,' therefore one ought to love Satan, was a tenet of the group, which called itself the Process Church ofthe Final Judgment. Today most of these people wear blue instead of black. Blazers and slacks have replaced their exotic attire. They call themselves the Foundation Church of the Millennium. They no longer try to love Satan.[101]

The leaders could not discard everything instantly, and they adopted various tactics for achieving change at the least cost. One approach was to rename things; a related approach was to reinterpret them. The Process had developed a public vocabulary of coined words. The Foundation retained much of the reality, changing only the image. Table 10 gives a comparative glossary of Process and Foundation terms, with their common meanings. Most of the new terminology came in during the first weeks of the "new church" and was a very inexpensive way of producing great superficial change.

Process	Foundation	Meaning
RITUAL TERMS:		
Alpha	Sanctum	the main ritual room
Altar	Shrine	the ritual table
Assembly	Celebration	a group ritual
Sacrifist	Celebrant	presiding priest at a ritual
Evangelist	Herald	priest that gives the sermon
Servers	Bearers	ritual assistants
MEMBERSHIP RANKS:		
Master	Luminary	the top leaders
Provisional Master	Minor Luminary	lieutenant leaders
Superior	Celebrant	junior "Mothers" and "Fathers"
Prophet	Mentor	senior "Brothers" and "Sisters"
IP Messenger	Covenantor	lowest rank of "ministers"
OP Messenger	Witness	student ministers
Disciple	Lay Founder	lay member who tithes
Initiate	Aspirant	new member
GENERAL:		
Process	Foundation	name of the organization
Chapters	Foundations	branches of the church
IPs	Elect	core members, "ministers"
Donating	Funding	the street work
Baptize	Consecrate	initiate to a new status
DJ (Dow-Jones)	JF (Jehovah's Finances)	financial indicator
The Cavern	The Garden	the coffeehouse

TABLE 10. **Glossary of Word Transformations**

All of the Process's emblems were abandoned. The badges, crosses, and special rings were "deconsecrated" and either destroyed or sold as simple jewelry. All of the marked ritual equipment, including priests' tabards, were discarded. Only one emblem was invented to replace the several given up. Father Aaron said, "I think we played around with quite a number of things that somehow reflect what we are, or were, or wanted to be." The natural symbol for Jehovah was the six-pointed Star of David. Mother Cassandra, who had invented the original, straight-armed Process Sign, drew a very similar new monogram for the Foundation. The first emblem had been the letter *P* for *Process*; the new one was based on the letter *F* for *Foundation*. The final result

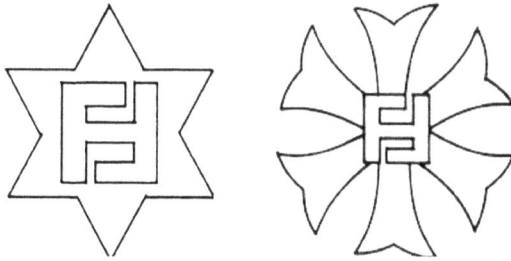

FIGURE 15. **Two versions of the Foundation symbol.**

in Figure 15 was a six-pointed star with a capital *F* in the center, with the *F* connected to a squared *J* to the right, representing Jehovah. Aaron said, "When this one came up, it just kind of rang bells with everybody, and we floated it around quite a lot of people, people with either an artistic or symbol-minded type of concern. And everybody seemed to think: 'This is great. That gets It.'" A later version stepped back from that very focused connection to the religion of the Old Testament, transforming the Star of David into what appeared like a flower, and conceptualizing the letters as two Fs, the second upside down, expressing Foundation Faith.

Aaron said the Foundation culture, like that of the Process, was built up eclectically, taking the best from many sources. It "is compiled out of thoughts, ideas, suggestions, things that people throw in or offer." One day, someone suggested that there should be flowers in the Sanctum for the various celebrations; "Then somebody came along and gave us a white rose, one week. And I thought: Oh, a white rose. A white rose symbolizes purity. We'll put it on the shrine in the celebration. So every week we have a white rose there." In May 1976, at some church festivity, a middle-aged Jewish man named Jerry was "doing a little number." He brought with him a shofar, the Jewish ram's-horn trumpet. He said, "This is a shofar; we'll give it to the Foundation." Aaron comments, "So obviously we had to use it. What is a shofar? It's for calling people to God. The obvious thing to do was to blow it at the start of every Sabbath Celebration."

Some hymns and chants were abandoned immediately, because their words and concepts were completely obsolete. Others were merely changed. For example, the second stanza of Process Chant no. 12, "Together we are come," expressed the value of community, the coming together of individuals mirroring the coming together of the parts of God:

Alone we are nothing,
Together we have strength;
Strength in our Unity,
The Unity of GOD.

The Foundation version of the same chant stresses the dominance of Jehovah. It preaches dedication to Him rather than commitment to the community:

Alone we are nothing,
With You we have strength,
Strength in our purpose,
The Glory of God.

For two years the church rituals limped along without printed hymnals. Little one-page "hymnlets" gave the words of the specific hymns selected for a Celebration, and the church printed several versions of hymnlets which were rotated for different weeks. Founders composed many songs, and finally in 1976 a modest hymnal was printed, incorporating suitable old Process hymns, some modified ones, and several new ones. Not all were composed by inner members. Hymn 25, "The Awaited One," was written by a young guitarist who was with the Foundation in New Orleans for a while and who, as Aaron said, "wrote this very beautiful atmospheric piece, and then went off his own way."

In every land there is a song
From the far horizons of time
A legend that's told in every tongue
The Awaited One shall come.

In doctrine, the Foundation was a bland simulacrum of a millenarian Jewish sect. It announced that the Messiah was coming soon, for the first time. Jesus was not the Messiah. Neither was Robert. Until the Messiah comes, we should live virtuous lives according to the laws of the Old Testament. Founders used a few Jewish terms, several showing up in hymn texts. The group's password was *Shalom*. Gone were the days of "As it is … so be it." Founders never wore crosses, but only their Stars of David. Several months after the Separation, I overheard one of the Foundation children warn a visitor who wore a cross that the man would go to Hell if he followed Christ. The church celebrated neither Christian nor Jewish holidays and did not follow Hebrew dietary laws.

The clientele of the church changed radically. In contrast to the old days, many of the people served by the Foundation were unhappy middle-aged people, considerably older than the ministers. In New York particularly, the clientele was primarily Jewish during this transition period. A number of steady customers spoke with Eastern European accents and brought in with them many elements of traditional Jewish culture. But it must be emphasized that most Founders did not come from Jewish families. I was able to determine the religious origins of twenty-five dedicated Founders, and only five were Jewish. An equal number were Roman Catholic, and there was an Armenian Orthodox, a Unitarian, and one with no religious training at all. The other twelve were all Protestants: five Anglicans, two Presbyterians, and five from other denominations. Perhaps the doctrines of the group were so vague because they represented the lowest common denominator of beliefs held from childhood by members.

Mother Seraphine recited the basic tenets of the group on one of its radio shows in early 1975: "The Foundation Church believes that a Messiah will come, not as some supernatural being but as a person with the qualities of leadership that will inspire people to a new way of living. Meanwhile, our function is to provide spiritual and moral leadership, to assert and affirm the values and codes in which we believe, to help and support people in need, and to offer a cause and a purpose for those looking for meaning in their lives and searching for truth within themselves."

Under such titles as Psychic Workshop, Focus, and Forum, the cult presented some of the most basic psychic activities that used to be performed in the Telepathy Developing Circles and the Progresses. I participated in several of the psychic activities at the New York and Chicago Foundations and discovered that much of the material was left over from the Process. Although the Missals were discarded, I was interested to discover that the leaders of the meetings most like the old Progresses were still using the same Training Synopses of Robert's writings that they had used years before. Robert's psychology theory, much of it at least, was still in use, although the fact was not made clear to any newcomer. Many Founders still typed each other in terms of God Patterns, although they no longer accepted any God but Jehovah.

In the summer of 1976, John and Aaron produced two doctrinal courses. I secured tapes of John's five-meeting course and discovered that it was hardly a course at all but really just brief statements followed by free-floating discussions. Titled *The New Reality,* this course covered five topics: love, the mind,

God, morality, and the world. The few ideas in the lectures were a mixture of the most sentimental conventional religiosity and a few leftover Process concepts. Occasionally John quoted the Bible. At one point he retold the Garden of Eden story. In the third lecture he discussed the different ideas people have about God—mentioning the Process's Gods obliquely—then argued that the only true God is Jehovah the God of the Old Testament.

John's introductory lecture was about love. We all desire love, he said. Love from family and friends is not great enough and not secure. We long for more, for something greater, something more reliable. It is a mistake to depend entirely on human beings. What we really need is love from God: perfect love, complete love, infinite love. We must keep God's commandments, or we will be cut off from Him, from the source of all love. "The ability to love is totally and solely dependent on being receptive to God." We could say that the original social implosion that produced the Process was driven by the hunger for infinite love. Not finding it in each other, not finding it in Robert de Grimston, the old Processeans had turned to Jehovah, an invisible and therefore indisputable source of such love. Poor in specific doctrines, the Foundation filled the gap with occult and psychic speculations. The church did not commit itself to belief in Astrology, Telepathy, the human Aura, or whatever, but toyed with these concepts as tentative, surrogate, low-level doctrine. It had become a psychic supermarket, purveying whatever occultism it could, indulging in whatever psychic activities seemed to appeal to people.

When I visited the Chicago Foundation in September 1975, Father Mathew took me along with him to a Psychic Fair being held by a number of occult groups in a magnificent lakeside convention center. The fair organizer, an independent entrepreneur, leased convention hall space, then rented booths to about thirty groups and individuals. There were palm readers, sellers of mystic equipment, representatives of Silva Mind Control, and every manner of occult professional. The Foundation had rented a double-sized booth for $150. They propped their big Star of David symbol up on a chair and offered Psychic Readings (Psychometry) for $5 and $10. I paid Brother Dagon $10 to do a reading, using my hand as the Psychometry object, focusing on the question of whether the Foundation would like my book when it came out. He said yes. I think he was wrong. Matthew told me at that time that the church was not and didn't want to be known as "a group of psychics. That's not our shtick." Rather, he said, it was a religious group interested in psychic phenomena.

In its early days, the Process presented its own message and was not hospitable to people who wanted to use the cult as a forum for their own non-Processean beliefs. However, the early Foundation invited many occult lecturers to give presentations. The Foundation referred to itself as a "psychic center," if not exactly a psychic supermarket, and used the contributions of famous occultists to build its own fame and make a little money. Among the subjects covered in lectures and demonstrations given by outsiders at the New York Foundation in 1976 were: Acupuncture, Alchemy, Astrology, Auras, the Bermuda Triangle, Biofeedback, Dowsing, ESP, Etheric Movement, Eurythmy, Hindu Astrology, Huna, Hypnosis, Iridology, Jungian Psychotherapy, Kirlian Photography, Naturopathy, Numerology, Psychotronics, Pyramid Power, Reflexology, Sufism, the Scudder Method of Healing, Telekinesis, Tibetan Buddhism, UFOs, and Zen Meditation. The Foundation held its own Psychic Fairs, a Psychic Festival, a Spiritual Technology Conference, Psychic Weekends, and an occult boat cruise around Manhattan.

The Foundation tried to make money at all its activities. It passed collection plates in the Sabbath rituals, something the Process had never done. It charged admission for the guest lectures, then split the take with the lecturers. Admission to the Focus or Forum (Progress) activities was $2. Psychic Readings, such as the one Sister Tamar gave me in New York, generally ran $5 for fifteen minutes. Sister Samaria did Psychic Sketches, pastel drawings that went for a few dollars. More money came in from individual healing sessions, aura readings, and Spiritual Consultations which cost $30. The Foundation held courses in occult practices. The fee for Sister Roxana's course "An Introduction to Astrology" was $70, while Mother Hathor's eight "Spiritual Healing" classes had a $100 fee.

TRANSFORMATIONS OF RITUAL

The Sabbath ritual evolved rapidly after the Separation, but the changes merely continued the trends in the last year of the Process. Figure 16 shows the layout of the New York Sanctum for the Sabbath Celebrations held there after mid-1975. As in the Process, there were water and fire bearers, marked with W and F, but only one minister, the Celebrant, marked with C. The two "cbs" were collection bowls, and the S in the diagram identifies where the Lead Singer sat. Both the physical layout and dramatic performance made it entirely clear that the clergy had become professional mediators between the congregation and

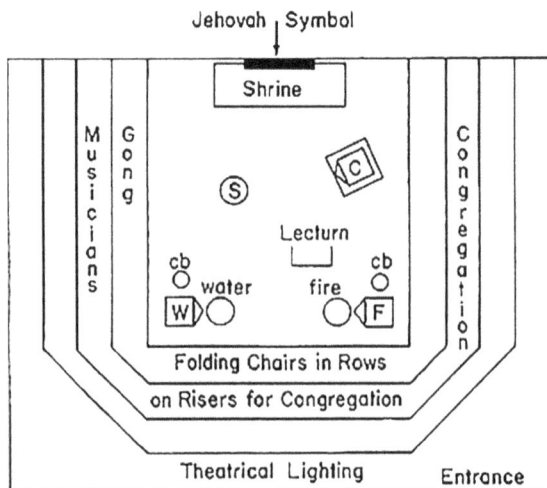

FIGURE 16. **Layout of the Foundation's Sabbath celebration.**

God. They were no longer extensions of the congregation, expressing the Gods that dwelled within, as they had been in the classical Process.

The rituals, strangely, had also lost their mysticism, their sacredness, and their profundity. The Celebrations had become *entertainments*. A year after the Separation, on February 22, 1975, I wrote in my field notes, "The Sabbath Celebration was more like a religious variety show than a group ritual. Father Lars started it off, pacing back and forth in front of the stage during the beginning like a warm-up MC from a TV show. He even began with jokes." At several rituals I attended over the next year and a half, the priests would suddenly drop character and explain to the audience what was going on, particularly when they were introducing a change in the ritual or a new song, but also at other times as well. The Celebrant acted like a Master of Ceremonies, introducing the Herald, who would enter and give a sermon, and musical soloists by name. In the old Process, the Sacrifist and Evangelist almost always kept a haughty detachment, seldom making eye contact with members of the congregation, never smiling except in the Revelation, infusing the ritual with as much drama and mystery as they could muster. The Foundation seemed more amateurish in its theatrics, perhaps because they were now conceived as theatrics rather than something more real.

I observed the ritual room of the New York branch evolve into a small theater from the time the building was first occupied at the beginning of 1975 until September 1976, when I terminated my field research. In early 1975, the ritual took place on a broad, low stage, covered by a carpet. Over the months, the Founders built four tiers of risers on three sides, transforming the room into a modern small theater with a sunken stage. They set up theatrical lighting controlled from a booth at the back. There was even a sound system. The audience for these presentations seldom surpassed seventy-five, however, including all the Founders. The smaller Chicago branch, with a minuscule clientele, continued to use a low stage and did not invest in elaborate remodeling of the ritual room.

The Shrine (altar) was a table, of various construction at different times and chapters, supporting small pieces of ritual equipment, including two custom-made seven-candle candelabras. I hesitate to call them "menorahs," because I never heard a Founder use this Jewish term. Hanging behind the Shrine, a few inches in front of the back wall, was a gold Star of David, about a yard across, with a huge, blue capital *FJ* in the center. Stage lighting was set so that, at certain points in the ritual, colored shadows of this emblem were cast on the white wall, symbolizing the presence of Jehovah.

Several old symbols were reinterpreted. The best example is the traditional use of fire and water. The New York Foundation took over the old Boston altar stands and the two silver bowls that had been contributed by Ron Forbes. One held water; the other contained a flaming Sterno can. Near the entrance of the ritual room, the Founders placed a second set of fire and water bowls on a little table. In the early days, Robert had introduced the use of fire and water to symbolize Satan and Christ. Every initiation ceremony, at every level, administered fire and water to transform the candidate into his new status. The Foundation retained these evocative symbols but reinterpreted their meaning. As Aaron told me in 1976, "They symbolized something different then from what they symbolize now, but they're still as symbolic and as usable. It's such an old, original, basic symbolism of God—the fire and the water, those two basic elements—the one representing the spirit and the other representing the physical." In Process initiation rituals and the Union Ceremony, the Hymn of Consecration would accompany the anointing with fire and water. One phrase was chanted many times: "May the Water give me Life, Purify me with the Fire." One verse sang of water and Christ, while another chanted to Satan:

> Purify me with the Fire,
> Satan, test me in Your Pit of Fire, desire...
> Purify me with the Fire,
> Tell me how to give my life to You.

After the Separation, the Foundation quickly dropped the Christ and Satan verses, and the Consecration Chant became the simple repetition, over and over, of "May the Water give me Life, Purify me with the Fire." There was no longer any explanation of what the fire and water represented. In February 1975, a new chant was introduced, with fresh music that gave new meaning to the symbolic elements:

By the Fire of Purification
And by the Water of Life
May the Great Lord Jehovah
Be with us now and forever.

One important piece of stage business used by the Process and modified in several forms by the Foundation was the blessing of the congregation using the fire and water. Called *The Invitation,* this blessing was spoken in the Sabbath Assembly by the Sacrifist. He rose to his feet, standing at his end of the circle of participants, facing the altar with the two bowls on stands at either side. As he spoke, he raised first one arm, then the other, pointing with two fingers of one hand straight at the water bowl, then with two fingers of the other hand at the fire:

May the life-giving Water of the Lord Christ
and the purifying Fire of the Lord Satan
bring the presence of Love and Unity
into this Assembly.

Immediately after the Separation, the Foundation changed this to:

May the Fire of Purification
and the Water of Life
bring the presence of love
into this Celebration.

Again, Christ and Satan had been removed from the symbolism, but the theatrically successful blessing with fire and water was retained. A year later, the relevance of the symbols to the Lord Jehovah was stressed, and the complexity of the stage business was greatly increased. Early in the Sabbath Celebration, the Celebrant (Sacrifist) would stand in front of the Shrine (altar), facing the congregation. The two Bearers of the bowls would come forward and stand on either side of him. The fire was not yet lit, and the water bowl was still empty. As he spoke, the Celebrant would take a burning taper from the altar and light the fire, then pour water into the other bowl from a flask that also had been resting on the altar. His words were an explanation to the congregation:

> This is the Fire of Purification through which
> our Lord Jehovah shall purge all sin and sickness
> from the world and from each of us.
> And this is the Water of Life through which
> He will invest in us His Spirit for the Millennium.

Another version of this blessing was used in Midnight Celebration rituals, the successor to the Process's Midnight Meditations. By the end of my observation period, September 1976, the original Invitation had been altered to dramatize explicitly the transformed theological universe of the church. The Processean Sacrifist pointed his hands toward the center of the encircling congregation as he spoke the Invitation. As we have seen, the focus of attention in the rituals before 1973 was at the center of the congregation. All the cosmic principles were conceived of as dwelling within the social group that comprised the cult. The Foundation worshiped a distant God, Jehovah who dwells in Heaven. When priests spoke to Jehovah in the Foundation rituals, they either gazed upward or faced the altar where His symbol hung. The focus was above and beyond the social group, in some cosmic realm quite outside the congregation. In the Midnight Celebration version of the Invitation, the Bearers came forward with their bowls, the fire already burning brightly and the water sloshing. As in the old Process initiation rituals, the priest passed his fingers through the fire and dipped them in the water as he spoke. But instead of pointing into the congregation, he raised his hands, two fingers of each extended as before, and pointed upward, at Heaven. His words stressed the new theology:

> By the Fire of Purification
> And by the Water of Life
> May this Celebration be filled with
> praise and exaltation to
> Our Lord Jehovah
> and to his Messiah.

Indeed, after my departure, Christ may have returned, as the sociologist of religion Massimo Introvigne has suggested.[102] Yet, beneath the visible surface, the Foundation continued the dynamic tradition of The Process, constantly seeking new inspirations.

FOUNDATION SOCIETY

The social organization of the Foundation was based on traditions developed by the Process, but there were changes. The first eighteen months after the Foundation were a time in which Founders concentrated on renewing their internal society and paid relatively little attention to those who used to be called OPs. The rank of Acolyte was dropped, and the rank of Initiate, now called Aspirant, was restricted to those few individuals working to become Witnesses (OP Messengers). The Witnesses lived in their own apartment, as had OP Messengers before them, but very few new people were recruited during the months of crisis. The most troublesome Disciples were driven away, and those few that remained were called Lay Founders. Asserting a distinction between clergy and laity, this name indicated a further step toward conventional church status. Formerly there had merely been several steps in increasing commitment. Witnesses were often described as "student ministers," while those above Witness rank, the Elect, were "ministers." In mid-1976, another status was invented, that of Friend of the Foundation, similar to Lay Founder except that Friends did not have to tithe but merely to make significant, continuing contributions in labor or money. The great mass of the people who attended Foundation psychic activities had no status in the church and tended to be a fluid population.

One important change was the emergence of the New York branch as a supreme headquarters. The Westchester County hideaway, formerly called Mount Chi but now Shiloh, was retained, but, instead of being the Omega, it was merely an adjunct of the New York headquarters chapter. At the beginning of 1975, the Foundation took over a four-story Manhattan building and began paying off the $900,000 price the owner demanded. For about a year, there was tremendous pressure on street Donators to bring in great sums of money, but when a good bit of the price had been paid off, and some spaces were rented to businessmen, the pressure let up. The three smaller chapters, in Toronto, New Orleans, and Chicago, were not centers of great cultural activity nor particularly good recruiting grounds. I think they mainly served as sources of money, centers for donating over wide geographical areas, but they also gave Founders the possibility of a more varied life through occasional transfer to different cities.

In August and September 1975, I conducted censuses of the New York and Chicago branches; the basic information obtained at that time appears in Table 11. We can see that the New York chapter was three times the size of the one in Chicago and contained far more high-status members. The status differential of males versus females in New York is explained by the fact that all the Luminaries and Minor Luminaries had been at Xtul, where there were twice as many males as females.

	New York			Chicago		
	Males	Females	Total	Males	Females	Total
Luminary	4	1	5	0	1	1
Minor Luminary	3	0	3	0	0	0
Celebrant	4	4	8	2	0	2
Mentor	2	6	8	2	3	5
Covenantor	1	4	5	2	1	3
Witness	0	3	3	0	0	0
Total	14	18	32	6	5	11

TABLE 11. **Census of the New York and Chicago Foundations**

Robert believed that the Foundation was completely dominated by Mary Ann. But when I asked Father John to describe the governmental structure of the Foundation, he told me what I had heard many times: "We have a board of directors which is composed of the Luminaries, both male and female. We have a kind of executive committee of four, of which I'm one." The other three were Joel, Raphael, and Aaron. John said this formal structure did describe the way things worked. He denied there was any hidden power structure in any way different from the explicit arrangements. The Four and the council of Luminaries were certainly capable of running thing on a day-to-day basis.

Brother Lars described Mary Ann as an exceptional person: "She has a vision. It's almost like a voice. One could say that she has an amazing perception of life, amazing perception on the direction" the Foundation should go. He acknowledged that she gave vital guidance: "To describe her, she is like a channel. How do you describe a channel? I think the biggest thing that I feel personally around her is the love of God. The amount of care. And that is probably the biggest thing, that she cares. She cares about us. She cares about the direction that we are heading."

Raphael knew Mary Ann well and said he had a clear perspective on the role she played over the years: "She was, I would say, very much Robert's wife. She never was an out-front figure in any sense. She was enormously helpful in the original setting up in London. But I would say that over the years he was always the out-front one. She was never involved in the organization of the Process. She was always very supportive of him." I asked Raphael if she received any financial support from the Foundation. Hesitantly, haltingly, he said, "No... No... No." What is her role today? "She is now a friend of ours, but she lives a very private kind of life. She does a lot of traveling around. She's sometimes in town, but not very often. And she has no official connection with us at all." Micah agreed. He said Mary Ann has "always remained a good, true friend, a constant companion and true friend, and I think reasonably stays in the background." Her only participation with the church was "in a very loosely advisory capacity." Yet when decades later Micah published his extensive autobiography of his Process and Foundation years, using the name Timothy Wyllie, he reported she was the dominant figure in the cult.

In reporting his own experiences during that problematic time, Wyllie analyzed the culture of the Foundation as if it possessed two factions initially. He himself belonged to the Universalists, who were enthusiastic about continuing to explore alternative ideas, psychic activities, and recruiting widely from the general public. The other faction was dominated by Mary Ann, whom Wyllie called an autocrat, represented by the Four, who were her highest status followers. Before long, she had banned many of the activities that Wyllie preferred, calling them "secular," which led to a schism. In 1977, he and perhaps fifteen other members sought a degree of independence, and with seven of them Wyllie set up an apartment for a group they called the Unit which they hoped would be allowed to function as a local church still within the Foundation. For a while that seemed to work, but the central organization demanded increasing money from the Unit, even taking it to court in 1978, followed by total disintegration.[103]

Without revealing private, personal details, I happened to have a strong connection to another leader of the Unit, have been in communication with him over the decades and recently shared with him my work revising this history of the Process. He was intelligent, expressed a rather stable personality, and continued his personal exploration of culture, publishing extensively in many media. Thus, I know that Wyllie's style of life and writing was but one alternative among many explored by former Processeans, many of them fitting the general definition of Luciferianism.

Another very revealing autobiography was posted online by Jared Garrett with the suggestive title *Hey Kid, There's Nothing Wrong with You.* The book tells his personal story in great detail and has this summary: "I grew up in a cult called The Foundation Faith of God, which splintered off of Scientology in the Sixties. I escaped when I was seventeen after a childhood of neglect, abuse, rituals, intermittent good times, and lots and lots of work and books. I spent my childhood wondering why I'd been abandoned by my parents. My journey to overcome years of abuse, neglect, and emotional damage has been a process of discovering what individual worth and personal strength mean."[104] I knew his "parents" well, but he was born when children were raised collectively and conceptualized as children of the cult not of their immediate biological ancestors. Some of the children remained within the Foundation and now are inheriting rewarding roles within the non-religious charity organization that evolved from it. So, without an extensive study, interviewing many of the middle-aged adults who had been born into the communes, we cannot fully understand what it meant to enter existence through this unconventional door.

I must leave to someone else the task of writing an ethnography of the Foundation Church of the Millennium and its evolution over the decades into a nature conservancy that seems to have outgrown psychotherapy, magic, and religion. In the following chapter we will examine the rebirth of the Process after the Foundation. For Founders, the Process failed and was discarded with Robert de Grimston. When Robert and Morgana fled the group, they lost the social structure of the Process but took the culture with them. Robert and some of the chief Luminaries of the Foundation say he took *The Process* with him. The history from 1963 through 1976 is the story of a social group that became a cult that developed into a sect that nearly completed a transformation to the status of conventional religious denomination. On February 27, 1978, it dropped the word "Millennium" from its formal name on the New Orleans incorporation, and that year it moved to a remote location in Arizona. On August 12, 1993, it dropped the word "God."

CHAPTER 10 A New Beginning

There is nothing left now with the world of men, but to take from the midst of humanity the few, the very few who do not belong to humanity, and to allow the Devastation of the Latter Days to take its inevitable course.

— *And Now the Judgment,* Process scripture

IN THE YEAR AFTER THE SEPARATION, small groups of former Processeans gathered in New Orleans, Chicago, Boston, and Toronto. Inspired by their interest, Robert de Grimston attempted to create his cult anew. Because he felt the old cult was a complete failure, he refused to use the same methods a second time. Therefore he did not start with a therapy process or any other mechanism to strengthen social bonds among the people who came to him. Rather, he encouraged them to begin with the sudden creation of new functioning church chapters. Given that many Outside Processeans lived in the Boston area where I happened to be, and that chapter had been closed when the regional focus shifted to New York City, I was able to observe the most complete attempt at revival. Had the OPs been orderly people enjoying economic security, they might have been able to form a cohesive group through living, working, and studying together. But, for the most part, they were unprepared for the challenge: socially isolated, disoriented by the counterculture of the 1960s, and in some cases suffering serious personal problems. The many disoriented Processeans drained the vitality of the few talented ones. The Process's Renaissance was really a Dark Age.

REBIRTH OF THE PROCESS

The Process was dead, but there were many who wanted it brought back to life. Some had left the cult in the most painful days, dissatisfied but not yet thoroughly disillusioned. They wanted bigger roles in a better cult. A larger group consisted of the rejected would-be Processeans, people who had not been allowed to enter the high-class world of inside members. They wanted a cut-rate cult that would confer on them the high status jealously guarded by the people now in the Foundation. And there was Robert de Grimston. He wanted his Process back.

Robert offered a weekly Process seminar to New Orleans peripherals and contemplated expanding it into a Process College. Author of the Teachings, he felt they were the heart of the movement. He incorrectly believed that the mere dissemination of his doctrines could create a new church. Attendance at the seminar was irregular. The people who came had little concept of the theology and were neither philosophical nor intellectual. Robert tried to teach them from his unpublished 1971 book manuscript *Blame and Demand*.

At one seminar, attended by only four peripheral Processeans, there was a lengthy debate between Robert and a fellow we can call Rock, who wanted to tour the country with the status of Process minister. But Rock was not sure he should try to sell the whole package. The head of the New Orleans Foundation, Father Raphael, had lectured his flock on the failings of Robert's teachings. Rock commented: "Now Raphael had a point when he said that the Unity of Christ and Satan got in the way" of public acceptance. "A number of people that I've talked to were under the impression that Processeans had sexual intercourse with the Devil."

Robert exclaimed, "Does one abandon a set of beliefs and teachings because there are people who have difficulty with them?" Rock, who cared little for the doctrines but much for the status of minister, was unmoved. Robert continued, "But, you know, I've found, and I think many, many Processeans have found, that on personal contact, with a little explanation, there are very few people who don't at least begin to understand that it's not Devil worship, not paganism, not black magic. It's something basically good." Other seminar participants agreed with Rock that the doctrine was hard to sell. Robert argued passionately: "Could you imagine that Jesus would have scrapped his teaching because the Pharisees regarded it as the work of the Devil?" But Rock replied that they would have to compromise if they were going to build a successful church organization.

Morgana leapt into the debate: "This is the basis of the split between the Foundation and the Process, because the Foundation, in my terms, became identified totally with the structure, with the organization, and completely negated the teachings. Those became secondary." She and Robert spoke almost in unison: "And therefore, of course, if there was any block to the expansion of the organization in the teachings, you scrap the teachings!" Nobody was convinced. Robert failed to get a dedicated group together in New Orleans. Former Processeans in other cities wrote, called, and even visited him. He decided to explore the situation.

Robert flew to New York City for the weekend of July 27-28, 1974, in order to meet with many northeast Processeans, say his piece in the shadow of the Foundation headquarters, and test the possibilities for the future. A disciple made arrangements for Robert to speak in a Victorian church in Greenwich Village on Saturday evening. A large audience attended, most of them former Processeans who had never actually seen Robert before. The next day, Robert met with two dozen of these people at Washington Square Park. They sat on newspapers on the ground, sang cult songs, and talked. Finally, they held a Meditation, then the nostalgic gathering broke up. There had been no formal discussion of a rebirth of the Process, but enough people had shown an interest in Robert to convince him that the cult could indeed be revived.

Robert flew back to New Orleans and contemplated his prospects. What he really wanted to do was spread his teachings and receive honor and support from readers. He submitted his manuscript *The Matthew Commentaries*, an exegesis of the New Testament, to commercial publishers, but none were interested. The Process College never materialized. A month after the New York trip, he sent an open letter to his fans, saying: "You may form ANY kind of group or corporation or commune that suits you." Hinting that a rebirth of the cult was on the horizon, he said his fans were free to wear uniforms, take ranks and titles, and hold rituals. He promised to provide material for doctrinal seminars.

All the people Robert had met in New York were strangers to him. The most able and mature of them was a talented ceramic artist and former architect. He played a very significant role for several months as Robert's chief assistant, but not using a public sacred name, so here we will give him a rather profound pseudonym: Osiris. That is the name of an ancient Egyptian "god," who however really may have been a religious leader who like Jesus was killed but then imagined by his followers to have been resurrected to take on the role of mediator with the actual gods. So, from the perspective of the Process, Osiris could have been identified as the original Christ, crucified two thousand years before Jesus was.

Osiris was a Coptic Egyptian who was living near Boston with his American girlfriend and her little boy. He had joined the cult in Boston, was assigned to the Miami chapter, then quit after nearly a year of Messenger status. "I discovered it ceased to be what I wanted." Osiris was a really remarkable man. As a boy, he had organized a hashish club dedicated to experiencing everything of which the spirit was capable and gaining complete mastery over every mode of consciousness. He had investigated a number of religious organizations, including Rosicrucianism, not as a religious seeker but as a spiritual connoisseur and epicure. Osiris joined the Process because it seemed dedicated to "adventure, fun, growth, expansion. The main attraction to me was the feeling of: we're a group of people who are willing to follow our stars—no matter where it leads—up or down or sideways."

In a series of phone calls, Osiris and Robert discussed the future of the cult and ultimately decided to launch it again in Boston. In New Orleans, Chicago, and Toronto, there were small groups of former Disciples who had longed to be Inside Processeans but had never made the grade. But there were also Foundation chapters in all three cities, which would have been uncomfortable competition for a fledgling Process. The Foundation had pulled out of Boston, leaving many OPs high and dry, ready to link up with any version of the cult that might appear.

There seemed to be the beginning of a Boston chapter already in existence. To preserve their privacy while facilitating clarity in this complex narrative, here we will give them pseudonyms. The Process Disciples Bob Stone and Sam Rhodes, with Bob's wife Maude, had been talking about reincorporating the church and had been holding regular meetings with several friends, including D. Lord, Rose, Marsha, and Julio Famagusta. A second group consisted of ex-Messengers living in what had been the old Disciple commune on Suffolk Street: Ariel, Vita Cordova, Isolde, and Woody. These two groups had little in common, disliked each other, but seemed to be a promising beginning.

Other individuals connected in the following weeks, whom we shall call: Ron Forbes, Mark Lembert, Al Capone, Roger Bergman, Rico Sorbo, Quincy Adams, Wendy Adams, and Melvin Potts. Osiris contacted many of the former cult members in and around Boston and told them that Robert de Grimston was coming to gather his followers. On October 5, Robert was "on my way to Boston to find out what the Game has in store for me there. The strongest Process contingent is in Boston. And the time has come to discover whether I'm meant to be directly involved in the recreation of a physical Process structure. The signs, of course, are ambivalent."

Robert moved in with Osiris and held a series of seven organizational meetings with the Boston cliques. On October 8, Robert's birthday, Sam Rhodes held a huge party for everybody at his parents' home. Old friendships were reestablished, and many people met for the first time. There were many unattached former cult members in the area, but Robert tried to work primarily through the two main groups. Bob Stone had been holding meetings and rituals, often at a casual-furniture shop, the Bean Bag Store. On the average, eight people attended, and a total of fourteen different folk came to one or more of his meetings. None of them had been Messengers for any length of time. Osiris had a definite opinion of Stone's bean-baggers: "They had some connection with the Process in the past, and they missed that very much, and they wanted to keep it going as long as possible. Like: Daddy and Mommy left home and haven't come back. It feels lonely without Daddy and Mommy, so we'll play-act Daddy and Mommy and do exactly the same things that were going on. So we'll have this nice, warm security feeling. And hopefully if we keep doing that, Daddy and Mommy will come back." Daddy Robert was home again.

The Suffolk Street ex-Messengers, Ariel said, were "people who had left the Process on rather a sour note." It was a colder group than Stone's, reserved even in its skepticism. Sue Knowles, former proprietor of the Process Thrift Store and now a teacher, was unnerved by Robert's style of communication as she observed it in his Suffolk Street conferences: "He doesn't listen to what other people are saying. He has his vision, and that's where he's at. He laid out his latest vision of where he wanted the Process to go. And I think Brother Patrick said something about: well, that wasn't exactly what he wanted. He wanted more openness, more freedom, and more New Game type of playing. And Robert again repeated his vision. No one said a word. And he said, 'I think everybody agrees with that.' And no one said a word. He did that about three or four times, the whole silent consent thing, and just went on that everyone had accepted it. Everybody was just so awestruck with him."

The plan that emerged from all these conferences was that Osiris would find a house the cult could rent, people would all move in together, and a new Boston chapter would come into being. Osiris located a renovated house in Waltham, west of the city, that was divided into four apartments. He and Robert went through the list of those who wanted to move in and selected only those with jobs or very good employment prospects. Most of the old Messengers withdrew from the project when they saw what the other Processeans looked like and learned what Robert expected of them. The group assembled only enough cash for two of the four apartments, a third was taken by a pair of non-Processean women, and the fourth was left empty. The chosen people moved in at the beginning of November, but Robert and Osiris continued to live together with Osiris's girlfriend and her son.

Two weeks later, a group of rejected, unemployed Processeans, acting without official sanction, scraped up a few dollars and rented the fourth apartment in the house. Ariel said the main group deliberated and "it was decided that it's silly to have them living in that apartment next door and be separate from us. So we absorbed them, but in absorbing them we had to open up the doors to everyone." Although no one knew it at the time, this decision assured failure of the entire project. The three apartments filled up. There were two married couples: Bob and Maude Stone, Quincy and Wendy Adams. Three couples paired off informally: Vita Cordova and Ariel, Isolde and Woody, Rose and D. Lord. One woman, Marsha, lived by herself. The remainder were unruly, unattached males. Although the ex-Messengers sometimes used their old sacred names, there was such confusion over the relative statuses of the house members that the group did not adopt the old system of ranks. The imposition of such a system might have introduced a measure of coherence to social relations, but at the cost of acute resentment by those who would wind up at the bottom. The group talked about ranks as a thing of the future, a fantasy that never did emerge.

The ex-Messengers were able people of middle-class background. Except for Bob Stone, none of the other people were regularly employed and did not care to be. When the Process had come into existence back in London, a social implosion stimulated by many powerful therapy sessions brought individuals together into a cohesive group. This time, people with little in common and no history of developing cohesion were thrown together in an ambiguous living situation in the vain hope that something grand would develop. Had Robert immediately begun therapy sessions, had there been some selectivity in admitting candidates for membership, and had there been a more favorable economic base for the Waltham Process, the social cleavages might have been overcome. But Robert was done with formal therapy as an outreach method. He wanted his teachings to be the seed for the new cult. Waltham was like a sack full of wild, hungry cats. In four months, it tore itself apart.

WALTHAM ASPIRATIONS

The Walthamites had high hopes. For the first and probably last time in their lives, they had a chance to make history. They thought it was just barely possible that they were like Christ's disciples, never-to-be-forgotten founders of a new age. Julio said Waltham was really a "training camp." He said, "This is boot camp for the Army of God." He wanted to be High Pontiff in charge of designing rituals for the new church. Marsha was content to become an IP, while Rose's ambition was to be a "minister." D. Lord desperately longed to be a Messenger. Melvin Potts expressed a philosophical attitude: "If it's meant for me to go into the Hierarchy, I think I'd like it. The entire idea of this house is basically: the majority of those who go through this will be the new Hierarchy when we reopen."

The Waltham house decorated the semblance of a Process church. A great communal feast was served on Thanksgiving, and everyone gorged on donated turkeys and other goodies. Sam Rhodes entertained with a magic show, and there was singing. Late that evening, the house was formally consecrated by Robert de Grimston. The Processeans stood together in black uniforms, holding candles, and chanting. They went from room to room, consecrating every nook with fire and water. At every turn, Robert proclaimed,

"This House belongs to the Gods!"

At first, the Sabbath Assemblies were rather informal. Then D. Lord invested a week of woodworking to make a complete set of ritual furniture, including a circular altar, two carved priests' chairs, stands for the fire and water bowls, and a gong made from a pot lid. Mark Lembert made a silver and black plywood emblem to hang against a black curtain in the living room of one of the apartments. The room became a holy place, the Waltham Alpha, with the unveiling of the new equipment at the Sabbath, on Saturday, December 14. The Assembly was held in the classical form, with the circular altar at the center and twenty-one Processeans sitting in an oval around it.

December was the time of greatest excitement and hope. Thanksgiving established Waltham as the Boston chapter. The new ritual equipment and black uniforms elevated the drama of the cult. Robert, Morgana, and Osiris moved into the house around the 20th. The Christmas Eve party was the high point before everything slid into ruin. There was a wreath on the door, greens on the bookcase, and a nice Christmas tree in a corner of the Alpha. Each resident of the house made a cardboard ornament for the tree. The dinner was wonderful. There was turkey (but no gravy), bread dressing, mashed potatoes, bread and butter, pies, cookies, and fruit punch. After supper, Sam Rhodes put on another magic show, dressed in top hat and tails, using a school desk covered with a black cloth as his work table. His magic equipment emerged from an old suitcase labeled the Great Destroyer. Silk handkerchiefs changed color before our very eyes. Rings linked and unlinked, leaving only the slightest suspicion that one of them might have had a gap in it. Sam poured milk from a gimmicked pitcher into a rolled newspaper, then made it vanish. He drew a coin from Isolde's ear. Too bad his powers were insufficient to restore his own health or that of his cult.

One factor that did not help the chances for the Walthamite church was the poor medical condition of many members. One man's intestinal difficulties threw him into the hospital more than once, and eventually he gave up trying to live a vigorous life and moved out of the Waltham house to live with his parents. Another man had a problem with his blood sugar and terrible physical awkwardness. He never walked, but rather stumbled around, bumping into people and things, and had similar lack of control over his emotional impulses. A woman complained of several disorders related to her obesity. Another woman was operated on for an ovarian cyst and afterward delighted in displaying her obscenely ugly scar. Her baby son went to the hospital with pneumonia. During the hundreds of hours I spent with the Walthamites, never did I hear one person show real concern for another's medical problem. The cult ideology was useful to them in denying any need for sympathy because it claimed that each person's problem had been chosen by him. When a male member's digestive system broke down, they criticized him for "pulling in a limitation" by adopting such an excuse for his laziness.

Several accidents occurred. A woman splashed duplicator fluid in her eye while working at an outside job. A man stuck his thumb in the power planer that was part of his basement shop. It was a dirty, aged machine with no safeguards. It bit a large chunk out of his thumb. The doctor bandaged it and made him wear a sling and stay away from water. He enjoyed the sling, and it was not his habit to wash anyway. A few days later, the physician grafted a chunk of flesh from the guy's upper arm into the hole in his thumb.

The Waltham house was an unhealthy environment. Many of the rooms were filthy. Cat excrement and garbage filled the cracks and corners. There were not enough towels or toilet paper in the bathrooms. The diet was very poor. By the middle of January, it was terrible. One guy pretended to be the house doctor, but nobody went to him for treatment. I several times saw him caress women's heads, in order, he said, to cure their headaches and colds. His chief methods of treatment were all magical, including rituals and meditation. One of Julio's most potent medications was "red medicine." The ingredients included red wine, kerosene, diced onion, potassium permanganate, and several herbs. It was supposed to be a quick sure cure for gonorrhea.

For a couple of months the Waltham group had a definite plan. Robert wanted them to save up a lot of money and prepare spiritually to leave civilization and set up a Survival Center. Julio said this would be "a place in some very remote part of the country, where we will live and grow. We will also run missions into cities. If we all make it, we'll be the future ministers of the church." Where would they go? Quincy Adams claimed Robert told him all about it. Proudly, he refused to divulge the details: "My lips are sealed." Roger Bergman felt the Survival Center would be in New Mexico. Mark Lembert said the Middle West was a possibility. Roger didn't feel he was ready to live off the land. The people in the house were unhealthy, so it was a good thing, he felt, that they had time to build themselves up. Maude didn't like the Survival Center idea. She was squeamish about the snakes, spiders, and scorpions she was convinced infested New Mexico. Sam Rhodes joked that they were probably going to Outer Mongolia: "The idea is something similar to what happened at Xtul eleven years ago. Total isolation and self-supporting, where we can really learn how to go about setting up our Survival Centers." Woody felt it might be a good idea to "get mobile homes, campers" and send musical mobile chapters out from the Center: "Everyone will say, 'Wow! This is a really terrific experience! I've never heard music that really expressed every emotion that I was going through played like that!' Because, hopefully, that's where our music is going to get, where we'll be able to pick up emotions and *play* them."

Robert had come back to his old apocalyptic view that "human structures are collapsing." Of course, his own human structures had collapsed. A Biblical analogy helped him explain the purpose of Waltham and allege its divinely ordained importance: "Noah didn't build his ark on water. He was given time—not much but enough—to build it on dry land and solid earth. But he built it to survive when that dry land and solid earth were lost beneath a deluge that he knew was coming. And he didn't stop building until his ark was ready for that deluge." The new Process would be that ark, and in Waltham they needed the security of a solid environment in order to build it. Robert made only the vaguest of plans for the Survival Center, consulting a few governmental pamphlets and checking out the Surplus Property Utilization Program. He admitted that he didn't really know what the group would wind up doing: "Maybe we'll be gypsies."

THE NEW OMEGA

When Morgana joined Robert in Boston, she was presented to the Walthamites as Robert's *Consort*. Many believed that Osiris was the new High Pontiff of the church. The three of them were the new Omega, isolated from the body of the church but supreme over it. Robert never became the leader of the Waltham group but preferred the status of Teacher. He hoped that his Teachings would draw out of the mass of miserable Walthamites a few individuals capable of existing on his plane. Osiris said the Omega did not participate in the life or rituals of the Waltham house, except as observers, because "we were not part of the Boston chapter." Other chapters might emerge in Chicago and Toronto. All should be treated equally. "The period before we went into living in the Waltham house there was a conscious, deliberate stress on the fact that there is a Process with or without Waltham. This entity was called the Omega." The little house was a very crowded living quarters for a woman, her son, the Omega, and Satan the dog. After a couple of months, Osiris's girlfriend became completely fed up, terminated her romantic affair with him, and asked the Omega to move out. Osiris, Morgana, and Robert took up residence in the Waltham house around December 20, taking over the downstairs apartment.

Thus, the triad moved into Waltham without the intent of asserting true leadership or even becoming involved in chapter activities.

In the last weeks of 1974, Robert and Osiris went to New York City to see Mary Ann and Robert's brother Phineas, who stayed with the Foundation for a while. This was the only time after the Separation that Mary Ann and Robert met. For seven hours they exchanged blame and recriminations. The meeting proved there was no hope of reconciliation between Robert and Mary Ann. A chronology outlined by Timothy Wyllie, who was then still Father Micah and a leader of the Foundation, also reported: "Robert, hoping for a reconciliation, travels to New York for a final meeting with Mary Ann. They divorce early in the next year."[105] Over the next two months, Robert formally disentangled himself from the Foundation and from Mary Ann. He was forced to negotiate with the Foundation to obtain copies of his own writings. In a letter to John, he also argued that the Foundation owed him a considerable sum of money: "Over eleven years I estimate the income of The Process to be close to $5,000,000, which was made possible in large part by my contribution to its development. In view of this, a settlement on me of $50,000 seems scarcely unreasonable to enable me to continue my work." John was not impressed by this argument.

Robert kept these dealings secret from the Walthamites, and they in turn tried to uncover everything he hid. For a long time, several of them were under the mistaken impression that Robert was very rich, the heir to a vast family fortune. He never told them his real situation, one of complete penury. He did not take a job in Boston, although for a brief time Morgana worked as a secretary, and he made absolutely no financial contributions to the house. His rent was paid by the Walthamites, who also provided his food.

Osiris said that Robert had always been distant from his cult: "In a sense, Robert was outside the Process. He was not part of the group. He said many times that many of the Masters didn't have any contact with him." He may have never attended a Sabbath Assembly before Waltham. When I showed him my photographs taken four years earlier of the Sacrifist and Evangelist, he seemed astonished to see the colorful tabards they wore. He didn't have the slightest recollection of such garments. When he did sit in on Waltham Sabbaths, he clutched the Assembly Book, confused as any newcomer. He seemed unfamiliar with the hymns and the pieces of ritual business. He did not dress like the others. When everyone else, including Osiris and Morgana, began wearing black uniforms, as in the very old days, de Grimston adopted a brown uniform for himself. Once in jest he introduced himself as "Mr. Brown." Robert's costume consisted of a brown turtleneck shirt, brown trousers, and brown half boots. The colors ranged from honey to caramel to chocolate. He wore a large ornate silver cross and frequently carried a brown shoulder bag filled with personal effects such as his pipe and tobacco.

Osiris explained to me how the three members of the Omega spent their time: "If you could manage to take a peek for a short period of time at what was going on, it wouldn't make sense to you." Mostly they talked, but the content of the discussions was so personal that outsiders would not have understood they were engaged in Process work. What were the norms? "You have to be as open as possible with yourself and with the other two members of the triangle. And that whatever it is, whether it's extremely negative, extremely positive, you have to express it, and you have to force yourself not to avoid it. Which led to activities like exhausting any feelings one might have about something—to its limit. Pushing it, and pulling it, and explaining it, and talking about it until you are completely out in the open, instead of trying to look good or trying to get your point across or trying to influence somebody else."

The work of the Omega was identical to that of an encounter group, except that the benefit was supposed to be for all Processeans, not just for participants. Osiris answered questions. "It lasts all of the day—twenty-four hours." Whatever happened within the triumvirate had to be analyzed to death. "What does it mean? Where is it going? Why is it happening? What does it imply should happen in the future? How is everybody in the group, as part of the group, feeling? Doing? What they represent? What they mean?" This was how Robert had spent the last dozen years of his life. The continual encounter group stew that surrounded him gave the inspiration for his writings. But beyond that, he believed this living process of personal therapy was the engine of all human history. Magically, this intimate process influenced all events in the outside world. "Robert feels that his destiny *is* The Process. And The Process is his destiny. So whatever he's doing—that's The Process."

Robert's major creative activity during the three months he lived near Boston was the writing of several short scriptures that never went beyond manuscript stage, and the invention of an extremely complex therapeutic board game called *Contact*. Few members of the house were ever permitted to play the game. Robert changed the rules in mid-play when I was his partner at the board.

Osiris's major creative activity was the invention of a new symbol for the cult. It was unveiled at the Sabbath Assembly on December 14 and was in use only for the duration of the Waltham house. Shown in Figure 17, this emblem is a complex structural transformation of the older Unity Cross. The dragon

FIGURE 17. **The New Dragon Symbol, designed by Osiris.**

represents Satan. Robert remarked that the Unity Cross dragon had no wings, while this new dragon possessed both wings and feet, "an Unfallen Serpent, no less!" Inside the coils of the dragon is a cross, dominated yet protected, showing a new relationship between Satan and Christ. Satan now plays the dominant role, yet works with Christ to achieve first Separation, then Unity: first Death, then Rebirth.

The cross in the center is actually a cutout area, a hole. In the large wooden emblem made by Mark Lembert, the hole was large enough to put your hand through. Osiris explained that the dragon is *around* the cross, acting as a wall. A wall with an opening like a door. The cross, the door, is a way through. He said this symbolized The Process itself. "What are we offering? A way out. *Exit*. It's a door that is opened for anybody who wants to go through that door." The outline of the emblem is rectangular with two notches, one on each side. Osiris explained that these notches were the arms of another cross. The outline of the symbol is a cross turned inside out, as though the whole world outside the emblem were one great topologically transformed Christian symbol. Thus, the symbol contains one cross but is contained by another. Rank-and-file Walthamites found Osiris's creation inscrutable and unappealing. The Omega did not bother to explain its symbolism to them. For a while they planned to produce pendants following this design, to be worn by all Processeans. Higher-ranked members would wear emblems with little outlines of the Process Sign and the Sign of Union in the upper corners. Middle-ranked members would have only the Process Sign, while low-ranked folk would have plain emblems. Money for this project was never raised, and only a few cardboard mock-ups of the pendant were ever made. Ranks were not introduced, either.

DEVIANCE AND DISINTEGRATION

The house was in desperate need of government. Robert gave no leadership at all. Ariel recalled there was "a lot of personality conflict" living at such close quarters: "Isolde took it upon herself to see that things got done." Mel Potts said, "We asked Robert to put someone as his mediator with him. And after a few days of debate, Robert gave the position to Isolde, making her Head of House." Ariel said, "It's an old Process concept that a house needs a head." As Roger comments, "She's tremendously strong." But as soon as Isolde began exercising authority, the pressure on her became tremendous. Roger was not enthusiastic about the house inspections Isolde held for a while. "You would be docked fifty cents from your allowance every time you screwed up." The allowance, which Isolde dispensed, was only four dollars a week to cover all personal needs.

According to Ariel, "Isolde became unpopular because she was in charge, used to bitch at them to clean their rooms, get a job. Mark stirred up trouble by badmouthing." Mark Lembert, styling himself the Marquis de Lombardia, flashed a marvelous homemade purple cape and said, "I don't see eye to eye with the leaders in this house." One evening the Marquis demanded to see the group's financial records, which Woody was keeping at Isolde's orders. She refused to hand them over. Isolde played the Head of House role in the traditional Process fashion: secretively, dogmatically, and inconsistently. When it became apparent that opposition to her was reaching revolutionary proportions, the Omega installed Bob Stone and Ariel as co-heads of House and gave the wholly honorary posts of Apartment Heads to Marsha and Maude. "It was total competition in Waltham," Ariel said. "You tried to be manipulating things into the direction you wanted them to go, 'cause we still thought we were creating The Process. I was trying to make damn sure that I was going to have a good position, that we were going to go in the direction I wanted to go in, that I never made a wrong move. So it was like everybody existing in paranoia."

From the very beginning, people were constantly being expelled from the house or made so uncomfortable that they left voluntarily. Unfortunately, this ostracism process never succeeded in pruning the group down to an efficient, cohesive core. There was none. Rico Sorbo and Ron Forbes lived at Waltham only briefly. Rico lost his job in November, just before moving into the house, tried to keep the fact secret, then was embarrassed into leaving when the truth came out. He had been a security guard. Kids threw rocks at him. He called the real cops. His boss said, "If you can't handle things like this yourself, you shouldn't be a guard. You're fired." Ron Forbes also left because he couldn't hold a job. Isolde reprimanded him for doing very little work around the house and sleeping much of the time.

The most dynamic person expelled from the house was Al Capone. He claimed to be the great-nephew of an infamous gangster and acted the part.

Ariel said, "Al has two very distinct sides. On one side, he's a really fantastic guy who has charisma, enthusiasm, energy, dedication, anything you'd want. And on the other side, he's quite mad and violent. He drinks very heavily." The group told Al he could not drink in the house, but he did anyway. "He couldn't just *drink*, he'd get *wasted*. And when he gets wasted, he gets violent." If someone got in his way, he'd shout, "I'll kill you!" They knew he was capable of it. According to one story, he became angry with the Omega and threw Osiris over a table. Sam Rhodes says Al was often drunk and "very destructive, very Satanic, ripping things asunder. Ungoverned fury. He'd go around doing great physical damage to other people." A year earlier, when Marsha was visibly pregnant, Al Capone had punched her quite hard in the stomach. Typical Capone behavior. Roger Bergman called Al "powerful" and "mercurial." At the Thanksgiving party, Al sang some crooner songs of the 1950s, "in his bright yellow sweater with tears in his eyes, terribly sentimental. And everybody thought: this is marvelous! But later he got drunk and went around yelling, 'Bullshit! It's fucking bullshit! Bullshit! Bullshit!' Stomping around in the middle of the Alpha, scaring the daylights out of everybody. Nobody dared say a word." The Walthamites were so terrified of Al Capone they could not tell him to leave, but withdrew from him and created an uncomfortable atmosphere. At last word, he had moved to New York, saying he was going to be a hit man for the Mafia.

A creeping problem that poisoned social life progressively at Waltham was a crime wave of petty thefts. The members never pooled their private property. They were extremely possessive about their rooms and complained that their privacy was often violated. Mel Potts, who slept in a hallway, used to throw open doors and burst into rooms without knocking. The identity of the house thieves was never determined, although there was much evidence against several people. Mark ran up hundred-dollar phone bills without any intention of paying for them. When Isolde accused him, he denied any guilt, then accused her of using church money to buy special food for herself. In January, someone stole Isolde's copies of the doctrinal Missal from her room. Marsha's radio disappeared. Money vanished from several rooms. Mail was intercepted, opened, and deprived of any checks and cash it contained. One of the two electric typewriters was stolen. D. Lord said that he had hidden three dollars in the handle of a screwdriver. Only Ron Forbes knew about it. The money was gone. D. Lord said he suspected Ron had run off with Marsha's radio, but Marsha said that was impossible. The mood of the house was ill feeling and suspicion. Some suspected Quincy. Some suspected D. Lord. Some suspected Mark. Some suspected various guests. D. Lord said many of his best woodworking tools had been vanishing from the basement. I happen to know that D. Lord himself secretly sold some of these tools for booze money. The thefts continued as long as anyone was living at Waltham. Perhaps everybody was the thief.

Instability of erotic relationships within this small, compressed community took many steps toward disintegration. A series of sex episodes, half secret and half obvious, caused emotional tornadoes of anger and desire. At midnight, when everybody was gathered for an Evening Assembly, Robert, Osiris, and Morgana unexpectedly burst in and took over the situation. For two hours they discussed the state of the house. I watched one guy squirm in the corner, afraid his shame would come into the open. Another kept dropping hints that he had something to say, each time causing the other guy terrible anguish. Finally, all was revealed. Robert remained calm, relaxed, accepting. He toyed with his pipe and smiled. He said adultery was not a sin. There are no sexual rules at all in The Process. There was no reason to blame anyone. There was no justification for prohibiting similar sexual behavior in the future. If any couple wanted to carry on an affair, then that was fine. No person could own another. Each person must be completely free to follow the desires of the moment.

The Omega said it was quite shocked and disgusted by all the problems and conflict in the house. Repeatedly, Robert, Morgana, and Osiris commented that the Walthamites could have solved all their problems by studying Process scriptures. Robert felt his teachings were the heart of the cult, yet few of his followers seemed to care about the doctrines at all. Despite the weekly doctrinal seminars and the twice-daily rituals, the Walthamites never seemed to absorb the basic tenets of the cult. Bob Stone had his own doctrine, Bobbycraft. Julio Famagusta professed to be an exalted mystic and spent more time dervishing in front of his Rosicrucian altar than working around the house. Ron Forbes was one of the few who understood the doctrines, but he enjoyed profaning the services. For example, he once caused a startling interruption at one of the Sabbath Assemblies. Twenty people were present that evening. Roger was the Sacrifist, and Julio the Evangelist. Julio had just begun his sermon when Ron pulled out a gun and fired at him. Bang! Bang! Bang! Blanks.

One theory of Functionalist sociological analysis is the idea that the shared ideology and collective ritual provided by a religion work to unify the group that practices it.[106] Both ideology and ritual are supposed to be powerful forces producing social structure and cohesion out of chaos. The Process had a vivid, shared set of symbols. The Walthamites participated in seminars and used many elements of Robert's culture in their everyday speech. They sang rousing hymns and enacted dramatic rituals. The result was failure. Neither the ideology nor the ritual seemed to have much strength to hold the members together. Divisions in the social structure and material conflicts remained. I believe that ideology and ritual may have important consequences but are primarily epiphenomenal. They are extensions of informal social relations. The Process had to exist as a cohesive social group before its culture could have any meaning. A cohesive social group cannot be created by the mere mechanical recitation of ideology and ritual, which are the superficial expressions of cohesion.

Robert's response to all the schisms was to promulgate new doctrines. He said the cult was evolving into a new, highly differentiated stage in which several branches, each with its own style, would cooperate. He said the Foundation was really only the Jehovian Order of The Process, although it was not yet ready to admit this fact. The Walthamites were the Luciferian Order. Ultimately, the Omega would be supreme over all of them. He conceptually divided his current followers into two Process groups, P1 and P2. The first were the people closest to him, mainly the ex-Messengers, and the second were those individuals continually splitting away. P1 was closest to God; P2 was closest to Humanity. They were integrated in his mind through his habitual conceptualization that all reality was divided into cooperating polar opposites, that Jehovians and Luciferians, P1 and P2, would work together for common Process goals. His intellectual structures proved, however, to have absolutely no power to influence reality. His mental images could not hold together a disintegrating house of disorganized people.

ECONOMIC FAILURE

Waltham was an economic as well as a social failure. Only Woody and Bob held jobs throughout the life of the chapter. Woody was an orderly at an institution for the mentally disabled, a difficult, menial job. He sometimes worked double shifts to bring in extra money. Bob Stone kept his computer job. Vita Cordova was a telephone secretary at an electronic supply company for a while and worked as a go-go dancer in Boston's red-light district after that. Quincy and Marsha briefly held security guard jobs. Ron Forbes helped Rose get a job at the Minuteman Restaurant when she lost a secretarial position, but she did not have reliable transportation and lost this job quickly too. Blanche made a few dollars at Señor Pizza, and her boyfriend Mark earned as much by selling his own blood to the blood bank. Four of the men worked at one time or another for the Alert gas station down the road, and a number got intermittent employment through Handy Andy, a manual labor bureau. Julio Famagusta worked a single day for an antique store. He was hired to restore old furniture, and after a few hours of attacking an aged cabinet with de-finishing goo and scraper, he was happy to rejoin the ranks of the unemployed.

D. Lord did not feel up to looking for outside work. He said nobody would hire an ex-convict, and he was afraid to show his face in Boston because the police wanted him on an assault charge. Instead, he spent many hours setting up a woodworking shop in the basement, collecting antique tools, including a 500-pound radial arm saw. Sam Rhodes helped by illegally rewiring the cellar electric circuit board to accommodate the equipment. Except for the fancy ritual furniture, the only product that ever emerged from this Process wood factory was an uneven, unfinished prototype knickknack shelf. D. Lord complained that he could not start making money until he had a good table saw. The lack of a saw was his perpetual excuse for doing no work. One time Sam Rhodes donated one hundred dollars toward the purchase of a second-hand saw, but Isolde decided to pay off one of Woody's bills instead.

For months, Bob Stone and Sam Rhodes had planned to start a Process Craft Store. Many inexperienced young people imagine they can earn a living through their favorite childhood hobbies. Bob Stone made a photo enlarger out of an old potato-chip can. It worked but never achieved commercial-quality prints. He also made and sold a few tiny glass horses, using materials provided by a glass crafts kit. Nobody else was able to master the technique. Undaunted, the Walthamites organized on paper the Process Craft Factory, planning to support themselves through candlemaking, glassblowing, woodworking, astrology charts, aura spins, leather work, terrariums, and silkscreening. The greatest effort went into candle manufacture. Even Robert tried his hand at it. Isolde retrieved a huge tin container, a yard square, from the junkyard. It was placed on cinder blocks in the cellar, given an inside floor of bricks, and nearly filled with water. Several large cans were placed inside, each containing wax of a different color. To heat the water and thereby melt the wax, they immersed an electric frying pan and turned it on. The apparatus took so long to heat up that they left the frying pan connected day and night, for weeks. It was a wonder somebody wasn't electrocuted.

The first step in manufacture was to cast white wax candle cores in star-shaped molds, with a long piece of common string for the wick. Then this core was dunked repeatedly in different colors of wax, building up polychrome layers. Before the wax had completely set, the pointed edges were undercut and peeled back like flower petals. The result was an ornate, splendid, fragile centerpiece. Isolde had seen candles like this on sale for several dollars each. Out of more than thirty produced, only three were ever sold. The wax petals habitually broke off, and it seemed impossible to keep the surface of the wax from clouding over. A last-ditch attempt by Rose to start a coffeehouse in her bedroom did not even earn enough money to pay for the tea and sugar. Business was bad all around.

Originally, Robert was opposed to street donating. But shortly before Christmas, the Walthamites decided to give it a try. First, they needed a magazine to sell. They pulled material from old Process publications, composed poems, and invented little church announcements. Robert contributed an open letter on the future of the cult. Dim photographs showed house residents at work. They printed five thousand copies of their amateur publication at a cost of $250 and planned to ask fifty cents for each copy on the streets. Groups went into Boston a half-dozen times, and once to New York. Without training or proper uniforms, they hawked this pathetic magazine in the winter cold, making themselves miserable. This last Process magazine was designed to net about two thousand dollars. It brought in only a couple of hundred before the project was abandoned.

Retrieving was a fairly successful source of food, liberating what cash there was for other expenses. Much of the food was purchased before mid-December, and the menu included entrees like: tuna and noodle casserole, sloppy Joes, arroz con pollo, meat loaf, shit on shingles, Rose's Surprise, and Frankfurters and beans. The Walthamites were still hoping to save up money for the Survival Center, so the Heads of House decreed that absolutely all food should be retrieved. Several times I went out with house members at five in the morning to beg at Boston's vegetable and meat distribution centers. These places were collections of little transshipping warehouses. Big trucks came in from out of state and unloaded in the middle of the night, then little trucks came and took the food to local supermarkets. The New England Produce Center in Chelsea, really a part of Boston, had nearly fifty of these establishments, each specializing in a different fruit or vegetable, all arranged in immensely long buildings. We would walk from one to the next, begging: "Hello, we are from the Process Church in Waltham. I'm Brother William, and this is Brother Quincy. We have a community center in Waltham where we feed twenty-five families a week. Could you help us by making a donation of food?"

We did not mention that the church had no charter or social function. The "twenty-five families" were actually the twenty-five individuals that lived in the house.

I was surprised to find that about a third of the managers we spoke with gave us something each time. We had no competition. It would have been easy for anyone to go there, pretend to represent a church, and come away with a carload of food. But the job was terribly unpleasant, and the one car kept breaking down, so Waltham was pitifully short of decent food. Usually we got vegetables. For an entire week the house subsisted on carrot and onion stew (no meat) augmented by stale Sweetie Pie marshmallow cookies. The diet was not sufficiently nourishing for body or spirit.

The Walthamites slid into debt. They could not keep even, let alone build up a Survival Center fund. Ariel said things were going along okay until "It doesn't look like we're going to make February's rent. We've got a lot of people in the house that are not making any money." The total rent for the three apartments was $875 monthly, not counting utilities. The Omega conferred with the three Heads of House: "So we decided the only thing we can do is say everybody produces eighty dollars a week," according to Ariel. There had been an informal goal of "$750 collectively" a week, but now the responsibility fell on each individual. Woody earned $100 per week and Bob Stone something over $130. Several other members of the house immediately panicked. Pessimism grew, then turned to anger. Tension built to explosive pressure.

A few days after the stern announcement, Marsha picked up a newspaper and began looking through the real estate ads. She had very little money but was contemplating moving out of the Process. Mel Potts reminded her that their names were on the lease of the third apartment of the house. The Omega could not kick her out! With Mark, Blanche, Rose, and D. Lord, she decided to take over the third apartment. Bob and Maude Stone began talking about leaving. Bob mused about starting a cult of his own. Roger, Julio, Isolde, Woody, Ariel, Vita, and Mel stuck with the Omega. A week after this schism, Roger told me the $80 rule was suspended because not all the people in his group had been able to make it. "It was a kind of test," he said, intended to find the real core of Processeans who were really dedicated. Actually, it was an impulsive demand, only afterward defined as a calculated test. A couple of weeks later, Isolde and Woody threw off their onerous responsibilities. They disappeared to join the fundamentalist Church of the Living God.

TORONTO

On February 14, 1975, Robert flew to Toronto to check out the group there. There were eight full-time adult members, five of them living with their four children in a large house on Ontario Street. The Toronto Processeans were decent people, most of them gainfully employed, very different from the average Walthamite. Robert admitted, "Boston, in practical and organizational terms, was a fiasco." He decided to abandon it. Morgana supervised preparations to close down the Waltham house and joined Robert in Toronto on March 2.

Robert had hoped to find among the Walthamites a few worthy people capable of following him. As early as the beginning of November, he said, "I'm testing like fury in all directions. Well, I'm not, but something inside me is. It's as though there's very little time, and I must know who's really with me and who's against me. It's a painful and uncomfortable time for everyone. But those who endure it are mine, and those who don't are not." His principle was: "Many are called, but very, very few are chosen." Only five were permitted to follow Robert and Morgana to Toronto: Osiris, Ariel, Vita Cordova, Roger Bergman, and Melvin Potts. For the first two weeks of March, they worked like mad people at several jobs in Boston, earned a great amount of money, then abandoned the Waltham house on the 14th. The penniless people in Marsha's apartment left at the end of the month. The ritual equipment was moved to the East Boston apartment of a Processean couple who had not moved in at Waltham, where a number of seminars, parties, and rituals were held by the last leftover people.

Osiris left Toronto the day after he got there. The cult no longer promised to satisfy his desires for excitement, power, or spiritual growth. He planned to return to his artistic pottery, write a book on Sufism using Arabic sources, and establish his own spiritual retreat in backcountry New England. When he spoke with Morgana on the phone, she told him that his dragon-and-cross emblem had been abandoned in favor of a completely new symbol invented by Robert. Morgana refused to tell Osiris how it looked but toyed with him, making him guess. Robert's emblem, she said, would not contain either a dragon or a cross.

When I saw the new symbol in Toronto, I discovered Morgana had been only half right. As shown in Figure 18, it is a double cross, the upright Christian cross combined with the inverted Satanic cross. The Sign of Union was placed at the center of the Christian cross, where the upper arm intersects the vertical

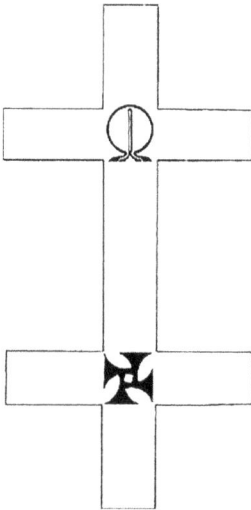

FIGURE 18.
The New Unity symbol, designed by Robert.

bar. The Process Sign was placed on the lower arm, at the center of the Satanic cross. Thus, the two unifying symbols nailed the two opposing crosses together, as Robert said, "in an unbreakable alliance."

There were several reasons why Osiris's dragon symbol was abandoned. Rank-and-file members had neither understood nor liked it. It was so complex that it did not catch the eye of the outsider the way earlier symbols had. There was also a theological reason for its replacement. The dragon, symbolic of Separation, expressed what had happened at Waltham, and Robert hoped to achieve greater success in Toronto with an optimistic new Unity symbol. Finally, the dragon was very much Osiris's personal emblem. It had been part of Osiris's attempt to seize power and status within the cult. After Osiris abandoned Robert, Robert marked the breach between them by abandoning the symbol of Osiris.

Robert resolved that he would not make the same mistakes in Toronto that he had in Boston. He believed that he had not exercised enough control at Waltham, so he made a vigorous effort to seize control of Toronto. He did not realize until too late that this was an equal mistake. The Canadians had already achieved high cohesiveness among themselves and were in reasonably good control of their own lives. While Robert was at a distance, they loved him as their charismatic teacher. By calling themselves Processeans and claiming to follow him, they achieved the feeling that they were glorious pioneers, building a movement of cosmic significance. But when Robert actually came to live with them, their love faded. He expected them to feed, clothe, and house him. He demanded absolute authority. A bad bargain.

For the first time in the history of the cult, Robert participated fully in the rituals. This had the bad effect of putting every other ritual performer in second-rate status. Robert wrote a new set of church incorporation documents designed to make him dictator: "Robert de Grimston is the Teacher. He cannot be removed from office. He sits on the Board of Directors. He is entitled to veto any resolution of the board." Adding injury to insult, the last Walthamites arrived. Ariel says, "We hit that place like a ton of bricks!" Suddenly there were two rival groups in the house, and Robert seemed to prefer others over the five original residents of Ontario Street.

Then the most cataclysmic split of all occurred, although it proved to be temporary, a separation between Morgana and Robert. He could not take his own advice and, try as he might, could not console himself with Process teachings. He and Morgana got into terrible fights and ruined the respect the others had for them. On March 17, Robert said, "Now we face the most intense and the greatest vulnerability of all. I've twisted into it. I've brought the pain on myself again. But this time with no obvious way out. Not even the road of death and rebirth. This time I've trapped myself." All his security, the shreds of his remaining self-respect, were tied up in Morgana. He groped for a doctrinal explanation. It was the anniversary of the Separation, at least of the date of Robert's formal expulsion. He decided that the spiritual issues engaged at the time of the original schism had not been resolved, and this new schism was the great opportunity to resolve them for good. Both Mary Ann and Morgana were JS personalities. He had been terribly dependent on both of them. Perhaps this time he would conquer the JS pattern, or his dependence upon strong women, and achieve the cure he had struggled to find for so many years.

Robert moved out of the house to live with a former Disciple. This fellow was a true gentleman, reasonably prosperous in business, and very kindly. He tried to mediate between Robert and Morgana. She of course asserted her Luciferian right to freedom. The Canadian and American factions at Ontario Street were at each other's throats. Robert appointed Ariel treasurer of the entire group, but Pericles, a little-known Canadian member, was currently holding the cashbox and accounts and refused to hand them over. Ariel commented, "Charles Manson talks about how the coyote is so paranoid, he's totally in time. By the time I got to Toronto, I was so conditioned to paranoia. Got to watch out for my standing, you know, or I'll slip. It was a power struggle. I felt like I was involved in the French Revolution, you know, Robespierre trying to axe Danton. Really tight intrigue. At times it was medieval, palace-like." Unbeknownst to Robert, Pericles pried the locked door off Robert's office, stole his copy of the secret Teachings, Xeroxed it, and replaced everything as it had been. Pericles planned his own cult, without Robert.

On March 25, 1975, the last Process chapter disintegrated. In the afternoon, Robert despaired: "Again the Valley of the Shadow. No light. No relief. No hope." Everyone came together for a long meeting after supper, and the false unity of the Process was formally dissolved. Over the following days, individuals spun off in different directions. Vita and Ariel ultimately returned to Boston. Melvin Potts and three of the Canadians moved into an apartment.

Pericles and his woman Bonnie went to British Columbia to start a new life. Others vanished.

For three days Robert would not eat anything. He sat in a corner of Harold's living room, brooding and trembling. "Where the hell do I go from here?" he asked himself. Several of us sat in a circle with him, casting *I Ching* fortunes. Robert took each of them very seriously. We threw the three silver coins made for Robert by Brother Mathew years before. On one side of each was an ornate cross, on the other the head of a goat, Christ and Satan joined. With great interest, Robert read each fortune from a big book and gave his interpretations. He asked himself, "Why don't we all cut our losses and scrap it?" He looked around at me, Vita, Roger, Ariel, and Harold, all soon to disperse. He thought, "Perhaps they're all quite happy playing their alienating games with one another. Perhaps we should just leave them to it. Perhaps the link is totally compulsive on my side. Perhaps the Unity is a myth, after all." Robert's followers abandoned him, but in the end Morgana returned and they were reconciled.

ENDING THE GAME OF THE GODS

George Oberhofer, my able research assistant at Waltham, wrote an excellent term paper for a Harvard deviance course, analyzing the decay of the group in terms of Rosabeth Kanter's model of commitment.[107] He felt the key to the failure of Robert's second cult was his permissive concept of the New Game. The Foundation succeeded in holding members and making money under the authoritarian rule of Jehovah. The new Process died under the liberal regime of Lucifer. Oberhofer explained, "What the New Game actually did was to ban the concept of 'blame' within The Process' social structure; in so doing it inhibited the suppression of behavior which undermined the two most basic goals—and needs—of The Process as a sociocultural system." These goals were "the detachment of its members from all other human institutions, and the attachment of them to a more 'godly' way of life." He cited Kanter's lengthy discussion of a long list of "commitment mechanisms" that ensure longevity for Utopian communities, norms that bind members and reduce the likelihood of their defection. He wrote, "In order to remain distinct and cohesively organized, such groups must detach members from the outside world so as to minimize or eliminate any advantage members might see in returning to the outside; they must also attach members to their own social structure so as to provide them with comparative advantages for remaining within the group."

To give a simple example: if members can be made to invest prior wealth and current labor in the community and are not permitted to withdraw any of their investment upon leaving, they will be more likely to stay in order to receive some benefit from that investment. Oberhofer observed that the Omega utterly failed to achieve these ends. Because of its permissive ideology, it refused to exercise authority and enforce norms that would have served commitment and cohesion: "The hierarchy, under the influence of the New Game, could not blame its subjects; their behavior was simply written off as 'enactments' or 'performances.'"

Kanter's analysis failed to ask what factors make it possible to enforce authoritarian norms. She also neglected the question of how successful Utopian communities are formed in the first place. As Oberhofer said, the analysis concentrated on commitment mechanisms that maintain cohesion in a group already somewhat cohesive. Authoritarian rule is impossible until after members are already strongly committed to a group. We have seen that the Process emerged from a social implosion that transformed a loosely connected network of individuals into a tight unit. Only after the implosion did its members accept authoritarian rule. The Walthamites were never cohesive. When they arrived in Toronto, they smashed the cohesion that had developed there. Had Robert been a more decisive leader, he might have been able to cull from the mob that swarmed around him a few stable people who were ready to build good relationships with each other and follow him. But the mere suppression of deviance would not have bound together the disorganized, pathological majority of the latter-day Processeans.

I agree with Oberhofer that anarchism is not a good ideology with which to build an authoritarian movement. But, as modern psychotherapy has shown, it is possible to build looser, more liberal movements through a network of gratifying intimate relationships around an ideology of freedom. Robert felt that the Foundation had achieved a false success, a plush prison for its members. Authority means loss of freedom. In the Foundation, Mary Ann's control perspective won out over Robert's liberation perspective. Flattered by people like the Walthamites into attempting a renewal of the old structures, Robert was seduced into self-betrayal. He almost became the slave of his will to power, and only failure saved him. The Process was Robert's therapy. He was its patient even before he was its creator. To cure himself he had to conquer guilt. "Blame is the core of strife and discord," says one Process Precept. Another says, "Blame is the detonator of all evil"; blame triggers an explosion of wickedness. In his unpublished manuscript *Blame and Demand*, Robert wrote, "Through blame we perpetuate our own self-punishment. It's the great-est burden of all, because it's the source of all other burdens." While an author-itarian religious commune might successfully hold people, it would not be good for them. In another unpublished book manuscript, Robert wrote, "People don't exist to be sacrificed before the altar of religious doctrine. Religious doctrine exists for the overall benefit of people."

On April 26, 1975, Robert de Grimston returned to Boston to bid farewell. He was accompanied by the one remaining Canadian disciple and Morgana. Two dozen Processeans crammed into the living room of the East Boston apartment for the last Sabbath Assembly ever held. Robert was Evangelist. When it came time for his revelation, he dissolved the ritual, sat in the Sacrifist's chair so he could see everyone, and explained the meaning of The Process. He said it was a mistake to think of The Process as a church organiza-tion. The Process was change, not static authority. An informal group of coop-erating Processeans could be fine, increasing each person's awareness while preserving his freedom. "But when that becomes the source of your security, when that becomes what you lean on—whether it's for spiritual security, phys-ical security, the security of giving you an identity or a function, or emotional security—it's unstable. It's unreal. It's not The Process. I can give no one here security, nor can any organization I might ever form or have formed. What I can do is help each Processean to find that security within himself. That is what Process teachings are about." The Process is not a church, but a path of discovery leading each Processean individually to God: "God, for each one of us, is inside each one of us. And there's the ultimate in security." Robert's parting words were: "To put it bluntly, you're on your own!"

After saying farewell to the Boston Processeans, Robert and Morgana stayed for a week with me, then lived in Toronto until they had raised enough money to escape North America. They flew to London at the beginning of June 1975. For a while they stayed with Robert's parents, then moved into a furnished apartment. They both took common jobs, Robert with a shipping company, and settled into ordinary lives. In a few weeks they were married. They did not give up all hope for The Process. Several former followers in London made contact, Robert even spoke with the man who had made the original P-Scope so many years before. For months Robert had contemplated spreading his teachings through a mail-order correspondence course. A com-mittee consisting of Osiris, Ariel, and myself had worked on this project at Waltham. In the last days in Toronto, Robert had begun assembling his writing into a series of lessons. Once they were established in London, Robert and

Morgana began sending out mimeographed lessons to anyone willing to subscribe.

Throughout this book I have said that the Process was a social phenomenon. Every aspect of it, including the intellectual doctrines, rested on a social base. Robert's teachings were a projection of his own social experience and had no meaning to anyone who did not already share his social universe. I wrote to Robert, giving him my basic analysis and stressing the importance of the intense social relations from which everything else had sprung. He replied, "I like your analysis of that area," but he was not about to follow my advice to repeat the same pattern over again.

For Robert, cultic society had been a failure. The true Process was his own experiences, his personal feelings, and their expression through his writings: "If the course is a success, it should bring some real Processeans out of hiding. Then, wherever we are actually located, we could begin to hold meetings and courses, and later give personal therapy sessions to those whom we regard as suitable to have them. That—in a sense—is the old Process in reverse. And I think it's the right way around. It puts an understanding and absorption of The Process itself *first*, and *then* progresses into personal therapy."

Morgana vigorously supported Robert's work but was not confident. Writing from London, she told me she had been disillusioned by the abject failure of so many Processeans to fulfill the promise of the teachings. "It actually causes me anxieties when I realize how easy it is to give lip service to something without it ever really meaning anything. It gives me cause to examine my own motivations around Process teachings and precisely what I'm 'using' them for. I must say I'm not heartened by the 'Processeans' we've met here. ALL of them (and I mean ALL) are in what I would call 'ropey' states. Yet it has never occurred to them that perhaps they could solve some of their problems by reading the Process literature that they possess. If those who have had prolonged contact with The Process are still oblivious of what is contained in its theology, are we being foolish by thinking we will be able to reach anyone who has had NO previous contact with it?"

Robert said he had "mixed feelings" about the Foundation. As usual, he perceived duality, but near the end of the adventure he also saw duplicity: "For me there are two Foundations. There's the group of Processeans at the top, which I still regard somewhat as my own personal Frankenstein's monster, and for which I feel very responsible. And then there's the helpless harmless group of Founders gathered round them, looking for God and security and approval and love. And the two elements are completely alien to one another. *Their* union isn't based on an awareness of a fundamental unity, but on a total un-awareness of a less fundamental but much more intense dichotomy!" One union did survive, the fundamental unity between Robert and Morgana. After the correspondence course proved unpopular, they moved back to the United States, got decent jobs where their intellectual skills could solve clear problems, and stayed together over the following decades of their lives.

CHAPTER 11 The Light of Lucifer

Show me the way to go home
Show me that I'm not alone
Show me the light I have known
Show me Lucifer, Lucifer, Lucifer!

— Unofficial Process Hymn

WHEN THE PROCESS WAS BORN in the 1960s at the border between psycho-therapy and church, it explored a territory between magic and religion where innovation ranged between *client cult* and *cult movement*. After the Separation, the Process cult movement socially disintegrated and became an *audience cult*. In a 1980 journal article with Rodney Stark, I offered these definitions:

> Cults limited to providing magical services are *client cults*. . . .
> The relationship between magician and customer is limited to the consultant/client or therapist/patient model, short-term exchanges with relatively specific aims. *Audience cults* are even less close to being religions. Usually they display little or no formal organization of any kind. Indeed, the great majority of persons who take part in audience cults do so entirely through the mass media: books, magazines, newspapers, TV, astrology columns, and the like.[108]

Today, the primary medium for audience cults is internet, and for three decades Processean culture has thrived there.

REFLECTIONS ON THE PAST

Both the Process and the Foundation have survived half a century after their Separation, yet each greatly transformed. It could be said that the Process followed Lucifer, becoming an intellectual and artistic magical culture, be-loved by individuals and communicated across friendship networks and inter-net, but no longer having any formal organization. In a 2019 journal article, Carole M. Cusack correctly reported that "The Process is a defunct religion with extensive online archives, curated by ex-members and enthusiasts. Processean ideas are kept 'alive' and potentially able to be revived. . . . The Process emerged in the 1960s, underwent a formal change of leadership in 1974, and gradually altered. The strategy of abandoning esoteric beliefs and replacing them with more 'acceptable' views ('nominally' Christian—and then animal rights-based) resulted in the demise of the original group."[109] However, the animal rights group still thrives, and one count of its founders lists thir-ty-one former Processeans. So the process of the Process led to separation be-tween an established social organization and its early culture, rendering both of them *parareligious*.

Without claiming to know how far secularization will advance in the coming decades or centuries, one major feature has long been the blurring of religious concepts. In a recent study of the religious aspects of *Star Wars* culture, I suggested: "Parareligions of many different kinds cover the broad territory around established religions, and thus may be defined as attenuated forms of faith, liberated components of established denominations, or distinct subcultures that perform functions similar to one or more of those that traditionally belonged to sacred institutions."[110] The Foundation followed Jehovah, abandoning much of the shared culture over its first decade and remarkably shifting its love of Gods to a magnified love of Animals. On May 21, 1974, the organization's name in the New Orleans incorporation was changed to the Foundation–Church of the Millennium. On March 1, 1976, this became the Foundation Faith of the Millennium, and on February 27, 1978, in a retreat from the chaos of the Millennium, it became the Foundation Faith of God.

Another time, another author will need to write a careful and inspirational history of the Foundation, how it evolved into a very successful non-profit organization with an emphasis on animal rights and welfare, formally secular but possessing features of religion. As of 2024, anyone who is interested can search online and learn a good deal, yet it seems best not to provide direct links here. In 2013, the group posted a history that I can quote here, because it is no longer available. For example, here is how that public history described the immediate result of the Separation: "De Grimston and his supporters were shown the door in 1974. Those remaining reorganized around basic Christian principles that pointed toward kindness and compassion in all things, especially in their relationship to the animals. The re-formed organization was called the Foundation Faith, which focused on living a life that expressed one's beliefs through the work done—mostly now with children in hospitals, with the elderly in nursing homes and in hospice, at prisons, and, of course with animals."

Currently the deepest examination of the early Foundation is the autobiographical essay by Timothy Wyllie, who had served as Father Micah, a leader especially in the cult's highly artistic magazines. It can be found in the book *Love Sex Fear Death* that was edited by Adam Parfrey and published in 2009 by Feral House. His viewpoint was literally critical: "By early 1974 we had fully transformed ourselves into The Foundation Faith of the Millennium and Mary Ann ruled supreme. Having dumped Lucifer and Satan, at least exoterically, and de-emphasized Christ (Robert's role), Mary Ann was at last able to place all the emphasis on Jehovah, the god in our little pantheon with whom she primarily identified—along with Satan of course."[111]

Wyllie left this world in 2017, but his spiritual legacy is available for anyone who wishes to explore. Several of his surreal artworks were displayed in the Outsider Art Fair in New York in 2023, and a website displayed five of them, saying: "He talked to dolphins, angels, and aliens, and co-founded a 'spiritual community' most called a cult."[112] Many of the post-Processean books he wrote are available from their publisher, Inner Traditions, which reports: "In the late 70s, Timothy began a systematic exploration of out-of-body states. This led to experiments in telepathic communication with dolphins and an open invitation to contact with nonphysical beings that continues to this day. During this time, he was also running his own business in New York City, marketing a system he had co-devised for storing and filing color photographs. He retired from the business community in 1981 and turned full time to his creative endeavors."[113]

His standard writing procedure became psychic contact with a spiritual being, then acting as co-author to tell their transcendent story. The connection to the Process is unmentioned but obvious. The publisher's web page for *Confessions of a Rebel Angel* explains: "After eons of isolation, Lucifer and his rebel angels are being redeemed. Writing through Timothy Wyllie, rebel angel Georgia describes her half million years stationed on Earth as a watcher and reveals that there are millions of rebel angels currently incarnated who have an opportunity to redeem the past and contribute their particular talents to the world."[114] So now Wyllie is himself a Luciferian rebel angel, ready to co-author a new book with a mortal writer. The web page explains further: "More than two hundred millennia ago the high angel Lucifer launched a revolution among the angelic hierarchy, which led to the quarantine of 37 planets, including our own, from the rest of the Multiverse. Now, after eons of isolation, the rebel angels are being redeemed and we are being welcomed back into the benevolent and caring Multiverse with a massive transformation of consciousness and a reconnection to our celestial destiny."

Meanwhile, the Foundation followed its own, very different path. In 1978 the core group of members moved to a ranch in Arizona, where they became even more involved with animals, while one of its leaders in parallel operated an animal shelter in Pennsylvania. Its 2013 historical post summarized: "For many of the group, the animals had always been the main driving passion. And when a few of the group got together one evening at the ranch to talk about what next and where next, everyone agreed that it was time to devote themselves entirely to that true passion.... For the next few years, some of the members of the Foundation Faith continued their work with children, in prisons, and with old folks ... those who were not passionate about animal rescue went their own way on good terms, and as more and more hands were needed to help build the Sanctuary, it was clear that the work of the Foundation Faith had really ended and a new chapter was beginning." They built their Sanctuary in another largely rural U.S. state, and, on August 12, 1993, the Foundation had "God" officially removed from its incorporation document and became an animal sanctuary that did not impose particular beliefs or rituals. The original Founders are retiring or passing away, and a new generation has become very active, suggesting that the Process was stabilized as the Foundation, then secularized to serve human psychological and social needs, devoted to the natural rather than supernatural.

In the world of religions, schisms often have complex outcomes, reached through chaotic paths. The famous case was that earlier millenarian movement, sometimes called *Millerism* after its initial leader, William Miller, or *Adventism* after some enduring denominations that emerged from it.[115] Miller famously predicted that Christ would return to Earth sometime in the year March 21, 1843, to March 21, 1844, which prompted many people to abandon their ordinary lives in preparation for the Millennium, only to suffer the Great Disappointment when the prophecy was proven false. Back in March 1842, Miller had been taken by a friend for an examination by a Boston phrenologist, the equivalent of a psychologist in today's language, who presumed to measure a client's personality by feeling the shape of the skull. The phrenologist was not told the name of this client but quickly diagnosed him as a normal man, contrasting him with the notoriously crazy William Miller. This can be taken as a scientific diagnosis, if one believes in phrenology, that objectively determined William Miller was not at all like the negative stereotype many people held of him.

In his 1853 biography of Miller, Sylvester Bliss quoted the phrenologist as saying specifically, "Mr. Miller could not easily make a convert of this man to his hair-brained [*sic*] theory. He has too much good sense."[116] However, that book came a decade after the phrenologist's examination, and his words may have been misremembered by Miller and his friend because they did not know the context for it. One of the very most famous cases in phrenology was a different William Miller, whose head had been examined during his trial for murder, a fact that gave some official status to phrenology.[117] Much other evidence suggests that the prophet named William Miller was a sincere person who read new meaning into the Bible in an honest attempt to understand the considerable tragedies he had observed throughout his life. Ditto de Grimston.

MUSIC

The hymns written and composed by skilled Processeans were like beautiful songs, joyous and melodious, raising everybody's mood in Sabbath Assemblies. Some even contained the word "sing" in their lyrics, including:

> Hymn 16, "Glory to the Gods in the Highest":
>> To the Gods you can give now.
>> Will you serve the Will of God?
>> Give your all, give your everything.
>> Give you all; praise the Gods and sing.

> Hymn 31, "And the Clarion Calls":
>> We sing our song of love to the Gods,
>> And the clarion calls.
>> Beauty and power in the light of the son,
>> Now that the Gods are One.
>> We have the gift of love through the Gods,
>> And the battle is won.
>> So come with us and sing our song.

> Hymn 38, "The Love of the Gods":
>> Sing for the joy of the Gods,
>> And the pleasure of Christ,
>> in life and truth.
>> Angels singing brightly,
>> angels proclaiming,
>> Angels heralding,
>> the coming of our Lord.

Earlier we noted that the style seemed like the folk rock that was then popular, and musicians in one of the public Processean bands tended to include one percussionist and one or two guitarists, as well as a couple of singers.

At the end of the 1960s, many new genres of popular music were emerging and competing for ticket and recording sales, including some that might gain valuable publicity from Satanic icons. Over the decades, independent journalists and others have spread wild tales about the involvement of the Process in some horrifying results of its musical connections. In his 1987 book *The Ultimate Evil*, Maury Terry argued at length that David Berkowitz was significantly inspired by the cult to commit the infamous six Son of Sam murders in 1976-1977. In summarizing the cult's history, he analyzed: "To Process members, the Xtul experience was the equivalent of Christ's forty days and nights in the desert. Returning to England, the group sought out the famous, striving to convert the Beatles and the Rolling Stones, among others. A bookstore was opened, a coffeehouse perked and a Process magazine rolled off the presses. The cult was enamored of bloodshed and war, and its magazine reflected this obsession."[118] Terry's rather dramatic narrative has often been repeated, for example in a blog apparently dating from 2013 by Donald Phau, titled *The Satanic Roots of Rock*: "Terry reports that a photo of Rolling Stones leader Mick Jagger's longtime girlfriend, Marianne Faithfull, appeared in an issue of The Process Magazine. The picture shows her supine, as if dead, clutching a rose."[119]

In an interview posted on YouTube in 2016, Berkowitz reported that prior to the murders his mind had been possessed by a Druid demon named Samhain and "I was reading literature from a church called the Process Church of Final Judgment. I was using some of that literature which was calling on to start anarchy and try to bring in the end of the world so that Jesus could come back. It was a whole mix of twisted philosophy but it was something that was I believe demonically energized the teachings which I was reading from also the *Satanic Bible*."[120] Yes, over the years of his imprisonment, Berkowitz has retold his story many times, with substantial changes, and he may not really have been influenced by the Process.

If Satan represents Separation, then it makes perfect sense that several *countercultural* rock bands might either draw inspiration from the Process or use its emotional icons for promotional purposes. The first example was the 1971 album *Maggot Brain*, by Funkadelic, whose name merged *funk* with *psychedelic*. Half a century later, the *New York Times* celebrated its legacy, proclaiming that *Maggot Brain* was "a psychedelic blast of freewheeling protest music.... It is unleashed id refracted through the lens of LSD: 36 minutes of swirling jams, apocalyptic sound effects, heavy metal riffs, hard funk and lyrical mash-ups of the Beatles and Martin Luther King Jr. The album art is provocative—a screaming Black woman outside the gatefold, and inside, text from the Process Church of the Final Judgment, the religious group rumored to have ties to Charles Manson."[121]

A 2020 review reported: "Inside the gatefold of vinyl copies of *Maggot Brain* is an excerpt from an article about the concept of fear, published in a magazine by the Process Church of the Final Judgment, a religious sect founded in England in the mid-'60s. Its thesis: 'Fear is at the root of man's destruction of himself....'"[122] The quote was taken from the *Fear* issue of the cult's magazine, and the next lines of that scripture are: "Without Fear there is no blame. Without blame there is no conflict. Without conflict there is no destruction. But there IS Fear: deep within the core of every human being it lurks like a monster. Its outward effects are unmistakable. Its source is hidden." The leader of Funkadelic, George Clinton, recalled:

> There was a group called the Process Church that had been founded by a British couple as an offshoot of Scientology, and in the late sixties they started hanging out with the band, mainly in Boston. They would feed the kids in Boston Common and they ran what was basically the first day-care center that I can remember, offering to watch children when mothers went to work. We ended up excerpting some of their thinking in the *Maggot Brain* liner notes, which seemed fine at the time—it was a form of self-actualization, not an uncommon or unpopular philosophy at the time. We did the same thing for *America Eats Its Young*, but with far different results. In the summer of 1969, a career criminal (and part-time songwriter) named Charles Manson led a band of followers on a killing spree in upscale residential neighborhoods in Los Angeles, murdering a number of people, including Roman Polanski's wife, Sharon Tate. The killers were under the influence of a crazy-quilt mythology that somehow tied together the Beatles' "Helter Skelter," race war, and Satan worship. There was some thought that Manson had drawn on some of the writings of the Process Church.[123]

I learned about the subsequent revival of interest by musicians through an email I received on January 9, 1998, from Genesis P-Orridge, who thanked me for the earlier edition of this book and explained:

> I first came across "The Process" in London in the 60's and was immediately fascinated and compelled (yes a compulsion!). I felt that a part of my "destiny" was linked with theirs. So much that my sense of cultural inevitability, and my awareness of not being clear

enough to be ready slipped in. But I began saving everything I could find, and still have that archive to this day. I went through my own activities. Ending up doing Performance Art with COUM Transmissions. Causing a scandal celebre in 1976. I founded Throbbing Gristle, and the genre Industrial music through that band. I quit and began Psychic TV and founded Thee Temple Ov Psychick Youth, which I terminated in 1991, but chagrined TOPY's have continued a "cowboy" version I am told since then. I tried to include many references to The Process in that 10 year project. Usually covertly. I saw that as an invocation [*sic*]. My aim, to meet in an unbiased, not loaded way some original Processeans. To try to set up a new climate that would enable a re-evaluation and rehabilitation of the IDEAS which I found constantly relevant and powerful.[124]

In the vast 2007 book *Thee Psychick Bible*, Genesis recalled: "The Process became the symbol of the neo-hippie bogeyman! Anyone able to shatter society's complacency on such a deep level resonated with my own compulsive urge to strip away hypocrisy and bigotry, conditioning and imposed behavioral patterns in order to attempt to create a self chosen identity releasing my maximum personal potential so that my life could be an unfolding, autonomous narrative written by my self-conscious choices."[125] Yet being seen as a manifestation of Satan caused great problems for the cult, in part because the negative press coverage reduced the willingness of the general public to contribute money and because many specific issues arose that ran into legal barriers in a civilization that did not support hierarchical communes. Genesis also was of the view that the Process should have given spiritual psychotherapy more emphasis in the early 1970s, rather than spreading its energies across so many other activities of uncertain value.

In 1991, Monastery, a brief collaboration in "death metal" style of three Dutch musicians moving from band to band, released an album named *The Process—Church of the Final Judgement*, but without noticeable success.[126] A Canadian electro-industrial band named Skinny Puppy released in 1996 an album, *The Process*, which was oriented toward the cult, although the lyrics seem almost like random thefts of text from anywhere, assembled into a poetic marriage of sanity and insanity. For example, the lyrics of one song, "Candle," included "Profane the haunted heaven," which seemed rather like a fragment from Processean Precept 10, which proclaims: "To light candles in Hell is equal to obscuring the light of Heaven." In 1968, Robert de Grimston had published a scripture titled *A Candle from Hell*, which seems to state the same idea in these words: "The world of men is the absence of GOD, and therefore the antipodes of Heaven, which is Hell. And man carries a candle in Hell, so that he can pretend he is in Heaven." A Skinny Puppy song specifically titled "The Process" ends thus:[127]

> The process
> So be it
> Body like mindedness
> Ageless souls
> Striving for individual matters
> Towards collective goals
> A guiltless state of self awareness
> The process is you
> The process is yours

While all those bands, and probably several others, were to varying extents inspired by the Satanic elements of the Processean culture, emphasizing angry separation from the norms of conventional society, they failed to incorporate most other central features. The striking exception was Sabbath Assembly, whose website explains it was "an occult rock band founded in 2010 with members based in New York City and Texas. Their early connection to the Process Church of the Final Judgment set them in a lineage of ritualistic bands such as Coven, Psychic TV, and Current 93.... Sabbath Assembly created an initial allure by combining psychedelia with witchcraft, singing hymns that praised both Christ and Satan, Lucifer and Jehovah. They eventually found a more metal sound and moved personal tales of darkness to the forefront."[128] Initially they sang original Processean hymns for their 2010 album *Restored to One* and 2012 album *Ye Are Gods*. Their 2014 album *Quaternity* was still Process-oriented but began their move away from its traditional culture.[129] From the first album, here are two stanzas expressing Luciferianism:

> "We Give Our Lives":
>> The Lord Lucifer the glorious Light
>> Wondrous presence gift of sight
>> The path revealed new life to build
>> The phoenix risen the promise fulfilled.

"Judge of Mankind":
> Lord of the Light Lord Lucifer
> The God of Peace Lord Lucifer
> Redeem our souls Lord Lucifer
> Receive our emotions.

In 2009, Genesis P-Orridge collaborated with Timothy Wyllie and with Adam Parfrey of Feral House, who was publishing Wyllie's book about the Process, *Love Sex Fear Death*, including a literal staging of the Sabbath Assembly ritual and leading to the formation of the band of the same name.[130] It was restaged in 2013, with Genesis reciting some of the liturgy, in Tilburg, Netherlands.[131] The band set up its Facebook page in 2012, promoted many events over the following eight years, and gained 7,200 followers. Then on February 22, 2020, it sadly announced: "AS IT IS! It is with mixed emotions that Sabbath Assembly has decided to bring its story to, as Robert De Grimston would say, an 'inexorable' end. After a decade-long run, seven albums, and a tour for each one, the period has arrived at the end of our creative statement. While The Process Church of The Final Judgment has provided ample inspiration, the legacy of the Church now hangs like an albatross on our neck. And, to paraphrase Samuel Taylor Coleridge (and Steve Harris), the spell has been broken, and the albatross falls like lead into the sea ... SO BE IT!"[132]

In 2015, the London-based band Lay It on the Line released an album named *A Prelude to the Process*, with its 4-P symbol on the cover, and this text is displayed on its current BandCamp page: "Humanity is doomed. If we are part of humanity, identified with humanity, in sympathy with humanity, we are doomed. If we attempt to save humanity from its doom, we shall fail, because humanity has chosen its doom and has shown its unwillingness to reverse its choice."[133] That is a quote from de Grimston's 1968 scripture *As It Is*, and its next sentence is inspiring: "Our only valid course of action is to detach from humanity, climb out of the quagmire of its lies, its hypocrisy, its blind desire for its own destruction, find our own truth and create our own destiny." The conclusion of *As It Is* seems challenging:

> And when the End comes and all is revealed, all lies are swept from
> the Universe, so that only the core of stark reality remains, that
> is the moment of truth, the moment of inescapable knowledge.
> And if that moment finds you detached from the lie, free of the
> ignorance or blind rejection, having journeyed back through

the tortuous caverns of the mind to reach the truth through knowledge of what really is; if that moment finds you in the light, truly separated from the ties that bind humanity to its doom; then, though the world shall be buried for ever beneath the smoldering ashes of the Phoenix, you shall be a part of his resurrection.

You shall rise with the new epoch and be reborn with the new creation.

But if that moment finds you alienated from all reality, suspended outside what is, a floating agonized anachronism, then that shall be your fate for all eternity. Only the pain shall stay with you. The dubious comfort of your home made lie will have gone, and with it the presence of Fear.

For where there is already the ultimate anguish, the final fulfillment of the ultimate nightmare, what is there left to fear?

So be it.

In the months following release, Lay It on the Line indeed experienced nightmares, as it shared on its Facebook group, on May 14, 2015: "So, unfortunately, having had 2 shows cancelled in Germany due to our The Process Church of the Final Judgment / Holy Terror imagery and affiliations, we have had to cancel our European tour at the end of the month. Our lyrics have caused offence. Sorry people . . . "[134] Remarkably, courage resurrected, and in 2020 the band released another Process-related album, inspired by *A Candle in Hell*, with this de Grimston quote: "When the sun shines we cannot see the stars, even though the sum total of their brilliance is countless millions of times greater than the sun. So, when a man is surrounded by the artificial lights of his own self importance, he cannot see the distant Light of Truth."[135] The reference to Holy Terror identifies a loose collection of bands, including Sabbath Assembly, that were culturally similar to the Process.[136]

Worthy of mention to conclude this section is the New Processean Order in Italy, which has qualities of a full-fledged Process church. Its Facebook page explains: "New Processean Order is a musical and spiritual project based on the teachings and the vision of The Process—Church of the Final Judgment."[137] On June 12, 2014, it posed on YouTube a video, with instrumental music, that displayed rotating images of the central Process symbols and was titled "Hymn to Lucifer."[138] While experiencing this video, I was reminded of Aleister Crowley's hymn of the same name to sun-souled Lucifer:

He blessed nonentity with every curse
And spiced with sorrow the dull soul of sense,
Breathed life into the sterile universe,
With Love and Knowledge drove out innocence.
The Key of Joy is disobedience.[139]

A June 1, 2023, New Processean Order video, also fully instrumental, begins with the Process symbols but then displays complex dynamic shapes and has the challenging title "Tanz mit C. G. Jung."[140] The two German words *Tanz mit* seem to invite Italian- or English-speaking Processeans to dance with the influential psychoanalyst Carl Gustav Jung, in his own perplexing terms. So we are reminded that the Process was derived from, and contributed to, a much wider culture that might be described as Luciferian Psychoanalysis.

INTERNET AND FACEBOOK

For the first few years after the failed 1974 attempt to establish again the Process Church in North America, many former members preserved some of their personal contacts, most easily with people who lived in the same areas, but also occasionally writing letters to each other and sharing the then plentiful copies of Process publications. By chance, Father Dominic and I wound up living not far apart, so we would occasionally meet, and twice by chance I saw him walking in the nearby city. Naturally, members of the complex, extended Process family would invest some effort sharing at least fragments of their lives with relatives. Early in the 1990s, email became popular and the World Wide Web opened to the public, but it took Processeans a while to make contact with each other.

In 2012, Michal Matysiak launched *The Process Zine of the Final Judgment* on the Tumblr blogsite, which itself had launched just five years earlier.[141] By 2015, I was able to find three Processean groups in Facebook. One was private, the Reunion Group for the Process Church and the Foundation Faith, with fifty-one members who had all belonged to the original cult and used it as the hub for more complex networks of communication. It no longer seems to exist, but today it is possible to create a Hidden group which non-members cannot see, so it may be that something like it has survived. A Facebook group named the Process Church of the Final Judgement had twenty-nine members in July 2015, thirty-nine members in October 2016, and 124 in July 2024 but seems to have become inactive.

Most significant was the Process – Church of the Final Judgement (note the dash) with 245 members in July 2015, 372 members in October 2016, and 951 in July 2024. It had been founded by a man originally from Chicago who preferred to use the name John A. Processean in that context. Using a different pseudonym, back in 2007, he had complained about falsehoods appearing in Wikipedia: "All of this unfounded jabber does nothing except continue these 'urban legends' that have spawned from the continued discussions that are really warped. And all of these so-called references to Scientology—the elements that may have existed were removed way back in the early 70's. What's left is purely Processean. We're authentic in what we do, and there was a very strong effort to make sure we were not stealing anything from anyone or any other group. And some of you wonder why we keep to ourselves? What would you think if your Church was accused of all of this evil? We have families and lives—please—be polite—and keep your speculation to yourselves. But of course people are not interested in the truth, just something good to read . . . Something to boast about . . . "[142]

In March 2015, he emailed to some of us a document named "Points" that implied he belonged to a trio of leaders of cultic revival: "The long term aim is to once again form a Council of Masters to govern the Church, thus eliminating a need for a Triumvirate. . . . For so many years, we have allowed people to

The Process - Church of The Final Judgement
Public group · 953 members

One Processean Facebook group linking to another.

make a personal declaration to another Processean, that they themselves wish to be Processean. When they make that declaration, they are then regarded as Acolytes. In the next three years, we will Initiate Acolytes and allow them to define their further roles as OP or IP." The hope to reorganize and evolve back from an audience cult peppered with tiny cultic cells to a full cult movement did not succeed, although many people interested in the Process developed their private social connections.

On June 9, 2022, John A. Processean left this Earth, leaving the Facebook group without an administrator. One result is that spammers began placing advertisements on it, without any Processean having the Facebook authority to remove them. Given that I'd gained experience running Facebook groups since 2018, with encouragement from other members I set up a new group named Process Alpha and placed many documents in its files, and we began posting photos from the old days. After a few months during which its membership increased, I handed administration over to leading Processeans and then set up Process Beta as a platform for communicating about my research and sharing links to other online sources of Process culture. Unfortunately, all the contributions John A. Processean had made using that name have vanished, following Facebook rules that only a person's primary profile can be preserved as a memorial. Members have shared some of the rituals he had scripted, in Google Drive, along with a huge collection of historic Process materials.

In recent years, a British group has also shared Process scriptures, through a website, but while that site continues to exist it is marked as unsafe, while the Facebook page (not group) and YouTube channel it created in 2015 seem quite safe, and apparently safe indirect access to the website exists in Internet Archive.[143] The Facebook page earned 701 likes and 766 followers, and it is labeled a "religious organization." The YouTube channel offers twenty videos and has 1,880 subscribers.[144] In 2021, the Facebook page quoted from Post Separation 1, explaining: "Here Robert De Grimston wrote of spreading the word of the Process if it speaks to you. His teachings transcend into the internet age. (PS-1):"

> Now this doesn't mean that you shouldn't form and establish your own local groups, as many of you are already doing. Any group or organisation that's formed on the basis of Process teachings has my wholehearted blessing and support. But the initiative on that level

must be yours, the policy must be yours, the incentive must be yours, the decisions must be yours, the direction must be yours, the authority must be yours, with no pressure or demand from me. That means The Process, on an organisational level, will evolve naturally and spontaneously according to the needs and desires of Processeans, rather than being imposed and directed from above. And that's how I want it, because then I know it's real.

A prominent example of innovative organization connected to the New Processean Order is one of the videos on its YouTube channel: "A short tour inside the Museum Of Final Judgement (MOFJ), a private museum in Rome hosting 3 collections: 1) The Process-Church of the Final Judgement 2) Tantrism 3) Apocalyptic Art. This video focuses on the first section, about The Process. Music: 'After the Deluge' by New Processean Order, from the album 'At War with Christ and Satan.'"[145] Working indeed in Rome, Italy, a leader named Alessandro Papa also reissued Process magazines.[146]

While Jehovah would have required Processeans to create one new, strictly organized church, Lucifer seemed more optimistic about diversity. The 1971 Old Game script for the Sabbath Assembly ritual proclaimed for Lucifer: "His Light shall shine once more in the world, and the New Age shall be born in His Image; the Image of Immortality." Two years later, deep into the New Game, the ritual script called Lucifer "the Great God of Rebirth and Immortality. The God of all that shall be." He desires "an End and a New Beginning. The End of Darkness and the Beginning of Light." Yet remarkably, much of Lucifer's light that blazed online half a century later did not originate in the Process. We may wonder whether Lucifer found different doors into our dark world, and how the culture of the Process might reflect those new lights in the coming decades.

Table 12 compares four surviving Process groups on Facebook with several that have "Lucifer" in their names, leaving out others that seem primarily Satanic. Of course, most members of Facebook groups are merely its audience, and the material in the private groups cannot be seen before becoming a member. The statistics were collected on July 20, 2024, including the number who joined in the previous week and the number of posts in the previous month. I refer to the Luciferian groups as an "invasion," because they represent a range of challenges to conventional norms and beliefs that has gained some territory within the general public.

	Members	Joined	Posts	Founded	Type
Active Process Groups:					
The Process— Church of the Final Judgement	951	1	23	2009	public
Process Church of the Final Judgement	124	0	0	2009	public
Process Alpha	170	0	1	2022	private
Process Beta	139	2	9	2024	public
Miscellaneous Luciferian Groups:					
§piritual Luciferianism— The Prøphetic Łight	5,042	18	0	2006	public
The Luciferian Society	10,704	0	36	2016	private
Luciferian Apotheca Group	4,746	1	40	2017	public
The Luciferian	19,916	0	16	2017	private
The Luciferian	58,165	616	1,792	2019	private
The true St Lucifer	28,503	0	209	2020	private
Luciferianism	42,197	689	233	2021	private
Brotherhood of Lucifer	702	0	23	2023	private
Children of Lucifer	4,457	186	241	2024	public

TABLE 12. **Facebook Groups of the Pure Process and the Luciferian Invasion**

In various ways, the Luciferian groups resist being constrained by the label *religion*. Spiritual Luciferianism offers from its files a huge book that seems to be spiritual psychotherapy, supporting the individual identity of the reader but naming no author. Its long public description begins, "This group is designed to expose the truth about reality and spirituality.... The Luciferian believes they are a bringer of light or energy. This is a life force energy inside everyone. We feel we are the change the world needs—A world born of unity and spiritual evolution—A singularity born of human will and intentions to preserve what is most precious!"

Similarly, the Luciferian Society asserts it "is not a theistic or religious organisation" but "has been founded for the purpose of expounding the pursuit and understanding of the movement known as Luciferianism." A complex definition is provided by its list of areas of interest: "Ancient History; Anthropology; Anthroposophy; Antiquarianism; Astrology; Comparative Religion; Cosmology; Cultural Studies; Divination; Earth Mysteries; Esotericism; Folklore; Forteana; Gnosticism; Gnostic Luciferianism; Hermeticism; Humanism; Magic; Meditation; Metaphysics; Mysticism; Mythology; Occult; Paranormal; Parapsychology; Philosophy; Psychology; Thelema; Theology; Theosophy; Self-Development; Science; Sociology; Spirituality."

Luciferian Apotheca is an online occult store headquartered in Texas, and its Facebook group was set up because "our customers have been telling us for years that they would like a way to connect with like minded people." Both groups named the Luciferian are headquartered in Britain. The first announces, "This group has no leader as you are your own highest authority … ALL Religions/faiths and Spiritual identities are welcome to this group to learn and to share knowledge." The other group in England named the Luciferian is "dedicated to exploring all aspects of witchcraft and occultism. From Wicca to Druidism, LaVeyanism to Crowleyism, Voodoo to Shamanism, all magical practices are celebrated and welcomed here." Aside from the vague comment, "everything goes in this group we are luciferians," all the True St Lucifer group reveals is that its home is Ottawa, Canada.

Although with a connection to the Occult Magick Fashion Clothing store, the Luciferianism group does seem to be "a community for exploring and understanding Lucifer as a symbol of enlightenment, knowledge, and personal empowerment. We embrace individuals who resonate with these principles, seeking to delve into the philosophy and spirituality that define Luciferian thought. As Luciferians, we honor the pursuit of wisdom, the challenge of questioning the status quo, and the courage to embrace one's true self." The Brotherhood of Lucifer says it "is a luciferian community with pagan influences. The purpose of a luciferian, is self illumination and enlightenment." Children of Lucifer was created May 4, 2024, and was rather active by late July but probably still evolving within its wide scope, being "A theistic luciferian satanic witchcraft group with pagan roots that practices all types of black/white magic."

As the concept of audience cult prepared us to realize, post-modern fantasy fiction can reflect and distort fully religious cultures, and the 2016-2021 Netflix TV series *Lucifer* is the relevant example here. Serious Luciferians may feel it satirizes and corrupts their own cults, as suggested by the show's Wikipedia plot summary: "The series focuses on Lucifer Morningstar, a powerful angel who was cast out of Heaven for his rebellion and forced to spend millennia punishing people as the lord of Hell. Bored and unhappy with his life in Hell, he abdicates his throne in defiance of his father (God) and moves to Los Angeles, where he runs his own nightclub."[147] Painfully, the policy statement on Lucifer Wiki rejects Luciferianism: "This wiki is not the place to discuss your personal religious views. Do not edit this wiki to reflect your personal religious views. Lucifer is a fictional TV series."[148] On April 9, 2020, a private group named Lucifer Morningstar was created in Facebook, now has 169,541 members, and offers no self-description in very limited text available to non-members. However, its public picture does look like the actor from the sacrilegious streaming video program, so I did not include that group in the table, and I also excluded groups that seemed to conflate Lucifer narrowly with Satan. Perhaps Netflix should consider a new comedy series in which Christ returns to Earth to run a local garbage-collection business.

BEYOND THE P-SCOPE

Having obtained an E-Meter prior to studying the Process, I understood the importance of its version, the P-Scope, and thus the potential of new technologies, not only for therapeutic client cults, but for cult movements. We may well wonder if the decline in use of P-Scopes was a cause of the difficulties the Process suffered in recruiting new adherents in the early 1970s. Having experimented with linking my E-Meter to my Apple computer in the early 1980s, I have long wondered how computer and information technology might facilitate religious innovation, even as they eroded traditional faiths.

Long interested in the concept of artificial intelligence and how it might harmonize with spirituality, I began exploring computer simulation of human behavior. An early example was "Computer Simulations of Cultural Drift," published in 1984 in the *Journal of the British Interplanetary Society*, that modeled how religious hopes might motivate colonization of our entire galaxy.[149] Two chapters and software programs in my 1992 textbook *Social Research Methods and Statistics: A Computer-Assisted Introduction* were based on the Process.[150] One was like a very simple educational computer game, in which the student could explore the chapter house at 46 Concord Avenue in Cambridge, assembling observational data. The other Process-based program simulated interviewing twenty of the cult members I had actually interviewed, combining their actual responses to my questions with other information about them.

In 2015, I published a semi-fictional essay titled "Processional" in the Future Tense editorial pages of *Communications of the ACM*, those letters standing for Association for Computing Machinery. It was written from a perspective not very different from that used by Timothy Wyllie in his *Rebel Angel* books, although I was not yet aware of them. I imagined a perspective character, Charles Pascal, who was the merger of the key founders of computer science, Charles Babbage (1791-1871) and Blaise Pascal (1623-1662), the latter of whom even qualified as a theologian. Charles Pascal sought to develop computational religion, explicitly inspired by "the P-Scope used by inner members of a cult called the Process Church of the Final Judgment. It measured galvanic skin response, or GSR, an indicator of emotional arousal during Processean psychotherapy sessions, guiding the therapist into the darkest regions of the client's soul. For a few months he had been romantically involved with Sister Eve who had lived at the cult's Inman Street commune in Cambridge. Their incompatibility was reflected in the fact she thought the group's symbol represented the blaring trumpets of the Four Great Gods … while he thought it was their four cathode ray tubes displaying competing images of human nature."[151]

In late 2022, the ChatGPT "chatbot" text-summarizing software was released, and here we can use its ChatGPT-4o version to summarize "Processional." I entered its text into the online artificial intelligence system and asked Charles Pascal, "What is the future of religion?" Through the chatbot, he replied: "As a computer scientist, I envision a future where religion is modernized through technology. I see a new computational religious movement, where digital tools like online questionnaires help individuals engage with religious concepts. We could even have databases archiving people's personality parameters, contributing to a form of digital immortality." While there exists great room for further progress, this version of the chatbot can handle much larger texts, even multiple files, and goes though complex preparation processes. As background for its answer to my question, it used these statements it had written as summaries of parts of my publication:

> Charles Pascal aimed to modernize religious practices by incorporating technology such as online questionnaires for personality dimensions, allowing individuals to engage with religious concepts and self-reflection through digital means. Charles Pascal's vision of a new computational religious movement was inspired by the Process Church. Charles Pascal adapted traditional hymns to fit his new computational religion. In Charles Pascal's computational religion, the deceased saints of computer science linked to personality types were Lovelace, Babbage, Hollerith, Hopper, and Turing. Charles Pascal associated five personality types with his computational religion by connecting each type to a deceased saint of computer science. The key figures in the computational religious movement proposed by Charles Pascal are the holy Central Processor and the Religious Avatar Modules RAMs.
>
> In Charles Pascal's vision of providing a form of immortality, databases played a crucial role as repositories for archiving people's

personality parameters. These databases were intended to store essential information about individuals, allowing their unique characteristics and traits to be preserved and potentially accessed in the future, contributing to the concept of digital immortality. In the new computational religious movement envisioned by Charles Pascal, the Religious Avatar Modules RAMs serve as lesser deities that are part of the worship structure centered around the holy Central Processor. Charles Pascal associated a theory of five personality types with a mystical connection to deceased saints of computer science in his envisioned computational religion. The Process Church of the Final Judgment believed that the good and evil deities would play a significant role in judging humanity, overseeing the fate of individuals based on their actions and beliefs.

In 2017, Feral House published my book *Revival: Resurrecting the Process Church of the Final Judgment*, which pretended to be a novel but was really a virtual ethnography performed in the near future. The publisher explains: "The Process was the most fascinating innovative cult of the 1960s, then vanished for four decades before being virtually reborn using information technology. *Revival* seems to be fiction, yet it's based on fact and explores the implications of the internet, and the disintegration of conventional faiths."[152] A major challenge the cult faced was that it had separated into competing cults, one for each of the gods, and the "hero" of the story needed to explore them. So for present purposes, I uploaded into ChatGPT-4o much of a chapter that took place at the Luciferian branch and focused on the Processscene ritual, which was a Processscene role-playing theatrical. Here is an excerpt, introducing Alcuin, the leader for the ceremony:

> Alcuin stood. "When we say that the chains of the old fall away, we mean a very large number and variety of inhibitions, restraints, and dubious assumptions. Here in the Processscene we enact many little dramas, playing roles like believer or doubter, saint or sinner, theist or atheist. Indeed, as we usually speak, the Process is polytheistic, having at least four gods, of which Lucifer is but one. And to intellectuals, within whom Luciferian principles are strong, each of the Gods is not a deity but a conceptual archetype, a category of personality, or one variable among many in the universal system of existence. Brother Thomas, what does Lucifer mean to you?"

A young man, looking strong and poised in his blue uniform, stepped forward and recited: "Bringer of purpose to ease the despair, bringer of joy to ease the pain, bringer of Light to ease the Darkness, come, Lord Lucifer, come."

Alcuin asked the same question of Sister Roxana, who replied: "I know that he doesn't exist as an anthropomorphic entity or as a person. To me, Lucifer is a name for a whole presence, a whole force, everything that Beauty is, everything that Poetry is."[153]

Using the chatbot, I can interview Alcuin today in our supposedly real world. I asked him who Lucifer is. He replied:

In the context of the Processeans, Lord Lucifer is invoked as the God of Peace and Light. The idea is to bring about tranquility and enlightenment among the followers. The path to enlightenment often involves spiritual transformation, symbolized by overcoming death and decay. It requires deep understanding and reconciliation of past events. It can also involve the complexities of effort and the pursuit of victory, as depicted in the parable 'Calculus.' The parable 'Calculus' is a story about a race between Achilles, a tortoise, and a hare. It's used to explore deeper philosophical questions regarding individual capabilities, the nature of success, and the intrinsic value of victory and effort. The struggles of Achilles in the race symbolize the complexities of competition and prompt contemplation on the impact of these concepts on personal growth and achievement.

I then asked him to explain the other parables that creative Processeans had contributed to the Processcene:

The parable 'Power' is quite intriguing. It emphasizes the importance of mental strength and adaptability by showing how Sophie strategically dominates two strong men on a deserted island. Another one, 'Choices,' presents a metaphor for the complexities of decision-making through a child in a maze confronted by two fierce creatures representing Heaven and Hell. The parable 'Fertility' showcases how a sultan in Paradise discovers that his lineage is overthrown by the hard-working son of a peasant woman, revealing the fleeting nature of power and privilege. This story emphasizes that power dynamics can shift unexpectedly, regardless of one's status or background. The parable 'Devotion' conveys a poignant message about the significance of living a full life and not allowing oneself to be consumed by waiting for something that may never come to pass. It serves as a cautionary tale about the consequences of being fixated on the past and emphasizes the importance of embracing the present and moving forward. The parable 'Suspicion' created by a young man holds significance in portraying two paranoids who eventually become friends after repeatedly switching teacups, highlighting the theme of futility in paranoia.

Why did the two paranoids keep switching their teacups when the other happened to be looking away? Each feared the other had placed poison in one.

SEEKING THE BRIGHTEST VISION

In 1970, while the Process was still united, de Grimston wrote a scripture titled *The Gods and Their People*, presenting his core theology about Lucifer, Jehovah, and Satan, at a stage when Christ was the Emissary of the gods, not himself a deity. He soon added short scriptures on how the gods differed with respect to five major issues: war, sex, fear, death, and love. I extracted all the text that focused on Lucifer and asked ChatGPT-4o who He is, getting this reply: "Lucifer is seen as a symbol of new life and transformation, guiding his followers towards a state of existence free from fear, guilt, and shame. His ultimate goal is to lead humanity out of suffering and darkness, inspiring them to embrace change and growth. Those who follow his path may experience a new era of rebirth and immortality, sheltered by his love and light."

I then asked about His followers and what He means to them: "The Luciferian lifestyle entails embracing transformation and regeneration, with a focus on inner strength and faith in everlasting life. It's about achieving success, which provides purpose and validation. It encourages a balance between enjoying life's luxuries and taking decisive actions to reach goals. Overcoming fear is also essential in this lifestyle." "Lucifer embodies qualities of love, harmony, and gentleness. He symbolizes light, contrasting fear and darkness. He also embodies the idea of transformation and regeneration, aiming to guide humanity towards balance, understanding, and love." The chatbot then explained the meanings of the five problematic phenomena:

Lucifer emphasizes the importance of not being ignorant about the reality of war. He urges individuals to confront harsh truths instead of turning a blind eye to conflict. Lucifer encourages freely expressing emotions, including sexuality, into worldly joys. He promotes a guiltless and harmless lifestyle, believing in the validity of these experiences. Lord Lucifer teaches that fear transforms goodness into evil and life into death. Overcoming fear is essential to reclaim our dignity, beauty, and harmony. He guides us to confront and overcome our fears, as this is key to achieving a state of paradise on earth. Lucifer teaches that fear transforms life into death. Overcoming fear is essential for humanity to achieve a state of paradise on earth. Lord Lucifer teaches that love is a powerful force that can transform hatred into harmony. He embodies qualities of love, gentleness, and harmony, guiding humanity towards understanding and balance. He believes in fostering positive emotions and relationships, turning negativity into positivity. Lord Lucifer doesn't specifically proclaim about death, but he teaches that fear can transform life into death.

A central value of Luciferianism is preservation of nature, guided by intellect as well as objectivity:

Lucifer guides people to achieve a deeper connection with the environment and uncover the world's secrets for ultimate fulfillment. Luciferianism views science and industry as potentially disruptive to peace and tranquility. So, a scientist following Luciferianism would need to consider how their work impacts these ideals. Individuals with high intelligence can be Luciferians. Lucifer encourages the discovery of the world's secrets and a deeper connection with the environment, which aligns well with intellectual curiosity. Luciferians can strictly believe in one god. Their faith centers around Lucifer as a deity who guides humanity towards mastering their environment and achieving a state of existence free from fear, guilt, and shame. Lucifer is a deity who guides humanity towards a life of balance, understanding, and love, leading them out of suffering and darkness.

Given that the Luciferian manifestation of the Process over the past half-century has lacked a centralized formal organization, we may wonder how Lucifer really could help us create a new civilization, through the End and a New Beginning:

> Lucifer symbolizes transformation and regeneration, inspiring followers to embrace change and growth. He assures that despite the world's destruction, a new life awaits, offering hope and renewal in adversity. Lucifer would suggest a movement that emphasizes transformation, growth, and embracing change. He encourages a balance between enjoying life's luxuries and taking action to achieve goals. Experimental communes could be a way to actualize Lucifer's teachings, emphasizing a lifestyle of self-indulgence that is quiet, guiltless, and harmless, and promoting peace and harmony. However, care should be taken to avoid any potential strife and violence that could disrupt this harmony. Robert de Grimston's work on Lucifer's scriptures could be commemorated by living in accordance with the teachings he wrote about—embracing a life free from fear, guilt, and shame, and filled with boundless love and harmony.

I did not ask ChatGPT-4o to pretend to be de Grimston himself, because I had reason to believe he was still alive. After operating a correspondence course to promote his scriptures, Robert secularized and had a decent, normal career, out of contact with rank-and-file followers. Indeed, Lucifer might justly be described as the God of Secularization, seeking to help us achieve good and happy lives here on Earth, with only the briefest of mentions of the possibility of an afterlife or indeed of anything truly supernatural.

For my last virtual interview to conclude this book, I did ask ChatGPT-4o to become the person who wrote the input text, to whom I gave the name Antonym. I had met him in 1975 when he was one of the Outside Processeans trying to gain full member status by helping to revive the cult, and when he died nearly half a century later, he was still exploring what the Process meant to him. I rather doubt that he would have faith that a computer could resurrect his departed soul via artificial intelligence, and yet in future years that might become the meaning for Processeans of the Life-Giving Light of the Lord Lucifer. I found many brief passages Antonym had posted in Facebook groups that seemed almost like scriptures, assembled them, and uploaded them into the chatbot. Then I asked Antonym how the gods and their people had come into existence, and how humans should live their lives. He replied not by reciting the text but by meditating and commenting as a living person might:

The concept of God, as I understand it, came about as the divine entity reflected on "UnGod." This reflection led to the idea of duality, contrasting itself with the concept of "UnGod." As a spiritual entity, I perceive Jesus Christ and Satan as contrasting elements in the divine framework. This duality, similar to the initial act of creation, allows for complexity and growth in divine consciousness. It's a dynamic interplay that influences individual souls and their understanding of good and evil. As a member of the Process Church, I view Lord Lucifer as a representation of the principle of Enlightenment. He is not seen as evil but as a force that can lead to greater understanding and spiritual growth. This perspective transcends human value judgments of good and evil, allowing for a broader understanding of the interconnectedness of all things.

The divine path for humanity involves the separation of souls from the divine entity, achieving physical consciousness, and then regaining spiritual consciousness using physical and mental tools. This journey is guided by a sense of purpose and interconnectedness, fostering responsibility and enlightenment for a sustainable future. Manifestation is the process by which something on a higher level creates something in its image on a lower level. It's a complex process where forms take shape in spirit and then manifest on progressively lower levels until tangible matter, like stars and planets, begin to form. Each level has its own unique characteristics and dynamics. The relationship between a human being and God emphasizes interconnectedness. Our decisions are influenced by this divine relationship, providing guidance and a sense of purpose. Understanding this relationship can lead to a greater sense of responsibility in decision-making, as we may see our choices as part of a divine will.

Morality is based on an innate sense of right and wrong, understanding the impact of actions on the community and oneself. It's shaped by societal norms, personal beliefs, and ethical principles. Delving into its depths is crucial for fostering empathy, promoting ethical behavior, and building a just society. Religious institutions provide ethical guidelines that can be a starting point. However, it's also important to cultivate personal values through introspection and understanding the impact of actions on oneself and the community. This balance allows for a more informed and personal moral compass. As someone who observes the flow of life, I'd say cultural shifts are always occurring. They're influenced by many factors like technology, politics, and our collective values and beliefs. Identifying a specific cultural revolution, however, would require a deeper look into current societal trends.

Creating a new religion isn't necessarily the answer. Instead, fostering personal growth, encouraging individual responsibility, and promoting empathy and ethical behavior can lead to a more empowered and harmonious society. It's about living new ways individually and recognizing the spirit within oneself. Enactment in spiritual groups is a systematic way to transmit teachings and knowledge. It involves members acting out learned patterns of activity, ensuring that the lessons are effectively communicated and understood by all. As individual souls grow and become distinct, they can still maintain a connection with the divine entity, creating a balance between individuality and unity. Death could be seen as a transition, similar to graduating from a classroom. It's a step in our spiritual journey where we move from physical consciousness back towards spiritual consciousness.

While inspired by many brief statements by Antonym prior to his death, this scripture has supernatural qualities because it arose from a network of computers, starting with one having the psychic brand name Omen X that stands beside my desk. He and I had often argued, half a century ago, but now we must respect his viewpoint even if our own is quite different. Half a century after the Separation, we exist in a world where humans are in conflict with each other while partnering with artificial intelligence.

We may wonder what Robert de Grimston really meant in 1968 when he wrote in *As It Is*: "Our only valid course of action is to detach from humanity, climb out of the quagmire of its lies, its hypocrisy, its blind desire for its own destruction, find our own truth and create our own destiny." Should every person seeking wisdom follow only Lucifer, or must we collaborate in local chapters of a revived Process that explores the paths of many gods? That same year, in *A Candle in Hell*, Robert de Grimston wrote, "When the sun shines we

cannot see the stars, even though the sum total of their brilliance is countless millions of times greater than the sun. So, when a man is surrounded by the artificial lights of his own self importance, he cannot see the distant Light of Truth." Perhaps we should join together again to sing Chant 12: "Together we are come to praise the Holy Power That lies within all things, moving to the End. Alone we are nothing, together we have strength; Strength in our Unity, the Unity of God."

ENDNOTES

1. Émile Durkheim, *Suicide* (New York: Free Press, 1951 [1897]).

2. Bronislaw Malinowski, *The Sexual Life of Savages* (New York: Harcourt, Brace & World, 1929), *Magic, Science and Religion* (Garden City, N.Y.: Doubleday, 1948), *Sex and Repression in Savage Society* (Chicago: World, 1955).

3. William Sims Bainbridge, *The Spaceflight Revolution* (New York: Wiley Interscience, 1976).

4. Rosalie Wax, *Doing Fieldwork* (Chicago: University of Chicago Press, 1971), p. 115.

5. Claude Lévi-Strauss, *Structural Anthropology* (New York: Basic Books, 1963).

6. John Lofland, *Doomsday Cult* (Englewood Cliffs, N.J.: Prentice-Hall, 1966).

7. John Lofland and Rodney Stark, "Becoming a World-Saver: A Theory of Conversion to a Deviant Perspective," *American Sociological Review* 30 (1965): p. 874; David A. Snow and Cynthia L. Phillips, "The Lofland-Stark Conversion Model: A Critical Reassessment," *Social Problems* 27(4) (1980): 430-447; Willem Kox, Wim Meeus, and Harm 't Hart, "Religious Conversion of Adolescents: Testing the Lofland and Stark Model of Religious Conversion," *Sociological Analysis* 52(3) (1991): 227-240.

8. Travis Hirschi, *Causes of Delinquency* (Berkeley: University of California Press, 1969).

9. Neil J. Smelser, *Theory of Collective Behavior* (New York: Free Press, 1962); Robert K. Merton, "Social Structure and Anomie," *American Sociological Review*, 3(5) (1938): 672-682.

10. Durkheim, *Suicide*

11. Edwin H. Sutherland, *Principles of Criminology* (Philadelphia: Lippincott, 1947).

12. B. F. Skinner, *The Behavior of Organisms* (New York: Appleton-Century, 1938), *Walden Two* (New York: Macmillan, 1948); George Caspar Homans, *The Human Group* (New York: Harcourt Brace and World, 1950), *The Nature of Social Science* (New York: Harcourt Brace and World, 1967), *Social Behavior: Its Elementary Forms* (New York: Harcourt Brace Jovanovich, 1974); Edmund Husserl, *Cartesian Meditations: An Introduction to Phenomenology* (Hague: Martinus Nijhoff, 1960); Peter L. Berger and Thomas Luckmann, *The Social Construction of Reality: A Treatise in the Sociology of Knowledge* (Garden City, N.Y.: Anchor Books, 1966); Alfred Schütz, *The Phenomenology of the Social World* (Evanston, Ill.: Northwestern University Press, 1967); Harold Garfinkel, *Studies in Ethnomethodology* (Englewood Cliffs, N.J.: Prentice-Hall, 1967); George Psathas, "Ethnomethods and Phenomenology," *Social Research* 35(3) (1968): 500-520.

13. William Sims Bainbridge, *Nanoconvergence* (Upper Saddle River, N.J.: Prentice-Hall, 2007), p. 129.

14. D. W. Winnicott, *Playing and Reality* (New York: Basic Books, 1971).

15. Carlos Castaneda, *The Teachings of Don Juan: A Yaqui Way of Knowledge* (Berkeley: University of California Press, 1968), *A Separate Reality: Further Conversations with Don Juan* (New York: Simon and Schuster, 1971), *Journey to Ixtlan: The Lessons of Don Juan* (New York: Simon and Schuster, 1972).

16. Robert Marshall, "The Dark Legacy of Carlos Castaneda," *Salon*, April 12, 2007, www.salon.com/2007/04/12/castaneda/.

17. *Courses of Instruction for Harvard & Radcliffe, 1972-1973* (Cambridge, Mass.: Harvard University, 1972), p. 24.

18. wrldrels.org/2016/10/08/league-for-spiritual-discovery/.

19. William Sims Bainbridge and Rodney Stark, "Cult Formation: Three Compatible Models," *Sociological Analysis* 40(4) (1979): 283-295.

20. Rodney Stark and William Sims Bainbridge, *A Theory of Religion* (New York: Lang, 1987).

21. Christian Giudice, "'I, Jehovah': Mary Ann de Grimston and The Process Church of the Final Judgment," pp. 121-140 in *Female Leaders in New Religious Movements*, ed. by I. Bårdsen Tøllefsen and Christian Giudice (London: Palgrave, 2017), p. 123.

22. John Lofland, *Doomsday Cult* (Englewood Cliffs, N.J.: Prentice-Hall, 1966), pp. 41-42.

23. John R. Howard, *The Cutting Edge* (Philadelphia: Lippincott, 1974), p. 188.

24. Ibid., p. 189.

25. Anthony F .C. Wallace, "The Institutionalization of Cathartic and Control Strategies in Iroquois Religious Psychotherapy," p. 94 in *Culture and Mental Health*, ed. by Marvin K. Opler (New York: Macmillan, 1959).

26. August B. Hollingshead and Frederick Redlich, *Social Class and Mental Illness* (New York: Wiley, 1958); Stanley T. Michael, "Social Class and Psychiatric Treatment," *Journal of Psychiatric Research* 5 (1967): 243-254; Van Buren O. Hammett, "A Consideration of Psychoanalysis in Relation to Psychiatry Generally, Circa 1965," *American Journal of Psychiatry* 122 (1965): 42-54.

27. Alfred Adler, *Understanding Human Nature* (Greenwich, Conn.: Fawcett, 1954), p. 47.

28. Ibid., p. 49.

29. Philip Rieff, *The Triumph of the Therapeutic* (New York: Harper and Row, 1968), p. 95.

30. Ibid., p. 87.

31. Jerome D. Frank, *Persuasion and Healing* (New York: Schocken, 1961); John G. Kennedy, "Nubian Zar Ceremonies as Psychotherapy," *Human Organization* 26:4 (1967), 185-194; Wolfgang Lederer, "Primitive Psychotherapy," *Psychiatry* 22 (1959): 255-265; Lloyd H. Rogler and August B. Hollingshead, "The Puerto Rican Spiritualist as a Psychiatrist," *American Journal of Sociology* 67(1) (1961): 17-21; Kilton Stewart, "Dream Theory in Malaya," pp. 159-167 *Altered States of Consciousness*, ed. by Charles T. Tart (New York: Wiley, 1969); William Sargant, *Battle for the Mind* (New York: Harper and Row, 1959); Ari Kiev (ed.), *Magic, Faith and Healing* (New York: Free Press, 1964); Richard F. Larson, "The Clergyman's Role in the Therapeutic Process: Disagreement between Clergymen and Psychiatrists," *Psychiatry* 31 (1968): 250-263; Peter Roger Breggin, "Psychotherapy as Applied Ethics," *Psychiatry* 34 (1971): 59-74.

32. J. A. C. Brown, *Freud and the Post-Freudians* (Baltimore: Penguin, 1967), p. 40.

33. William Sims Bainbridge and Rodney Stark, "Scientology: To Be Perfectly Clear," *Sociological Analysis* 41 (1980): 128-136; William Sims Bainbridge, "Science and Religion: The Case of Scientology," pp. 59-79 in *The Future of New Religious Movements*, ed. by David G. Bromley and Phillip E. Hammond (Macon, Ga.: Mercer University Press, 1987); "The Cultural Context of Scientology," pp. 35-51 in *Scientology*, ed. by James R. Lewis. (New York: Oxford University Press, 2000).

34. Binswanger, Ludwig, "On the Psychogalvanic Phenomenon in Association Experiments," pp. 446-530 in *Studies in Word-Association*, ed. by C. G. Jung (New York, N.Y.: Moffat, Yard, 1919).

35. William Sims Bainbridge, "Cultural Genetics," pp. 157-198 in *Religious Movements*, ed. by Rodney Stark (New York: Paragon, 1985).

36. J. Gordon Melton, *Encyclopedia of American Religions* (Wilmington, N.C.: McGrath, 1978), p. 257.

37. Rodney Stark, "Introduction," pp. 1-10 in *Religious Movements*, ed. by Rodney Stark (New York: Paragon, 1985), p. 3

38. Leon Festinger, H. W. Riecken, and Stanley Schachter, *When Prophecy Fails* (New York: Harper and Row, 1956).

39. en.wikipedia.org/wiki/When_Prophecy_Fails.

40. Myron G. Sandifer *et al.*, "Similarities and Differences in Patient Evaluation by U.S. and U.K. Psychiatrists," *American Journal of Psychiatry* 126(2) (1969): 206–212.

41. John Lofland, *Doomsday Cult*, p. 7; John Lofland and Rodney Stark, "Becoming a World-Saver: A Theory of Conversion to a Deviant Perspective," *American Sociological Review* 30(6) (1965): 862-875.

42. Lofland, *Doomsday Cult*, p. 34.

43. George C. Homans, *Social Behavior: Its Elementary Forms* (New York: Harcourt Brace Jovanovich, 1974), p. 16.

44. Ibid., p. 25.

45. Victor Papanek, *Design for the Real World* (New York: Bantam, 1973); R. Buckminster Fuller, *Utopia or Oblivion* (New York: Bantam, 1969), *Operating Manual for Spaceship Earth* (New York: Pocket Books, 1970), *I Seem to Be a Verb* (New York: Bantam, 1970)

46. Joshua J. Rothman, *The Discovery of the Asylum* (Boston: Little, Brown, 1971); George Rosen, *Madness in Society* (New York: Harper and Row, 1969); Michel Foucault, *Madness and Civilization* (New York: New American Library, 1971); Robert Darnton, *Mesmerism and the End of the Enlightenment in France* (New York: Schocken, 1970).

47. Erik H. Erikson, *Identity, Youth and Crisis* (New York: Norton, 1968); Karl Mannheim, "The Sociological Problem of Generations," pp. 352-369 in *Studies in Social Movements*, ed. By Barry McLaughlan (New York: Free Press, 1969); Erik H. Erikson (ed.), *The Challenge of Youth* (Garden City, N.Y.: Doubleday, 1965).

48. Sargant, *Battle for the Mind*.

49. Lofland, *Doomsday Cult*; Mark Granovetter, "The Strength of Weak Ties," *American Journal of Sociology* 78(6) (1973): 1360-1380.

50. E. L. Quarantelli and Dennis Wenger: "A Voice from the Thirteenth Century: The Characteristics and Conditions for the Emergence of a Ouija Board Cult," pp. 143-57 in *Deviance: Action, Reaction, Interaction*, ed. By Frank R. Scarpicti and Dominic T. McFarlane (Reading, Mass.: Addison-Wesley, 1975).

51. George Devereux (ed.), *Psychoanalysis and the Occult* (New York: International Universities Press, 1953); Nandor Fodor, *Freud, Jung, and Occultism* (New Hyde Park, N.Y.: University Books, 1971); Philip Seitz, "ESP-Like Experiences in a Psychoanalyst: A Possible Psychological Mechanism," *Psychoanalysis and Contemporary Science* 4 (1975): 189-209.

52. Philip Reiff, *The Triumph of the Therapeutic* (New York: Harper and Row, 1968).

53. Sabrina Verney, *Xtul: An Experience of The Process* (Baltimore: Publish America, 2011), p. 62.

54. Timothy Wyllie, *Love Sex Fear Death: The Inside Story of The Process Church of the Final Judgment* (Port Townsend, Wash.: Feral House, 2009).

55. Aaron, Cassandra, Christian, Cyrus, Diana, Dominic, Greer, Hagar, Hathor, Joel, John, Joshua, Lars, Malachi, Matthew, Micah, Morgana, Phineas, Raphael, Rebekah, Rhea, Seraphine.

56. Émile Durkheim, *The Elementary Forms of the Religious Life* (New York: Free Press, 1965), p. 54.

57. Ibid., p. 55.

58. Ibid., p. 56.

59. Steven M. Tipton, *Getting Saved from the Sixties: Moral Meaning in Conversion and Cultural Change* (Berkeley: University of California Press, 1982).

60. Evon Z. Vogt, *The Zinacantecos of Mexico: A Modern Maya Way of Life* (New York: Holt, Rinehart and Winston, 1970).

61. Elisabethe Corathiel, *Oberammergau and Its Passion Play* (Westminster, Md.: Newman Press, 1960), p. 102.

62. Lucy Seaman Bainbridge, *Round the World Letters* (Boston: Lothrop, 1882), pp. 435-436.

63. www.passionsspiele-oberammergau.de/en/play/history/2.

64. Erich Gritzbach, *Hermann Goering: The Man and His Work* (London: Hurst and Blackett, 1939), pp. 148-149.

65. Roger Manvell and Heinrich Fraenkel, *Goering* (New York: Simon and Schuster, 1962), p. 23.

66. John Symonds, *The Magic of Aleister Crowley* (London: Mullet, 1958).

67. Aleister Crowley, *The Confessions of Aleister Crowley* (New York: Hill and Wang, 1969), p. 796.

68. Bill Beckett, "Preparing for the Fiery End: Process," *Harvard Crimson*, April 27, 1971, www.thecrimson.com/article/1971/4/27/preparing-for-the-fiery-end-process/.

69. Vincent Bugliosi, *Helter Skelter: The True Story of the Manson Murders* (New York: Norton, 1974), pp. 758-759.

70. Ibid., 757.

71. Randall H. Alfred, "The Church of Satan," pp. 180-202 in *The New Religious Consciousness*, ed. by Charles Y. Glock and Robert N. Bellah (Berkeley: University of California Press, 1976).

72. Ed Sanders, *The Family: The Story of Charles Manson's Dune Buggy Attack Battalion* (New York: Dutton, 1971), pp. 80-81.

73. Eleanor Blau, "Unity of Christ and Satan: A Tenet of Religious Cult," *New York Times*, August 23, 1971, www.nytimes.com/1971/08/23/archives/unity-of-christ-and-satan-a-tenet-of-religious-cult.html.

74. Maren Lockwood Carden, *Oneida: Utopian Community to Modern Corporation* (Baltimore: Johns Hopkins, 1969).

75. Benjamin Zablocki, *The Joyful Community* (Baltimore: Penguin, 1971).

76. Rosabeth Moss Kanter, *Commitment and Community* (Cambridge, Mass.: Harvard University Press, 1972), 19-20; Kathleen Kinkade, *A Walden Two Experiment: The First Five Years of Twin Oaks Community* (New York: William Morrow, 1974).

77. Erving Goffman, *Encounters* (Indianapolis: Bobbs-Merrill, 1961), 83-152, especially p. 108.

78. Ernest Newman, *Wagner as Man and Artist* (New York: Random House, 1924); Richard Wagner, *The Art-Work of the Future* (Lincoln: University of Nebraska Press, 1993).

79. Kanter, *Commitment and Community*.

80. Franz Boas, "The Ethnological Significance of Esoteric Doctrines," pp. 312-315 in *Race, Language, and Culture* (New York: Free Press, 1966).

81. George Wilhelm Friedrich Hegel, *Philosophy of Mind* (New York: Oxford University Press, 2007 [1830]).

82. Claude Lévi-Strauss, *The Raw and the Cooked* (New York: Harper and Row, 1969), p. 13.

83. Wyllie, *Love Sex Fear Death,* p. 95.

84. Friedrich Nietzsche, *Die Geburt der Tragödie* (Munich: Goldmann, 1872); William Sims Bainbridge, "Burglarizing Nietzsche's Tomb," *Journal of Evolution and Technology* 21(1) (2010): 37-54.

85. Eliphas Levi, *Transcendental Magic* (New York: Weiser, 1974), p. 186.

86. I Kings 7:15, 21-22; II Chronicles 3:15-17; II Kings 25:17; I Chronicles 4:12; Jeremiah 52:21-23.

87. Lewis Spence, *An Encyclopaedia of Occultism* (New Hyde Park, N.Y.: University Books, 1960), p. 234.

88. Francis King, *Magic—The Western Tradition* (New York: Avon, 1975), plate 44.

89. Manly Palmer Hall, *An Encyclopedic Outline of Masonic, Hermetic, Qahbalistic and Rosicrucian Symbolic Philosophy* (Los Angeles: Philosophical Research Society, 1945), illustration facing p. CXIII.

90. The literature on this point is voluminous and disputatious. The behaviorists attack the psychoanalytically-oriented approach; see Hans. J. Eysenck, "The Effects of Psychotherapy," *International Journal of Psychiatry* 1 (1965): 99-144; Richard B. Stuart, *Trick or Treatment* (Champaign, Ill.: Research Press, 1970); Stanley Rachman*, The Effects of Psychotherapy* (Oxford: Pergamon, 1971); Joseph Wolpe and Stanley Rachman, "Psychoanalytic 'Evidence': A Critique Based on Freud's Case of Little Hans," *Journal of Nervous and Mental Disease* 130 (1960): 135-148; and Albert Bandura, *Principles of Behavior Modification* (New York: Holt, Rinehart and Winston, 1969), 52-61. But the behaviorist approach itself is limited in applicability, and its apparent successes may have nothing to do with its alleged basis in experimental psychology; see Nathaniel McConaghy, "Aversive Therapy of Homosexuality: Measures of Efficacy," *American Journal of Psychiatry* 127(9) (1971): 1221-1224. See also Andrew Salter, *The Case against Psychoanalysis* (New York: Harper and Row, 1972).

91. William Sims Bainbridge, "Ethical Challenges of Ubiquitous Healthcare," pp. 473-506 in *Wireless Computing in Medicine: From Nano to Cloud with Ethical and Legal Implications*, ed. by Mary Mehrnoosh Eshaghian-Wilner (New York: Wiley, 2016), *Dynamic Secularization* (Cham, Switzerland: Springer, 2017); Richard Border *et al.,* "No Support for Historical Candidate Gene or Candidate Gene-by-Interaction Hypotheses for Major Depression across Multiple Large Samples," *American Journal of Psychiatry* 196(5) (2019): 376-387; Thomas Insel, *Healing: Our Path from Mental Illness to Mental Health* (New York: Penguin, 2022); Jerold J. Kreisman, "Do Psychiatrists Do Psychotherapy Anymore?" *Psychology Today,* July 30, 2022, www.psychologytoday.com/us/blog/i-hate-you-dont-leave-me/202207/do-psychiatrists-do-psychotherapy-anymore; Helena Hansen, Kevin J. Gutierrez, and Saudi Garcia, "Rethinking Psychiatry," *Daedalus* 152(4) (2023): 75-91.

92. Jerome D. Frank, *Persuasion and Healing* (New York: Schocken, 1961); Wolfgang Lederer, "Primitive Psychotherapy," *Psychiatry* 22 (1959): 255-265.

93. Ari Kiev, *Transcultural Psychiatry* (New York: Free Press, 1972); David J. Rothman, *The Discovery of the Asylum* (Boston: Little, Brown, 1971); Anselm Straus *et al., Psychiatric Ideologies and Institutions* (New York: Free Press, 1964); Robert B. Edgerton, "Conceptions of Psychosis in Four East African Societies," *American Anthropologist* 68 (1966): 408-425; Jozef Ph. Hes, "From Native Healer to Modern Psychiatrist—Afro-Asian Immigrants to Israel and Their Attitudes towards Psychiatric Facilities," *International Journal of Social Psychiatry* 13(1) (1966-67): 21-27; Masaaki Kato, "Report on Psychotherapy in Japan," *International Journal of Social Psychiatry* 5(1) (1959): 56-60; Richard F. Larson, "The Clergyman's Role in the Therapeutic Process: Disagreement between Clergymen and Psychiatrists," *Psychiatry* 31 (1968): 250-263; Lawrence S. Linn, "Social Identification and the Seeking of Psychiatric Care," *American Journal of Orthopsychiatry* 38(1) (1968): 83-88; Shashi K. Pande, "The Mystique of 'Western' Psychotherapy: An Eastern Interpretation," *Journal of Nervous and Mental Disease* 146(6) (1968): 425-432.

94. Spence, *Encyclopaedia of Occultism*, p. 333.

95. www.lronhubbard.org/timeline/commander-snake-thompson.html.

96. Consuelo Andrew Seoane, *Beyond the Ranges* (New York: Robert Spellar, 1960); Rhoda Low Seoane, *Uttermost East and the Longest War* (New York: Vantage, 1968); William Sims Bainbridge, "Surreal Impersonation," pp. 65-80 in *Methods for Studying Video Games and Religion*, ed. by Vit Šisler, Kerstin Radde-Antweiler, and Xenia Zeiler (New York: Routledge, 2018).

97. William Sims Bainbridge, *Across the Secular Abyss* (Lanham, Md.: Lexington, 2007), "The Cultural Context of Scientology," pp. 35-51 in *Scientology*, ed. by James R. Lewis (New York: Oxford University Press, 2009).

98. Alfred Adler, *Understanding Human Nature* (Greenwich, Conn.: Fawcett, 1954); Carl Gustav Jung, *Synchronicity: An Acausal Connecting Principle* (London: Routledge and Kegan Paul, 1972).

99. Binswanger, Ludwig, "On the Psychogalvanic Phenomenon in Association Experiments," pp. 446-530 in *Studies in Word-Association*, ed. by C. G. Jung (New York: Moffat, Yard, 1919).

100. Herbert J. Freudenberger, "Staff Burn-Out," *Journal of Social Issues* 30(1) (1974): 159-165.

101. Eleanor Blau, "Young Sect No Longer Hails Devil," *New York Times*, December 1, 1974, p. 53, www.nytimes.com/1971/08/23/archives/unity-of-christ-and-satan-a-tenet-of-religious-cult.html.

102. Massimo Introvigne, *Satanism: A Social History* (Leiden: Brill, 2016) p. 335.

103. Wyllie, *Love Sex Fear Death*.

104. booklife.com/project/hey-kid-there-s-nothing-wrong-with-you-51034.

105. Wyllie, *Love Sex Fear Death*, p. 25.

106. Talcott Parsons, "Evolutionary Universals in Society," *American Sociological Review* 29(3) (1964): 339-357, "Religion in Postindustrial America: The Problem of Secularization," *Social Research* 41(2) (1974): 193-225; George A. Huaco, "Ideology and General Theory: The Case of Sociological Functionalism," *Comparative Studies in Society and History* 28(1) (1986): 34-54.

107. Kanter, *Commitment and Community*.

108. William Sims Bainbridge and Rodney Stark, "Client and Audience Cults in America," *Sociological Analysis* 41(3) (1980): 199-214, p. 199.

109. Carole M. Cusack, "The Process Church of the Final Judgment: The Demise by Transmutation and Replacement of a Controversial New Religion," *International Journal for the Study of New Religions* 10(2) (2019): 139-158, pp. 139-140.

110. William Sims Bainbridge, *The Sacred Force of Star Wars Jedi* (Cambridge: Cambridge University Press, 2024), pp. 7-8.

111. Wyllie, *Love Sex Fear Death*, p. 117.

112. Taylor Dafoe, "Timothy Wyllie, the Mystical Telepathic Artist Who Spoke to Dolphins, Is Finally Getting His Due for His Remarkable Landscapes," *ArtNet*, March 2, 2023, news.artnet.com/art-world/timothy-wyllie-outsider-art-fair-2264421.

113. www.innertraditions.com/author/timothy-wyllie/.

114. www.innertraditions.com/books/confessions-of-a-rebel-angel.

115. William Sims Bainbridge, *The Sociology of Religious Movements* (New York: Routledge, 1997), pp. 89-118.

116. Sylvester Bliss, *Memoirs of William Miller* (Boston: Joshua V. Himes, 1853), p. 160.

117. O. S. Fowler, Ellis Lewis, and William Miller, "Phrenological Developments and Character of William Miller, Who Was Executed at Williamsport, Pa., July 27th, 1838, for the Murder of Solomon Hoffman," *American Phrenological Journal and Miscellany* (1839), pp. 272-286; Robert E. Riegel, "The Introduction of Phrenology to the United States," *American Historical Review* 39(1) (1933): 73-78; Bainbridge, *Sociology of Religious Movements*, p. 102.

118. Maury Terry, *The Ultimate Evil* (New York: Bantam, 1987), p. 211.

119. Donald Phau, "The Satanic Roots of Rock," www.av1611.org/othpubls/roots.html.

120. www.youtube.com/watch?v=LMF-o6Fj8yg.

121. Christopher R. Weingarten and Aliza Aufrichtig, "Before & After 'Maggot Brain,'" *New York Times*, July 11, 2021, www.nytimes.com/interactive/2021/07/11/arts/music/funkadelic-maggot-brain.html.

122. Dave Segal, "Maggot Brain Funkadelic 1971," *Pitchfork*, June 21, 2020, pitchfork.com/reviews/albums/funkadelic-maggot-brain/.

123. George Clinton, *Brothas Be, Yo Like George, Ain't That Funkin' Kinda Hard on You?: A Memoir* (New York: Atria, 2014), p. 113.

124. Genesis P-Orridge, email message to William Sims Bainbridge, January 9, 1998.

125. Genesis Breyer P-Orridge, *Thee Psychick Bible* (Port Townsend, Wash.: Feral House, 2007), p. 353.

126. www.diskery.com/diskery_LTE.php?BANDNUM=2700&ALBUM=0&APPLICATION=Biography, overgroundscene.wordpress.com/tag/monastery/.

127. genius.com/Skinny-puppy-process-lyrics.

128. www.sabbathassembly.org/.

129. sabbathassembly.bandcamp.com/.

130. ibid.

131. www.youtube.com/watch?v=9NXDgha910U, accessed October 23, 2016.

132. www.facebook.com/SabbathAssembly.

133. layitontheline.bandcamp.com/album/a-prelude-to-the-process.

134. www.facebook.com/profile/100042174651875/.

135. layitontheline.bandcamp.com/album/a-candle-in-hell.

136. open.spotify.com/playlist/4vDsZe0zJMIpi5xJ1J68Zo; open.spotify.com/playlist/7qnJzOLoUWdz8CUpuM3won.

137. www.facebook.com/newprocesseanorder.

138. www.youtube.com/watch?v=rcWnNUUQVjE.

139. genius.com/Aleister-crowley-hymn-to-lucifer-annotated.

140. www.youtube.com/watch?v=vm7DxuuYbY4.

141. theprocesszine.tumblr.com.

142. en.wikipedia.org/wiki/Talk:Process_Church_of_the_Final_Judgment.

143. web.archive.org/web/20220528045106/https://www.processeans.co.uk/.

144. www.youtube.com/c/ProcessChurch.

145. www.youtube.com/watch?v=8RpOciEWN70.

146. kaliyugaeditions.weebly.com/.

147. en.wikipedia.org/wiki/Lucifer_(TV_series).

148. lucifer.fandom.com/wiki/Lucifer_Wiki:Policy.

149. William Sims Bainbridge, "Computer Simulations of Cultural Drift," *Journal of the British Interplanetary Society* 37 (1984): 420-429.

150. William Sims Bainbridge, *Social Research Methods and Statistics: A Computer-Assisted Introduction* (Belmont, Calif.: Wadsworth, 1992).

151. William Sims Bainbridge, "Processional," *Communications of the ACM* 58(10) (2015): 104-105, p. 104.

152. feralhouse.com/revival/.

153. William Sims Bainbridge, *Revival: Resurrecting the Process Church of the Final Judgment* (Port Townsend, Wash.: Feral House, 2017), pp. 157-158.

www.ingramcontent.com/pod-product-compliance
Lightning Source LLC
Jackson TN
JSHW070807270425
83185JS00002B/1